CHOICES

Ninth Edition

Freshman Seminar

Edited by

Roberta L. McFadden

Mount Saint Mary's University
Emmitsburg, Maryland

Copley Custom Textbooks

An imprint of XanEdu Custom Publishing

ISBN 13: 978-1-58152-659-2
ISBN 10: 1-58152-659-8

Cover art by Meaghan Conlon: *The pictures I used were some my sister took. To me, the picture on the cover of a single seed atop its stalk is very similar to a college freshman. It is the first time you are on your own, getting ready to head into the real world. Yet you are still connected, and have not completely learned how to fly yet. The back cover represents a later stage—the end of the four years of college. The seedlings, now ready to detach from home, fly away and plant themselves in a new world where they will eventually grow and bloom.*

Acknowledgments:

pp. 3–13: "Expelled" by John Cheever, appeared in the *New Republic*, July 19, 1982.

pp. 14–37: From *Flow: The Psychology of Optimal Experience* by Mihaly Csikzentmihalyi. Copyright © 1990 by Mihaly Csikzentmihalyi. Reprinted by permission of HarperCollins Publishers, Inc.

pp. 38–42: From *Dorothy Day: Selected Writings* by Dorothy Day. Copyright © 1983, 1992, 2005 by Orbis Books. Reprinted by permission of the publisher via the Copyright Clearance Center.

pp. 43–61: Copyright © 1997 by *Harper's Magazine*. All rights reserved. Reproduced from the September issue by special permission.

pp. 62–76: From *Pedagogy of the Oppressed* by Paulo Freire. Copyright © 1970. Reprinted by permission of The Continuum International Publishing Group, Inc.

Copley Custom Textbooks
An imprint of XanEdu Custom Publishing
138 Great Road
Acton, MA 01720
800-562-2147

Contents

Preface

As the Freshman Seminar program celebrates more than twenty years at Mount St. Mary's University, the Seminar faculty offer this ninth edition of *Choices*. We build on the work of many who have contributed to and shaped this volume of readings since 1987. Our goal is to select works that engage your mind and spirit as you explore the central themes of education, work, and values in our program. We hope that you gain not only new knowledge as you analyze and discuss these readings, but also new confidence in making the important choices in your life.

This text represents a joint effort by the entire Freshman Seminar faculty, but special recognition is due the thoughtful and meticulous efforts of the 2008–2009 *Choices* sub-committee: our colleagues Christine Blackshaw, Carl Glover, Curtis Johnson (chair), and Carmen Schmersahl. My deep appreciation to you and all who helped bring this ninth edition of *Choices* to its final form.

Roberta L. McFadden
Mount St. Mary's University
Fall 2009

Our Mission

Mount St. Mary's is a Catholic institution of higher education dedicated to liberal learning in the pursuit of truth. Mount St. Mary's, mindful of its role in the Church's mission to the world and respectful of the religious liberty of all, affirms the values and beliefs central to the Catholic vision of the person and society, and seeks to deepen understanding of our faith and its practice in just and compassionate engagement with the world.

In order to enable individuals to understand and to challenge or embrace the cultural forces operating on them, Mount St. Mary's, in all its curricular and co-curricular programs, encourages each student to undertake free and rigorous inquiry leading to a reflective and creative understanding of the traditions which shape the communities in which we live.

Mount St. Mary's strives to graduate men and women who cultivate a mature spiritual life, who live by high intellectual and moral standards, who respect the dignity of other persons, who see and seek to resolve the problems facing humanity, and who commit themselves to live as responsible citizens.

Goals and Objectives of the Undergraduate Program

Through all its undergraduate programs, curricular and co-curricular, Mount Saint Mary's strives to graduate students who have developed

1. An understanding of the Western humanist tradition, including its American expression, particularly as that tradition has been interpreted in Catholic thought and practice. [primarily a goal of the core curriculum]

   To fulfill this goal, Mount Saint Mary's expects students to

   a. complete a sequenced and integrated core curriculum rooted in the Western humanist tradition and the Catholic contribution to it;
   b. cultivate an active understanding of the Christian humanist dialogue of faith and reason;
   c. deepen their understanding of the major developments of Western history and culture, including the methods of inquiry and verification practiced in the humanities and sciences;
   d. deepen their understanding of the created universe and of the human role within it;
   e. deepen their understanding of the creative arts;
   f. deepen their understanding of how the culture of the U.S. has emerged from and influenced the Western tradition;
   g. achieve perspective on the Western humanist tradition by investigating at least one culture that has developed outside or beyond the dominant traditions of the West.

2. The skills of analysis, communication, and problem solving that enable them to appreciate, critique and contribute to that tradition. [primarily a goal of the core, supplemented by the major and other studies]

   To fulfill this goal, Mount Saint Mary's expects students to

   a. become skilled readers, writers and speakers;
   b. comprehend and skillfully employ quantitative reasoning;
   c. demonstrate proficiency through the first-year college level in a foreign language;
   d. skillfully employ contemporary research methods, including the resources of information technology;
   e. recognize and evaluate claims of intellectual authority.

3. An understanding of the purposes, methods, and substance of a particular intellectual discipline. [primarily a goal of the major supplemented by the core and other studies]

   To fulfill this goal, Mount Saint Mary's expects students to

   a. complete an undergraduate major;
   b. connect study in that major with learning in the core curriculum and electives;
   c. understand the relationship of that study to civic and professional life, for example, by participating in internships, community service, inter-cultural experiences, or study abroad.

4. An understanding of the nature of the good and a commitment to its practice, particularly in regard to justice, dignity, and freedom and responsibility in human communities. [a goal of the full curriculum and co-curriculum]

   To fulfill this goal, Mount Saint Mary's expects students to

   a. develop this understanding of the good as presented in classical, Christian, and modern thought;
   b. honor the dignity and worth of persons of different racial and cultural heritages;
   c. honor their human nature—body, mind, and spirit—as a gift to be nurtured individually as well as in honest, responsible, and compassionate relationships;
   d. address the pressing questions of social justice and human need.

5. The personal synthesis of learning and the capacity for life-long inquiry that constitute the ultimate goal of a liberal education. [a goal of the full curriculum and co-curriculum]

   To fulfill this goal, Mount Saint Mary's expects students to

   a. seek to integrate learning across courses and disciplines within the core curriculum;
   b. connect core learning with learning in the major;
   c. explore and extend their own intellectual and vocational strengths and interests through study and co-curricular activities beyond the core and major;
   d. connect the whole of their learning, in class and out, to their lives as scholars, professionals, citizens, and people of faith.

Key Questions to Ask about a Reading

- Who is the author?

- Who is the intended audience?

- When was the work written?

- What is the purpose of the work?

- What are the central ideas of the work?

- What does the author wish to happen to the reader after reading the work?

- How has this reading changed me?

Sr. Mary Kate, a Sister of St. Joseph of Springfield for over twenty-seven years, taught junior high and high school in various schools in Texas and Massachusetts for sixteen years before obtaining her Ph.D. in biblical studies at The Catholic University of America. She has spent the last eight and a half years teaching at the Mount as a member of the theology department. Her most recent publication, "Biblical Justice," is the lead chapter in Brazos Press' The Heart of Catholic Social Teaching, *edited by David M. McCarthy.*

Vocation Story

Sr. Mary Kate Birge

1   This past Sunday, at my community's Transfer of Leadership celebration, I saw my novice director. It was the first time we had met since before I had begun my doctoral studies in 1995. Even then our meetings had only been chanced, sporadic moments at very large congregational events since her leaving community two months after I made first vows. I was delighted that she was here, and hurried to greet her. We only had a few moments to speak in a very crowded chapel, busy with the happy and noisy sounds of folks moving from chapel to dining room to continue the celebration. After warmly embracing me, Carol came directly to the heart of the matter, as was always her wont, "So, you have become a scholar and teacher, what you had hoped for so long ago. Are you happy?"

2   I had forgotten, forgotten that even then I had known and been clear what I had wanted, had hoped against hope to do: to study and teach the Word. I remember when I was in grade school (today we would say middle school) and junior high being "hungry" for God in some strange and inexplicable way, and I knew I wanted to learn more about him (well, my feminist consciousness had not yet been raised!). I thought studying Latin would do that, bring me closer to knowing God, so I started studying Latin as soon as I could—eighth grade, in fact. I discovered that I was very good at learning Latin and that I liked it a lot. Words, their meanings, the way they changed with the simple addition of a prefix or a suffix, the infinite

number of images they could create had captured me. I was hooked. And I wanted more.

3   By the time I had reached sophomore year in high school, I had become a very bookish young woman. I knew clearly that, come college, I would major in Spanish, minor in Latin, teach for a while, and then spend the rest of my life doing social work, most appropriate employment for a nun, something about which I was also very sure I would do (although I wasn't exactly shouting these last plans from the roof top—it was way too weird, even for me).

4   In English class that year we had numerous novels to read for which we then had to write book reports. I never minded the reading of novels; in fact, I wallowed in reading, especially reading novels. A friend had recommended that I read Chaim Potok's *The Chosen* since I liked reading; a book report was coming up in class. So, next time I was in the school bookstore, I picked up a ninety-five cent paperback copy and began to read it in study that afternoon. I couldn't put it down; I was captured—again—but this time not just by words. Here were two high school students doing something amazing with ancient languages and prayer and God; they were passionate about establishing the meaning of the text, and not just any text either. The text had to do with God. They argued and shouted and appealed to arcane Aramaic grammar rules because the text mattered to them, because God mattered to them. My mouth was watering with desire; I could taste the words as the characters on the page speaking them in my mind's imagination. Even now my heart still beats faster as I remember those first moments of longing and hope.

5   I finished the book later that day (long after I had gone to bed that night, probably under the covers with the help of a flashlight). And I remember closing the book and feeling sad that the story was over, and sad that I couldn't do the same thing that Reuven and Danny had done. "I wish I could do that in my religion," I whispered silently to myself. And a "still, small voice," I suspect the same one Elijah heard that day on Mount Horeb, seemed to say in my mind's ear, "You can do that, if you want to."

6   All of that came flooding back to me as I heard Carol's statement and her question. I smiled, grinned even, nodding and said, "Yes, I am a scholar and teacher, and I am very happy."

John Cheever was born May 27, 1912, in Quincy, Mass., and died June 18, 1982, of cancer. He attended Thayer Academy in South Braintree, but was expelled for low marks. "Expelled," a story based upon his prep school experiences, was published in The New Republic *when Cheever was only seventeen. After serving in the Army Signal Corps in World War II, he went on to a distinguished career as an author. For forty years he was considered one of America's finest short story writers, especially gifted at capturing the foibles and frustrations of suburban life. When a collection of his best work,* The Stories of John Cheever, *was published in 1979, it received the Pulitzer Prize, the National Book Critics Circle Award, and the American Book Award. His daughter, Susan Cheever, has written a fine memoir about the troubled life of her father,* Home before Dark *(1984).*

Expelled

John Cheever

1   It didn't come all at once. It took a very long time. First I had a skirmish with the English department and then all the other departments. Pretty soon something had to be done. The first signs were cordialities on the part of the headmaster. He was never nice to anybody unless he was a football star, or hadn't paid his tuition, or was going to be expelled. That's how I knew.

2   He called me down to his office with the carved chairs arranged in a semicircle and the brocade curtains resting against the vacant windows. All about him were pictures of people who had got scholarships at Harvard. He asked me to sit down.

3   "Well, Charles," he said, "some of the teachers say you aren't getting very good marks."

4   "Yes," I said, "that's true." I didn't care about the marks.

5   "But Charles," he said, "you know the scholastic standard of this school is very high and we have to drop people when their work becomes unsatisfactory." I told him I knew that also.

Then he said a lot of things about the traditions, and the elms, and the magnificent military heritage from our West Point founder.

6   It was very nice outside of his room. He had his window pushed open halfway and one could see the lawns pulling down to the road behind the trees and the bushes. The gravy-colored curtains were too heavy to move about in the wind, but some papers shifted around on his desk. In a little while I got up and walked out. He turned and started to work again. I went back to my next class.

7   The next day was very brilliant and the peach branches were full against the dry sky. I could hear people talking and a phonograph playing. The sounds came through the peach blossoms and crossed the room. I lay in bed and thought about a great many things. My dreams had been thick. I remembered two converging hills, some dry apple trees, and a broken blue egg cup. That is all I could remember.

8   I put on knickers and a soft sweater and headed toward school. My hands shook on the wheel. I was like that all over.

9   Through the cloudy trees I could see the protrusion of the new tower. It was going to be a beautiful new tower and it was going to cost a great deal of money. Some thought of buying new books for the library instead of putting up a tower, but no one would see the books. People would be able to see the tower five miles off when the leaves were off the trees. It would be done by fall.

10   When I went into the building the headmaster's secretary was standing in the corridor. She was a nice sort of person with brown funnels of hair furrowed about a round head. She smiled. I guess she must have known.

The Colonel

11   Every morning we went up into the black chapel. The brisk headmaster was there. Sometimes he had a member of the faculty with him. Sometimes it was a stranger.

12   He introduced the stranger, whose speech was always the same. In the spring life is like a baseball game. In the fall it is like football. That is what the speaker always said.

13   The hall is damp and ugly with skylights that rattle in the rain. The seats are hard and you have to hold a hymnbook in your lap. The hymnbook often slips off and that is embarrassing.

14   On Memorial Day they have the best speaker. They have a mayor or a Governor. Sometimes they have a Governor's second. There is very little preference.

15   The Governor will tell us what a magnificent country we have. He will tell us to beware of the Red menace. He will want to tell us that the goddam foreigners should have gone home a hell of a long time ago. That they should have stayed in their own goddam countries if they didn't like ours. He will not dare say this though.

16   If they have a mayor the speech will be longer. He will tell us that our country is beautiful and young and strong. That the War is over, but that if there is another war we must fight. He will tell us that war is a masculine trait that has brought present civilization to its fine condition. Then he will leave us and help stout women place lilacs on graves. He will tell them the same thing.

17   One Memorial Day they could not get a Governor or a mayor. There was a colonel in the same village who had been to war and who had a chest thick with medals. They asked him to speak. Of course he said, he would like to speak.

18   He was a thin colonel with a soft nose that rested quietly on his face. He was nervous and pushed his wedding ring about his thin finger. When he was introduced he looked at the audience sitting in the uncomfortable chairs. There was silence and the dropping of hymnbooks like the water spouts in the aftermath of a heavy rain.

19   He spoke softly and quickly. He spoke of war and what he had seen. Then he had to stop. He stopped and looked at the boys. They were staring at their boots. He thought of the empty rooms in the other buildings. He thought of the rectangles of empty desks. He thought of the curtains on the stage and the four Windsor chairs behind him. Then he started to speak again.

20   He spoke as quickly as he could. He said war was bad. He said that there would never be another war. That he himself should stop it if he could. He swore. He looked at the young faces.

They were all very clean. The boys' knees were crossed and their soft pants hung loosely. He thought of the empty desks and began to whimper.

21 The people sat very still. Some of them felt tight as though they wanted to giggle. Everybody looked serious as the clock struck. It was time for another class.

22 People began to talk about the colonel after lunch. They looked behind them. They were afraid he might hear them.

23 It took the school several weeks to get over all this. Nobody said anything, but the colonel was never asked again. If they could not get a Governor or a mayor they could get someone besides a colonel. They made sure of that.

Margaret Courtwright

24 Margaret Courtwright was very nice. She was slightly bald and pulled her pressed hair down across her forehead. People said that she was the best English teacher in this part of the country, and when boys came back from Harvard they thanked her for the preparation she had given them. She did not like Edgar Guest, but she did like Carl Sandburg. She couldn't seem to understand the similarity. When I told her people laughed at Galsworthy she said that people used to laugh at Wordsworth. She did not believe people were still laughing at Wordsworth. That was what made her so nice.

25 She came from the West a long time ago. She taught school for so long that people ceased to consider her age. After having seen twenty-seven performances of "Hamlet" and after having taught it for sixteen years, she became a sort of immortal. Her interpretation was the one accepted on college-board papers. That helped everyone a great deal. No one had to get a new interpretation.

26 When she asked me for tea I sat in a walnut armchair with grapes carved on the head and traced and retraced the arms on the tea caddy. One time I read her one of my plays. She thought it was wonderful. She thought it was wonderful because she did not understand it and because it took two hours to read. When I had finished, she said, "You know that thing just took right hold of me. Really it just swept me right along. I think it's fine that you like to write. I once had a Japanese pupil who

liked to write. He was an awfully nice chap until one summer he went down to Provincetown. When he came back he was saying that he could express a complete abstraction. Fancy . . . a complete abstraction. Well, I wouldn't hear of it and told him how absurd it all was and tried to start him off with Galsworthy again, but I guess he had gone just too far. In a little while he left for New York and then Paris. It was really too bad. One summer in Provincetown just ruined him. His marks fell down . . . he cut classes to go to symphony. . . ." She went into the kitchen and got a tray of tarts.

27 The pastries were flaky and covered with a white coating that made them shine in the dead sunlight. I watched the red filling burst the thin shells and stain the triangles of bright damask. The tarts were good. I ate most of them.

28 She was afraid I would go the way of her Japanese pupil. She doubted anyone who disagreed with Heine on Shakespeare and Croce on expression.

29 One day she called me into her antiseptic office and spoke to me of reading Joyce. "You know, Charles," she said, "this sex reality can be quite as absurd as a hypercritical regard for such subjects. You know that, don't you? Of course, you do." Then she went out of the room. She had straight ankles and wore a gold band peppered with diamond chips on her ring finger. She seemed incapable of carrying the weight of the folds in her clothing. Her skirt was askew, either too long in front or hitching up on the side. Always one thing or the other.

30 When I left school she did not like it. She was afraid I might go too near Provincetown. She wished me good luck and moved the blotter back and forth on her desk. Then she returned to teaching "Hamlet."

31 Late in February Laura Driscoll got fired for telling her history pupils that Sacco and Vanzetti were innocent. In her farewell appearance the headmaster told everyone how sorry he was that she was going and made it all quite convincing. Then Laura stood up, told the headmaster that he was a damned liar, and waving her fan-spread fingers called the school a hell of a dump where everyone got into a rut.

32 Miss Courtwright sat closely in her chair and knew it was true. She didn't mind much. Professor Rogers with his

antifeminization movement bothered her a little, too. But she knew that she had been teaching school for a long time now and no movement was going to put her out of a job overnight—what with all the boys she had smuggled into Harvard and sixteen years of "Hamlet."

Laura Driscoll

33   History classes are always dead. This follows quite logically, for history is a dead subject. It has not the death of dead fruit or dead textiles or dead light. It has a different death. There is not the timeless quality of death about it. It is dead like scenery in the opera. It is on cracked canvas and the paint has faded and peeled and the lights are too bright. It is dead like old water in a zinc bathtub.

34   "We are going to study ancient history this year," the teacher will tell the pupils. "Yes, ancient history will be our field.

35   "Now of course, this class is not a class of children any longer. I expect the discipline to be the discipline of well bred young people. We shall not have to waste any time on the scolding of younger children. No. We shall just be able to spend all our time on ancient history.

36   "Now about questions. I shall answer questions if they are important. If I do not think them important I shall not answer them, for the year is short, and we must cover a lot of ground in a short time. That is, if we all cooperate and behave and not ask too many questions we shall cover the subject and have enough time at the end of the year for review.

37   "You may be interested in the fact that a large percentage of this class was certified last year. I should like to have a larger number this year. Just think, boys: wouldn't it be fine if a very large number—a number larger than last year—was certified? Wouldn't that be fine? Well, there's no reason why we can't do it if we all cooperate and behave and don't ask too many questions.

38   "You must remember that I have twelve people to worry about and that you have only one. If each person will take care of his own work and pass in his notebook on time it will save me a lot of trouble. Time and trouble mean whether you get into college or not, and I want you all to get into college.

39 "If you will take care of your own little duties, doing what is assigned to you and doing it well, we shall all get along fine. You are a brilliant-looking group of young people, and I want to have you all certified. I want to get you into college with as little trouble as possible.

40 "Now about the books. . . ."

41 I do not know how long history classes have been like this. One time or another I suppose history was alive. That was before it died its horrible fly-dappled unquivering death.

42 Everyone seems to know that history is dead. No one is alarmed. The pupils and the teachers love dead history. They do not like it when it is alive. When Laura Driscoll dragged history into the classroom, squirming and smelling of something bitter, they fired Laura and strangled the history. It was too tumultuous. Too turbulent.

43 In history one's intellect is used for mechanical speculation on a probable century or background. One's memory is applied to a list of dead dates and names. When one begins to apply one's intellect to the mental scope of the period, to the emotional development of its inhabitants, one becomes dangerous. Laura Driscoll was terribly dangerous. That's why Laura was never a good history teacher.

44 She was not the first history teacher I had ever had. She is not the last I will have. But she is the only teacher I have ever had who could feel history with an emotional vibrance—or, if the person was too oblique, with a poetic understanding. She was five feet four inches tall, brown-haired, and bent-legged from horseback riding. All the boys thought Laura Driscoll was a swell teacher.

45 She was the only history teacher I have ever seen who was often ecstatical. She would stand by the boards and shout out her discoveries on the Egyptian cultures. She made the gargoylic churnings of Chartres in a heavy rain present an applicable meaning. She taught history as an interminable flood of events viewed through the distortion of our own immediacy. She taught history in the broad-handed rhythms of Hauptmann's drama, in the static melancholy of Egypt moving before its own shadow down the long sand, in the fluted symmetry of the Doric culture. She taught history as a

hypothesis from which we could extract the evaluation of our own lives.

46   She was the only teacher who realized that, coming from the West, she had little business to be teaching these children of New England.

47   "I do not know what your reaction to the sea is," she would say. "For I have come from a land where there is no sea. My elements are the fields, the sun, the plastic cadence of the clouds and the cloudlessness. You have been brought up by the sea. You have been coached in the cadence of the breakers and the strength of the wind.

48   "My emotional viewpoints will differ from yours. Do not let me impose my perceptions upon you."

49   However, the college-board people didn't care about Chartres as long as you knew the date. They didn't care whether history was looked at from the mountains or the sea. Laura spent too much time on such trivia and all of her pupils didn't get into Harvard. In fact, very few of her pupils got into Harvard, and this didn't speak well for her.

50   While the other members of the faculty chattered over Hepplewhite legs and Duncan Phyfe embellishments, Laura was before five-handed Siva or the sexless compassion glorious in its faded polychrome. Laura didn't think much of America. Laura made this obvious and the faculty heard about it. The faculty all thought America was beautiful. They didn't like people to disagree.

51   However, the consummation did not occur until late in February. It was cold and clear and the snow was deep. Outside the windows there was the enormous roaring of broken ice. It was late in February that Laura Driscoll said Sacco and Vanzetti were undeserving of their treatment.

52   This got everyone all up in the air. Even the headmaster was disconcerted.

53   The faculty met.

54   The parents wrote letters.

55   Laura Driscoll was fired.

"Miss Driscoll," said the headmaster during her last chapel at the school, "has found it necessary to return to the West. In the few months that we have had her with us, she has been a staunch friend of the academy, a woman whom we all admire and love and who, we are sure, loves and admires the academy and its elms as we do. We are all sorry Miss Driscoll is leaving us. . . ."

57 Then Laura got up, called him a damned liar, swore down the length of the platform and walked out of the building.

58 No one ever saw Laura Driscoll again. By the way everyone talked, no one wanted to. That was all late in February. By March the school was quiet again. The new history teacher taught dates. Everyone carefully forgot about Laura Driscoll.

59 "She was a nice girl," said the headmaster, "but she really wasn't made for teaching history. . . . No, she really wasn't a born history teacher."

Five Months Later

60 The spring of five months ago was the most beautiful spring I have ever lived in. The year before I had not known all about the trees and the heavy peach blossoms and the tea-colored brooks that shook down over the brown rocks. Five months ago it was spring and I was in school.

61 In school the white limbs beyond the study hall shook out a greenness, and the tennis courts became white and scalding. The air was empty and hard, and the vacant wind dragged shadows over the road. I knew all this only from the classrooms.

62 I knew about the trees from the window frames. I knew the rain only from the sounds on the roof. I was tired of seeing spring with walls and awnings to intercept the sweet sun and the hard fruit. I wanted to go outdoors and see the spring. I wanted to feel and taste the air and be among the shadows. That is perhaps why I left school.

63 In the spring I was glad to leave school. Everything outside was elegant and savage and fleshy. Everything inside was slow and cool and vacant. It seemed a shame to stay inside.

64 But in a little while the spring went. I was left outside and there was no spring. I did not want to go in again. I would not have gone in again for anything. I was sorry, but I was not sorry over the fact that I had gone out. I was sorry that the outside and the inside could not have been open to one another. I was sorry that there were roofs on the classrooms and trousers on the legs of the instructors to insulate their contacts. I was not sorry that I had left school. I was sorry that I left for the reasons that I did.

65 If I had left because I had to go to work or because I was sick it would not have been so bad. Leaving because you are angry and frustrated is different. It is not a good thing to do. It is bad for everyone.

66 Of course it was not the fault of the school. The headmaster and faculty were doing what they were supposed to do. It was just a preparatory school trying to please the colleges. A school that was doing everything the colleges asked it to do.

67 It was not the fault of the school at all. It was the fault of the system—the noneducational system, the college-preparatory system. That was what made the school so useless.

68 As a college-preparatory school it was a fine school. In five years they could make raw material look like college material. They could clothe it and breed it and make it say the right things when the colleges asked it to talk. That was its duty.

69 They weren't prepared to educate anybody. They were members of a college-preparatory system. No one around there wanted to be educated. No sir.

70 They presented the subjects the colleges required. They had math, English, history, languages, and music. They once had had an art department but it had been dropped. "We have enough to do," said the headmaster, "just to get all these people into college without trying to teach them art. Yes sir, we have quite enough to do as it is."

71 Of course there were literary appreciation and art appreciation and musical appreciation, but they didn't count for much. If you are young, there is very little in Thackeray that is parallel to your own world. Van Dyke's "Abbé Scaglia" and the fretwork of Mozart quartets are not for the focus of your ears and

eyes. All the literature and art that holds a similarity to your life is forgotten. Some of it is even forbidden.

72 Our country is the best country in the world. We are swimming in prosperity and our President is the best president in the world. We have larger apples and better cotton and faster and more beautiful machines. This makes us the greatest country in the world. Unemployment is a myth. Dissatisfaction is a fable. In preparatory school America is beautiful. It is the gem of the ocean and it is too bad. It is bad because people believe it all. Because they become indifferent. Because they marry and reproduce and vote and they know nothing. Because the tempered newspaper keeps its eyes ceilingwards and does not see the dirty floor. Because all they know is the tempered newspaper.

73 But I will not say any more. I do not stand in a place where I can talk.

74 And now it is August. The orchards are stinking ripe. The tea-colored brooks run beneath the rocks. There is sediment on the stone and no wind in the willows. Everyone is preparing to go back to school. I have no school to go back to.

75 I am not sorry. I am not at all glad.

76 It is strange to be so very young and to have no place to report to at nine o'clock. That is what education has always been. It has been laced curtseys and perfumed punctualities.

77 But now it is nothing. It is symmetric with my life. I am lost in it. That is why I am not standing in a place where I can talk.

78 The school windows are being washed. The floors are thick with fresh oil.

79 Soon it will be time for the snow and the symphonies. It will be time for Brahms and the great dry winds.

*M*ihaly Csikszentmihalyi (1934–), a professor and former chair of the Department of Psychology at the University of Chicago, has been engaged in studies related to optimal experience, or "flow," for more than twenty-five years. His research has generated interest in not only the academic world but has also appeared in numerous popular publications such as Psychology Today, *the* New York Times, *the* Washington Post, *the* Chicago Tribune, Omni, *and* Newsweek. *In addition to* Flow, *he wrote* Beyond Boredom and Anxiety, *and co-authored* The Creative Vision, The Meaning of Things, *and* Being Adolescent. *Professor Csikszentmihalyi has participated in a number of television programs in both Europe and America, including several appearances on the popular PBS series* Nova.

Work as Flow

Mihaly Csikszentmihalyi

1   Like other animals, we must spend a large part of our existence making a living: calories needed to fuel the body don't appear magically on the table, and houses and cars don't assemble themselves spontaneously. There are no strict formulas, however, for how much time people actually have to work. It seems, for instance, that the early hunter-gatherers, like their present-day descendants living in the inhospitable deserts of Africa and Australia, spent only three to five hours each day on what we would call working—providing for food, shelter, clothing, and tools. They spent the rest of the day in conversation, resting, or dancing. At the opposite extreme were the industrial workers of the nineteenth century, who were often forced to spend twelve-hour days, six days a week, toiling in grim factories or dangerous mines.

2   Not only the quantity of work, but its quality has been highly variable. There is an old Italian saying: "*Il lavoro nobilita l'uomo, e lo rende simile alle bestie*"; or, "Work gives man nobility, and turns him into an animal." This ironic trope may be a comment on the nature of all work, but it can also be interpreted to mean that work requiring great skills and that is done freely refines the complexity of the self; and, on the other hand, that there are few

14

things as entropic as unskilled work done under compulsion. The brain surgeon operating in a shining hospital and the slave laborer who staggers under a heavy load as he wades through the mud are both working. But the surgeon has a chance to learn new things every day, and every day he learns that he is in control and that he can perform difficult tasks. The laborer is forced to repeat the same exhausting motions, and what he learns is mostly about his own helplessness.

3　Because work is so universal, yet so varied, it makes a tremendous difference to one's overall contentment whether what one does for a living is enjoyable or not. Thomas Carlyle was not far wrong when he wrote, "Blessed is he who has found his work; let him ask no other blessedness." Sigmund Freud amplified somewhat on this simple advice. When asked for his recipe for happiness, he gave a very short but sensible answer: "Work and love." It is true that if one finds flow in work, and in relations with other people, one is well on the way toward improving the quality of life as a whole. In this chapter we shall explore how jobs can provide flow, and in the following one we shall take up Freud's other main theme—enjoying the company of others.

Autotelic Workers

4　As punishment for his ambition, Adam was sentenced by the Lord to work the earth with the sweat of his brow. The passage of Genesis (3:17) that relates this event reflects the way most cultures, and especially those that have reached the complexity of "civilization," conceive of work—as a curse to be avoided at all costs. It is true that, because of the inefficient way the universe operates, it requires a lot of energy to realize our basic needs and aspirations. As long as we didn't care how much we ate, whether or not we lived in solid and well-decorated homes, or whether we could afford the latest fruits of technology, the necessity of working would rest lightly on our shoulders, as it does for the nomads of the Kalahari desert. But the more psychic energy we invest in material goals, and the more improbable the goals grow to be, the more difficult it becomes to make them come true. Then we need increasingly high inputs of labor, mental and physical, as well as inputs of natural resources, to satisfy escalating expectations. For much of history, the great majority of people who lived at the periphery of "civilized" societies had to give up any hope of enjoying life in order to make the dreams of the few who had found a way of exploiting them come true. The achievements that set civilized nations apart from the more primitive—such as the Pyramids, the Great Wall of China, the Taj Mahal, and the temples, palaces, and dams of antiquity—were usually built with the energy of slaves forced to realize their rulers' ambitions. Not surprisingly, work acquired a rather poor reputation.

5   With all due respect to the Bible, however, it does not seem to be true that work necessarily needs to be unpleasant. It may always have to be hard, or at least harder than doing nothing at all. But there is ample evidence that work can be enjoyable, and that indeed, it is often the most enjoyable part of life.

6   Occasionally cultures evolve in such a way as to make every-day productive chores as close to flow activities as possible. There are groups in which both work and family life are challenging yet harmoniously integrated. In the high mountain valleys of Europe, in Alpine villages spared by the Industrial Revolution, communities of this type still exist. Curious to see how work is experienced in a "traditional" setting representative of farming life-styles that were prevalent everywhere up to a few generations ago, a team of Italian psychologists led by Professor Fausto Massimini and Dr. Antonella Delle Fave recently interviewed some of their inhabitants, and have generously shared their exhaustive transcripts.

7   The most striking feature of such places is that those who live there can seldom distinguish work from free time. It could be said that they work sixteen hours a day each day, but then it could also be argued that they never work. One of the inhabitants, Serafina Vinon, a seventy-six-year-old woman from the tiny hamlet of Pont Trentaz, in the Val d'Aosta region of the Italian Alps, still gets up at five in the morning to milk her cows. Afterward she cooks a huge breakfast, cleans the house, and, depending on the weather and time of year, either takes the herd to the meadows just below the glaciers, tends the orchard, or cards some wool. In summer she spends weeks on the high pastures cutting hay, and then carries huge bales of it on her head the several miles down to the barn. She could reach the barn in half the time if she took a direct route; but she prefers following invisible winding trails to save the slopes from erosion. In the evening she may read, or tell stories to her great-grandchildren, or play the accordion for one

of the parties of friends and relatives that assemble at her house a few times a week.

8 Serafina knows every tree, every boulder, every feature of the mountains as if they were old friends. Family legends going back many centuries are linked to the landscape: On this old stone bridge, when the plague of 1473 had exhausted itself, one night the last surviving woman of Serafina's village, with a torch in her hand, met the last surviving man of the village further down the valley. They helped each other, got married, and became the ancestors of her family. It was in that field of raspberries that her grandmother was lost when she was a little girl. On this rock, standing with a pitchfork in his hand, the Devil threatened Uncle Andrew during the freak snowstorm of '24.

9 When Serafina was asked what she enjoys doing most in life, she had no trouble answering: milking the cows, taking them to the pasture, pruning the orchard, carding wool . . . in effect, what she enjoys most is what she has been doing for a living all along. In her own words: "It gives me a great satisfaction. To be outdoors, to talk with people, to be with my animals . . . I talk to everybody—plants, birds, flowers, and animals. Everything in nature keeps you company; you see nature progress every day. You feel clean and happy: too bad that you get tired and have to go home. . . . even when you have to work a lot it is very beautiful."

10 When she was asked what she would do if she had all the time and money in the world, Serafina laughed—and repeated the same list of activities: she would milk the cows, take them to pasture, tend the orchard, card wool. It is not that Serafina is ignorant of the alternatives offered by urban life: she watches television occasionally and reads newsmagazines, and many of her younger relatives live in large cities and have comfortable life-styles, with cars, appliances, and exotic vacations. But their more fashionable and modern way of life does not attract Serafina; she is perfectly content and serene with the role she plays in the universe.

11 Ten of the oldest residents of Pont Trentaz, ranging from sixty-six to eighty-two years of age, were interviewed; all of them gave responses similar to Serafina's. None of them drew a sharp distinction between work and free time, all mentioned

work as the major source of optimal experiences, and none would want to work less if given a chance.

12   Most of their children, who were also interviewed, expressed the same attitude toward life. However, among the grandchildren (aged between twenty and thirty-three years), more typical attitudes toward work prevailed: given a chance they would have worked less, and spent more time instead in leisure—reading, sports, traveling, seeing the latest shows. Partly this difference between the generations is a matter of age; young people are usually less contented with their lot, more eager for change, and more intolerant of the constraints of routine. But in this case the divergence also reflects the erosion of a traditional way of life, in which work was meaningfully related to people's identities and to their ultimate goals. Some of the young people of Pont Trentaz might in their old age come to feel about their work as Serafina does; probably the majority will not. Instead, they will keep widening the gap between jobs that are necessary but unpleasant, and leisure pursuits that are enjoyable but have little complexity.

13   Life in this Alpine village has never been easy. To survive from day to day each person had to master a very broad range of difficult challenges ranging from plain hard work, to skillful crafts, to the preservation and elaboration of a distinctive language, of songs, of artworks, of complex traditions. Yet somehow the culture has evolved in such a way that the people living in it find these tasks enjoyable. Instead of feeling oppressed by the necessity to work hard, they share the opinion of Giuliana B., a seventy-four-year-old lady: "I am free, free in my work, because I do whatever I want. If I don't do something today I will do it tomorrow. I don't have a boss, I am the boss of my own life. I have kept my freedom and I have fought for my freedom."

14   Certainly, not all preindustrial cultures were this idyllic. In many hunting or farming societies life was harsh, brutish, and short. In fact, some of the Alpine communities not far from Pont Trentaz were described by foreign travelers of the last century as riddled with hunger, disease, and ignorance. To perfect a life-style capable of balancing harmoniously human goals with the resources of the environment is as rare a feat as building one of the great cathedrals that fill visitors with awe. We can't generalize from one successful example to

all preindustrial cultures. But by the same token even one exception is sufficient to disprove the notion that work must always be less enjoyable than freely chosen leisure.

15   But what about the case of an urban laborer, whose work is not so clearly tied to his subsistence? Serafina's attitude, as it happens, is not unique to traditional farming villages. We can occasionally find it around us in the midst of the turmoils of the industrial age. A good example is the case of Joe Kramer, a man we interviewed in one of our early studies of the flow experience. Joe was in his early sixties, a welder in a South Chicago plant where railroad cars are assembled. About two hundred people worked with Joe in three huge, dark, hangar-like structures where steel plates weighing several tons move around suspended from overhead tracks, and are welded amid showers of sparks to the wheelbases of freight cars. In summer it is an oven, in winter the icy winds of the prairie howl through. The clanging of metal is always so intense that one must shout into a person's ear to make oneself understood.

16   Joe came to the United States when he was five years old, and he left school after fourth grade. He had been working at this plant for over thirty years, but never wanted to become a foreman. He declined several promotions, claiming that he liked being a simple welder, and felt uncomfortable being anyone's boss. Although he stood on the lowest rung of the hierarchy in the plant, everyone knew Joe, and everyone agreed that he was the most important person in the entire factory. The manager stated that if he had five more people like Joe, his plant would be the most efficient in the business. His fellow workers said that without Joe they might as well shut down the shop right now.

17   The reason for his fame was simple: Joe had apparently mastered every phase of the plant's operation, and he was now able to take anyone's place if the necessity arose. Moreover, he could fix any broken-down piece of machinery, ranging from huge mechanical cranes to tiny electronic monitors. But what astounded people most was that Joe not only could perform these tasks, but actually enjoyed it when he was called upon to do them. When asked how he had learned to deal with complex engines and instruments without having had any formal training, Joe gave a very disarming answer. Since childhood he

had been fascinated with machinery of every kind. He was especially drawn to anything that wasn't working properly: "Like when my mother's toaster went on the fritz, I asked myself: 'If I were that toaster and I didn't work, what would be wrong with me?'" Then he disassembled the toaster, found the defect, and fixed it. Ever since, he has used this method of empathic identification to learn about and restore increasingly complex mechanical systems. And the fascination of discovery has never left him; now close to retirement, Joe still enjoys work every day.

18 Joe has never been a workaholic, completely dependent on the challenges of the factory to feel good about himself. What he did at home was perhaps even more remarkable than his transformation of a mindless, routine job into a complex, flow-producing activity. Joe and his wife live in a modest bungalow on the outskirts of the city. Over the years they bought up the two vacant lots on either side of their house. On these lots Joe built an intricate rock garden, with terraces, paths, and several hundred flowers and shrubs. While he was installing underground sprinklers, Joe had an idea: What if he had them make rainbows? He looked for sprinkler heads that would produce a fine enough mist for this purpose, but none satisfied him; so he designed one himself, and built it on his basement lathe. Now after work he could sit on the back porch, and by touching one switch he could activate a dozen sprays that turned into as many small rainbows.

19 But there was one problem with Joe's little Garden of Eden. Since he worked most days, by the time he got home the sun was usually too far down the horizon to help paint the water with strong colors. So Joe went back to the drawing board, and came back with an admirable solution. He found floodlights that contained enough of the sun's spectrum to form rainbows, and installed them inconspicuously around the sprinklers. Now he was really ready. Even in the middle of the night, just by touching two switches, he could surround his house with fans of water, light, and color.

20 Joe is a rare example of what it means to have an "autotelic personality," or the ability to create flow experiences even in the most barren environment—an almost inhumane workplace, a weed-infested urban neighborhood. In the entire railroad plant, Joe appeared to be the only man who had the

vision to perceive challenging opportunities for action. The rest of the welders we interviewed regarded their jobs as burdens to be escaped as promptly as possible, and each evening as soon as work stopped they fanned out for the saloons that were strategically placed on every third corner of the grid of streets surrounding the factory, there to forget the dullness of the day with beer and camaraderie. Then home for more beer in front of the TV, a brief skirmish with the wife, and the day—in all respects similar to each previous one—was over.

21 One might argue here that endorsing Joe's life-style over that of his fellow workers is reprehensibly "elitist." After all, the guys in the saloon are having a good time, and who is to say that grubbing away in the backyard making rainbows is a better way to spend one's time? By the tenets of cultural relativism the criticism would be justifiable, of course. But when one understands that enjoyment depends on increasing complexity, it is no longer possible to take such radical relativism seriously. The quality of experience of people who play with and transform the opportunities in their surroundings, as Joe did, is clearly more developed as well as more enjoyable than that of people who resign themselves to live within the constraints of the barren reality they feel they cannot alter.

22 The view that work undertaken as a flow activity is the best way to fulfill human potentialities has been proposed often enough in the past, by various religious and philosophical systems. To people imbued with the Christian worldview of the Middle Ages it made sense to say that peeling potatoes was just as important as building a cathedral, provided they were both done for the greater glory of God. For Karl Marx, men and women constructed their being through productive activities; there is no "human nature," he held, except that which we create through work. Work not only transforms the environment by building bridges across rivers and cultivating barren plains; it also transforms the worker from an animal guided by instincts into a conscious, goal-directed, skillful person.

23 One of the most interesting examples of how the phenomenon of flow appeared to thinkers of earlier times is the concept of *Yu* referred to about 2,300 years ago in the writings of the Taoist scholar Chuang Tzu. *Yu* is a synonym for the right way of following the path, or *Tao*: it has been translated into English as "wandering"; as "walking without touching the ground";

or as "swimming," "flying," and *"flowing."* Chuang Tzu believed that to *Yu* was the proper way to live—without concern for external rewards, spontaneously, with total commitment—in short, as a total autotelic experience.

24 As an example of how to live by *Yu*—or how to flow—Chuang Tzu presents, in the Inner Chapters of the work which has come down to us bearing his name, a parable of a humble worker. This character is Ting, a cook whose task was to butcher the meat at the court of Lord Hui of Wei. Schoolchildren in Hong Kong and Taiwan still have to memorize Chuang Tzu's description: "Ting was cutting up an ox for Lord Wen-hui. At every touch of his hand, every heave of his shoulder, every move of his feet, every thrust of his knee—zip! zoop! He slithered the knife along with a zing, and all was in perfect rhythm, as though he were performing the dance of the Mulberry Grove or keeping time to the Ching-shou music."

25 Lord Wen-hui was fascinated by how much flow (or *Yu*) his cook found in his work, and so he complimented Ting on his great skill. But Ting denied that it was a matter of skill: "What I care about is the Way, which goes beyond skill." Then he described how he had achieved his superb performance: a sort of mystical, intuitive understanding of the anatomy of the ox, which allowed him to slice it to pieces with what appeared to be automatic ease: "Perception and understanding have come to a stop and spirit moves where it wants."

26 Ting's explanation may seem to imply that *Yu* and flow are the result of different kinds of processes. In fact, some critics have emphasized the differences: while flow is the result of a conscious attempt to master challenges, *Yu* occurs when the individual gives up conscious mastery. In this sense they see flow as an example of the "Western" search for optimal experience, which according to them is based on changing objective conditions (e.g., by confronting challenges with skills), whereas *Yu* is an example of the "Eastern" approach, which disregards objective conditions entirely in favor of spiritual playfulness and the transcendence of actuality.

27 But how is a person to achieve this transcendental experience and spiritual playfulness? In the same parable, Chuang Tzu offers a valuable insight to answer this question, an insight that has given rise to diametrically opposite interpretations. In

Watson's translation, it reads as follows: "However, whenever I come to a complicated place, I size up the difficulties, tell myself to watch out and be careful, keep my eyes on what I'm doing, work very slowly, and move my knife with the greatest of subtlety, until—flop! the whole thing comes apart like a clod of earth crumbling to the ground. I stand there holding the knife and look all around me, completely satisfied and reluctant to move on, and then I wipe off the knife and put it away."

28   Now some earlier scholars have taken this passage to refer to the working methods of a mediocre carver who does not know how to *Yu*. More recent ones such as Watson and Graham believe that it refers to Ting's own working methods. Based on my knowledge of the flow experience, I believe the latter reading must be the correct one. It demonstrates, even after all the obvious levels of skill and craft (*chi*) have been mastered, the *Yu* still depends on the discovery of new challenges (the "complicated place" or "difficulties" in the above quotation), and on the development of new skills ("watch out and be careful, keep my eyes on what I'm doing . . . move my knife with the greatest of subtlety").

29   In other words, the mystical heights of the *Yu* are not attained by some superhuman quantum jump, but simply by the gradual focusing of attention on the opportunities for action in one's environment, which results in a perfection of skills that with time becomes so thoroughly automatic as to seem spontaneous and otherworldly. The performances of a great violinist or a great mathematician seem equally uncanny, even though they can be explained by the incremental honing of challenges and skills. If my interpretation is true, in the flow experience (or *Yu*) East and West meet: in both cultures ecstasy arises from the same sources. Lord Wen-hui's cook is an excellent example of how one can find flow in the most unlikely places, in the most humble jobs of daily life. And it is also remarkable that over twenty-three centuries ago the dynamics of this experience were already so well known.

30   The old woman who farms in the Alps, the welder in South Chicago, and the mythical cook from ancient China have this in common: their work is hard and unglamorous, and most people would find it boring, repetitive, and meaningless. Yet these individuals transformed the jobs they had to do into complex activities. They did this by recognizing opportunities

for action where others did not, by developing skills, by focusing on the activity at hand, and allowing themselves to be lost in the interaction so that their selves could emerge stronger afterward. Thus transformed, work becomes enjoyable, and as the result of a personal investment of psychic energy, it feels as if it were freely chosen, as well.

Autotelic Jobs

31   Serafina, Joe, and Ting are examples of people who have developed an autotelic personality. Despite the severe limitations of their environment they were able to change constraints into opportunities for expressing their freedom and creativity. Their method represents one way to enjoy one's job while making it richer. The other is to change the job itself, until its conditions are more conducive to flow, even for people who lack autotelic personalities. The more a job inherently resembles a game—with variety, appropriate and flexible challenges, clear goals, and immediate feedback—the more enjoyable it will be regardless of the worker's level of development.

32   Hunting, for instance, is a good example of "work" that by its very nature had all the characteristics of flow. For hundreds of thousands of years chasing down game was the main productive activity in which humans were involved. Yet hunting has proven to be so enjoyable that many people are still doing it as a hobby, after all practical need for it has disappeared. The same is true of fishing. The pastoral mode of existence also has some of the freedom and flowlike structure of earliest "work." Many contemporary young Navajos in Arizona claim that following their sheep on horseback over the mesas is the most enjoyable thing they ever do. Compared to hunting or herding, farming is more difficult to enjoy. It is a more settled, more repetitive activity, and the results take much longer to appear. The seeds planted in spring need months to bear fruit. To enjoy agriculture one must play within a much longer time frame than in hunting: while the hunter may choose his quarry and method of attack several times each day, the farmer decides what crops to plant, where, and in what quantity only a few times each year. In order to succeed, the farmer must make lengthy preparations, and endure chancy periods of waiting helplessly for the weather to cooperate. It is not surprising to learn that populations of nomads or hunters, when forced to

become farmers, appear to have died out rather than submitting themselves to that ostensibly boring existence. Yet many farmers also eventually learned to enjoy the more subtle opportunities of their occupation.

33   The crafts and cottage industries that before the eighteenth century occupied most of the time left free from farming were reasonably well designed in terms of providing flow. English weavers, for example, had their looms at home, and worked with their entire family according to self-imposed schedules. They set their own goals for production, and modified them according to what they thought they could accomplish. If the weather was good, they quit so they could work in the orchard or the vegetable garden. When they felt like it they would sing a few ballads, and when a piece of cloth was finished they all celebrated with a wee drink.

34   This arrangement still functions in some parts of the world that have been able to maintain a more humane pace of production, despite all the benefits of modernization. For instance, Professor Massimini and his team have interviewed weavers in the province of Biella, in northern Italy, whose pattern of working resembles that of the fabled English weavers of over two centuries ago. Each of these families owns two to ten mechanical looms that can be supervised by a single person. The father may watch the looms early in the morning, then call in his son to take over while he goes looking for mushrooms in the forest or stops by the creek to fish for trout. The son runs the machines until he gets bored, at which point the mother takes over.

35   In their interviews, every member of the families listed weaving as the most enjoyable activity they did—more than traveling, more than going to discos, more than fishing, and certainly more than watching TV. The reason that working was so much fun is that it was continually challenging. Family members designed their own patterns, and when they had had enough of one kind they would switch to another. Each family decided what type of cloth to weave, where to buy the materials, how much to produce, and where to sell it. Some families had customers as far away as Japan and Australia. Family members were always traveling to manufacturing centers to keep abreast of new technical developments, or to buy necessary equipment as cheaply as possible.

36   But throughout most of the Western world such cozy arrange-
     ments conducive to flow were brutally disrupted by the inven-
     tion of the first power looms, and the centralized factory sys-
     tem they spawned. By the middle of the eighteenth century
     family crafts in England were generally unable to compete
     with mass production. Families were broken up, workers had
     to leave their cottages and move en masse into ugly and
     unwholesome plants, rigid schedules lasting from dawn to
     dusk were enforced. Children as young as seven years of age
     had to work themselves to exhaustion among indifferent or
     exploitive strangers. If the enjoyment of work had any credi-
     bility before, it was effectively destroyed in that first frenzy of
     industrialization.

37   Now we have entered a new, postindustrial age, and work is
     said to be becoming benign again: the typical laborer now sits
     in front of a bank of dials, supervising a computer screen in a
     pleasant control room, while a band of savvy robots down the
     line do whatever "real" work needs to be done. In fact, most
     people are not engaged in production any longer; they work in
     the so-called "service sector," at jobs that would surely appear
     like pampered leisure to the farmers and factory workers of
     only a few generations ago. Above them are the managers and
     professionals, who have great leeway in making whatever
     they want to of their jobs.

38   So work can be either brutal and boring, or enjoyable and excit-
     ing. In just a few decades, as happened in England in the 1740s,
     the average working conditions can change from being rela-
     tively pleasant to a nightmare. Technological innovations such as
     the waterwheel, the plow, the steam engine, electricity, or the sil-
     icon chip can make a tremendous difference in whether work
     will be enjoyable or not. Laws regulating the enclosure of the
     commons, the abolition of slavery, the abolition of apprentices,
     or the institution of the forty-hour week and of minimum wages
     can also have a great impact. The sooner we realize that the qual-
     ity of the work experience can be transformed at will, the sooner
     we can improve this enormously important dimension of life.
     Yet most people still believe that work is forever destined to
     remain "the curse of Adam."

39   In theory, any job could be changed so as to make it more
     enjoyable by following the prescriptions of the flow model. At
     present, however, whether work is enjoyable or not ranks

quite low among the concerns of those who have the power to influence the nature of a given job. Management has to care for productivity first and foremost, and union bosses have to keep safety, security, and compensations uppermost in their minds. In the short run these priorities might well conflict with flow-producing conditions. This is regrettable, because if workers really enjoyed their jobs they would not only benefit personally, but sooner or later they would almost certainly produce more efficiently and reach all the other goals that now take precedence.

40   At the same time, it would be erroneous to expect that if all jobs were constructed like games, everyone would enjoy them. Even the most favorable external conditions do not guarantee that a person will be in flow. Because optimal experience depends on a subjective evaluation of what the possibilities for action are, and of one's own capacities, it happens quite often that an individual will be discontented even with a potentially great job.

41   Let us take as an example the profession of surgery. Few jobs involve so much responsibility, or bestow so much status on its practitioners. Certainly if challenges and skills are significant factors, then surgeons must find their job exhilarating. And in fact many surgeons say that they are addicted to their work, that nothing else in their lives compares with it in terms of enjoyment, that anything that takes them away from the hospital—a Caribbean vacation, a night at the opera—feels like a waste of time.

42   But not every surgeon is as enthusiastic about his job. Some grow so bored by it that they take up drinking, gambling, or a fast life-style to forget its drudgery. How can such widely diverging views of the same profession be possible? One reason is that surgeons who settle down for well-paid but repetitive routines soon begin to feel their tedium. There are surgeons who only cut out appendices, or tonsils; a few even specialize in piercing earlobes. Such specialization can be lucrative, but it makes enjoying the job more difficult. At the other extreme, there are competitive supersurgeons who go off the deep end in the other direction, constantly needing new challenges, wanting to perform spectacular new surgical procedures until they finally can't meet the expectations they have set for themselves. Surgical pioneers burn out for the opposite

reason of the routine specialist: they have accomplished the impossible once, but they haven't found a way to do it again.

43   Those surgeons who enjoy their work usually practice in hospitals that allow variety and a certain amount of experimentation with the latest techniques, and that make research and teaching part of the job. The surgeons who like what they do mention money, prestige, and saving lives as being important to them, but they state that their greatest enthusiasm is for the intrinsic aspects of the job. What makes surgery so special for them is the feeling one gets from the activity itself. And the way they describe that feeling is in almost every detail similar to the flow experiences reported by athletes, artists, or the cook who butchered the meat for the Lord of Wei.

44   The explanation for this is that surgical operations have all the characteristics that a flow activity should have. Surgeons mention, for instance, how well defined their goals are. An internist deals with problems that are less specific and localized, and a psychiatrist with even more vague and ephemeral symptoms and solutions. By contrast the surgeon's task is crystal-clear: to cut out the tumor, or set the bone, or get some organ pumping away again. Once that task is accomplished he can sew up the incision, and turn to the next patient with the sense of a job well done.

45   Similarly surgery provides immediate and continuous feedback. If there is no blood in the cavity, the operation is going well; then the diseased tissue comes out, or the bone is set; the stitches take (or not, if that is the case), but throughout the process one knows exactly how successful one is, and if not, why not. For this reason alone, most surgeons believe that what they are doing is so much more enjoyable than any other branch of medicine, or any other job on earth.

46   At another level, there is no lack of challenges in surgery. In the words of one surgeon: "I get intellectual enjoyment—like the chess player or the academic who studies ancient Mesopotamian toothpicks. . . . The craft is enjoyable, like carpentry is fun. . . . The gratification of taking an extremely difficult problem and making it go." And another: "It's very satisfying and if it is somewhat difficult it is also exciting. It's very nice to make things work again, to put things in their right place so that it looks like it should, and fits neatly. This is very

pleasant, particularly when the group works together in a smooth and efficient manner: then the aesthetics of the whole situation can be appreciated."

47   This second quote indicates that the challenges of an operation are not limited to what the surgeon must do personally, but include coordinating an event that involves a number of additional players. Many surgeons comment on how exhilarating it is to be part of a well-trained team that functions smoothly and efficiently. And of course there is always the possibility of doing things better, of improving one's skills. An eye surgeon commented, "You use fine and precise instruments. It is an exercise in art. . . . It all rests on how precisely and artistically you do the operation." Remarked another surgeon, "It is important to watch for details, to be neat and technically efficient. I don't like to waste motion and so try to make the operation as well planned and thought out as possible. I'm particular about how the needle is held, where the stitches are placed, the type of suture, and so on—things should look the best and seem easy."

48   The way surgery is practiced helps block out distractions, and concentrates all one's attention on the procedure. The operating theater is indeed like a stage, with spotlights illuminating the action and the actors. Before an operation surgeons go through steps of preparation, purification, and dressing up in special garments—like athletes before a contest, or priests before a ceremony. These rituals have a practical purpose, but they also serve to separate celebrants from the concerns of everyday life, and focus their minds on the event to be enacted. Some surgeons say that on the mornings before an important operation they put themselves on "automatic pilot" by eating the same breakfast, wearing the same clothes, and driving to the hospital by the same route. They do so not because they are superstitious, but because they sense that this habitual behavior makes it easier for them to devote their undivided attention to the challenge ahead.

49   Surgeons are lucky. Not only are they paid well, not only do they bask in respect and admiration, but they also have a job built according to the blueprint of flow activities. Not-withstanding all these advantages, there are surgeons who go out of their minds because of boredom, or because they are reaching after unattainable power and fame. What this indicates is

that important as the structure of a job is, by itself it won't determine whether or not a person performing that job will find enjoyment in it. Satisfaction in a job will also depend on whether or not a worker has an autotelic personality. Joe the welder enjoyed tasks that few would regard as providing opportunities for flow. At the same time some surgeons manage to hate a job that seems to have been intentionally created to provide enjoyment.

50   To improve the quality of life through work, two complementary strategies are necessary. On the one hand jobs should be redesigned so that they resemble as closely as possible flow activities—as do hunting, cottage weaving, and surgery. But it will also be necessary to help people develop autotelic personalities like those of Serafina, Joe, and Ting, by training them to recognize opportunities for action, to hone their skills, to set reachable goals. Neither one of these strategies is likely to make work much more enjoyable by itself; in combination, they should contribute enormously to optimal experience.

The Paradox of Work

51   It is easier to understand the way work affects the quality of life when we take the long view, and compare ourselves with people from different times and cultures. But eventually we have to look more closely at what is happening here and now. Ancient Chinese cooks, Alpine farmers, surgeons, and welders help illuminate the potential inherent in work, but they are not, after all, very typical of the kind of job most people do nowadays. What is work like for average American adults today?

52   In our studies we have often encountered a strange inner conflict in the way people relate to the way they make their living. On the one hand, our subjects usually report that they have had some of their most positive experiences while on the job. From this response it would follow that they would wish to be working, that their motivation on the job would be high. Instead, even when they feel good, people generally say that they would prefer not to be working, that their motivation on the job is low. The converse is also true: when supposedly enjoying their hard-earned leisure, people generally report surprisingly low moods; yet they keep on wishing for more leisure.

53   For example, in one study we used the Experience Sampling Method to answer the question: Do people report more instances of flow at work or in leisure? The respondents, over a hundred men and women working full-time at a variety of occupations, wore an electronic pager for one week, and whenever the pager beeped in response to signals sent at eight random times each day for a week, they filled out two pages of a booklet to record what they were doing and how they felt at the moment they were signaled. Among other things, they were asked to indicate, on ten-point scales, how many challenges they saw at the moment, and how many skills they felt they were using.

54   A person was counted as being in flow every time he or she marked both the level of challenges and the level of skills to be above the mean level for the week. In this particular study over 4,800 responses were collected—an average of about 44 per person per week. In terms of the criterion we had adopted, 33 percent of these responses were "in flow"—that is, above the mean personal weekly level of challenges and skills. Of course, this method of defining flow is rather liberal. If one only wished to include extremely complex flow experiences— say, those with the highest levels of challenges and skills—perhaps fewer than 1 percent of the responses would qualify as flow. The methodological convention adopted here to define flow functions somewhat like a microscope: depending on the level of magnification used, very different detail will be visible.

55   As expected, the more time a person spent in flow during the week, the better was the overall quality of his or her reported experience. People who were more often in flow were especially likely to feel "strong," "active," "creative," "concentrated," and "motivated." What was unexpected, however, is how frequently people reported flow situations at work, and how rarely in leisure.

56   When people were signaled while they were actually working at their jobs (which happened only about three-fourths of the time, because, as it turned out, the remaining one-fourth of the time on the job these average workers were daydreaming, gossiping, or engaged in personal business), the proportion of responses in flow was a high 54 percent. In other words, about half the time that people are working they feel they are confronting above-average challenges, and using above-average

skills. In contrast, when engaged in leisure activities such as reading, watching TV, having friends over, or going to a restaurant, only 18 percent of the responses ended up in flow. The leisure responses were typically in the range we have come to call *apathy*, characterized by below-average levels of both challenges and skills. In this condition, people tend to say that they feel passive, weak, dull, and dissatisfied. When people were working, 16 percent of the responses were in the apathy region; in leisure, over half (52 percent).

57   As one would expect, managers and supervisors were significantly more often in flow at work (64 percent) than were clerical workers (51 percent) and blue-collar workers (47 percent). Blue-collar workers reported more flow in leisure (20 percent) than clerical workers (16 percent) and managers (15 percent) did. But even workers on the assembly lines reported they were in flow more than twice as often at work as in leisure (47 percent versus 20 percent). Conversely, apathy was reported at work more often by blue-collar workers than by managers (23 percent versus 11 percent), and in leisure more often by managers than by blue-collar workers (61 percent versus 46 percent).

58   Whenever people were in flow, either at work or in leisure, they reported it as a much more positive experience than the times they were not in flow. When challenges and skills were both high they felt happier, more cheerful, stronger, more active; they concentrated more; they felt more creative and satisfied. All these differences in the quality of experience were very significant statistically, and they were more or less the same for every kind of worker.

59   There was only a single exception to this general trend. One of the questions in the response booklet asked respondents to indicate, again on a ten-point scale from no to yes, their answer to the following question: "Did you wish you had been doing something else?" The extent to which a person answers this with a no is generally a reliable indication of how motivated he or she is at the moment of the signal. The results showed that people wished to be doing something else to a much greater extent when working than when at leisure, and this regardless of whether they were in flow. In other words, motivation was low at work even when it provided flow, and it was high in leisure even when the quality of experience was low.

60   Thus we have the paradoxical situation: On the job people feel skillful and challenged, and therefore feel more happy, strong, creative, and satisfied. In their free time people feel that there is generally not much to do and their skills are not being used, and therefore they tend to feel more sad, weak, dull, and dissatisfied. Yet they would like to work less and spend more time in leisure.

61   What does this contradictory pattern mean? There are several possible explanations, but one conclusion seems inevitable: when it comes to work, people do not heed the evidence of their senses. They disregard the quality of immediate experience, and base their motivation instead on the strongly rooted cultural stereotype of what work is *supposed* to be like. They think of it as an imposition, a constraint, an infringement of their freedom, and therefore something to be avoided as much as possible.

62   It could be argued that although flow at work is enjoyable, people cannot stand high levels of challenge all the time. They need to recover at home, to turn into couch potatoes for a few hours each day even though they don't enjoy it. But comparative examples seem to contradict this argument. For instance the farmers of Pont Trentaz work much harder, and for longer hours, than the average American, and the challenges they face in their daily round require at least as high levels of concentration and involvement. Yet they don't wish to be doing something else while working, and afterward, instead of relaxing, they fill their free time with demanding leisure activities.

63   As these findings suggest, the apathy of many of the people around us is not due to their being physically or mentally exhausted. The problem seems to lie more in the modern worker's relation to his job, with the way he perceives his goals in relation to it.

64   When we feel that we are investing attention in a task against our will, it is as if our psychic energy is being wasted. Instead of helping us reach our own goals, it is called upon to make someone else's come true. The time channeled into such a task is perceived as time subtracted from the total available for our life. Many people consider their jobs as something they have to do, a burden imposed from the outside, an effort that takes life away from the ledger of their existence. So even though the

momentary on-the-job experience may be positive, they tend to discount it, because it does not contribute to their own long-range goals.

65   It should be stressed, however, that "dissatisfaction" is a relative term. According to large-scale national surveys conducted between 1972 and 1978, only 3 percent of American workers said they were very dissatisfied with their jobs, while 52 percent said they were very satisfied—one of the highest rates in industrialized nations. But one can love one's job and still be displeased with some aspects of it, and try to improve what is not perfect. In our studies we find that American workers tend to mention three main reasons for their dissatisfaction with their jobs, all of which are related to the quality of experience typically available to them at work—even though, as we have just seen, their experience at work tends to be better than it is at home. (Contrary to popular opinion, salary and other material concerns are generally not among their most pressing concerns.) The first and perhaps most important complaint concerns the lack of variety and challenge. This can be a problem for everyone, but especially for those in lower-level occupations in which routine plays a major role. The second has to do with conflicts with other people on the job, especially bosses. The third reason involves burnout: too much pressure, too much stress, too little time to think for oneself, too little time to spend with the family. This is a factor that particularly troubles the higher echelons—executives and managers.

66   Such complaints are real enough, as they refer to objective conditions, yet they can be addressed by a subjective shift in one's consciousness. Variety and challenge, for instance, are in one sense inherent characteristics of jobs, but they also depend on how one perceives opportunities. Ting, Serafina, and Joe saw challenges in tasks that most people would find dull and meaningless. Whether a job has variety or not ultimately depends more on a person's approach to it than on actual working conditions.

67   The same is true of the other causes of dissatisfaction. Getting along with co-workers and supervisors might be difficult, but generally can be managed if one makes the attempt. Conflict at work is often due to a person's feeling defensive out of a fear of losing face. To prove himself he sets certain goals for how others should treat him, and then expects rigidly that others

will fulfill those expectations. This rarely happens as planned, however, because others also have an agenda for their own rigid goals to be achieved. Perhaps the best way to avoid this impasse is to set the challenge of reaching one's goals while helping the boss and colleagues reach theirs; it is less direct and more time-consuming than forging ahead to satisfy one's interests regardless of what happens to others, but in the long run it seldom fails.

68 Finally, stresses and pressures are clearly the most subjective aspects of a job, and therefore the ones that should be most amenable to the control of consciousness. Stress exists only if we experience it; it takes the most extreme objective conditions to cause it directly. The same amount of pressure will wilt one person and be a welcome challenge to another. There are hundreds of ways to relieve stress, some based on better organization, delegation of responsibility, better communication with co-workers and supervisors; others are based on factors external to the job, such as improved home life, leisure patterns, or inner disciplines like transcendental meditation.

69 These piecemeal solutions may help, but the only real answer to coping with work stress is to consider it part of a general strategy to improve the overall quality of experience. Of course this is easier said than done. To do so involves mobilizing psychic energy and keeping it focused on personally forged goals, despite inevitable distractions. Various ways of coping with external stress will be discussed later, in chapter 9. Now it may be useful to consider how the use of leisure time contributes—or fails to contribute—to the overall quality of life.

The Waste of Free Time

70 Although, as we have seen, people generally long to leave their places of work and get home, ready to put their hardearned free time to good use, all too often they have no idea what to do there. Ironically, jobs are actually easier to enjoy than free time, because like flow activities they have built-in goals, feedback, rules, and challenges, all of which encourage one to become involved in one's work, to concentrate and lose oneself in it. Free time, on the other hand, is unstructured, and requires much greater effort to be shaped into something that can be enjoyed. Hobbies that demand skill, habits that set goals and limits, personal interests, and especially inner discipline help

to make leisure what it is supposed to be—a chance for *re-cre-ation*. But on the whole people miss the opportunity to enjoy leisure even more thoroughly than they do with working time. Over sixty years ago, the great American sociologist Robert Park already noted: "It is in the improvident use of our leisure, I suspect, that the greatest wastes of American life occur."

71   The tremendous leisure industry that has arisen in the last few generations has been designed to help fill free time with enjoyable experiences. Nevertheless, instead of using our physical and mental resources to experience flow, most of us spend many hours each week watching celebrated athletes playing in enormous stadiums. Instead of making music, we listen to platinum records cut by millionaire musicians. Instead of making art, we go to admire paintings that brought in the highest bids at the latest auction. We do not run risks acting on our beliefs, but occupy hours each day watching actors who pretend to have adventures, engaged in mock-meaningful action.

72   This vicarious participation is able to mask, at least temporarily, the underlying emptiness of wasted time. But it is a very pale substitute for attention invested in real challenges. The flow experience that results from the use of skills leads to growth; passive entertainment leads nowhere. Collectively we are wasting each year the equivalent of millions of years of human consciousness. The energy that could be used to focus on complex goals, to provide for enjoyable growth, is squandered on patterns of stimulation that only mimic reality. Mass leisure, mass culture, and even high culture when only attended to passively and for extrinsic reasons—such as the wish to flaunt one's status—are parasites of the mind. They absorb psychic energy without providing substantive strength in return. They leave us more exhausted, more disheartened than we were before.

73   Unless a person takes charge of them, both work and free time are likely to be disappointing. Most jobs and many leisure activities—especially those involving the passive consumption of mass media—are not designed to make us happy and strong. Their purpose is to make money for someone else. If we allow them to, they can suck out the marrow of our lives, leaving only feeble husks. But like everything else, work and leisure can be appropriated for our needs. People who learn to enjoy their work, who do not waste their free time, end up

feeling that their lives as a whole have become much more worthwhile. "The future," wrote C. K. Brightbill, "will belong not only to the educated man, but to the man who is educated to use his leisure wisely."

Dorothy Day (1897–1980) was a journalist and radical, mother and grandmother, a Catholic convert, labor activist, pacifist, and spiritual writer. She was all of these at once, but none of these in ways that we might expect. She prayed to the saints, and has been called a saint. When asked if she might be a saint, she would reply that she did not want to be dismissed so easily. Like many saints, her uncompromising faith made her marginal to her times; yet, from the margins her life captured the imagination of the age. In New York City in 1933, she and Peter Maurin founded the Catholic Worker Movement, which lives by voluntary poverty and practices spiritual and corporal works of mercy. Today, Catholic Workers and their houses of hospitality welcome the poor in cities throughout the U.S. Catholic historian David O'Brien has called Day "the most significant, interesting, and influential person in the history of American Catholicism."

Poverty and Precarity

Dorothy Day

1   It is hard to write about poverty.

2   We live in a slum neighborhood. It is becoming ever more crowded with Puerto Ricans, those who have the lowest wages in the city, who do the hardest work, who are small and undernourished from generations of privation and exploitation.

3   It is hard to write about poverty when the backyard at Chrystie Street still has the furniture piled to one side that was put out on the street in an eviction in a next-door tenement.

4   How can we say to these people, "Rejoice and be exceedingly glad, for great is your reward in heaven," when we are living comfortably in a warm house, sitting down to a good table, decently clothed? Maybe not so decently. I had occasion to visit the city shelter last month where homeless families are cared for. I sat there for a couple of hours, contemplating poverty and destitution—a family with two of the children asleep in the parents' arms and four others sprawling against them; another young couple, the mother pregnant. I made myself known to a young man in charge. (I did not want to appear to be spying on

them when all I wanted to know was the latest on the apartment situation for homeless families.) He apologized for making me wait, explaining that he had thought I was one of the clients.

5   We need always to be thinking and writing about poverty, for if we are not among its victims its reality fades from us. We must talk about poverty, because people insulated by their own comfort lose sight of it. So many decent people come in to visit and tell us how their families were brought up in poverty, and how, through hard work and cooperation, they managed to educate all the children—even raise up priests and nuns to the Church. They contend that healthful habits and a stable family situation enable people to escape from the poverty class, no matter how mean the slum they may once have been forced to live in. So why can't everybody do it? No, these people don't know about the poor. Their conception of poverty is of something neat and well ordered as a nun's cell.

6   And maybe no one can be told; maybe they will have to experience it. Or maybe it is a grace which they must pray for. We usually get what we pray for, and maybe we are afraid to pray for it. And yet I am convinced that it is the grace we most need in this age of crisis, this time when expenditures reach into the billions to defend "our American way of life." Maybe this defense itself will bring down upon us the poverty we are afraid to pray for.

7   I well remember our first efforts when we started publishing our paper. We had no office, no equipment but a typewriter which was pawned the first month. We wrote the paper on park benches and the kitchen table. In an effort to achieve a little of the destitution of our neighbors, we gave away our furniture and sat on boxes. But as fast as we gave things away people brought more. We gave blankets to needy families and when we started our first House of Hospitality people gathered together what blankets we needed. We gave away food and more food came in—exotic food, some of it: a haunch of venison from the Canadian Northwest, a can of oysters from Maryland, a container of honey from Illinois. Even now it comes in, a salmon from Seattle, flown across the continent; nothing is too good for the poor.

8   No one working with *The Catholic Worker* gets a salary, so our
    readers feel called upon to give and help us keep the work
    going. And then we experience a poverty of another kind, a
    poverty of reputation. It is said often and with some scorn,
    "Why don't they get jobs and help the poor that way? Why are
    they living off others, begging?"

9   I can only explain to such critics that it would complicate
    things to give a salary to Roger for his work of fourteen hours
    a day in the kitchen, clothes room, and office; to pay Jane a
    salary for running the women's house and Beth and Annabelle
    for giving out clothes, for making stencils all day and helping
    with the sick and the poor, and then have them all turn the
    money right back in to support the work. Or to make it more
    complicated, they might all go out and get jobs, and bring the
    money home to pay their board and room and the salaries of
    others to run the house. It is simpler just to be poor. It is sim-
    pler to beg. The main thing is not to hold on to anything.

10 But the tragedy is that we do, we all do hold on—to our books,
    our tools, such as typewriters, our clothes; and instead of
    rejoicing when they are taken from us we lament. We protest
    when people take our time or privacy. We are holding on to
    these "goods" too.

11 Occasionally, as we start thinking of poverty—often after read-
    ing the life of such a saint as Benedict Joseph Labre—we dream
    of going out on our own, living with the destitute, sleeping on
    park benches or in the city shelter, living in churches, sitting
    before the Blessed Sacrament as we see so many doing from the
    Municipal Lodging House around the corner. And when such
    thoughts come on warm spring days when the children are
    playing in the park, and it is good to be out on the city streets,
    we know that we are only deceiving ourselves, for we are only
    dreaming of a form of luxury. What we want is the warm sun,
    and rest, and time to think and read, and freedom from the
    people who press in on us from early morning until late at
    night. No, it is not simple, this business of poverty.

12 "Precarity," or precariousness, is an essential element in true vol-
    untary poverty, a saintly priest from Martinique has written us.
    "True poverty is rare," he writes. "Nowadays religious commu-
    nities are good, I am sure, but they are mistaken about poverty.
    They accept, admit, poverty on principle, but everything must

be good and strong, buildings must be fireproof. Precarity is everywhere rejected, and precarity is an essential element of poverty. This has been forgotten. Here in our monastery we want precarity in everything except the church. These last days our refectory was near collapsing. We have put several supplementary beams in place and thus it will last maybe two or three years more. Someday it will fall on our heads and that will be funny. Precarity enables us better to help the poor. When a community is always building, enlarging, and embellishing, there is nothing left over for the poor. We have no right to do so as long as there are slums and breadlines somewhere."

13 Over and over again in the history of the Church the saints have emphasized poverty. Every religious community, begun in poverty and incredible hardship, but with a joyful acceptance of hardship by the rank-and-file priests, brothers, monks, or nuns who gave their youth and energy to good works, soon began to "thrive." Property was extended until holdings and buildings accumulated; and although there was still individual poverty in the community, there was corporate wealth. It is hard to remain poor.

14 One way to keep poor is not to accept money which is the result of defrauding the poor. Here is a story of St. Ignatius of Sardinia, a Capuchin recently canonized. Ignatius used to go out from his monastery with a sack to beg from the people of the town, but he would never go to a merchant who had built up his fortune by defrauding the poor. Franchino, the rich man, fumed every time the saint passed his door. His concern, however, was not the loss of the opportunity to give alms, but fear of public opinion. He complained at the friary, whereupon the Father Guardian ordered St. Ignatius to beg from the merchant the next time he went out.

15 "Very well," said Ignatius obediently. "If you wish it, Father, I will go, but I would not have the Capuchins dine on the blood of the poor."

16 The merchant received Ignatius with great flattery and gave him generous alms, asking him to come again in the future. But hardly had Ignatius left the house with his sack on his shoulder when drops of blood began oozing from the sack. They trickled down on Franchino's doorstep and ran down through the street to the monastery. Everywhere Ignatius went, a trickle of blood

followed him. When he arrived at the friary, he laid the sack at the Father Guardian's feet. "What is this?" gasped the Guardian. "This," St. Ignatius said, "is the blood of the poor."

17   This story appeared in the last column written by a great Catholic layman, a worker for social justice, F. P. Kenkel, editor of *Social Justice Review* in St. Louis (and always a friend of Peter Maurin's).

18   Mr. Kenkel's last comment was that the universal crisis in the world today was created by love of money. "The Far East and the Near East [and he might have said all Africa and Latin America also] together constitute a great sack from which blood is oozing. The flow will not stop as long as our interests in those people are dominated largely by financial and economic considerations."

19   Voluntary poverty, Peter Maurin would say, is the answer. Through voluntary poverty we will have the means to help our brothers. We cannot even see our brothers in need without first stripping ourselves. It is the only way we have of showing our love.

*M*ark Edmundson is a professor of English literature at the Universi-ty of Virginia. He is also a contributing editor to Harper's maga-zine, where the following article, "The Uses of a Liberal Arts Education," appeared in September, 1997. In it he offers a brief overview of the dangers inherent in what he sees as risk-free exchanges between students and teach-ers in today's college classrooms, where education has become equated with entertainment rather than with challenges to the intellect. Edmundson is the author of numerous articles and several books, including Teacher, the One Who Made the Difference (2002) and Literature against Philos-ophy, Plato to Derrida: A Defence of Poetry (1995).

On the Uses of a Liberal Education

As Lite Entertainment
for Bored College Students

Mark Edmundson

1   Today is evaluation day in my Freud class, and everything has changed. The class meets twice a week, late in the afternoon, and the clientele, about fifty undergraduates, tends to drag in and slump, looking disconsolate and a little lost, waiting for a jump start. To get the discussion moving, they usually require a joke, an anecdote, an off-the-wall question—When you were a kid, were your Halloween getups ego costumes, id costumes, or superego costumes? That sort of thing. But today, as soon as I flourish the forms, a buzz rises in the room. Today they write their assessments of the course, their assessments of me, and they are without a doubt wide-awake. "What is your evalua-tion of the instructor?" asks question number eight, entreating them to circle a number between five (excellent) and one (poor, poor). Whatever interpretive subtlety they've acquired during the term is now out the window. Edmundson: one to five, stand and shoot.

2   And they do. As I retreat through the door—I never stay around for this phase of the ritual—I look over my shoulder and see them toiling away like the devil's auditors. They're pitched into high writing gear, even the ones who struggle to

43

squeeze out their journal entries word by word, stoked on a procedure they have by now supremely mastered. They're playing the informed consumer, letting the provider know where he's come through and where he's not quite up to snuff.

3   But why am I so distressed, bolting like a refugee out of my own classroom, where I usually hold easy sway? Chances are the evaluations will be much like what they've been in the past—they'll be just fine. It's likely that I'll be commended for being "interesting" (and I am commended, many times over), that I'll be cited for my relaxed and tolerant ways (that happens, too), that my sense of humor and capacity to connect the arcana of the subject matter with current culture will come in for some praise (yup). I've been hassled this term, finishing a manuscript, and so haven't given their journals the attention I should have, and for that I'm called—quite civilly, though—to account. Overall, I get off pretty well.

4   Yet I have to admit that I do not much like the image of myself that emerges from these forms, the image of knowledgeable, humorous detachment and bland tolerance. I do not like the forms themselves, with their number ratings, reminiscent of the sheets circulated after the TV pilot has just played to its sample audience in Burbank. Most of all I dislike the attitude of calm consumer expertise that pervades the responses. I'm disturbed by the serene belief that my function—and, more important, Freud's, or Shakespeare's, or Blake's—is to divert, entertain, and interest. Observes one respondent, not at all unrepresentative: "Edmundson has done a fantastic job of presenting this difficult, important & controversial material in an enjoyable and approachable way."

5   Thanks but no thanks. I don't teach to amuse, to divert, or even, for that matter, to be merely interesting. When someone says she "enjoyed" the course—and that word crops up again and again in my evaluations—somewhere at the edge of my immediate complacency I feel encroaching self-dislike. That is not at all what I had in mind. The off-the-wall questions and the sidebar jokes are meant as lead-ins to stronger stuff—in the case of the Freud course, to a complexly tragic view of life. But the affability and the one-liners often seem to be all that land with the students; their journals and evaluations leave me little doubt.

6　I want some of them to say that they've been changed by the course. I want them to measure themselves against what they've read. It's said that some time ago a Columbia University instructor used to issue a harsh two-part question. One: What book did you most dislike in the course? Two: What intellectual or characterological flaws in you does that dislike point to? The hand that framed that question was surely heavy. But at least it compels one to see intellectual work as a confrontation between two people, student and author, where the stakes matter. Those Columbia students were being asked to relate the quality of an encounter, not rate the action as though it had unfolded on the big screen.

7　Why are my students describing the Oedipus complex and the death drive as being interesting and enjoyable to contemplate? And why am I coming across as an urbane, mildly ironic, endlessly affable guide to this intellectual territory, operating without intensity, generous, funny, and loose?

8　Because that's what works. On evaluation day, I reap the rewards of my partial compliance with the culture of my students and, too, with the culture of the university as it now operates. It's a culture that's gotten little exploration. Current critics tend to think that liberal-arts education is in crisis because universities have been invaded by professors with peculiar ideas: deconstruction, Lacanianism, feminism, queer theory. They believe that genius and tradition are out and that P.C., multiculturalism, and identity politics are in because of an invasion by tribes of tenured radicals, the late millennial equivalents of the Visigoth hordes that cracked Rome's walls.

9　But mulling over my evaluations and then trying to take a hard, extended look at campus life both here at the University of Virginia and around the country eventually led me to some different conclusions. To me, liberal-arts education is as ineffective as it is now not chiefly because there are a lot of strange theories in the air. (Used well, those theories can be illuminating.) Rather, it's that university culture, like American culture writ large, is, to put it crudely, ever more devoted to consumption and entertainment, to the using and using up of goods and images. For someone growing up in America now, there are few available alternatives to the cool consumer worldview. My students didn't ask for that view, much less create it, but they bring a consumer weltanschauung to school, where it exerts a

powerful, and largely unacknowledged, influence. If we want
to understand current universities, with their multiple woes,
we might try leaving the realms of expert debate and fine ideas
and turning to the classrooms and campuses, where a new
kind of weather is gathering.

10   From time to time I bump into a colleague in the corridor and
we have what I've come to think of as a Joon Lee fest. Joon Lee
is one of the best students I've taught. He's endlessly curious,
has read a small library's worth, seen every movie, and knows
all about showbiz and entertainment. For a class of mine he
wrote an essay using Nietzsche's Apollo and Dionysus to analyze the pop group The Supremes. A trite, cultural-studies bon-
bon? Not at all. He said striking things about conceptions of
race in America and about how they shape our ideas of beauty.
When I talk with one of his other teachers, we run on about the
general splendors of his work and presence. But what
inevitably follows a JL fest is a mournful reprise about the
divide that separates him and a few other remarkable students
from their contemporaries. It's not that some aren't nearly as
bright—in terms of intellectual ability, my students are all that
I could ask for. Instead, it's that Joon Lee has decided to follow
his interests and let them make him into a singular and rather
eccentric man; in his charming way, he doesn't mind being at
odds with most anyone.

11   It's his capacity for enthusiasm that sets Joon apart from what
I've come to think of as the reigning generational style.
Whether the students are sorority/fraternity types, grunge afi-
cionados, piercer/tattooers, black or white, rich or middle class
(alas, I teach almost no students from truly poor backgrounds),
they are, nearly across the board, very, very self-contained. On
good days they display a light, appealing glow; on bad days,
shuffling disgruntlement. But there's little fire, little passion to
be found.

12   This point came home to me a few weeks ago when I was wandering across the university grounds. There, beneath a classi-
cally cast portico, were two students, male and female, having
a rip-roaring argument. They were incensed, bellowing at each
other, headstrong, confident, and wild. It struck me how rarely
I see this kind of full-out feeling in students anymore. Strong
emotional display is forbidden. When conflicts arise, it's generally understood that one of the parties will say something

sarcastically propitiating ("whatever" often does it) and slouch away.

13 How did my students reach this peculiar state in which all passion seems to be spent? I think that many of them have imbibed their sense of self from consumer culture in general and from the tube in particular. They're the progeny of 100 cable channels and omni-present Blockbuster outlets. TV, Marshall McLuhan famously said, is a cool medium. Those who play best on it are low-key and nonassertive; they blend in. Enthusiasm, à la Joon Lee, quickly looks absurd. The form of character that's most appealing on TV is calmly self-interested though never greedy, attuned to the conventions, and ironic. Judicious timing is preferred to sudden self-assertion. The TV medium is inhospitable to inspiration, improvisation, failures, slipups. All must run perfectly.

14 Naturally, a cool youth culture is a marketing bonanza for producers of the right products, who do all they can to enlarge that culture and keep it grinding. The Internet, TV, and magazines now teem with what I call persona ads, ads for Nikes and Reeboks and Jeeps and Blazers that don't so much endorse the capacities of the product per se as show you what sort of person you will be once you've acquired it. The Jeep ad that features hip, outdoorsy kids whipping a Frisbee from mountaintop to mountaintop isn't so much about what jeeps can do as it is about the kind of people who own them. Buy a Jeep and be one with them. The ad is of little consequence in itself, but expand its message exponentially and you have the central thrust of current consumer culture—buy in order to be.

15 Most of my students seem desperate to blend in, to look right, not to make a spectacle of themselves. (Do I have to tell you that those two students having the argument under the portico turned out to be acting in a role-playing game?) The specter of the uncool creates a subtle tyranny. It's apparently an easy standard to subscribe to, this Letterman-like, Tarantino-like cool, but once committed to it, you discover that matters are rather different. You're inhibited, except on ordained occasions, from showing emotion, stifled from trying to achieve anything original. You're made to feel that even the slightest departure from the reigning code will get you genially ostracized. This is a culture tensely committed to a laid-back norm.

16   Am I coming off like something of a crank here? Maybe. Oscar
      Wilde, who is almost never wrong, suggested that it is perilous
      to promiscuously contradict people who are much younger
      than yourself. Point taken. But one of the lessons that consumer
      hype tries to insinuate is that we must never rebel against the
      new, never even question it. If it's new—a new need, a new
      product, a new show, a new style, a new generation—it must
      be good. So maybe, even at the risk of winning the withered,
      brown laurels of crankdom, it pays to resist newness-worship
      and cast a colder eye.

17   Praise for my students? I have some of that too. What my stu-
      dents are, at their best, is decent. They are potent believers in
      equality. They help out at the soup kitchen and volunteer to
      tutor poor kids to get a stripe on their résumés, sure. But they
      also want other people to have a fair shot. And in their com-
      mitment to fairness they are discerning; there you see them at
      their intellectual best. If I were on trial and innocent, I'd want
      them on the jury.

18   What they will not generally do, though, is indict the current
      system. They won't talk about how the exigencies of capitalism
      lead to a reserve army of the unemployed and nearly inevitable
      misery. That would be getting too loud, too brash. For the per-
      vading view is the cool consumer perspective, where passion
      and strong admiration are forbidden. "To stand in awe of noth-
      ing, Numicus, is perhaps the one and only thing that can make
      a man happy and keep him so," says Horace in the Epistles,
      and I fear that his lines ought to hang as a motto over the uni-
      versity in this era of high consumer capitalism.

19   It's easy to mount one's high horse and blame the students for
      this state of affairs. But they didn't create the present culture of
      consumption. (It was largely my own generation, that of the
      Sixties, that let the counterculture search for pleasure devolve
      into a quest for commodities.) And they weren't the ones
      responsible, when they were six and seven and eight years old,
      for unplugging the TV set from time to time or for hauling off
      and kicking a hole through it. It's my generation of parents
      who sheltered these students, kept them away from the hard
      knocks of everyday life, making them cautious and overfragile,
      who demanded that their teachers, from grade school on, flat-
      ter them endlessly so that the kids are shocked if their college
      profs don't reflexively suck up to them.

20   Of course, the current generational style isn't simply derived
     from culture and environment. It's also about dollars. Students
     worry that taking too many chances with their educations will
     sabotage their future prospects. They're aware of the fact that a
     drop that looks more and more like one wall of the Grand
     Canyon separates the top economic tenth from the rest of the
     population. There's a sentiment currently abroad that if you
     step aside for a moment, to write, to travel, to fall too hard in
     love, you might lose position permanently. We may be on a
     conveyor belt, but it's worse down there on the filth-strewn
     floor. So don't sound off, don't blow your chance.

21   But wait. I teach at the famously conservative University of
     Virginia. Can I extend my view from Charlottesville to encom-
     pass the whole country, a whole generation of college stu-
     dents? I can only say that I hear comparable stories about class-
     room life from colleagues everywhere in America. When I visit
     other schools to lecture, I see a similar scene unfolding. There
     are, of course, terrific students everywhere. And they're all the
     better for the way they've had to strive against the existing con-
     formity. At some of the small liberal-arts colleges, the tradition
     of strong engagement persists. But overall, the students strike
     me as being sweet and sad, hovering in a nearly suspended
     animation.

22   Too often now the pedagogical challenge is to make a lot from
     a little. Teaching Wordsworth's "Tintern Abbey," you ask for
     comments. No one responds. So you call on Stephen. Stephen:
     "The sound, this poem really flows." You: "Stephen seems
     interested in the music of the poem. We might extend his com-
     ment to ask if the poem's music coheres with its argument. Are
     they consistent? Or is there an emotional pain submerged here
     that's contrary to the poem's appealing melody?" All right, it's
     not usually that bad. But close. One friend describes it as
     rebound teaching: they proffer a weightless comment, you hit
     it back for all you're worth, then it comes dribbling out again.
     Occasionally a professor will try to explain away this intellec-
     tual timidity by describing the students as perpetrators of post-
     modern irony, a highly sophisticated mode. Everything's a
     slick counterfeit, a simulacrum, so by no means should any
     phenomenon be taken seriously. But the students don't have
     the urbane, Oscar Wilde-type demeanor that should go with
     this view. Oscar was cheerful funny, confident, strange. (Wilde,

mortally ill, living in a Paris flophouse: "My wallpaper and I are fighting a duel to the death. One or the other of us has to go.") This generation's style is considerate, easy to please, and a touch depressed.

23   Granted, you might say, the kids come to school immersed in a consumer mentality—they're good Americans, after all—but then the university and the professors do everything in their power to fight that dreary mind-set in the interest of higher ideals, right? So it should be. But let us look at what is actually coming to pass.

24   Over the past few years, the physical layout of my university has been changing. To put it a little indecorously, the place is looking more and more like a retirement spread for the young. Our funds go to construction, into new dorms, into renovating the student union. We have a new aquatics center and ever-improving gyms, stocked with StairMasters and Nautilus machines. Engraved on the wall in the gleaming aquatics building is a line by our founder, Thomas Jefferson, declaring that everyone ought to get about two hours' exercise a day. Clearly even the author of the Declaration of Independence endorses the turning of his university into a sports-and-fitness emporium.

25   But such improvements shouldn't be surprising. Universities need to attract the best (that is, the smartest and the richest) students in order to survive in an ever more competitive market. Schools want kids whose parents can pay the full freight, not the ones who need scholarships or want to bargain down the tuition costs. If the marketing surveys say that the kids require sports centers, then, trustees willing, they shall have them. In fact, as I began looking around, I came to see that more and more of what's going on in the university is customer driven. The consumer pressures that beset me on evaluation day are only a part of an overall trend.

26   From the start, the contemporary university's relationship with students has a solicitous, nearly servile tone. As soon as someone enters his junior year in high school, and especially if he's living in a prosperous zip code, the informational material—the advertising—comes flooding in. Pictures, testimonials, videocassettes, and CD ROMs (some bidden, some not) arrive

at the door from colleges across the country, all trying to capture the student and his tuition cash. The freshman-to-be sees photos of well-appointed dorm rooms; of elaborate phys-ed facilities; of fine dining rooms; of expertly kept sports fields; of orchestras and drama troupes; of students working alone (no overbearing grown-ups in range), peering with high seriousness into computers and microscopes; or of students arrayed outdoors in attractive conversational garlands.

27   Occasionally—but only occasionally, for we usually photograph rather badly; in appearance we tend at best to be styleless—there's a professor teaching a class. (The college catalogues I received, by my request only, in the late Sixties were austere affairs full of professors' credentials and course descriptions; it was clear on whose terms the enterprise was going to unfold.) A college financial officer recently put matters to me in concise, if slightly melodramatic, terms: "Colleges don't have admissions offices anymore, they have marketing departments." Is it surprising that someone who has been approached with photos and tapes, bells and whistles, might come in thinking that the Freud and Shakespeare she had signed up to study were also going to be agreeable treats?

28   How did we reach this point? In part the answer is a matter of demographics and (surprise) of money. Aided by the G.I. bill, the college-going population in America dramatically increased after the Second World War. Then came the baby boomers, and to accommodate them, schools continued to grow. Universities expand easily enough, but with tenure locking faculty in for lifetime jobs, and with the general reluctance of administrators to eliminate their own slots, it's not easy for a university to contract. So after the baby boomers had passed through—like a fat meal digested by a boa constrictor—the colleges turned to energetic promotional strategies to fill the empty chairs. And suddenly college became a buyer's market. What students and their parents wanted had to be taken more and more into account. That usually meant creating more comfortable, less challenging environments, places where almost no one failed, everything was enjoyable, and everyone was nice.

29   Just as universities must compete with one another for students, so must the individual departments. At a time of rank economic anxiety, the English and history majors have to

contend for students against the more success-insuring branches, such as the sciences and the commerce school. In 1968, more than 21 percent of all the bachelor's degrees conferred in America were in the humanities; by 1993, that number had fallen to about 13 percent. The humanities now must struggle to attract students, many of whose parents devoutly wish they would study something else.

30   One of the ways we've tried to stay attractive is by loosening up. We grade much more softly than our colleagues in science. In English, we don't give many Ds, or Cs for that matter. (The rigors of Chem 101 create almost as many English majors per year as do the splendors of Shakespeare.) A professor at Stanford recently explained grade inflation in the humanities by observing that the undergraduates were getting smarter every year; the higher grades simply recorded how much better they were than their predecessors. Sure.

31   Along with softening the grades, many humanities departments have relaxed major requirements. There are some good reasons for introducing more choice into curricula and requiring fewer standard courses. But the move, like many others in the university now, jibes with a tendency to serve—and not challenge—the students. Students can also float in and out of classes during the first two weeks of each term without making any commitment. The common name for this time span—shopping period—speaks volumes about the consumer mentality that's now in play. Usually, too, the kids can drop courses up until the last month with only an innocuous "W" on their transcripts. Does a course look too challenging? No problem. Take it pass-fail. A happy consumer is, by definition, one with multiple options, one who can always have what he wants. And since a course is something the students and their parents have bought and paid for, why can't they do with it pretty much as they please?

32   A sure result of the university's widening elective leeway is to give students more power over their teachers. Those who don't like you can simply avoid you. If the clientele dislikes you en masse, you can be left without students, period. My first term teaching I walked into my introduction to poetry course and found it inhabited by one student, the gloriously named Bambi

Lynn Dean. Bambi and I chatted amiably awhile, but for all that she and the pleasure of her name could offer, I was fast on the way to meltdown. It was all a mistake, luckily, a problem with the scheduling book. Everyone was waiting for me next door. But in a dozen years of teaching I haven't forgotten that feeling of being ignominiously marooned. For it happens to others, and not always because of scheduling glitches. I've seen older colleagues go through hot embarrassment at not having enough students sign up for their courses: they graded too hard, demanded too much, had beliefs too far out of keeping with the existing disposition. It takes only a few such instances to draw other members of the professoriat further into line.

33 And if what's called tenure reform—which generally just means the abolition of tenure—is broadly enacted, professors will be yet more vulnerable to the whims of their customer-students. Teach what pulls the kids in, or walk. What about entire departments that don't deliver? If the kids say no to Latin and Greek, is it time to dissolve classics? Such questions are being entertained more and more seriously by university administrators.

34 How does one prosper with the present clientele? Many of the most successful professors now are the ones who have "decentered" their classrooms. There's a new emphasis on group projects and on computer-generated exchanges among the students. What they seem to want most is to talk to one another. A classroom now is frequently an "environment," a place highly conducive to the exchange of existing ideas, the students' ideas. Listening to one another, students sometimes change their opinions. But what they generally can't do is acquire a new vocabulary, a new perspective, that will cast issues in a fresh light.

35 The Socratic method—the animated, sometimes impolite give-and-take between student and teacher—seems too jagged for current sensibilities. Students frequently come to my office to tell me how intimidated they feel in class; the thought of being embarrassed in front of the group fills them with dread. I remember a student telling me how humiliating it was to be corrected by the teacher, by me. So I asked the logical question: "Should I let a major factual error go by so as to save discomfort?" The student—a good student, smart and earnest—said that was a tough question. He'd need to think about it.

36   Disturbing? Sure. But I wonder, are we really getting students ready for Socratic exchange with professors when we push them off into vast lecture rooms, two and three hundred to a class, sometimes face them with only grad students until their third year, and signal in our myriad professorial ways that we often have much better things to do than sit in our offices and talk with them? How bad will the student-faculty ratios have to become, how teeming the lecture courses, before we hear students righteously complaining, as they did thirty years ago, about the impersonality of their schools, about their decline into knowledge factories? "This is a firm," said Mario Savio at Berkeley during the Free Speech protests of the Sixties, "and if the Board of Regents are the board of directors, . . . then . . . the faculty are a bunch of employees and we're the raw material. But we're a bunch of raw material that don't mean . . . to be made into any product."

37   Teachers who really do confront students, who provide significant challenges to what they believe, can be very successful, granted. But sometimes such professors generate more than a little trouble for themselves. A controversial teacher can send students hurrying to the deans and the counselors, claiming to have been offended. ("Offensive" is the preferred term of repugnance today, just as "enjoyable" is the summit of praise.) Colleges have brought in hordes of counselors and deans to make sure that everything is smooth, serene, unflustered, that everyone has a good time. To the counselor, to the dean, and to the university legal squad, that which is normal, healthy, and prudent is best.

38   An air of caution and deference is everywhere. When my students come to talk with me in my office, they often exhibit a Franciscan humility. "Do you have a moment?" "I know you're busy. I won't take up much of your time." Their presences tend to be very light; they almost never change the temperature of the room. The dress is nondescript: clothes are in earth tones; shoes are practical—cross-trainers, hiking boots, work shoes, Dr. Martens, with now and then a stylish pair of raised-sole boots on one of the young women. Many, male and female both, peep from beneath the bills of monogrammed baseball caps. Quite a few wear sports, or even corporate, logos, sometimes on one piece of clothing but occasionally (and disconcertingly) on more. The walk is slow; speech is careful, sweet,

a bit weary, and without strong inflection. (After the first live-ly week of the term, most seem far in debt to sleep.) They are almost unfailingly polite. They don't want to offend me; I could hurt them, savage their grades.

39 Naturally, there are exceptions, kids I chat animatedly with, who offer a joke, or go on about this or that new CD (almost never a book, no). But most of the traffic is genially sleepwalk-ing. I have to admit that I'm a touch wary, too. I tend to hold back. An unguarded remark, a joke that's taken to be off-color, or simply an uncomprehended comment can lead to difficul-ties. I keep it literal. They scare me a little, these kind and melancholy students, who themselves seem rather frightened of their own lives.

40 Before they arrive, we ply the students with luscious ads, guar-anteeing them a cross between summer camp and lotusland. When they get here, flattery and nonstop entertainment are available, if that's what they want. And when they leave? How do we send our students out into the world? More and more, our administrators call the booking agents and line up one or another celebrity to usher the graduates into the millennium. This past spring, Kermit the Frog won himself an honorary degree at Southampton College on Long Island; Bruce Willis and Yogi Berra took credentials away at Montclair State; Arnold Schwarzenegger scored at the University of Wisconsin-Superior. At Wellesley, Oprah Winfrey gave the commence-ment address. (Wellesley—one of the most rigorous academic colleges in the nation.) At the University of Vermont, Whoopi Goldberg laid down the word. But why should a worthy administrator contract the likes of Susan Sontag, Christopher Hitchens, or Robert Hughes—someone who might actually say something, something disturbing, something "offensive"—when he can get what the parents and kids apparently want and what the newspapers will softly commend—more lite entertainment, more TV?

41 Is it a surprise, then, that this generation of students—steeped in consumer culture before going off to school, treated as potent customers by the university well before their date of arrival, then pandered to from day one until the morning of the final kiss-off from Kermit or one of his kin—are inclined to see the books they read as a string of entertainments to be placidly enjoyed or languidly cast down? Given the way

universities are now administered (which is more and more to say, given the way that they are currently marketed), is it a shock that the kids don't come to school hot to learn, unable to bear their own ignorance? For some measure of self-dislike, or self-discontent—which is much different than simple depression—seems to me to be a prerequisite for getting an education that matters. My students, alas, usually lack the confidence to acknowledge what would be their most precious asset for learning: their ignorance.

42 Not long ago, I asked my Freud class a question that, however hoary, never fails to solicit intriguing responses: Who are your heroes? Whom do you admire? After one remarkable answer, featuring T. S. Eliot as hero, a series of generic replies rolled in, one gray wave after the next: my father, my best friend, a doctor who lives in our town, my high school history teacher. Virtually all the heroes were people my students had known personally, people who had done something local, specific, and practical, and had done it for them. They were good people, unselfish people, these heroes, but most of all they were people who had delivered the goods.

43 My students' answers didn't exhibit any philosophical resistance to the idea of greatness. It's not that they had been primed by their professors with complex arguments to combat genius. For the truth is that these students don't need debunking theories. Long before college, skepticism became their habitual mode. They are the progeny of Bart Simpson and David Letterman, and the hyper-cool ethos of the box. It's inane to say that theorizing professors have created them, as many conservative critics like to do. Rather, they have substantially created a university environment in which facile skepticism can thrive without being substantially contested.

44 Skeptical approaches have potential value. If you have no all-encompassing religious faith, no faith in historical destiny, the future of the West, or anything comparably grand, you need to acquire your vision of the world somewhere. If it's from literature, then the various visions literature offers have to be inquired into skeptically. Surely it matters that women are denigrated in Milton and in Pope, that some novelistic voices assume an overbearing godlike authority, that the poor are, in

this or that writer, inevitably cast as clowns. You can't buy all of literature wholesale if it's going to help draw your patterns of belief.

45 But demystifying theories are now overused, applied mechanically. It's all logocentrism, patriarchy, ideology. And in this the student environment—laid-back, skeptical, knowing—is, I believe, central. Full-out debunking is what plays with this clientele. Some have been doing it nearly as long as, if more crudely than, their deconstructionist teachers. In the context of the contemporary university, and cool consumer culture, a useful intellectual skepticism has become exaggerated into a fundamentalist caricature of itself. The teachers have buckled to their students' views.

46 At its best, multiculturalism can be attractive as well-deployed theory. What could be more valuable than encountering the best work of far-flung cultures and becoming a citizen of the world? But in the current consumer environment, where flattery plays so well, the urge to encounter the other can devolve into the urge to find others who embody and celebrate the right ethnic origins. So we put aside the African novelist Chinua Achebe's abrasive, troubling Things Fall Apart and gravitate toward hymns on Africa, cradle of all civilizations.

47 What about the phenomenon called political correctness? Raising the standard of civility and tolerance in the university has been—who can deny it?—a very good thing. Yet this admirable impulse has expanded to the point where one is enjoined to speak well—and only well—of women, blacks, gays, the disabled, in fact of virtually everyone. And we can owe this expansion in many ways to the student culture. Students now do not wish to be criticized, not in any form. (The culture of consumption never criticizes them, at least not overtly.) In the current university, the movement for urbane tolerance has devolved into an imperative against critical reaction, turning much of the intellectual life into a dreary Sargasso Sea. At a certain point, professors stopped being usefully sensitive and became more like careful retailers who have it as a cardinal point of doctrine never to piss the customers off.

48 To some professors, the solution lies in the movement called cultural studies. What students need, they believe, is to form a critical perspective on pop culture. It's a fine idea, no doubt.

Students should be able to run a critical commentary against the stream of consumer stimulations in which they're immersed. But cultural-studies programs rarely work, because no matter what you propose by way of analysis, things tend to bolt downhill toward an uncritical discussion of students' tastes, into what they like and don't like. If you want to do a Frankfurt School-style analysis of Braveheart, you can be pretty sure that by mid-class Adorno and Horkheimer will be consigned to the junk heap of history and you'll be collectively weighing the charms of Mel Gibson. One sometimes wonders if cultural studies hasn't prospered because, under the guise of serious intellectual analysis, it gives the customers what they most want—easy pleasure, more TV. Cultural studies becomes nothing better than what its detractors claim it is—Madonna studies—when students kick loose from the critical perspective and groove to the product, and that, in my experience teaching film and pop culture, happens plenty.

49   On the issue of genius, as on multiculturalism and political correctness, we professors of the humanities have, I think, also failed to press back against our students' consumer tastes. Here we tend to nurse a pair of—to put it charitably—disparate views. In one mode, we're inclined to a programmatic debunking criticism. We call the concept of genius into question. But in our professional lives per se, we aren't usually disposed against the idea of distinguished achievement. We argue animatedly about the caliber of potential colleagues. We support a star system, in which some professors are far better paid, teach less, and under better conditions than the rest. In our own profession, we are creating a system that is the mirror image of the one we're dismantling in the curriculum. Ask a professor what she thinks of the work of Stephen Greenblatt, a leading critic of Shakespeare, and you'll hear it for an hour. Ask her what her views are on Shakespeare's genius and she's likely to begin questioning the term along with the whole "discourse of evaluation." This dual sensibility may be intellectually incoherent. But in its awareness of what plays with students, it's conducive to good classroom evaluations and, in its awareness of where and how the professional bread is buttered, to self-advancement as well.

50   My overall point is this: It's not that a leftwing professorial coup has taken over the university. It's that at American universities,

left-liberal politics have collided with the ethos of consumerism. The consumer ethos is winning.

51   Then how do those who at least occasionally promote genius and high literary ideals look to current students? How do we appear, those of us who take teaching to be something of a performance art and who imagine that if you give yourself over completely to your subject you'll be rewarded with insight beyond what you individually command?

52   I'm reminded of an old piece of newsreel footage I saw once. The speaker (perhaps it was Lenin, maybe Trotsky) was haranguing a large crowd. He was expostulating, arm waving, carrying on. Whether it was flawed technology or the man himself, I'm not sure, but the orator looked like an intricate mechanical device that had sprung into fast-forward. To my students, who mistrust enthusiasm in every form, that's me when I start riffing about Freud or Blake. But more and more, as my evaluations showed, I've been replacing enthusiasm and intellectual animation with stand-up routines, keeping it all at arm's length, praising under the cover of irony.

53   It's too bad that the idea of genius has been denigrated so far, because it actually offers a live alternative to the demoralizing culture of hip in which most of my students are mired. By embracing the works and lives of extraordinary people, you can adapt new ideals to revise those that came courtesy of your parents, your neighborhood, your clan—or the tube. The aim of a good liberal-arts education was once, to adapt an observation by the scholar Walter Jackson Bate, to see that "we need not be the passive victims of what we deterministically call 'circumstances' (social, cultural, or reductively psychological-personal), but that by linking ourselves through what Keats calls an 'immortal free-masonry' with the great we can become freer—freer to be ourselves, to be what we most want and value."

54   But genius isn't just a personal standard; genius can also have political effect. To me, one of the best things about democratic thinking is the conviction that genius can spring up anywhere. Walt Whitman is born into the working class and thirty-six years later we have a poetic image of America that gives a passionate dimension to the legalistic brilliance of the Constitution. A democracy needs to constantly develop, and to do so it

requires the most powerful visionary minds to interpret the present and to propose possible shapes for the future. By continuing to notice and praise genius, we create a culture in which the kind of poetic gamble that Whitman made—a gamble in which failure would have entailed rank humiliation, depression, maybe suicide—still takes place. By rebelling against established ways of seeing and saying things, genius helps us to apprehend how malleable the present is and how promising and fraught with danger is the future. If we teachers do not endorse genius and self-overcoming, can we be surprised when our students find their ideal images in TV's latest persona ads?

55   A world uninterested in genius is a despondent place, whose sad denizens drift from coffee bar to Prozac dispensary, unfired by ideals, by the glowing image of the self that one might become. As Northrop Frye says in a beautiful and now dramatically unfashionable sentence, "The artist who uses the same energy and genius that Homer and Isaiah had will find that he not only lives in the same palace of art as Homer and Isaiah, but lives in it at the same time." We ought not to deny the existence of such a place simply because we, or those we care for, find the demands it makes intimidating, the rent too high.

56   What happens if we keep trudging along this bleak course? What happens if our most intelligent students never learn to strive to overcome what they are? What if genius, and the imitation of genius, become silly, outmoded ideas? What you're likely to get are more and more one-dimensional men and women. These will be people who live for easy pleasures, for comfort and prosperity, who think of money first, then second, and third, who hug the status quo; people who believe in God as a sort of insurance policy (cover your bets); people who are never surprised. They will be people so pleased with themselves (when they're not in despair at the general pointlessness of their lives) that they cannot imagine humanity could do better. They'll think it their highest duty to clone themselves as frequently as possible. They'll claim to be happy, and they'll live a long time.

57   It is probably time now to offer a spate of inspiring solutions. Here ought to come a list of reforms, with due notations about a core curriculum and various requirements. What the

traditionalists who offer such solutions miss is that no matter what our current students are given to read, many of them will simply translate it into melodrama, with flat characters and predictable morals. (The unabated capitalist culture that conservative critics so often endorse has put students in a position to do little else.) One can't simply wave a curricular wand and reverse acculturation.

58   Perhaps it would be a good idea to try firing the counselors and sending half the deans back into their classrooms, dismantling the football team and making the stadium into a playground for local kids, emptying the fraternities, and boarding up the student-activities office. Such measures would convey the message that American colleges are not northern outposts of Club Med. A willingness on the part of the faculty to defy student conviction and affront them occasionally—to be usefully offensive—also might not be a bad thing. We professors talk a lot about subversion, which generally means subverting the views of people who never hear us talk or read our work. But to subvert the views of our students, our customers, that would be something else again.

59   Ultimately, though, it is up to individuals—and individual students in particular—to make their own way against the current sludgy tide. There's still the library, still the museum, there's still the occasional teacher who lives to find things greater than herself to admire. There are still fellow students who have not been cowed. Universities are inefficient, cluttered, archaic places, with many unguarded corners where one can open a book or gaze out onto the larger world and construe it freely. Those who do as much, trusting themselves against the weight of current opinion, will have contributed something to bringing this sad dispensation to an end. As for myself, I'm canning my low-key one-liners; when the kids' TV-based tastes come to the fore, I'll aim and shoot. And when it's time to praise genius, I'll try to do it in the right style, full-out, with faith that finer artistic spirits (maybe not Homer and Isaiah quite, but close, close), still alive somewhere in the ether, will help me out when my invention flags, the students doze, or the dean mutters into the phone. I'm getting back to a more exuberant style; I'll be expostulating and arm waving straight into the millennium, yes I will.

Paulo Freire's work connecting educational theory with the politics of liberation had as its original focus the improvement of the quality of life of the poor in his native Brazil. His notion of liberation pedagogy has subsequently won him world-wide acclaim. This selection is the second chapter of his best known work, the Pedagogy of the Oppressed *(1970). Its basic thesis is that education is never a neutral process. Either it furthers the goal of human liberation, or it reinforces social tendencies that restrict human freedom. Until his death in 1997, Freire devoted most of his time to writing and lecturing, but taught occasionally at the Pontificia Universidade Catolica de São Paulo. Among the many honors awarded him were the UNESCO Peace Prize in 1986 and the Organization of American States Simon Rodriguez Prize for Education in 1992. His work is now the subject of a yearly conference entitled the "Pedagogy of the Oppressed."*

The Banking Concept of Education

Paulo Freire

1   A careful analysis of the teacher-student relationship at any level, inside or outside the school, reveals its fundamentally *narrative* character. This relationship involves a narrating Subject (the teacher) and patient, listening objects (the students). The contents, whether values or empirical dimensions of reality, tend in the process of being narrated to become lifeless and petrified. Education is suffering from narration sickness.

2   The teacher talks about reality as if it were motionless, static, compartmentalized, and predictable. Or else he expounds on a topic completely alien to the existential experience of the students. His task is to "fill" the students with the contents of his narration—contents which are detached from reality, disconnected from the totality that engendered them and could give them significance. Words are emptied of their concreteness and become a hollow, alienated, and alienating verbosity.

3   The outstanding characteristic of this narrative education, then, is the sonority of words, not their transforming power. "Four times four is sixteen; the capital of Pará is Belém." The student records, memorizes, and repeats these phrases without

perceiving what four times four really means, or realizing the true significance of "capital" in the affirmation "the capital of Pará is Belém," that is, what Belém means for Pará and what Pará means for Brazil.

4 Narration (with the teacher as narrator) leads the students to memorize mechanically the narrated content. Worse yet, it turns them into "containers," into "receptacles" to be "filled" by the teacher. The more completely he fills the receptacles, the better a teacher he is. The more meekly the receptacles permit themselves to be filled, the better students they are.

5 Education thus becomes an act of depositing, in which the students are the depositories and the teacher is the depositor. Instead of communicating, the teacher issues communiqués and makes deposits which the students patiently receive, memorize, and repeat. This is the "banking" concept of education, in which the scope of action allowed to the students extends only as far as receiving, filing, and storing the deposits. They do, it is true, have the opportunity to become collectors or cataloguers of the things they store. But in the last analysis, it is men themselves who are filed away through the lack of creativity, transformation, and knowledge in this (at best) misguided system. For apart from inquiry, apart from the praxis, men cannot be truly human. Knowledge emerges only through invention and re-invention, through the restless, impatient, continuing, hopeful inquiry men pursue in the world, with the world, and with each other.

6 In the banking concept of education, knowledge is a gift bestowed by those who consider themselves knowledgeable upon those whom they consider to know nothing. Projecting an absolute ignorance onto others, a characteristic of the ideology of oppression, negates education and knowledge as processes of inquiry. The teacher presents himself to his students as their necessary opposite; by considering their ignorance absolute, he justifies his own existence. The students, alienated like the slave in the Hegelian dialectic, accept their ignorance as justifying the teacher's existence—but, unlike the slave, they never discover that they educate the teacher.

7 The *raison d'être* of libertarian education, on the other hand, lies in its drive towards reconciliation. Education must begin with the solution of the teacher-student contradiction, by

reconciling the poles of the contradiction so that both are simultaneously teachers *and* students.

8   This solution is not (nor can it be) found in the banking concept. On the contrary, banking education maintains and even stimulates the contradiction through the following attitudes and practices, which mirror oppressive society as a whole:

   (a) the teacher teaches and the students are taught;
   (b) the teacher knows everything and the students know nothing;
   (c) the teacher thinks and the students are thought about;
   (d) the teacher talks and the students listen—meekly;
   (e) the teacher disciplines and the students are disciplined;
   (f) the teacher chooses and enforces his choice, and the students comply;
   (g) the teacher acts and the students have the illusion of acting through the action of the teacher;
   (h) the teacher chooses the program content, and the students (who were not consulted) adapt to it;
   (i) the teacher confuses the authority of knowledge with his own professional authority, which he sets in opposition to the freedom of the students;
   (j) the teacher is the Subject of the learning process, while the pupils are mere objects.

9   It is not surprising that the banking concept of education regards men as adaptable, manageable beings. The more students work at storing the deposits entrusted to them, the less they develop the critical consciousness which would result from their intervention in the world as transformers of that world. The more completely they accept the passive role imposed on them, the more they tend simply to adapt to the world as it is and to the fragmented view of reality deposited in them.

10   The capability of banking education to minimize or annul the students' creative power and to stimulate their credulity serves the interests of the oppressors, who care neither to have the world revealed nor to see it transformed. The oppressors use their "humanitarianism" to preserve a profitable situation. Thus they react almost instinctively against any experiment in education which stimulates the critical faculties and is not content with a partial view of reality but always seeks out the ties which link one point to another and one problem to another.

11 Indeed, the interests of the oppressors lie in "changing the consciousness of the oppressed, not the situation which oppresses them"; [1] for the more the oppressed can be led to adapt to that situation, the more easily they can be dominated. To achieve this end, the oppressors use the banking concept of education in conjunction with a paternalistic social action apparatus, within which the oppressed receive the euphemistic title of "welfare recipients." They are treated as individual cases, as marginal men who deviate from the general configuration of a "good, organized, and just" society. The oppressed are regarded as the pathology of the healthy society, which must therefore adjust these "incompetent and lazy" folk to its own patterns by changing their mentality. These marginals need to be "integrated," "incorporated" into the healthy society that they have "forsaken."

12 The truth is, however, that the oppressed are not "marginals," are not men living "outside" society. They have always been "inside"—inside the structure which made them "beings for others." The solution is not to "integrate" them into the structure of oppression, but to transform that structure so that they can become "beings for themselves." Such transformation, of course, would undermine the oppressors' purposes; hence their utilization of the banking concept of education to avoid the threat of student *conscientização* (conciousness raising).

13 The banking approach to adult education, for example, will never propose to students that they critically consider reality. It will deal instead with such vital questions as whether Roger gave green grass to the goat, and insist upon the importance of learning that, on the contrary, *R*oger gave green grass to the *r*abbit. The "humanism" of the banking approach masks the effort to turn men into automatons—the very negation of their ontological vocation to be more fully human.

14 Those who use the banking approach, knowingly or unknowingly (for there are innumerable well-intentioned banker-clerk teachers who do not realize that they are serving only to dehumanize), fail to perceive that the deposits themselves contain contradictions about reality. But, sooner or later, these contradictions may lead formerly passive students to turn against their domestication and the attempt to domesticate reality. They may discover through existential experience that their present way of life is irreconcilable with their vocation to

become fully human. They may perceive through their relations with reality that reality is really a *process*, undergoing constant transformation. If men are searchers and their ontological vocation is humanization, sooner or later they may perceive the contradiction in which banking education seeks to maintain them, and then engage themselves in the struggle for their liberation.

15   But the humanist, revolutionary educator cannot wait for this possibility to materialize. From the outset, his efforts must coincide with those of the students to engage in critical thinking and the quest for mutual humanization. His efforts must be imbued with a profound trust in men and their creative power. To achieve this, he must be a partner of the students in his relations with them.

16   The banking concept does not admit to such partnership—and necessarily so. To resolve the teacher-student contradiction, to exchange the role of depositor, prescriber, domesticator, for the role of student among students would be to undermine the power of oppression and serve the cause of liberation.

17   Implicit in the banking concept is the assumption of a dichotomy between man and the world: man is merely *in* the world, not *with* the world or with others; man is spectator, not re-creator. In this view, man is not a conscious being *(corpo conciente)*; he is rather the possessor of a consciousness: an empty "mind" passively open to the reception of deposits of reality from the world outside. For example, my desk, my books, my coffee cup, all the objects before me—as bits of the world which surrounds me—would be "inside" me, exactly as I am inside my study right now. This view makes no distinction between being accessible to consciousness and entering consciousness. The distinction, however, is essential: the objects which surround me are simply accessible to my consciousness, not located within it. I am aware of them, but they are not inside me.

18   It follows logically from the banking notion of consciousness that the educator's role is to regulate the way the world "enters into" the students. His task is to organize a process which already occurs spontaneously, to "fill" the students by making deposits of information which he considers to constitute true knowledge.[2] And since men "receive" the world as

passive entities, education should make them more passive still, and adapt them to the world. The educated man is the adapted man, because he is better "fit" for the world. Translated into practice, this concept is well suited to the purposes of the oppressors, whose tranquility rests on how well men fit the world the oppressors have created, and how little they question it.

19　The more completely the majority adapt to the purposes which the dominant minority prescribe for them (thereby depriving them of the right to their own purposes), the more easily the minority can continue to prescribe. The theory and practice of banking education serve this end quite efficiently. Verbalistic lessons, reading requirements,[3] the methods for evaluating "knowledge," the distance between the teacher and the taught, the criteria for promotion: everything in this ready-to-wear approach serves to obviate thinking.

20　The bank-clerk educator does not realize that there is no true security in his hypertrophied role, that one must seek to live *with* others in solidarity. One cannot impose oneself, nor even merely co-exist with one's students. Solidarity requires true communication, and the concept by which such an educator is guided fears and proscribes communication.

21　Yet only through communication can human life hold meaning. The teacher's thinking is authenticated only by the authenticity of the students' thinking. The teacher cannot think for his students, nor can he impose his thought on them. Authentic thinking, thinking that is concerned about *reality*, does not take place in ivory tower isolation, but only in communication. If it is true that thought has meaning only when generated by action upon the world, the subordination of students to teachers becomes impossible.

22　Because banking education begins with a false understanding of men as objects, it cannot promote the development of what Fromm calls "biophily," but instead produces its opposite: "necrophily."

> While life is characterized by growth in a structured, functional manner, the necrophilous person loves all that does not grow, all that is mechanical. The necrophilous person is driven by the desire to transform the organic into the inorganic, to approach life mechanically, as if all living persons were things. . . . Memory,

rather than experience; having, rather than being, is what counts. The necrophilous person can relate to an object—a flower or a person—only if he possesses it; hence a threat to his possession is a threat to himself; if he loses possession he loses contact with the world. . . . He loves control, and in the act of controlling he kills life.[4]

23   Oppression—overwhelming control—is necrophilic; it is nourished by love of death, not life. The banking concept of education, which serves the interests of oppression, is also necrophilic. Based on a mechanistic, static, naturalistic, spatialized view of consciousness, it transforms students into receiving objects. It attempts to control thinking and action, leads men to adjust to the world, and inhibits their creative power.

24   When their efforts to act responsibly are frustrated, when they find themselves unable to use their faculties, men suffer. "This suffering due to impotence is rooted in the very fact that the human equilibrium has been disturbed."[5] But the inability to act which causes men's anguish also causes them to reject their impotence, by attempting

> . . . to restore [their] capacity to act. But can [they], and how? One way is to submit to and identify with a person or group having power. By this symbolic participation in another person's life, [men have] the illusion of acting, when in reality [they] only submit to and become a part of those who act.[6]

25   Populist manifestations perhaps best exemplify this type of behavior by the oppressed, who, by identifying with charismatic leaders, come to feel that they themselves are active and effective. The rebellion they express as they emerge in the historical process is motivated by that desire to act effectively. The dominant elites consider the remedy to be more domination and repression, carried out in the name of freedom, order, and social peace (that is, the peace of the elites). Thus they can condemn—logically, from their point of view—"the violence of a strike by workers and [can] call upon the state in the same breath to use violence in putting down the strike."[7]

26   Education as the exercise of domination stimulates the credulity of students, with the ideological intent (often not perceived by educators) of indoctrinating them to adapt to the world of oppression. This accusation is not made in the naïve hope that the dominant elites will thereby simply abandon the

practice. Its objective is to call the attention of true humanists to the fact that they cannot use banking educational methods in the pursuit of liberation, for they would only negate that very pursuit. Nor may a revolutionary society inherit these methods from an oppressor society. The revolutionary society which practices banking education is either misguided or mistrusting of men. In either event, it is threatened by the specter of reaction.

27 Unfortunately, those who espouse the cause of liberation are themselves surrounded and influenced by the climate which generates the banking concept, and often do not perceive its true significance or its dehumanizing power. Paradoxically, then, they utilize this same instrument of alienation in what they consider an effort to liberate. Indeed, some "revolutionaries" brand as "innocents," "dreamers," or even "reactionaries" those who would challenge this educational practice. But one does not liberate men by alienating them. Authentic liberation—the process of humanization—is not another deposit to be made in men. Liberation is a praxis: the action and reflection of men upon their world in order to transform it. Those truly committed to the cause of liberation can accept neither the mechanistic concept of consciousness as an empty vessel to be filled, nor the use of banking methods of domination (propaganda, slogans—deposits) in the name of liberation.

28 Those truly committed to liberation must reject the banking concept in its entirety, adopting instead a concept of men as conscious beings, and consciousness as consciousness intent upon the world. They must abandon the educational goal of deposit-making and replace it with the posing of the problems of men in their relations with the world. "Problem-posing" education, responding to the essence of consciousness—*intentionality*—rejects communiqués and embodies communication. It epitomizes the special characteristic of consciousness: being *conscious of*, not only as intent on objects but as turned in upon itself in a Jasperian "split"—consciousness as consciousness *of* consciousness.

29 Liberating education consists in acts of cognition, not transferrals of information. It is a learning situation in which the cognizable object (far from being the end of the cognitive act) intermediates the cognitive actors—teacher on the one hand and students on the other. Accordingly, the practice of

problem-posing education entails at the outset that the teacher-student contradiction be resolved. Dialogical relations—indispensable to the capacity of cognitive actors to cooperate in perceiving the same cognizable object—are otherwise impossible.

30   Indeed, problem-posing education, which breaks with the vertical patterns characteristic of banking education, can fulfill its function as the practice of freedom only if it can overcome the above contradiction. Through dialogue, the teacher-of-the-students and the students-of-the-teacher cease to exist and a new term emerges: teacher-student with students-teachers. The teacher is no longer merely the-one-who-teaches, but one who is himself taught in dialogue with the students, who in turn while being taught also teach. They become jointly responsible for a process in which all grow. In this process, arguments based on "authority" are no longer valid; in order to function, authority must be *on the side of* freedom, not *against* it. Here, no one teaches another, nor is anyone self-taught. Men teach each other, mediated by the world, by the cognizable objects which in banking education are "owned" by the teacher.

31   The banking concept (with its tendency to dichotomize everything) distinguishes two stages in the action of the educator. During the first, he cognizes a cognizable object while he prepares his lessons in his study or his laboratory; during the second, he expounds to his students about that object. The students are not called upon to know, but to memorize the contents narrated by the teacher. Nor do the students practice any act of cognition, since the object towards which that act should be directed is the property of the teacher rather than a medium evoking the critical reflection of both teacher and students. Hence in the name of the "preservation of culture and knowledge" we have a system which achieves neither true knowledge nor true culture.

32   The problem-posing method does not dichotomize the activity of the teacher-student: he is not "cognitive" at one point and "narrative" at another. He is always "cognitive," whether preparing a project or engaging in dialogue with the students. He does not regard cognizable objects as his private property, but as the object of reflection by himself and the students. In this way, the problem-posing educator constantly re-forms his reflections in the reflection of the students. The students—no

longer docile listeners—are now critical co-investigators in dialogue with the teacher. The teacher presents the material to the students for their consideration, and re-considers his earlier considerations as the students express their own. The role of the problem-posing educator is to create, together with the students, the conditions under which knowledge at the level of the *doxa* is superseded by true knowledge, at the level of the *logos*.

33   Whereas banking education anesthetizes and inhibits creative power, problem-posing education involves a constant unveiling of reality. The former attempts to maintain the *submersion* of consciousness; the latter strives for the *emergence* of consciousness and *critical intervention* in reality.

34   Students, as they are increasingly posed with problems relating to themselves in the world and with the world, will feel increasingly challenged and obliged to respond to that challenge. Because they apprehend the challenge as interrelated to other problems within a total context, not as a theoretical question, the resulting comprehension tends to be increasingly critical and thus constantly less alienated. Their response to the challenge evokes new challenges, followed by new understandings; and gradually the students come to regard themselves as committed.

35   Education as the practice of freedom—as opposed to education as the practice of domination—denies that man is abstract, isolated, independent, and unattached to the world; it also denies that the world exists as a reality apart from men. Authentic reflection considers neither abstract man nor the world without men, but men in their relations with the world. In these relations consciousness and world are simultaneous: consciousness neither precedes the world nor follows it.

> La conscience et le monde sont donnés d'un même coup: extérieur par essence à la conscience, le monde est, par essence relatif à elle.[8] [Conciousness and the world are given at the same time: by nature exterior to conciousness, the world is in essence relative to it.]

In one of our culture circles in Chile, the group was discussing (based on a codification[9]) the anthropological concept of culture. In the midst of the discussion, a peasant who by banking standards was completely ignorant said: "Now I see that without man there is no world." When the educator responded:

"Let's say, for the sake of argument, that all the men on earth were to die, but that the earth itself remained, together with trees, birds, animals, rivers, seas, the stars . . . wouldn't all this be a world?" "Oh no," the peasant replied emphatically. "There would be no one to say: 'This is a world'."

36   The peasant wished to express the idea that there would be lacking the consciousness of the world which necessarily implies the world of consciousness. *I* cannot exist without a *not-I*. In turn, the *not-I* depends on that existence. The world which brings consciousness into existence becomes the world of that consciousness. Hence, the previously cited affirmation of Sartre: *"La conscience et le monde sont donnés d'un même coup."*

37   As men, simultaneously reflecting on themselves and on the world, increase the scope of their perception, they begin to direct their observations towards previously inconspicuous phenomena:

> In perception properly so-called, as an explicit awareness [*Gewahren*], I am turned towards the object, to the paper, for instance. I apprehend it as being this here and now. The apprehension is a singling out, every object having a background in experience. Around and about the paper lie books, pencils, ink-well, and so forth, and these in a certain sense are also "perceived", perceptually there, in the "field of intuition"; but whilst I was turned towards the paper there was no turning in their direction, nor any apprehending of them, not even in a secondary sense. They appeared and yet were not singled out, were not posited on their own account. Every perception of a thing has such a zone of background intuitions or background awareness, if "intuiting" already includes the state of being turned towards, and this also is a "conscious experience", or more briefly a "consciousness of" all indeed that in point of fact lies in the co-perceived objective background. [10]

38   That which had existed objectively but had not been perceived in its deeper implications (if indeed it was perceived at all) begins to "stand out," assuming the character of a problem and therefore of challenge. Thus, men begin to single out elements from their "background awarenesses" and to reflect upon them. These elements are now objects of men's consideration, and, as such, objects of their action and cognition.

39   In problem-posing education, men develop their power to perceive critically *the way they exist* in the world *with which* and *in*

which they find themselves; they come to see the world not as a static reality, but as a reality in process, in transformation. Although the dialectical relations of men with the world exist independently of how these relations are perceived (or whether or not they are perceived at all), it is also true that the form of action men adopt is to a large extent a function of how they perceive themselves in the world. Hence, the teacher-student and the students-teachers reflect simultaneously on themselves and the world without dichotomizing this reflection from action, and thus establish an authentic form of thought and action.

40 Once again, the two educational concepts and practices under analysis come into conflict. Banking education (for obvious reasons) attempts, by mythicizing reality, to conceal certain facts which explain the way men exist in the world; problem-posing education sets itself the task of demythologizing. Banking education resists dialogue; problem-posing education regards dialogue as indispensable to the act of cognition which unveils reality. Banking education treats students as objects of assistance; problem-posing education makes them critical thinkers. Banking education inhibits creativity and domesticates (although it cannot completely destroy) the *intentionality* of consciousness by isolating consciousness from the world, thereby denying men their ontological and historical vocation of becoming more fully human. Problem-posing education bases itself on creativity and stimulates true reflection and action upon reality, thereby responding to the vocation of men as beings who are authentic only when engaged in inquiry and creative transformation. In sum: banking theory and practice, as immobilizing and fixating forces, fail to acknowledge men as historical beings; problem-posing theory and practice take man's historicity as their starting point.

41 Problem-posing education affirms men as beings in the process of *becoming*—as unfinished, uncompleted beings in and with a likewise unfinished reality. Indeed, in contrast to other animals who are unfinished, but not historical, men know themselves to be unfinished; they are aware of their incompletion. In this incompletion and this awareness lie the very roots of education as an exclusively human manifestation. The unfinished character of men and the transformational character of reality necessitate that education be an ongoing activity.

42   Education is thus constantly remade in the praxis. In order to *be*, it must *become*. Its "duration" (in the Bergsonian meaning of the word) is found in the interplay of the opposites *permanence* and *change*. The banking method emphasizes permanence and becomes reactionary; problem-posing education—which accepts neither a "well-behaved" present nor a predetermined future—roots itself in the dynamic present and becomes revolutionary.

43   Problem-posing education is revolutionary futurity. Hence it is prophetic (and, as such, hopeful). Hence, it corresponds to the historical nature of man. Hence, it affirms men as beings who transcend themselves, who move forward and look ahead, for whom immobility represents a fatal threat, for whom looking at the past must only be a means of understanding more clearly what and who they are so that they can more wisely build the future. Hence, it identifies with the movement which engages men as beings aware of their incompletion—an historical movement which has its point of departure, its Subjects and its objective.

44   The point of departure of the movement lies in men themselves. But since men do not exist apart from the world, apart from reality, the movement must begin with the men-world relationship. Accordingly, the point of departure must always be with men in the "here and now," which constitutes the situation within which they are submerged, from which they emerge, and in which they intervene. Only by starting from this situation—which determines their perception of it—can they begin to move. To do this authentically they must perceive their state not as fated and unalterable, but merely as limiting—and therefore challenging.

45   Whereas the banking method directly or indirectly reinforces men's fatalistic perception of their situation, the problem-posing method presents this very situation to them as a problem. As the situation becomes the object of their cognition, the naïve or magical perception which produced their fatalism gives way to perception which is able to perceive itself even as it perceives reality, and can thus be critically objective about that reality.

46   A deepened consciousness of their situation leads men to apprehend that situation as an historical reality susceptible of

transformation. Resignation gives way to the drive for transformation and inquiry, over which men feel themselves to be
in control. If men, as historical beings necessarily engaged
with other men in a movement of inquiry, did not control that
movement, it would be (and is) a violation of men's humanity.
Any situation in which some men prevent others from engaging in the process of inquiry is one of violence. The means used
are not important; to alienate men from their own
decision-making is to change them into objects.

47 This movement of inquiry must be directed towards humanization—man's historical vocation. The pursuit of full humanity,
however, cannot be carried out in isolation or individualism, but
only in fellowship and solidarity; therefore it cannot unfold in
the antagonistic relations between oppressors and oppressed.
No one can be authentically human while he prevents others
from being so. Attempting *to be more* human, individualistical-
ly, leads to *having more,* egotistically: a form of dehumaniza-
tion. Not that it is not fundamental *to have* in order *to be*
human. Precisely because it *is* necessary, some men's *having*
must not be allowed to constitute an obstacle to others' *having,*
must not consolidate the power of the former to crush the latter.

48 Problem-posing education, as a humanist and liberating praxis,
posits as fundamental that men subjected to domination must
fight for their emancipation. To that end, it enables teachers and
students to become Subjects of the educational process by
overcoming authoritarianism and an alienating intellectual-
ism; it also enables men to overcome their false perception of
reality. The world—no longer something to be described with
deceptive words—becomes the object of that transforming
action by men which results in their humanization.

49 Problem-posing education does not and cannot serve the
interests of the oppressor. No oppressive order could permit
the oppressed to begin to question: Why? While only a revolutionary society can carry out this education in systematic
terms, the revolutionary leaders need not take full power
before they can employ the method. In the revolutionary
process, the leaders cannot utilize the banking method as an
interim measure, justified on grounds of expediency, with
the intention of *later* behaving in a genuinely revolutionary

fashion. They must be revolutionary—that is to say, dialogical—from the outset.

Notes

[1] Simone de Beauvoir, *La Pensée de Droite, Aujord'hui* (Paris); ST, *El Pensamiento politico de la Derecha* (Buenos Aires, 1963), p. 34.

[2] This concept corresponds to what Sartre calls the "digestive" or "nutritive" concept of education, in which knowledge is "fed" by the teacher to the students to "fill them out." See Jean-Paul Sartre, "Une idée fundamentale de la phénomenologie de Husserl: L'intentionalité." *Situations I* (Paris, 1947).

[3] For example, some professors specify in their reading lists that a book should be read from pages 10 to 15—and do this to "help" their students!

[4] Fromm, *op. cit.*, p. 41.

[5] *Ibid.*, p. 31.

[6] *Ibid.*

[7] Reinhold Niebuhr, *Moral Man and Immoral Society* (New York, 1960), p. 130.

[8] Sartre, *op. cit.*, p. 32.

[9] See Chapter 3.—Translator's note.

[10] Edmund Husserl, *Ideas—General Introduction to Pure Phenomenology* (London, 1969), pp. 105–106.

Philip Hallie (1922–1994) was born in Chicago, Illinois. After his undergraduate degree at Grinnell College (1946), he received his M.A. from Harvard (1948) and his Ph.D. from Oxford University (1951). From 1948–1950 Hallie was a Fulbright scholar. A professor of philosophy at Wesleyan University, his published works include The Paradox of Cruelty *(1969), and* Lest Innocent Blood Be Shed *(1979). In* Lest Innocent Blood Be Shed, *Philip Hallie explores the theme of goodness by telling the story of the people of Le Chambon in France who, along with their Protestant minister André Trocmé, helped 6,000 Jews escape from the Nazis.*

From Cruelty to Goodness

Philip Hallie

1   I am a student of ethics, of good and evil; but my approach to these two rather melodramatic terms is skeptical. I am in the tradition of the ancient Greek *skeptikoi*, whose name means "inquirers" or "investigators." And what we investigate is relationships among particular facts. What we put into doubt are the intricate webs of high-level abstractions that passed for philosophizing in the ancient world, and that still pass for philosophizing. My approach to good and evil emphasizes not abstract common nouns like "justice," but proper names and verbs. Names and verbs keep us close to the facts better than do our highfalutin common nouns. Names refer to particular people, and verbs connect subjects with predicates *in time*, while common nouns are above all this.

2   One of the words that is important to me is my own name. For me, philosophy is personal; it is closer to literature and history than it is to the exact sciences, closer to the passions, actions, and common sense of individual persons than to a dispassionate technical science. It has to do with the personal matter of wisdom. And so ethics for me is personal—my story, and not necessarily (though possibly) yours. It concerns particular people at particular times.

3   But ethics is more than such particulars. It involves abstractions, that is, rules, laws, ideals. When you look at the ethical magnates of history you see in their words and deeds two sorts of ethical rules: negative and positive. The negative rules are scattered throughout the Bible, but Moses brought down from Mount Sinai the main negative ethical rules of the West: Thou shalt not murder; thou shalt not betray. . . . The positive injunctions are similarly spread throughout the Bible. In the first chapter of the book of Isaiah we are told to ". . . defend the fatherless, plead for the widow. . . ." The negative ethic forbids certain actions; the positive ethic demands certain actions. To follow the negative ethic is to be decent, to have clean hands. But to follow the positive ethic, to be one's brother's keeper, is to be more than decent—it is to be active, even aggressive. If the negative ethic is one of decency, the positive one is the ethic of riskful, strenuous nobility.

4   In my early studies of particularized ethical terms, I found myself dwelling upon negative ethics, upon prohibitions. And among the most conspicuous prohibitions I found embodied in history was the prohibition against deliberate harmdoing, against cruelty. "Thou shalt not be cruel" had as much to do with the nightmare of history as did the prohibitions against murder and betrayal. In fact, many of the Ten Commandments—especially those against murder, adultery, stealing, and betrayal—were ways of prohibiting cruelty.

5   Early in my research it became clear that there are various approaches to cruelty, as the different commandments suggest. For instance, there is the way reflected in the origins of the word "cruel." The Latin *crudus* is related to still older words standing for bloodshed, or raw flesh. According to the etymology of the word, cruelty involves the spilling of blood.

6   But modern dictionaries give the word a different meaning. They define it as "disposed to giving pain." They emphasize awareness, not simply bloodshed. After all, they seem to say, you cannot be cruel to a dead body. There is no cruelty without consciousness.

7   And so I found myself studying the kinds of awareness associated with the hurting of human beings. It is certainly true that for millennia in history and literature people have been torturing each other not only with hard weapons but also with hard words.

8   Still, the word "pain" seemed to be a simplistic and superficial way of describing the many different sorts of cruelty. In Reska Weiss's *Journey Through Hell* (London, 1961) there is a brief passage of one of the deepest cruelties that Nazis perpetrated upon extermination camp inmates. On a march

> Urine and excreta poured down the prisoners' legs, and by nightfall the excrement, which had frozen to our limbs, gave off its stench. . . .

9   And Weiss goes on to talk not in terms of "pain" or bloodshed, but in other terms:

> . . . We were really no longer human beings in the accepted sense. Not even animals, but putrefying corpses moving on two legs. . . .

10   There is one factor that the idea of "pain" and the simpler idea of bloodshed do not touch: cruelty, not playful, quotidian teasing or ragging, but cruelty (what the anti-cruelty societies usually call "substantial cruelty") involves the maiming of a person's dignity, the crushing of a person's self-respect. Bloodshed, the idea of pain (which is usually something involving a localizable occurrence, localizable in a tooth, in a head, in short, in the body), these are superficial ideas of cruelty. A whip, bleeding flesh, these are what the journalists of cruelty emphasize, following the etymology and dictionary meaning of the word. But the depths of an understanding of cruelty lie in the depths of an understanding of human dignity and of how you can maim it without bloodshed, and often without localizable bodily pain.

11   In excremental assault, in the process of keeping camp inmates from wiping themselves or from going to the latrine, and in making them drink water from a toilet bowl full of excreta (and the excreta of the guards at that) localizable pain is nothing. Deep humiliation is everything. We human beings believe in hierarchies, whether we are skeptics or not about human value. There is a hierarchical gap between shit and me. We are even above using the word. We are "above" walking around besmirched with feces. Our dignity, whatever the origins of that dignity may be, does not permit it. In order to be able to want to live, in order to be able to walk erect, we must respect ourselves as beings "higher" than our feces. When we feel that we are not "higher" than dirt or filth, then our lives are maimed at the very center, in the very depths, not merely in

some localizable portion of our bodies. And when our lives are so maimed we become things, slaves, instruments. From ancient times until this moment, and as long as there will be human beings on this planet, there are those who know this and will use it, just as the Roman slave owners and the Southern American slave owners knew it when—one time a year—they encouraged the slaves to drink all the alcohol they could drink so that they could get bestially drunk and then even more bestially sick afterwards, under the eyes of their generous owners. The self-hatred, the loss of self-respect that the Saturnalia created in ancient Rome, say, made it possible to continue using the slaves as things, since they themselves came to think of themselves as things, as subhuman tools of the owners and the overseers.

12   Institutionalized cruelty, I learned, is the subtlest kind of cruelty. In episodic cruelty the victim knows he is being hurt, and his victimizer knows it too. But in a persistent pattern of humiliation that endures for years in a community, both the victim and the victimizer find ways of obscuring the harm that is being done. Blacks come to think of themselves as inferior, even esthetically inferior (black is "dirty"); and Jews come to think of themselves as inferior, even esthetically (dark hair and aquiline noses are "ugly"), so that the way they are being treated is justified by their "actual" inferiority, by the inferiority they themselves feel.

13   A similar process happens in the minds of the victimizers in institutionalized cruelty. They feel that since they are superior, even esthetically ("to be blonde is to be beautiful"), they deserve to do what they wish, deserve to have these lower creatures under their control. The words of Heinrich Himmler, head of the Nazi SS, in Posen in the year 1943 in a speech to his SS subordinates in a closed session, show how institutionalized cruelty can obscure harmdoing:

> . . . the words come so easily. "The Jewish people will be exterminated," says every party member, "of course. It's in our program . . . extermination. We'll take care of it." And then they come, these nice 80 million Germans, and every one of them has his decent Jew. Sure the others are swine, but his one is a fine Jew . . . Most of you will know what it means to have seen 100 corpses together, or 500 to 1000. To have made one's way through that, and . . . to have remained a decent person throughout, that is what has made us hard. That is a page of glory in our history. . . .

14   In this speech he was making a sharp distinction between the
      program of crushing the Jews and the personal sentiments of
      individual Germans. The program stretched over years; per-
      sonal sentiments were momentary. He was pleading for the
      program, for institutionalized destruction.

15   But one of the most interesting parts of the speech occurs
      toward the end of it:

> . . . in sum, we can say that we fulfilled the heaviest of tasks
> [destroying the Jews] in love to our people. And we suffered no
> harm in our essence, in our soul, in our character . . .

16   Commitment that overrides all sentimentality transforms cru-
      elty and destruction into moral nobility, and commitment is
      the lifeblood of an institution.

Cruelty and the Power Relationships

17   But when I studied all these ways that we have used the word
      "cruelty," I was nagged by the feeling that I had not penetrat-
      ed into its inner structure. I was classifying, sorting out symp-
      toms; but symptoms are signals, and what were the symptoms
      signals of? I felt like a person who had been studying cancer
      by sorting out brief pains from persistent pains, pains in the
      belly from pains in the head. I was being superficial, and I was
      not asking the question, "What are the forces behind these
      kinds of cruelty?" I felt that there were such forces, but as yet
      I had not touched them.

18   Then one day I was reading in one of the great autobiogra-
      phies of western civilization, Frederick Douglass's *Life and
      Times*. The passage I was reading was about Douglass's
      thoughts on the origins of slavery. He was asking himself:
      "How could these whites keep us enslaved?" And he sudden-
      ly realized:

> My faculties and powers of body and soul are not my own, but
> are the property of a fellow-mortal in no sense superior to me,
> except that he has the physical power to compel me to be owned
> and controlled by him. By the combined physical force of the
> community I am his slave—a slave for life.

19   And then I saw that a disparity in power lay at the center of
      the dynamism of cruelty. If it was institutional cruelty it was in
      all likelihood a difference involving both verbal and physical
      power that kept the cruelty going. The power of the majority

and the weakness of a minority were at the center of the institutional cruelty of slavery and of Nazi anti-Semitism. The whites not only outnumbered the blacks in America, but had economic and political ascendancy over them. But just as important as these "physical" powers was the power that words like "nigger" and "slave" gave the white majority. Their language sanctified if it did not create their power ascendancy over the blacks, and one of the most important projects of the slave-holders and their allies was that of seeing to it that the blacks themselves thought of themselves in just these powerless terms. They utilized the language to convince not only the whites but the blacks themselves that blacks were weak in mind, in will power, and in worth. These words were like the excremental assault in the killing camps of the Nazis: they diminished both the respect the victimizers might have for their victims and the respect the victims might have for themselves.

20   It occurred to me that if a power differential is crucial to the idea of cruelty, then when that power differential is maintained, cruelty will tend to be maintained, and when that power differential is eliminated, cruelty will tend to be eliminated. And this seemed to work. In all kinds of cruelty, violent and polite, episodic and institutional, when the victim arms himself with the appropriate strength, the cruelty diminishes or disappears. When Jews joined the Bush Warriors of France, the Maquis, and became powerful enough to strike at Vichy or the Nazis, they stopped being victims of French and Nazi cruelty. When Frederick Douglass learned to use the language with great skill and expressiveness, and when he learned to use his physical strength against his masters, the power differential between him and his masters diminished, and so did their cruelty to him. In his autobiography he wrote:

> A man without force is without the essential dignity of humanity. Human nature is so constituted that it cannot honor a helpless man, though it can pity him, and even this it cannot do long if signs of power do not arise.

21   When I looked back at my own childhood in Chicago, I remembered that the physical and mental cruelties that I suffered in the slums of the southwest side when I was about ten years old sharply diminished and finally disappeared when I learned how to defend myself physically and verbally. It is

exactly this lesson that Douglass learned while growing up in the cruel institution of slavery.

22　Cruelty then, whatever else it is, is a kind of power relationship, an imbalance of power wherein the stronger party becomes the victimizer and the weaker becomes the victim. And since many general terms are most swiftly understood in relationship with their opposites (just as "heavy" can be understood most handily in relationship with what we mean by "light") the opposite of cruelty lay in a situation where there is no imbalance of power. The opposite of cruelty, I learned, was freedom from that unbalanced power relationship. Either the victim should get stronger and stand up to the victimizer, and thereby bring about a balance of their powers, or the victim should free himself from the whole relationship by flight.

23　In pursuing this line of thought, I came to believe that, again, dictionaries are misleading: many of them give "kindness" as the antonym for "cruelty." In studying slavery in America and the concentration camps of central Europe I found that kindness could be the ultimate cruelty, especially when it was given within that unbalanced power relationship. A kind overseer or a kind camp guard can exacerbate cruelty, can remind his victim that there are other relationships than the relationship of cruelty, and can make the victim deeply bitter, especially when he sees the self-satisfied smile of his victimizer. He is being cruelly treated when he is given a penny or a bun after having endured the crushing and grinding of his mental and bodily well-being. As Frederick Douglass put it:

> The kindness of the slave-master only gilded the chain. It detracted nothing from its weight or strength. The thought that men are for other and better uses than slavery throve best under the gentle treatment of a kind master.

24　No, I learned, the opposite of cruelty is not kindness. The opposite of the cruelty of the overseer in American slavery was not the kindness of that overseer for a moment or for a day. An episodic kindness is not the opposite of an institutionalized cruelty. The opposite of institutionalized cruelty is freedom from the cruel relationship.

25　It is important to see how perspectival the whole meaning of cruelty is. From the perspective of the SS guard or the southern overseer, a bit of bread, a smile is indeed a diminution of cruelty. But in the relationship of cruelty, the point of view of the victimizer is of only minor importance; it is the point of view of the victim that is authoritative. The victim feels the suffering in his own mind and body, whereas the victimizer, like Himmler's "hard" and "decent" Nazi, can be quite unaware of that suffering. The sword does not feel the pain that it inflicts. Do not ask it about suffering.

Goodness Personified in Le Chambon

26   All these considerations drove me to write my book *The Paradox of Cruelty*. But with the book behind me, I felt a deep discontent. I saw cruelty as an embodiment, a particular case of evil. But if cruelty is one of the main evils of human history, why is the opposite of cruelty not one of the key goods of human history? Freedom from the cruel relationship, either by escaping it or by redressing the imbalance of power, was not essential to what western philosophers and theologians have thought of as goodness. Escape is a negative affair. Goodness has something positive in it, something triumphantly affirmative.

27   Hoping for a hint of goodness in the very center of evil, I started looking closely at the so-called "medical experiments" of the Nazis upon children, usually Jewish and Gypsy children, in the death camps. Here were the weakest of the weak. Not only were they despised minorities, but they were, as individuals, still in their non-age. They were dependents. Here the power imbalance between the cruel experimenters and their victims was at its greatest. But instead of seeing light or finding insight by going down into this hell, into the deepest depth of cruelty, I found myself unwillingly becoming part of the world I was studying. I found myself either yearning to be viciously cruel to the victimizers of the children, or I found myself feeling compassion for the children, feeling their despair and pain as they looked up at the men and women in white coats cutting off their fingertips one at a time, or breaking their slender bones, or wounding their internal organs. Either I became a would-be victimizer or one more Jewish victim, and in either case I was not achieving insight, only misery, like so many other students of the Holocaust. And when I was trying to be "objective" about my studies, when I was

succeeding at being indifferent to both the victimizers and the victims of these cruel relationships, I became cold; I became another monster who could look upon the maiming of a child with an indifferent eye.

28 To relieve this unending suffering, from time to time I would turn to the literature of the French resistance to the Nazis. I had been trained by the U. S. Army to understand it. The resistance was a way of trying to redress the power imbalance between Hitler's Fortress Europe and Hitler's victims, and so I saw it as an enemy of cruelty. Still, its methods were often cruel like the methods of most power struggles, and I had little hope of finding goodness here. We soldiers violated the negative ethic forbidding killing in order, we thought, to follow the positive ethic of being our brothers' keepers.

29 And then one gray April afternoon I found a brief article on the French village of Le Chambon-sur-Lignon. I shall not analyze here the tears of amazement and gladness and release from despair—in short, of joy—that I shed when I first read that story. Tears themselves interest me greatly—but not the tears of melancholy hindsight and existential despair; rather the tears of awe you experience when the realization of an ideal suddenly appears before your very eyes or thunders inside your mind; these tears interest me.

30 And one of the reasons I wept at first reading about Le Chambon in those brief, inaccurate pages was that at last I had discovered an embodiment of goodness in opposition to cruelty. I had discovered in the flesh and blood of history, in people with definite names in a definite place at a definite time in the nightmare of history, what no classical or religious ethicist could deny was goodness.

31 The French Protestant village of Le Chambon, located in the Cevennes Mountains of southeastern France, and with a population of about 3,500, saved the lives of about 6,000 people, most of them Jewish children whose parents had been murdered in the killing camps of central Europe. Under a national government which was not only collaborating with the Nazi conquerors of France but frequently trying to outdo the Germans in anti-Semitism in order to please their conquerors, and later under the day-to-day threat of destruction by the German Armed SS, they started to save children in the winter of 1940,

the winter after the fall of France, and they continued to do so until the war in France was over. They sheltered the refugees in their own homes and in various houses they established especially for them; and they took many of them across the terrible mountains to neutral Geneva, Switzerland, in the teeth of French and German police and military power. The people of Le Chambon are poor, and the Huguenot faith to which they belong is a diminishing faith in Catholic and atheist France; but their spiritual power, their capacity to act in unison against the victimizers who surrounded them, was immense, and more than a match for the military power of those victimizers.

32   But for me as an ethicist the heart of the matter was not only their special power. What interested me was that they obeyed *both* the negative and the positive injunctions of ethics; they were good not only in the sense of trying to be their brothers' keepers, protecting the victim, "defending the fatherless," to use the language of Isaiah; they were also good in the sense that they obeyed the negative injunctions against killing and betraying. While those around them—including myself—were murdering in order presumably, to help mankind in some way or other, they murdered nobody, and betrayed not a single child in those long and dangerous four years. For me as an ethicist they were the embodiment of unambiguous goodness.

33   But for me as a student of cruelty they were something more: they were an embodiment of the opposite of cruelty. And so, somehow, at last, I had found goodness in opposition to cruelty. In studying their story, and in telling it in *Lest Innocent Blood Be Shed*, I learned that the opposite of cruelty is not simply freedom from the cruel relationship; it is *hospitality*. It lies not only in something negative, an absence of cruelty or of imbalance; it lies in unsentimental, efficacious love. The opposite of the cruelties of the camps was not the liberation of the camps, the cleaning out of the barracks and the cessation of the horrors. All of this was the *end* of the cruelty relationship, not the opposite of that relationship. And it was not even the end of it, because the victims would never forget and would remain in agony as long as they remembered their humiliation and suffering. No, the opposite of cruelty was not the liberation of the camps, not freedom; it was the hospitality of the people of Chambon, and of very few others during the Holocaust. The opposite of cruelty was the kind of goodness that happened in Chambon.

34   Let me explain the difference between liberation and hospitality by telling you about a letter I received a year ago from a woman who had been saved by the people of Le Chambon when she was a young girl. She wrote:

> Never was there a question that the Chambonnais would not share all they had with us, meager as it was. One Chambonnais once told me that even if there was less, they still would want more for us.

35   And she goes on:

> It was indeed a very different attitude from the one in Switzerland, which while saving us also resented us so much.
>
> If today we are not bitter people like most survivors it can only be due to the fact that we met people like the people of Le Chambon, who showed to us simply that life can be different, that there are people who care, that people can live together and even risk their own lives for their fellow man.

36   The Swiss liberated refugees and removed them from the cruel relationship; the people of Le Chambon did more. They taught them that goodness could conquer cruelty, that loving hospitality could remove them from the cruel relationship. And they taught me this, too.

37   It is important to emphasize that cruelty is not simply an episodic, momentary matter, especially institutional cruelty like that of Nazism or slavery. As we have seen throughout this essay, not only does it persist while it is being exerted upon the weak; *it can persist in the survivors* after they have escaped the power relationship. The survivors torture themselves, continue to suffer, continue to maim their own lives long after the actual torture is finished. The self-hatred and rage of the blacks and the despair of the native Americans and the Jews who have suffered under institutional crushing and maiming are continuations of original cruelties. And these continuations exist because only a superficial liberation from torture has occurred. The sword has stopped falling on their flesh in the old obvious ways, but the wounds still bleed. I am not saying that the village of Chambon healed these wounds—they go too deep. What I am saying is that the people I have talked to who were once children in Le Chambon have more hope for their species and more respect for themselves as human beings than most other survivors I have met. The

enduring hospitality they met in Le Chambon helped them find realistic hope in a world of persisting cruelty.

38   What was the nature of this hospitality that saved and deeply changed so many lives? It is hard to summarize briefly what the Chambonnais did, and above all how they did it. The morning after a new refugee family came to town they would find on their front door a wreath with *"Bienvenue!"* "Welcome!" painted on a piece of cardboard attached to the wreath. Nobody knew who had brought the wreath; in effect, the whole town had brought it.

39   It was mainly the women of Chambon who gave so much more than shelter to these, the most hated enemies of the Nazis. There was Madame Barraud, a tiny Alsatian, who cared for the refugee boys in her house with all the love such a tiny body could hold, and who cared for the way they felt day and night. And there were others.

40   But there was one person without whom Le Chambon could not have become the safest place in Europe for Jews: the Huguenot minister of the village, André Trocmé. Trocmé was a passionately religious man. He was massive, more than six feet tall, blonde, with a quick temper. Once long after the war, while he was lecturing on the main project of his life, the promotion of the idea of nonviolence in international relations, one of the members of his audience started to whisper a few words to his neighbor. Trocmé let this go on for a few moments, then interrupted his speech, walked up to the astonished whisperer, raised his massive arm, pointed toward the door, and yelled, "Out! Out! Get out!" And the lecture was on nonviolence.

41   The center of his thought was the belief that God showed how important man was by becoming Himself a human being, and by becoming a particular sort of human being who was the embodiment of sacrificially generous love. For Trocmé, every human being was like Jesus, had God in him or her, and was just as precious as God Himself. And when Trocmé with the help of the Quakers and others organized his village into the most efficient rescue machine in Europe, he did so not only to save the Jews, but also to save the Nazis and their collaborators. He wanted to keep them from blackening their souls with more evil—he wanted to save them, the victimizers, from evil.

42   One of the reasons he was successful was that the Huguenots
      had been themselves persecuted for hundreds of years by the
      kings of France, and they knew what persecution was. In fact,
      when the people of Chambon took Jewish children and whole
      families across the mountains of southeastern France into neu-
      tral Switzerland, they often followed pathways that had been
      taken by Huguenots in their flight from the Dragoons of the
      French kings.

43   A particular incident from the story of Le Chambon during the
      Nazi occupation of France will explain succinctly why he was
      successful in making the village a village of refuge. But before
      I relate the story, I must point out that the people of the village
      did not think of themselves as "successful," let alone as
      "good." From their point of view, they did not do anything
      that required elaborate explanation. When I asked them why
      they helped these dangerous guests, they invariably answered,
      "What do you mean, 'Why'? Where else could they go? How
      could you turn them away? What is so special about being
      ready to help *(prête à servir)*? There was nothing else to do."
      And some of them laughed in amazement when I told them
      that I thought they were "good people." They saw no alterna-
      tive to their actions and to the way they acted, and therefore
      they saw what they did as necessary, not something to be
      picked out for praise. Helping these guests was for them as
      natural as breathing or eating—one does not think of alterna-
      tives to these functions; they did not think of alternatives to
      sheltering people who were endangering not only the lives of
      their hosts but the lives of all the people of the village.

44   And now the story. One afternoon a refugee woman knocked
      on the door of a farmhouse outside the village. The farmers
      around the village proper were Protestants like most of the
      others in Chambon, but with one difference: they were mostly
      "Darbystes," followers of a strange Scot named Darby, who
      taught their ancestors in the nineteenth century to believe
      every word of the Bible, and indeed, who had them memorize
      the Bible. They were literal fundamentalists. The farm-woman
      opened the door to the refugee and invited her into the kitchen
      where it was warm. Standing in the middle of the floor the
      refugee, in heavily accented French, asked for eggs for her chil-
      dren. In those days of very short supplies, people with chil-
      dren often went to the farmers in the "gray market" (neither

black nor exactly legal) to get necessary food. This was early in 1941, and the farmers were not yet accustomed to the refugees. The farm-woman looked into the eyes of the shawled refugee and asked, "Are you Jewish?" The woman started to tremble, but she could not lie, even though that question was usually the beginning of the end of life for Jews in Hitler's Fortress Europe. She answered, "Yes."

45   The woman ran from the kitchen to the staircase nearby, and while the refugee trembled with terror in the kitchen, she called up the stairs, "Husband, children, come down, come down! We have in our house at this very moment a representative of the Chosen People!"

46   Not all the Protestants in Chambon were Darbyste fundamentalists; but almost all were convinced that people are the children of God, and are as precious as God Himself. Their leaders were Huguenot preachers and their following of the negative and positive commandments of the Bible came in part from their personal generosity and courage, but also in part from the depths of their religious conviction that we are all children of God, and we must take care of each other lovingly. This combined with the ancient and deep historical ties between the Huguenots and the Jews of France and their own centuries of persecution by the Dragoons and Kings of France helped make them what they were, "always ready to help," as the Chambonnais saying goes.

A Choice of Perspectives

47   We have come a long way from cruelty to the people of Chambon, just as I have come a long way in my research from concrete evil to concrete goodness. Let me conclude with a point that has been alternately hinted at and stressed in the course of this essay.

48   A few months after *Lest Innocent Blood Be Shed* was published I received a letter from Massachusetts that opened as follows:

> I have read your book, and I believe that you mushy-minded moralists should be awakened to the facts. Nothing happened in Le Chambon, nothing of any importance whatsoever.

> The Holocaust, dear Professor, was like a geological event, like an earthquake. No person could start it; no person could change it; and no person could end it. And no small group of persons could do so either. It was the armies and the nations that performed

actions that counted. Individuals did nothing. You sentimental-
ists have got to learn that the great masses and big political ideas
make the difference. Your people and the people they saved simply do not exist . . .

49 Now between this position and mine there is an abyss that no
amount of shouted arguments or facts can cross. And so I shall
not answer this letter with a tightly organized reply. I shall
answer it only by telling you that one of the reasons institutional cruelty exists and persists is that people believe that
individuals can do nothing, that only vast ideologies and
armies can act meaningfully. Every act of institutional cruelty—Nazism, slavery, and all the others—lives not with people
in the concrete, but with abstractions that blind people to individuals. Himmler's speech to the SS leadership in 1943 is full
of phrases like "exterminating a bacillus," and "The Jewish
people will be exterminated." And in that speech he attacks
any German who believes in "his decent Jew." Institutional
cruelty, like other misleading approaches to ethics, blinds us to
the victim's point of view; and when we are blind to that point
of view we can countenance and perpetrate cruelty with
impunity.

50 I have told you that I cannot and will not try to refute the letter from Massachusetts. I shall only summarize the point of
view of this essay with another story.

51 I was lecturing a few months ago in Minneapolis, and when I
finished talking about the Holocaust and the village of Le
Chambon, a woman stood up and asked me if the village of Le
Chambon was in the Department of Haute-Loire, the high
sources of the Loire River. Obviously she was French, with her
accent; and all French people know that there are many villages called "Le Chambon" in France, just as any American
knows that there are many "Main Streets" in the United States.
I said that Le Chambon was indeed in the Haute-Loire.

52 She said, "Then you have been speaking about the village that
saved all three of my children. I want to thank you for writing
this book, not only because the story will now be permanent,
but also because I shall be able to talk about those terrible days
with Americans now, for they will understand those days better than they have. You see, you Americans, though you sometimes cross the oceans, live on an island here as far as war is
concerned . . ."

53   Then she asked to come up and say one sentence. There was
     not a sound, not even breathing, to be heard in the room. She
     came to the front of the room and said, "The Holocaust was
     storm, lightning, thunder, wind, rain, yes. And Le Chambon
     was the rainbow."

54   Only from her perspective can you understand the cruelty and
     the goodness I have been talking about, not from the point of
     view of the gentleman from Massachusetts. You must choose
     which perspective is best, and your choice will have much to
     do with your feelings about the preciousness of life, and not
     only the preciousness of other people's lives. If the lives of others
     are precious to you, your life will become more precious to you.

Eric Donald Hirsch, Jr., was born on March 22, 1928 in Memphis, Tennessee. He received his B.A. from Cornell University in 1950 and his M.A. (1953) and Ph.D. (1957) from Yale. Since 1960 he has taught in the Department of English at the University of Virginia. Hirsch has published a wide range of books on literary criticism and theory including Wordsworth and Schelling: A Typological Study of Romanticism *(1960),* Innocence and Experience: An Introduction to Blake *(1964),* Validity in Interpretation *(1967),* The Aims of Interpretation *(1976), and* The Philosophy of Composition *(1977). By far his most famous book, however, is the controversial best-seller* Cultural Literacy: What Every American Needs to Know *(1987). The book argues that because Americans do not share the same cultural terms and concepts, they are incapable of fully participating in society. Hirsch subsequently founded the Cultural Literacy Foundation, an organization which promotes the teaching of core knowledge in schools. In 1958 Hirsch married Mary Pope. They have three children and live in Charlottesville, Virginia.*

Cultural Literacy: What Every American Needs to Know

E. D. Hirsch, Jr.

1   My son is a high school teacher. In one of his classes he mentioned to his students that Latin is a dead language, no longer spoken. One girl raised her hand to challenge my son's claim. "But what do they speak in Latin America?" she demanded.

2   More and more of our young people don't know things we assume they know. What they do know is ephemeral and narrowly confined to their own generation. Many young people lack the information that writers of American books and newspapers have traditionally taken for granted among their readers.

3   According to a 1985 Foundations of Literacy study, two thirds of the 17-year-old students tested could not place the Civil War in the correct half-century; a third did not know that the Declaration of Independence was signed between 1750 and 1800; a third did not know that Columbus sailed for the New World

93

before 1750; three-fourths could not identify Walt Whitman or Thoreau or e. e. cummings or Carl Sandburg. And one-half of our high-school seniors did not recognize the names of Winston Churchill or Joseph Stalin.

4   We have long accepted literacy as a paramount aim of schooling. But only recently have some begun to realize that literacy is far more than a skill, and that it requires large amounts of specific information.

5   Where communications fail, so do undertakings. That is the moral of the story of the Tower of Babel. To grasp the words on a page, we have to know a lot of information that isn't on the page.

6   Several reading specialists have observed that "world knowledge" is essential to the development of reading and writing skills. I call this knowledge *cultural literacy*, the network of information that all competent readers possess. It is background information that enables them to read a book or an article with an adequate level of comprehension, getting the point, grasping the implications.

7   Clearly our schools have failed to fulfill their fundamental responsibility to provide students with this world knowledge. In view of the immense importance of cultural literacy for speaking, listening, reading and writing, why has the need for a definite, shared body of information been so rarely mentioned in discussions of education?

8   One reason we have ignored cultural literacy is that it was something we have been able to take for granted. We ignore the air we breathe until it is thin or foul. Only when we run into cultural illiteracy are we shocked into recognizing the importance of the information that we had unconsciously assumed.

9   To be sure, a minimal level of information is possessed by any normal person who lives in the United States and speaks elementary English. But this elementary level of information isn't sufficient to read newspapers or make informed civic decisions. Cultural literacy lies *above* the everyday levels of knowledge that everyone possesses and *below* the expert level known only to specialists. It is that middle ground of cultural knowledge writers assume to be possessed by the "common reader." It

includes information that we have traditionally expected our children to receive in school, but which they no longer do.

10　It will not do to blame television. Watching television does reduce reading and often encroaches on homework. But schools have children for six or seven hours a day, five days a week, nine months a year, for 13 years or more.

11　It is the American public school's cafeteria-style curriculum, combined with our unwillingness to place demands on students, that has resulted in a steady diminishment of commonly shared information between generations and between young people themselves. Those who graduate from the same school have often studied different subjects, and those who graduate from different schools have often studied different material even when their courses have carried the same titles. It would be hard to invent a better recipe for cultural fragmentation.

12　Current educational theorists hold that specific information is irrelevant to "language arts skills." They believe that reading and writing, like baseball and skating, are neutral, technical skills that can be developed by proper coaching and practice. Texts now used to teach reading and writing are screened not for the information they convey but for their readability scores.

13　The technical-skill idea becomes an oversimplification once students start reading for meaning rather than for cracking the alphabetic code. The trouble is that every text is different, and even the most elementary text implies information that it takes for granted and doesn't explain. Knowing such information is *the* decisive skill of reading.

14　Some have objected that teaching the traditional literate culture means teaching elitist material. That is an illusion. Literate culture is the most democratic culture in our land: it excludes nobody; it cuts across generations and social groups and classes.

15　Middle-class children are likely to acquire mainstream literate culture by daily encounters with literate people. But less-privileged children are denied these consistent interchanges. The most straightforward antidote to their deprivation is to make the essential information readily available inside the schools.

16   Background knowledge does not take care of itself. Reading and writing are cumulative skills; the more we read, the more necessary knowledge we gain for further reading.

17   I'm not suggesting that we teach our children exactly what our grandparents learned. It's obvious that the content of cultural literacy changes over the years. But stability, not change, is the chief characteristic of cultural literacy. Although historical and technical terms may follow the ebb and flow of events, the more stable elements of our national vocabulary, like George Washington, the Gettysburg Address, Hamlet and the Declaration of Independence, have persisted.

I spend a lot of time with teenagers, and frequently conduct focus groups to learn about their attitudes. Recently, a 19-year-old junior at the University of Southern California sat with me while I watched Guadalcanal Diary on TV. She was genuinely shocked to learn that the United States had fought a war against the Japanese. ("Who won?")

In fact I have not yet found a single student who could tell me the years when the Civil War, World War I and World War II were fought. Not one could name all the Presidents since World War II. Only one could even place the correct decade in which Dwight Eisenhower was President.

Of the teenagers with whom I work, only two could approximately identify Thomas Jefferson. Only a few could articulate in any way at all why life in a free country is different from life in a nonfree country.

In a state of such astonishing ignorance, young Americans may well not be prepared for even the most basic national responsibility—understanding what the society is about and why it must be preserved.

—Benjamin J. Stein in *Public Opinion*

Let me give some concrete examples of the kinds of core information I mean. American readers are assumed to have a general knowledge of the following people (I give just the beginning of a list): John Adams, Susan B. Anthony, Benedict Arnold, Daniel Boone, John Brown, Aaron Burr, John C. Calhoun, Henry Clay, James Fenimore Cooper, Lord Cornwallis, Davy Crockett, Emily Dickinson, Stephen A. Douglas, Frederick Douglass, Jonathan Edwards, Ralph Waldo Emerson, Benjamin Franklin, Robert Fulton, Ulysses S. Grant, Alexander Hamilton and Nathaniel Hawthorne. Most of us know rather little about these people, but that little is of crucial importance, because it enables writers and speakers to assume a starting point from which they can treat in detail what they wish to focus on.

19   Because literate people mention such names in passing, usually without explanation, children should acquire them as part of their intellectual equipment. Many such items of literate culture are arbitrary, but that does not make them dispensable.

20   Children also need to understand elements of our literary and mythic heritage that are often alluded to without explanation. For example: Adam and Eve, Cain and Abel, Noah and the Flood, David and Goliath, the Twenty-third Psalm, Humpty Dumpty, Jack and Jill, Cinderella, Jack and the Beanstalk, Peter Pan and Pinocchio. Also: Achilles, Adonis, Aeneas, Agamemnon, Antigone and Apollo, as well as Robin Hood, Paul Bunyan, Satan, Sodom and Gomorrah, the Ten Commandments.

21   A curriculum reform designed to teach young children the basics of cultural literacy will require radical changes in textbooks. But from a historical perspective, this would not be novel in conception. Here is an excerpt from the preface to one of the volumes of *Everyday Classics* by A. H. Thorndike and F. T. Baker. This was one of the most popular elementary schoolbooks in America in the early part of this century. (I have italicized a few phrases to show how fully aware they were of the need for teaching shared content in the days before the dominance of educational formalism.)

> *We have chosen what is common, established, almost proverbial; what has become indisputably "classic," what, in brief,* every child in the land ought so know, *because it is good,* and because other people know it.

The educational worth of such materials calls for no defense. In an age when the need of unifying our people is keenly felt, the value of a common stock of knowledge, a common set of ideals, is obvious.

22   Of course, we must present material to children in an interesting way. Dry incompetence is not the necessary alternative to lively ignorance. And very young children *are* interested in adult information long before they can make sense of it. Children don't have to be forced to memorize facts, they do it anyway. The great oversight of a watered-down curriculum for early grades is that while children are busily remembering what they experience in school, their school materials are often not worth remembering.

23   Many Americans who have graduated from high school in the recent past have been deprived of the cultural vocabulary that was commonly possessed by educated persons in past generations. Some repair work is necessary for them and for the members of the current school generation. They must be reintroduced to the cultural vocabulary that continues to be the foundation for literate national communication.

24   I have in mind the Founding Fathers' idea of an informed citizenry. This is the basic principle that underlies our national system of education in the first place—that people in a democracy can be entrusted to decide all important matters for themselves because they can deliberate and communicate with one another. Economic issues can be discussed in public. The moral dilemmas of new medical knowledge can be weighed. The broad implications of technological change can become subjects of informed public discourse.

25   This ideal is a basic principle of the American republic, and must once again become a primary responsibility of our schools.

*A*rlie Russell Hochschild (1940–) is professor of sociology at the University of California, Berkeley. Raised in Maryland, as a child she began to question how individuals control emotional displays in everyday life. She is known as the founder of the sociology of emotions, a branch that seeks to understand not only what people think, but also how people feel. She has researched and written on topics related to family-work struggles, global care work, and the relationship between culture and emotion. She wrote The Commercialization of Intimate Life: Notes from Home and Work (2003), The Time Bind: When Work Becomes Home and Home Becomes Work (1997), The Second Shift: Working Parents and the Revolution at Home (1989), The Managed Heart: The Commercialization of Human Feeling (1983), and The Unexpected Community (1973), and is the author of numerous articles and essays related to market culture. She also established and is the director of the Center for Working Families at the University of California.

There's No Place Like Work

Arlie Russell Hochschild

1   We are used to thinking that work is where most people feel like "just a number" or "a cog in a machine." It is where they have to be "on," have to "act," where they are least secure and most harried.

2   But new management techniques so pervasive in corporate life have helped transform the workplace into a more appreciative, personal sort of social world. Meanwhile, at home the divorce rate has risen, and the emotional demands have become more baffling and complex. In addition to teething, tantrums and the normal developments of growing children, the needs of elderly parents are creating more tasks for the modern family—as are the blending, unblending, reblending of new stepparents, stepchildren, exes and former in-laws.

3   This idea began to dawn on me during one of my first interviews with an Amerco worker. Linda Avery, a friendly, 38-year-old mother, is a shift supervisor at an Amerco plant. When I meet her in the factory's coffee-break room over a couple of Cokes, she is wearing blue jeans and a pink jersey, her hair

pulled back in a long, blond ponytail. Linda's husband, Bill, is a technician in the same plant. By working different shifts, they manage to share the care of their 2-year-old son and Linda's 16-year-old daughter from a previous marriage. "Bill works the 7 A.M. to 3 P.M. shift while I watch the baby," she explains. "Then I work the 3 P.M. to 11 P.M. shift and he watches the baby. My daughter works at Walgreen's after school."

4 Linda is working overtime, and so I begin by asking whether Amerco required the overtime, or whether she volunteered for it. "Oh, I put in for it," she replies. I ask her whether, if finances and company policy permitted, she'd be interested in cutting back on the overtime. She takes off her safety glasses, rubs her face and, without answering my question explains: "I get home, and the minute I turn the key, my daughter is right there. Granted, she needs somebody to talk to about her day. . . . The baby is still up. He should have been in bed two hours ago, and that upsets me. The dishes are piled in the sink. My daughter comes right up to the door and complains about anything her stepfather said or did, and she wants to talk about her job. My husband is in the other room hollering to my daughter, 'Tracy, I don't ever get any time to talk to your mother, because you're always monopolizing her time before I even get a chance!' They all come at me at once."

5 Linda's description of the urgency of demands and the unarbitrated quarrels that await her homecoming contrast with her account of arriving at her job as a shift supervisor: "I usually come to work early, just to get away from the house. When I arrive, people are there waiting. We sit, we talk, we joke. I let them know what's going on, who has to be where, what changes I've made for the shift that day. We sit and chitchat for 5 or 10 minutes. There's laughing, joking, fun."

6 For Linda, home has come to feel like work and work has come to feel a bit like home. Indeed, she feels she can get relief from the "work" of being at home only by going to the "home" of work. Why has her life at home come to seem like this? Linda explains it this way: "My husband's a great help watching our baby. But as far as doing housework or even taking the baby when I'm at home, no. He figures he works five days a week; he's not going to come home and clean. But he doesn't stop to think that I work seven days a week. Why should I have to come home and do the housework without help from anybody

else? My husband and I have been through this over and over again. Even if he would just pick up from the kitchen table and stack the dishes for me, that would make a big difference. He does nothing. On his weekends off, he goes fishing. If I want any time off, I have to get a sitter. He'll help out if I'm not here, but the minute I am, all the work at home is mine."

7   With a light laugh, she continues: "So I take a lot of overtime. The more I get out of the house, the better I am. It's a terrible thing to say, but that's the way I feel."

8   When Bill feels the need for time off, to relax, to have fun, to feel free, he climbs in his truck and takes his free time without his family. Largely in response, Linda grabs what she also calls "free time"—at work. Neither Linda nor Bill Avery wants more time together at home, not as things are arranged now.

9   How do Linda and Bill Avery fit into the broader picture of American family and work life? Current research suggests that however hectic their lives, women who do paid work feel less depressed, think better of themselves and are more satisfied than women who stay at home. One study reported that women who work outside the home feel more valued at home than housewives do. Meanwhile, work is where many women feel like "good mothers." As Linda reflects: "I'm a good mom at home, but I'm a better mom at work. At home, I get into fights with Tracy. I want her to apply to a junior college, but she's not interested. At work, I think I'm better at seeing the other person's point of view."

10   Many workers feel more confident they could "get the job done" at work than at home. One study found that only 59 percent of workers feel their "performance" in the family is "good or unusually good," while 86 percent rank their performance on the job this way.

11   Forces at work and at home are simultaneously reinforcing this "reversal." The lure of work has been enhanced in recent years by the rise of company cultural engineering—in particular, the shift from Frederick Taylor's principles of scientific management to the Total Quality principles originally set out by W. Edwards Deming. Under the influence of a Taylorist world view, the manager's job was to coerce the worker's mind and body, not to appeal to the worker's heart. The Taylorized

worker was de-skilled, replaceable and cheap, and as a consequence felt bored, demeaned and unappreciated.

12   Using modern participative management techniques, many companies now train workers to make their own work decisions, and then set before their newly "empowered" employees moral as well as financial incentives. At Amerco, the Total Quality worker is invited to feel recognized for job accomplishments. Amerco regularly strengthens the familylike ties of coworkers by holding "recognition ceremonies" honoring particular workers or management production teams. Amerco employees speak of "belonging to the Amerco family," and proudly wear their "Total Quality" pins or "High Performance Team" T-shirts, symbols of their loyalty to the company and of its loyalty to them. . . .

13   If Total Quality calls for "re-skilling" the worker in an "enriched" job environment, technological developments have long been de-skilling parents at home. Over the centuries, store-bought goods have replaced homespun cloth, homemade soap and home-baked foods. Day care for children, retirement homes for the elderly, even psychotherapy are, in a way, commercial substitutes for jobs that a mother once did at home. Even family-generated entertainment has, to some extent, been replaced by television, video games and the VCR. I sometimes watched Amerco families sitting together after their dinners, mute but cozy, watching sitcoms in which television mothers, fathers and children related in an animated way to one another while the viewing family engaged in relational loafing.

14   The one "skill" still required of family members is the hardest one of all—the emotional work of forging, deepening or repairing family relationships. It takes time to develop this skill, and even then things can go awry. Family ties are complicated. People get hurt. Yet as broken homes become more common—and as the sense of belonging to a geographical community grows less and less secure in an age of mobility—the corporate world has created a sense of "neighborhood," of "feminine culture," of family at work. Life at work can be insecure; the company can fire workers. But workers aren't so secure at home, either. Many employees have been working for Amerco for 20 years but are on their second or third marriages or relationships. The shifting balance between these two "divorce rates" may be the

most powerful reason why tired parents flee a world of unre-
solved quarrels and unwashed laundry for the orderliness,
harmony and managed cheer of work. People are getting their
"pink slips" at home.

15 Amerco workers have not only turned their offices into
"home" and their homes into workplaces; many have also
begun to "Taylorize" time at home, where families are suc-
cumbing to a cult of efficiency previously associated mainly
with the office and factory. Meanwhile, work time, with its ever
longer hours, has become more hospitable to sociability—periods of talking with friends on E-mail, patching up quarrels,
gossiping. Within the long workday of many Amerco employees are great hidden pockets of inefficiency while, in the far
smaller number of waking weekday hours at home, they are,
despite themselves, forced to act increasingly time-conscious
and efficient.

16 The Averys respond to their time bind at home by trying to
value and protect "quality time." A concept unknown to their
parents and grandparents, "quality time" has become a powerful symbol of the struggle against the growing pressures at
home. . . .

17 Quality time holds out the hope that scheduling intense periods of togetherness can compensate for an overall loss of time
in such a way that a relationship will suffer no loss of quality.
But this is just another way of transferring the cult of efficiency from office to home. We must now get our relationships in good repair in less time. Instead of nine hours a day
with a child, we declare ourselves capable of getting "the
same result" with one intensely focused hour. . . .

18 Part of modern parenthood seems to include coping with the
resistance of real children who are not so eager to get their
cereal so fast. Some parents try desperately not to appease
their children with special gifts or smooth-talking promises
about the future. But when time is scarce, even the best parents
find themselves passing a system-wide familial speed-up
along to the most vulnerable workers on the line. Parents are
then obliged to try to control the damage done by a reversal of
worlds. They monitor mealtime, homework time, bedtime trying to cut out "wasted" time.

19   In response, children often protest the pace, the deadlines, the
grand irrationality of "efficient" family life. Children dawdle.
They refuse to leave places when it's time to leave. They insist
on leaving places when it's not time to leave. Surely, this is part
of the usual stop-and-go of childhood itself, but perhaps, too, it
is the plea of children for more family time, and more control
over what time there is. This only adds to the feeling that life at
home has become hard work.

20   Instead of trying to arrange shorter or more flexible work
schedules, Amerco parents often avoid confronting the reality
of the time bind. Some minimize their ideas about how much
care a child, a partner or they themselves "really need." They
make do with less time, less attention, less understanding and
less support at home than they once imagined possible. They
emotionally downsize life. In essence, they deny the needs of
family members and they themselves become emotional
ascetics. If they once "needed" time with each other, they are
now increasingly "fine" without it. . . .

21   Obviously, not everyone, not even a majority of Americans, is
making a home out of work and a workplace out of home. But
in the working world, it is a growing reality and one we need
to face. Increasing numbers of women are rediscovering a great
male secret—that work can be an escape from the pressures of
home, pressures that the changing nature of work itself [is]
only intensifying. Neither men nor women are going to take up
"family friendly" policies, whether corporate or governmental,
as long as the current realities of work and home remain as
they are. For a substantial number of time-bound parents, the
stripped-down home and the neighborhood devoid of community are simply losing out to the pull of the workplace.

Elizabeth Holtry (b. 1970) graduated from the University of Maryland with a B.A. in studio art, and earned her M.F.A. in painting from the University of Cincinnati. She is an associate professor of art at Mount St. Mary's University, where she has taught since 2001. She is also a painter whose work has been exhibited regionally and nationally. In the following essay, she describes how she discovered her call to become an artist and educator.

Mr. Yoder Discovers "Liz's" Magic Pencil

Elizabeth Holtry

1   I could not muster anything above a whisper until third grade. Frequent moves due to my father's military career, coupled with my small stature, only exacerbated my shyness and lack of confidence. When I picked up my first drawing implement, however, I realized that some people communicate better through pictures. Mrs. Lippi, my third grade teacher, noticed my artistic talent for the first time when I drew a picture of a giraffe to accompany a story we read for class. In perfect teacher cursive, she wrote "Nice giraffe!" and "Pretty good for a lefty!" on my paper. I was actually right-handed, but I broke my arm a week before school started, after falling out of a tree trying to reach for some bizarre seed pods.

2   Our busy elementary school curriculum, laden with reading, writing, arithmetic, music, and physical education, left little time for formal art instruction. With my attention focused elsewhere, art wasn't exactly a priority for me. Intensely curious and active, I spent my childhood free time pursuing solitary interests such as horseback riding, crabbing, fishing, sewing, exploring nature, and sculpting sand creatures on the beach; nevertheless, I taught myself how to express my passion for horses through rather life like pencil drawings.

3   Once I started playing the flute in sixth grade, my nascent art career went on hiatus for a few years. Because of my passion for flute playing, I earned the band's coveted first chair position by the time I reached eighth grade. I cherished the close

105

friendships I made through band, and I loved practicing my instrument in private. Performing in front of a group of people and trying to cope with the catty competition among adolescent flutists determined to steal my chair, however, made me nervous. To make matters worse, membership in the high school Wind Ensemble compelled me to participate in the dreaded marching band. Wearing itchy, malodorous polyester uniforms while performing contrived half-time routines on the football field proved nightmarish for this shy, introverted adolescent. An auspicious move to Maryland in tenth grade offered a chance to make a clean break from small town Virginia life and my mortifying band experience.

4 Although I felt, and still feel, guilty for quitting something I had spent years striving to master, the notion of playing with a bunch of geeky strangers in a scary new high school seemed like a betrayal (a fourteen-year-old can rationalize anything!). I recalled my horse drawings from fifth grade and decided to take a painting and drawing course with tall, round-bellied, Mr. Olin Yoder. The odor of his tobacco pipe hung in the air around him and his peaches and cream face. A 60-something Swiss former Mennonite, topped with a mop of curly white hair, Mr. Yoder spoke with a booming voice that quickly oscillated between sharp staccato and melodic lyricism. On that first day of class he explained the class goals, expectations, and rules like a well-rehearsed ringmaster. I trembled. His enveloping comic presence overwhelmed me despite his ability to pass quite convincingly for Santa Claus. When I tore my eyes away from this man to survey the reactions of my classmates, I noticed the peculiar assortment of free spirits, disaffected burnouts, curious immigrant kids, and creepy punks. I did not know what to make of this underground freak show; surely I did not fit into any of those categories. But at least I escaped the performance anxiety-inducing band.

5 For our first project, Mr. Yoder instructed us to draw one of four artfully constructed still lifes sprinkled around the room. The drab, lifeless clay pots sitting at the end of my table beckoned me, for choosing those meant I need not abandon my safe spot at the back of the room. Feeling ashamed of my lonely-looking drawing, I covered my paper and cowered as Mr. Yoder approached to assess my progress. He smiled and gently pulled my hand away. After a moment that dragged on long enough in my mind to unleash myriad apprehensions, he

addressed me with a derivation of my name no one ever used with me, "Why Liz," and exclaimed, "You have a magic pencil!" My face flushed hot as he lifted the paper to show the class. In that moment, though, he elevated my sense of my own individuality, right along with my drawing, and made me feel special. Whether that first drawing deserved such praise is beside the point—he wanted to pull me out of my protective cocoon, and it worked. At the same time, his new nickname for me became my studio art name, used solely by Mr. Yoder. My confidence grew, and a string of art courses followed.

6   My journey into the art world led to summer art programs, exhibitions, awards, and acceptance letters to prestigious art schools. I routinely skipped lunch so I could paint and listen to Mr. Yoder drolly tell stories about artists or his exotic travels. He lent me art books, while I procured my own stash of quality art supplies. He let me store them in his office, secure from the tendency of things around school to wander away from their rightful owners. Mr. Yoder provided a unique safe haven in that basement art room. The pungent odor of acrylic paints, the gentle hum of conversation, and the clutter of art book and detritus used for still life made the art room cozy. I felt grateful for what had become crucial sustenance to my spirit.

7   Mr. Yoder, a seasoned and perceptive teacher, knew when to offer encouragement or to administer academic smelling salts. While I obsessed over meticulously rendered details, Mr. Yoder would admonish, "Free, be free!" and "Don't tickle your painting to death!" Rich laughter always followed his constructive criticism, making me feel safe in this new enclave. These comments still echo in my mind; years later, I catch myself using his idiomatic expressions in my own teaching. From Mr. Yoder, I learned about perseverance, patience, humility, tolerance, and hard work. In his own eccentric, pipe-tobacco smelling, mop-topped way, he taught me to believe in myself and how to overcome "masterpiece syndrome." And invaluably, he showed me that process and product are equally important. Mr. Yoder modeled how to teach with fancifulness and gusto, and in so doing inspired me to become a teacher. He encouraged me to creep out of my cocoon and reveal my inner eccentricity. I discovered my voice, my passion, and my home in his art room—my vocation within a vocation. After two decades, I still keep in touch with Mr. Yoder, and he still teases me about my magic pencil.

*P*ope John Paul II (1920–2005) was born Karol Wojtyla in the Polish town of Wadowice. He was ordained to the priesthood in 1946. He finished his doctorate in theology in 1948. In 1964, he was appointed archbishop of Krakow by Pope Paul VI, who made him a cardinal June 26, 1967. He took part in Vatican Council II (1962–1965) where he made an important contribution to drafting the Constitution Gaudium et spes.

He was Pope from October 16, 1978 to April 2, 2005; his pontificate, one of the longest in the history of the Church, lasted nearly twenty-seven years. Among many other accomplishments, he established World Youth Days; nineteen WYDs celebrated during his pontificate brought together millions of young people from all over the world. His most important Documents include fourteen Encyclicals, fifteen Apostolic Exhortations, eleven Apostolic Constitutions, and forty-five Apostolic Letters. He also was the author of five books.

Laborem Exercens: On Human Work

Pope John Paul II

Venerable Brothers and Dear Sons and Daughters,

1 Through work man must earn his daily bread[1] and contribute to the continual advance of science and technology and, above all, to elevating unceasingly the cultural and moral level of the society within which he lives in community with those who belong to the same family. And work means any activity by man, whether manual or intellectual, whatever its nature or circumstances; it means any human activity that can and must be recognised as work, in the midst of all the many activities of which man is capable and to which he is predisposed by his very nature, by virtue of humanity itself. Man is made to be in the visible universe an image and likeness of God himself,[2] and he is placed in it in order to subdue the earth.[3] From the beginning therefore he is *called to work. Work is one of the characteristics that distinguish* man from the rest of creatures, whose activity for sustaining their lives cannot be called work. Only man is capable of work, and only man works, at the same time by work occupying his existence on earth. Thus work bears a particular mark of man and of humanity, the mark of a person

operating within a community of persons. And this mark decides its interior characteristics; in a sense it constitutes its very nature.

I. Introduction

1. *Human Work on the Ninetieth Anniversary of* Rerum Novarum

2   Since 15 May of the present year was the *ninetieth anniversary* of the publication by the great Pope of the "social question", Leo XIII, of the decisively important Encyclical which begins with the words *Rerum Novarum*, I wish to devote this document to *human work* and, even more, to *man* in the vast context of the reality of work. As I said in the Encyclical *Redemptor Hominis*, published at the beginning of my service in the See of Saint Peter in Rome, man "is the primary and fundamental way for the Church",[4] precisely because of the inscrutable mystery of Redemption in Christ; and so it is necessary to return constantly to this way and to follow it ever anew in the various aspects in which it shows us all the wealth and at the same time all the toil of human existence on earth.

3   Work is one of these aspects, a perennial and fundamental one, one that is always relevant and constantly demands renewed attention and decisive witness. Because fresh *questions* and *problems* are always arising, there are always fresh hopes, but also fresh fears and threats, connected with this basic dimension of human existence: man's life is built up every day from work, from work it derives its specific dignity, but at the same time work contains the unceasing measure of human toil and suffering, and also of the harm and injustice which penetrate deeply into social life within individual nations and on the international level. While it is true that man eats the bread produced by the work of his hands[5]—and this means not only the daily bread by which his body keeps alive but also the bread of science and progress, civilization and culture—it is also a perennial truth that he eats this bread by *"the sweat of his face"*,[6] that is to say, not only by personal effort and toil but also in the midst of many tensions, conflicts and crises, which, in relationship with the reality of work, disturb the life of individual societies and also of all humanity.

4   We are celebrating the ninetieth anniversary of the Encyclical *Rerum Novarum* on the eve of new developments in technological, economic and political conditions which, according to many experts, will influence the world of work and production no less than the industrial revolution of the last century. There are many factors of a general nature: the widespread introduction of automation into many spheres of production, the increase in the cost of energy and raw materials, the growing realization that the heritage of nature is limited and that it is being intolerably polluted, and the emergence on the political scene of peoples who, after centuries of subjection, are demanding their rightful place among the nations and in international decision-making. These new conditions and demands will require a reordering and adjustment of the structures of the modern economy and of the distribution of work. Unfortunately, for millions of skilled workers these changes may perhaps mean unemployment, at least for a time, or the need for retraining. They will very probably involve a reduction or a less rapid increase in material well-being for the more developed countries. But they can also bring relief and hope to the millions who today live in conditions of shameful and unworthy poverty.

5   It is not for the Church to analyse scientifically the consequences that these changes may have on human society. But the Church considers it her task always to call attention to the dignity and rights of those who work, to condemn situations in which that dignity and those rights are violated, and to help to guide the above-mentioned changes so as to ensure authentic progress by man and society.

2. *In the Organic Development of the Church's Social Action*

6   It is certainly true that work, as a human issue, is at the very centre of the "social question" to which, for almost a hundred years, since the publication of the above-mentioned Encyclical, the Church's teaching and the many undertakings connected with her apostolic mission have been especially directed. The present reflections on work are not intended to follow a different line, but rather to be in organic connection with the whole tradition of this teaching and activity. At the same time, however, I am making them, according to the indication in the Gospel, in order to bring out *from the heritage of the Gospel "what*

*is new and what is old".*⁷ Certainly, work is part of "what is old"—as old as man and his life on earth. Nevertheless, the general situation of man in the modern world, studied and analysed in its various aspects of geography, culture and civilization, calls for the discovery of the *new meanings of human work*. It likewise calls for the formulation of the *new tasks* that in this sector face each individual, the family, each country, the whole human race, and, finally, the Church herself.

7   During the years that separate us from the publication of the Encyclical *Rerum Novarum*, the social question has not ceased to engage the Church's attention. Evidence of this are the many documents of the Magisterium issued by the Popes and by the Second Vatican Council, pronouncements by individual Episcopates, and the activity of the various centres of thought and of practical apostolic initiatives, both on the international level and at the level of the local Churches. It is difficult to list here in detail all the manifestations of the commitment of the Church and of Christians in the social question, for they are too numerous. As a result of the Council, the main coordinating centre in this field is the *Pontifical Commission Justice and Peace*, which has corresponding bodies within the individual Bishops' Conferences. The name of this institution is very significant. It indicates that the social question must be dealt with in its whole complex dimension. Commitment to justice must be closely linked with commitment to peace in the modern world. This twofold commitment is certainly supported by the painful experience of the two great world wars which in the course of the last ninety years have convulsed many European countries and, at least partially, countries in other continents. It is supported, especially since the Second World War, by the permanent threat of a nuclear war and the prospect of the terrible self-destruction that emerges from it.

8   If we follow the *main line of development of the documents* of the supreme Magisterium of the Church, we find in them an explicit confirmation of precisely such a statement of the question. The key position, as regards the question of world peace, is that of John XXIII's Encyclical *Pacem in Terris*. However, if one studies the development of the question of social justice, one cannot fail to note that, whereas during the period between *Rerum Novarum* and Pius XI's *Quadragesimo Anno* the Church's teaching concentrates mainly on the just solution of

the "labour question" within individual nations, in the next period the Church's teaching widens its horizon to take in the whole world. The disproportionate distribution of wealth and poverty and the existence of some countries and continents that are developed and of others that are not call for a levelling out and for a search for ways to ensure just development for all. This is the direction of the teaching in John XXIII's Encyclical *Mater et Magistra,* in the Pastoral Constitution *Gaudium et Spes* of the Second Vatican Council, and in Paul VI's Encyclical *Populorum Progressio.*

9   This trend of development of the Church's teaching and commitment in the social question exactly corresponds to the objective recognition of the state of affairs. While in the past *the "class" question* was especially highlighted as the centre of this issue, in more recent times it is *the "world" question* that is emphasised. Thus, not only the sphere of class is taken into consideration but also the world sphere of inequality and injustice, and as a consequence, not only the class dimension but also the world dimension of the tasks involved in the path towards the achievement of justice in the modern world. A complete analysis of the situation of the world today shows in an even deeper and fuller way the meaning of the previous analysis of social injustices; and it is the meaning that must be given today to efforts to build justice on earth, not concealing thereby unjust structures but demanding that they be examined and transformed on a more universal scale.

3.   *The Question of Work, the Key to the Social Question*

10   In the midst of all these processes—those of the diagnosis of objective social reality and also those of the Church's teaching in the sphere of the complex and many-sided social question— *the question of human work* naturally appears many times. This issue is, in a way, a *constant factor* both of social life and of the Church's teaching. Furthermore, in this teaching attention to the question goes back much further than the last ninety years. In fact the Church's social teaching finds its source in Sacred Scripture, beginning with the Book of Genesis and especially in the Gospel and the writings of the Apostles. From the beginning it was part of the Church's teaching, her concept of man and life in society, and, especially, the social morality which she worked out according to the needs of the different ages. This

traditional patrimony was then inherited and developed by the teaching of the Popes on the modern "social question", beginning with the Encyclical *Rerum Novarum*. In this context, study of the question of work, as we have seen, has continually been brought up to date while maintaining that Christian basis of truth which can be called ageless.

11 While in the present document we return to this question once more—without however any intention of touching on all the topics that concern it—this is not merely in order to gather together and repeat what is already contained in the Church's teaching. It is rather in order to highlight—perhaps more than has been done before—the fact that human work is *a key*, probably *the essential key*, to the whole social question, if we try to see that question really from the point of view of man's good. And if the solution—or rather the gradual solution—of the social question, which keeps coming up and becomes ever more complex, must be sought in the direction of "making life more human",[8] then the key, namely human work, acquires fundamental and decisive importance.

II. Work and Man

4. *In the Book of Genesis*

12 The Church is convinced that work is a fundamental dimension of man's existence on earth. She is confirmed in this conviction by considering the whole heritage of the many sciences devoted to man: anthropology, palaeontology, history, sociology, psychology and so on; they all seem to bear witness to this reality in an irrefutable way. But the source of the Church's conviction is above all the revealed word of God, and therefore what is *a conviction of the intellect* is also *a conviction of faith*. The reason is that the Church—and it is worthwhile stating it at this point—believes in man: she *thinks of man* and addresses herself to him *not only* in the light of historical experience, not only with the aid of the many methods of scientific knowledge, but in the first place in the light of the revealed word of the living God. Relating herself to man, she seeks *to express* the eternal *designs* and transcendent *destiny* which *the living God*, the Creator and Redeemer, has linked with him.

13 The Church finds *in the very first pages of the Book of Genesis* the source of her conviction that work is a fundamental dimension of human existence on earth. An analysis of these texts makes us aware that they express—sometimes in an archaic way of manifesting thought—the fundamental truths about man, in the context of the mystery of creation itself. These truths are decisive for man from the very beginning, and at the same time they trace out the main lines of his earthly existence, both in the state of original justice and also after the breaking, caused by sin, of the Creator's original covenant with creation in man. When man, who had been created "in the image of God. . . . male and female",[9] hears the words: "Be fruitful and *multiply, and fill the earth and subdue it*",[10] even though these words do not refer directly and explicitly to work, beyond any doubt they indirectly indicate it as an activity for man to carry out in the world. Indeed, they show its very deepest essence. Man is the image of God partly through the mandate received from his Creator to subdue, to dominate, the earth. In carrying out this mandate, man, every human being, reflects the very action of the Creator of the universe.

14 Work understood as a "transitive" activity, that is to say an activity beginning in the human subject and directed towards an external object, presupposes a specific dominion by man over "the earth", and in its turn it confirms and develops this dominion. It is clear that the term "the earth" of which the biblical text speaks is to be understood in the first place as that fragment of the visible universe that man inhabits. By extension, however, it can be understood as the whole of the visible world insofar as it comes within the range of man's influence and of his striving to satisfy his needs. The expression "subdue the earth" has an immense range. It means all the resources that the earth (and indirectly the visible world) contains and which, through the conscious activity of man, can be discovered and used for his ends. And so these words, placed at the beginning of the Bible, *never cease to be relevant*. They embrace equally the past ages of civilization and economy, as also the whole of modern reality and future phases of development, which are perhaps already to some extent beginning to take shape, though for the most part they are still almost unknown to man and hidden from him.

15 While people sometimes speak of periods of "acceleration" in the economic life and civilization of humanity or of individual

nations, linking these periods to the progress of science and technology and especially to discoveries which are decisive for social and economic life, at the same time it can be said that none of these phenomena of "acceleration" exceeds the essential content of what was said in that most ancient of biblical texts. As man, through his work, becomes more and more the master of the earth, and as he confirms his dominion over the visible world, again through his work, he nevertheless remains in every case and at every phase of this process within the Creator's original ordering. And this ordering remains necessarily and indissolubly linked with the fact that man was created, as male and female, "in the image of God". This *process is,* at the same time, *universal:* it embraces all human beings, every generation, every phase of economic and cultural development, and *at the same time* it is a process that takes place *within each human being,* in each conscious human subject. Each and every individual is at the same time embraced by it. Each and every individual, to the proper extent and in an incalculable number of ways, takes part in the giant process whereby man "subdues the earth" through his work.

5. *Work in the Objective Sense: Technology*

16 This universality and, at the same time, this multiplicity of the process of "subduing the earth" throw light upon human work, because man's dominion over the earth is achieved in and by means of work. There thus emerges the meaning of *work in an objective sense,* which finds expression in the various epochs of culture and civilization. Man dominates the earth by the very fact of domesticating animals, rearing them and obtaining from them the food and clothing he needs, and by the fact of being able to extract various natural resources from the earth and the seas. But man "subdues the earth" much more when he begins to cultivate it and then to transform its products, adapting them to his own use. Thus agriculture constitutes through human work a primary field of economic activity and an indispensable factor of production. Industry in its turn will always consist in linking the earth's riches—whether nature's living resources, or the products of agriculture, or the mineral or chemical resources—with man's work, whether physical or intellectual. This is also in a sense true in the sphere of what are called service industries, and also in the sphere of research, pure or applied.

17   In industry and agriculture man's work has today in many
      cases ceased to be mainly manual, for the toil of human hands
      and muscles is aided by *more and more highly perfected machin-
      ery*. Not only in industry but also in agriculture we are wit-
      nessing the transformations made possible by the gradual
      development of science and technology. Historically speaking,
      this, taken as a whole, has caused great changes in civilization,
      from the beginning of the "industrial era" to the successive
      phases of development through new technologies, such as the
      electronics and the microprocessor technology in recent years.

18   While it may seem that in the industrial process it is the
      machine that "works" and man merely supervises it, making it
      function and keeping it going in various ways, it is also true
      that for this very reason industrial development provides
      grounds for reproposing in new ways the question of human
      work. Both the original industrialization that gave rise to what
      is called the worker question and the subsequent industrial
      and post-industrial changes show in an eloquent manner that,
      even in the age of ever more mechanised "work", *the proper
      subject of work continues to be man.*

19   The development of industry and of the various sectors con-
      nected with it, even the most modern electronics technology,
      especially in the fields of miniaturization, communications and
      telecommunications and so forth, shows how vast is the role of
      technology, that ally of work that human thought has pro-
      duced, in the interaction between the subject and object of
      work (in the widest sense of the word). Understood in this case
      not as a capacity or aptitude for work, but rather as a *whole set
      of instruments* which man uses in his work, technology is
      undoubtedly man's ally. It facilitates his work, perfects, accel-
      erates and augments it. It leads to an increase in the quantity of
      things produced by work, and in many cases improves their
      quality. However, it is also a fact that, in some instances, tech-
      nology can cease to be man's ally and become almost his
      enemy, as when the mechanisation of work "supplants" him,
      taking away all personal satisfaction and the incentive to cre-
      ativity and responsibility, when it deprives many workers of
      their previous employment, or when, through exalting the
      machine, it reduces man to the status of its slave.

20   If the biblical words "subdue the earth" addressed to man from
      the very beginning are understood in the context of the whole

modern age, industrial and post-industrial, then they undoubtedly include also *a relationship with technology,* with the world of machinery which is the fruit of the work of the human intellect and a historical confirmation of man's dominion over nature.

21 The recent stage of human history, especially that of certain societies, brings a correct affirmation of technology as a basic coefficient of economic progress; but, at the same time, this affirmation has been accompanied by and continues to be accompanied by the raising of essential questions concerning human work in relationship to its subject, which is man. These questions are particularly *charged with content and tension of an ethical and an ethical and social character.* They therefore constitute a continual challenge for institutions of many kinds, for States and governments, for systems and international organizations; they also constitute a challenge for the Church.

6. *Work in the Subjective Sense: Man as the Subject of Work*

22 In order to continue our analysis of work, an analysis linked with the word of the Bible telling man that he is to subdue the earth, we must concentrate our attention on *work in the subjective sense,* much more than we did on the objective significance, barely touching upon the vast range of problems known intimately and in detail to scholars in various fields and also, according to their specializations, to those who work. If the words of the Book of Genesis to which we refer in this analysis of ours speak of work in the objective sense in an indirect way, they also speak only indirectly of the subject of work; but what they say is very eloquent and is full of great significance.

23 Man has to subdue the earth and dominate it, because as the "image of God" he is a person, that is to say, a subjective being capable of acting in a planned and rational way, capable of deciding about himself, and with a tendency to self-realization. As *a person, man is therefore the subject of work.* As a person he works, he performs various actions belonging to the work process; independently of their objective content, these actions must all serve to realize his humanity, to fulfil the calling to be a person that is his by reason of his very humanity. The principal truths concerning this theme were recently recalled by the

Second Vatican Council in the Constitution *Gaudium et Spes,* especially in Chapter One, which is devoted to man's calling.

24   And so this "dominion" spoken of in the biblical text being meditated upon here refers not only to the objective dimension of work but at the same time introduces us to an understanding of its subjective dimension. Understood as a process whereby man and the human race subdue the earth, work corresponds to this basic biblical concept only when throughout the process man manifests himself and confirms himself *as the one who "dominates".* This dominion, in a certain sense, refers to the subjective dimension even more than to the objective one: this dimension conditions *the very ethical nature* of work. In fact there is no doubt that human work has an ethical value of its own, which clearly and directly remains linked to the fact that the one who carries it out is a person, a conscious and free subject, that is to say a subject that decides about himself.

25   This truth, which in a sense constitutes the fundamental and perennial heart of Christian teaching on human work, has had and continues to have primary significance for the formulation of the important social problems characterizing whole ages.

26   *The ancient world* introduced its own typical differentiation of people into classes according to the type of work done. Work which demanded from the worker the exercise of physical strength, the work of muscles and hands, was considered unworthy of free men, and was therefore given to slaves. By broadening certain aspects that already belonged to the Old Testament, Christianity brought about a fundamental change of ideas in this field, taking the whole content of the Gospel message as its point of departure, especially the fact that the one who, while *being God,* became like us in all things[11] devoted most of the years of his life on earth to *manual work* at the carpenter's bench. This circumstance constitutes in itself the most eloquent "Gospel of work", showing that the basis for determining the value of human work is not primarily the kind of work being done but the fact that the one who is doing it is a person. The sources of the dignity of work are to be sought primarily in the subjective dimension, not in the objective one.

27   Such a concept practically does away with the very basis of the ancient differentiation of people into classes according to the kind of work done. This does not mean that, from the

objective point of view, human work cannot and must not be rated and qualified in any way. It only means that *the primary basis of the value of work is man himself,* who is its subject. This leads immediately to a very important conclusion of an ethical nature: however true it may be that man is destined for work and called to it, in the first place work is "for man" and not man "for work". Through this conclusion one rightly comes to recognize the pre-eminence of the subjective meaning of work over the objective one. Given this way of understanding things, and presupposing that different sorts of work that people do can have greater or lesser objective value, let us try nevertheless to show that each sort is judged above all by *the measure of the dignity* of the subject of work, that is to say the person, *the individual who carries it out.* On the other hand: independently of the work that every man does, and presupposing that this work constitutes a purpose—at times a very demanding one—of his activity, this purpose does not possess a definitive meaning in itself. In fact, in the final analysis it is always man who is *the purpose of the work,* whatever work it is that is done by man—even if the common scale of values rates it as the merest "service", as the most monotonous even the most alienating work.

7. *A Threat to the Right Order of Values*

28 It is precisely these fundamental affirmations about work that always emerged from the wealth of Christian truth, especially from the very message of the "Gospel of work", thus creating the basis for a new way of thinking, judging and acting. In the modern period, from the beginning of the industrial age, the Christian truth about work had to oppose the various trends of *materialistic and economistic* thought.

29 For certain supporters of such ideas, work was understood and treated as a sort of "merchandise" that the worker—especially the industrial worker—sells to the employer, who at the same time is the possessor of the capital, that is to say, of all the working tools and means that make production possible. This way of looking at work was widespread especially in the first half of the nineteenth century. Since then, explicit expressions of this sort have almost disappeared, and have given way to more human ways of thinking about work and evaluating it. The interaction between the worker and the tools and means of

production has given rise to the development of various forms of capitalism—parallel with various forms of collectivism—into which other socioeconomic elements have entered as a consequence of new concrete circumstances, of the activity of workers' associations and public authorities, and of the emergence of large transnational enterprises. Nevertheless, the *danger* of treating work as a special kind of merchandise", or as an impersonal "force" needed for production (the expression "workforce" is in fact in common use) *always exists,* especially when the whole way of looking at the question of economics is marked by the premises of materialistic economism.

30 A systematic opportunity for thinking and evaluating in this way, and in a certain sense a stimulus for doing so, is provided by the quickening process of the development of a one-sidedly materialistic civilization, which gives prime importance to the objective dimension of work, while the subjective dimension—everything in direct or indirect relationship with the subject of work—remains on a secondary level. In all cases of this sort, in every social situation of this type, there is a confusion or even a reversal of the order laid down from the beginning by the words of the Book of Genesis: *man is treated as an instrument of production,*[12] whereas he—he alone, independently of the work he does—ought to be treated as the effective subject of work and its true maker and creator. Precisely this reversal of order, whatever the programme or name under which it occurs, should rightly be called "capitalism"—in the sense more fully explained below. Everybody knows that capitalism has a definite historical meaning as a system, an economic and social system, opposed to "socialism" or "communism". But in the light of the analysis of the fundamental reality of the whole economic process—first and foremost of the production structure that work is—it should be recognized that the error of early capitalism can be repeated wherever man is in a way treated on the same level as the whole complex of the material means of production, as an instrument and not in accordance with the true dignity of his work—that is to say, where he is not treated as subject and maker, and for this very reason as the true purpose of the whole process of production.

31 This explains why the analysis of human work in the light of the words concerning man's "dominion" over the earth goes to the very heart of the ethical and social question. This concept

should also find *a central place* in the whole *sphere of social and economic policy,* both within individual countries and in the wider field of international and intercontinental relationships, particularly with reference to the tensions making themselves felt in the world not only between East and West but also between North and South. Both John XXIII in the Encyclical *Mater et Magistra* and Paul VI in the Encyclical *Populorum Progressio* gave special attention to these dimensions of the modern ethical and social question.

8. Worker Solidarity

32   When dealing with human work in the fundamental dimension of its subject, that is to say, the human person doing the work, one must make at least a summary evaluation of developments during the ninety years since *Rerum Novarum* in relation to the subjective dimension of work. Although the subject of work is always the same, that is to say man, nevertheless wide-ranging changes take place in the objective aspect. While one can say that, by reason of its subject, *work is one single thing* (one and unrepeatable every time), yet when one takes into consideration its objective directions one is forced to admit that *there exist many works,* many different sorts of work. The development of human civilization brings continual enrichment in this field. But at the same time, one cannot fail to note that in the process of this development not only do new forms of work appear but also others disappear. Even if one accepts that on the whole this is a normal phenomenon, it must still be seen whether certain ethically and socially dangerous irregularities creep in, and to what extent.

33   It was precisely one such *wide-ranging anomaly* that gave rise in the last century to what has been called "the worker question", sometimes described as "the proletariat question". This question and the problems connected with it gave rise to a just social reaction and caused the impetuous emergence of a great burst of solidarity between workers, first and foremost industrial workers. The call to solidarity and common action addressed to the workers—especially to those engaged in narrowly specialized, monotonous and depersonalized work in industrial plants, when the machine tends to dominate man— was important and eloquent from the point of view of social ethics. It was the reaction *against the degradation of man as the*

subject of work, and against the unheard-of accompanying exploitation in the field of wages, working conditions and social security for the worker. This reaction united the working world in a community marked by great solidarity.

34 Following the lines laid dawn by the Encyclical *Rerum Novarum* and many later documents of the Church's Magisterium, it must be frankly recognized that the reaction against the system of injustice and harm that cried to heaven for vengeance[13] and that weighed heavily upon workers in that period of rapid industrialization was justified *from the point of view of social morality.* This state of affairs was favoured by the liberal socio-political system, which, in accordance with its "economistic" premises, strengthened and safeguarded economic initiative by the possessors of capital alone, but did not pay sufficient attention to the rights of the workers, on the grounds that human work is solely an instrument of production, and that capital is the basis, efficient factor and purpose of production.

35 From that time, worker solidarity, together with a clearer and more committed realization by others of workers' rights, has in many cases brought about profound changes. Various forms of neo-capitalism or collectivism have developed. Various new systems have been thought out. Workers can often share in running businesses and in controlling their productivity, and in fact do so. Through appropriate associations, they exercise influence over conditions of work and pay, and also over social legislation. But at the same time various ideological or power systems, and new relationships which have arisen at various levels of society, *have allowed flagrant injustices to persist or have created new ones.* On the world level, the development of civilization and of communications has made possible a more complete diagnosis of the living and working conditions of man globally, but it has also revealed other forms of injustice, much more extensive than those which in the last century stimulated unity between workers for particular solidarity in the working world. This is true in countries which have completed a certain process of industrial revolution. It is also true in countries where the main working milieu continues to be *agriculture* or other similar occupations.

36 Movements of solidarity in the sphere of work—a solidarity that must never mean being closed to dialogue and collaboration with others—can be necessary also with reference to the

condition of social groups that were not previously included in such movements but which, in changing social systems and conditions of living, are undergoing *what is in effect "proletarianization"* or which actually already find themselves in a "proletariat" situation, one which, even if not yet given that name, in fact deserves it. This can be true of certain categories or groups of the working "intelligentsia", especially when ever wider access to education and an ever increasing number of people with degrees or diplomas in the fields of their cultural preparation are accompanied by a drop in demand for their labour. This *unemployment of intellectuals* occurs or increases when the education available is not oriented towards the types of employment or service required by the true needs of society, or when there is less demand for work which requires education, at least professional education, than for manual labour, or when it is less well paid. Of course, education in itself is always valuable and an important enrichment of the human person; but in spite of that, "proletarianization" processes remain possible.

37 For this reason, *there must be continued study of the subject of work* and of the subject's living conditions. In order to achieve social justice in the various parts of the world, in the various countries, and in the relationships between them, there is a need for ever new *movements of solidarity of* the workers and *with* the workers. This solidarity must be present whenever it is called for by the social degrading of the subject of work, by exploitation of the workers, and by the growing areas of poverty and even hunger. The Church is firmly committed to this cause, for she considers it her mission, her service, a proof of her fidelity to Christ, so that she can truly be the "Church of the poor". And the "poor" appear under various forms; they appear in various places and at various times; in many cases they appear as a *result of the violation of the dignity of human work:* either because the opportunities for human work are limited as a result of the scourge of unemployment, or because a low value is put on work and the rights that flow from it, especially the right to a just wage and to the personal security of the worker and his or her family.

9. *Work and Personal Dignity*

38 Remaining within the context of man as the subject of work, it is now appropriate to touch upon, at least in a summary way,

certain problems that *more closely define the dignity of human work,* in that they make it possible to characterize more fully its specific moral value. In doing this we must always keep in mind the biblical calling to "subdue the earth",[14] in which is expressed the will of the Creator that work should enable man to achieve that "dominion" in the visible world that is proper to him.

39   God's fundamental and original intention with regard to man, whom he created in his image and after his likeness,[15] was not withdrawn or cancelled out even when man, having broken the original covenant with God, heard the words: "In the sweat of your face you shall eat bread".[16] These words refer to *the sometimes heavy toil* that from then onwards has accompanied human work; but they do not alter the fact that work is the means whereby man *achieves that "dominion"* which is proper to him over the visible world, by "subjecting" the earth. Toil is something that is universally known, for it is universally experienced. It is familiar to those doing physical work under sometimes exceptionally laborious conditions. It is familiar not only to agricultural workers, who spend long days working the land, which sometimes "bears thorns and thistles",[17] but also to those who work in mines and quarries, to steel-workers at their blast-furnaces, to those who work in builders' yards and in construction work, often in danger of injury or death. It is likewise familiar to those at an intellectual workbench; to scientists; to those who bear the burden of grave responsibility for decisions that will have a vast impact on society. It is familiar to doctors and nurses, who spend days and nights at their patients' bedside. It is familiar to women, who, sometimes without proper recognition on the part of society and even of their own families, bear the daily burden and responsibility for their homes and the upbringing of their children. *It is familiar to all workers* and, since work is a universal calling, it is familiar to everyone.

40   And yet, in spite of all this toil—perhaps, in a sense, because of it—work is a good thing for man. Even though it bears the mark of a *bonum arduum,* in the terminology of Saint Thomas,[18] this does not take away the fact that, as such, it is a good thing for man. It is not only good in the sense that it is useful or something to enjoy; it is also good as being something worthy, that is to say, something that corresponds to man's dignity, that expresses this dignity and increases it. If one wishes to define

more clearly the ethical meaning of work, it is this truth that one must particularly keep in mind. Work is a good thing for man—a good thing for his humanity—because through work man *not only transforms nature*, adapting it to his own needs, but he also *achieves fulfilment* as a human being and indeed, in a sense, becomes "more a human being".

41 Without this consideration it is impossible to understand the meaning of the virtue of industriousness, and more particularly it is impossible to understand why industriousness should be a virtue: for virtue, as a moral habit, is something whereby man becomes good as man.[19] This fact in no way alters our justifiable anxiety that in work, whereby *matter* gains in *nobility, man* himself should not experience a lowering of his own dignity.[20] Again, it is well known that it is possible to use work in various ways *against man*, that it is possible to punish man with the system of forced labour in concentration camps, that work can be made into a means for oppressing man, and that in various ways it is possible to exploit human labour, that is to say the worker. All this pleads in favour of the moral obligation to link industriousness as a virtue with *the social order of work*, which will enable man to become, in work, "more a human being" and not be degraded by it not only because of the wearing out of his physical strength (which, at least up to a certain point, is inevitable), but especially through damage to the dignity and subjectivity that are proper to him.

10. *Work and Society: Family and Nation*

42 Having thus confirmed the personal dimension of human work, we must go on to the second *sphere of values* which is necessarily linked to work. Work constitutes a foundation for the formation of *family life*, which is a natural right and something that man is called to. These two spheres of values—one linked to work and the other consequent on the family nature of human life—must be properly united and must properly permeate each other. In a way, work is a condition for making it possible to found a family, since the family requires the means of subsistence which man normally gains through work. Work and industriousness also influence the whole *process of education* in the family, for the very reason that everyone "becomes a human being" through, among other things, work, and becoming a human being is precisely the main purpose of the whole

process of education. Obviously, two aspects of work in a sense come into play here: the one making family life and its upkeep possible, and the other making possible the achievement of the purposes of the family, especially education. Nevertheless, these two aspects of work are linked to one another and are mutually complementary in various points.

43   It must be remembered and affirmed that the family constitutes one of the most important terms of reference for shaping the social and ethical order of human work. The teaching of the Church has always devoted special attention to this question, and in the present document we shall have to return to it. In fact, the family is simultaneously a *community made possible by work* and the first *school of work*, within the home, for every person.

44   The third sphere of values that emerges from this point of view—that of the subject of work—concerns the *great society* to which man belongs on the basis of particular cultural and historical links. This society—even when it has not yet taken on the mature form of a nation—is not only the great "educator" of every man, even though an indirect one (because each individual absorbs within the family the contents and values that go to make up the culture of a given nation); it is also a great historical and social incarnation of the work of all generations. All of this brings it about that man combines his deepest human identity with membership of a nation, and intends his work also to increase the common good developed together with his compatriots, thus realizing that in this way work serves to add to the heritage of the whole human family, of all the people living in the world.

45   These three spheres are always *important for human work* in its subjective dimension. And this dimension, that is to say, the concrete reality of the worker, takes precedence over the objective dimension. In the subjective dimension there is realized, first of all, that "dominion" over the world of nature to which man is called from the beginning according to the words of the Book of Genesis. The very process of "subduing the earth", that is to say work, is marked in the course of history, and especially in recent centuries, by an immense development of technological means. This is an advantageous and positive phenomenon, on condition that the objective dimension of work does not gain the upper hand over the subjective dimension, depriving man of his dignity and inalienable rights or reducing them.

III. Conflict between Labour and Capital in the Present Phase of History

11. *Dimensions of the Conflict*

46 The sketch of the basic problems of work outlined above draws inspiration from the texts at the beginning of the Bible and in a sense forms the very framework of the Church's teaching, which has remained unchanged throughout the centuries within the context of different historical experiences. However, the experiences preceding and following the publication of the Encyclical *Rerum Novarum* form a background that endows that teaching with particular expressiveness and the eloquence of living relevance. In this analysis, work is seen as a great reality with a fundamental influence on the shaping in a human way of the world that the Creator has entrusted to man; it is a reality closely linked with man as the subject of work and with man's rational activity. In the normal course of events this reality fills human life and strongly affects its value and meaning. Even when it is accompanied by toil and effort, work is still something good, and so man develops through love for work. This entirely *positive and creative, educational and meritorious character of man's work* must be the basis for the judgments and decisions being made today in its regard in spheres that include *human rights*, as is evidenced by the international *declarations* on work and the many *labour codes* prepared either by the competent legislative institutions in the various countries or by organizations devoting their social, or scientific and social, activity to the problems of work. One organization fostering such initiatives on the international level is the International Labour Organization, the oldest specialized agency of the United Nations Organization.

47 In the following part of these considerations I intend to return in greater detail to these important questions, recalling at least the basic elements of the Church's teaching on the matter. I must however first touch on a very important field of questions in which her teaching has taken shape in this latest period, the one marked and in a sense symbolized by the publication of the Encyclical *Rerum Novarum*.

48 Throughout this period, which is by no means yet over, the issue of work has of course been posed on the basis of the great *conflict* that in the age of, and together with, industrial

development emerged *between "capital" and "labour"*, that is to say between the small but highly influential group of entrepreneurs, owners or holders of the means of production, and the broader multitude of people who lacked these means and who shared in the process of production solely by their labour. The conflict originated in the fact that the workers put their powers at the disposal of the entrepreneurs, and these, following the principle of maximum profit, tried to establish the lowest possible wages for the work done by the employees. In addition there were other elements of exploitation, connected with the lack of safety at work and of safeguards regarding the health and living conditions of the workers and their families.

49   This conflict, interpreted by some as a socioeconomic *class conflict*, found expression in the *ideological conflict* between liberalism, understood as the ideology of capitalism, and Marxism, understood as the ideology of scientific socialism and communism, which professes to act as the spokesman for the working class and the worldwide proletariat. Thus the real conflict between labour and capital was transformed into *a systematic class struggle,* conducted not only by ideological means but also and chiefly by political means. We are familiar with the history of this conflict and with the demands of both sides. The Marxist programme, based on the philosophy of Marx and Engels, sees in class struggle the only way to eliminate class injustices in society and to eliminate the classes themselves. Putting this programme into practice presupposes *the collectivization of the means of production* so that, through the transfer of these means from private hands to the collectivity, human labour will be preserved from exploitation.

50   This is the goal of the struggle carried on by political as well as ideological means. In accordance with the principle of "the dictatorship of the proletariat", the groups that as political parties follow the guidance of Marxist ideology aim by the use of various kinds of influence, including revolutionary pressure, to win *a monopoly of power in each society,* in order to introduce the collectivist system into it by eliminating private ownership of the means of production. According to the principal ideologists and leaders of this broad international movement, the purpose of this programme of action is to achieve the social revolution and to introduce socialism and, finally, the communist system throughout the world.

51 As we touch on this extremely important field of issues, which constitute not only a theory but a whole fabric of socioeconomic, political, and international life in our age, we cannot go *into the details*, nor is this necessary, for they are known both from the vast literature on the subject and by experience. Instead, we must leave the context of these issues and go back to the fundamental issue of human work, which is the main subject of the considerations in this document. It is clear, indeed, that this issue, which is of such importance for man—it constitutes one of the fundamental dimensions of his earthly existence and of his vocation—can also be explained only by taking into account the full context of the contemporary situation.

12. *The Priority of Labour*

52 The structure of the present-day situation is deeply marked by many conflicts caused by man, and the technological means produced by human work play a primary role in it. We should also consider here the prospect of worldwide catastrophe in the case of a nuclear war, which would have almost unimaginable possibilities of destruction. In view of this situation we must first of all recall a principle that has always been taught by the Church: *the principle of the priority of labour over capital.* This principle directly concerns the process of production: in this process labour is always a primary *efficient cause*, while capital, the whole collection of means of production, remains a mere *instrument* or instrumental cause. This principle is an evident truth that emerges from the whole of man's historical experience.

53 When we read in the first chapter of the Bible that man is to subdue the earth, we know that these words refer to all the resources contained in the visible world and placed at man's disposal. However, these resources *can serve man only through work*. From the beginning there is also linked with work the question of ownership, for the only means that man has for causing the resources hidden in nature to serve himself and others is his work. And to be able through his work to make these resources bear fruit, man takes over ownership of small parts of the various riches of nature: those beneath the ground, those in the sea, on land, or in space. He takes all these things over by making them his workbench. He takes them over through work and for work.

54   The same principle applies in the successive phases of this process, in which *the first phase* always remains the relationship of man with *the resources and riches of nature.* The whole of the effort to acquire knowledge with the aim of discovering these riches and specifying the various ways in which they can be used by man and for man teaches us that everything that comes from man throughout the whole process of economic production, whether labour or the whole collection of means of production and the technology connected with these means (meaning the capability to use them in work), presupposes these riches and resources of the visible world, riches and resources *that man finds* and does not create. In a sense man finds them already prepared, ready for him to discover them and to use them correctly in the productive process. In every phase of the development of his work man comes up against the leading role of *the gift made* by "nature", that is to say, in the final analysis, by *the Creator.* At the beginning of man's work is the mystery of creation. This affirmation, already indicated as my starting point, is the guiding thread of this document, and will be further developed in the last part of these reflections.

55   Further consideration of this question should confirm our conviction of *the priority of human labour over* what in the course of time we have grown accustomed to calling *capital.* Since the concept of capital includes not only the natural resources placed at man's disposal but also the whole collection of means by which man appropriates natural resources and transforms them in accordance with his needs (and thus in a sense humanizes them), it must immediately be noted that *all these means are the result of the historical heritage of human labour.* All the means of production, from the most primitive to the ultramodern ones—it is man that has gradually developed them: man's experience and intellect. In this way there have appeared not only the simplest instruments for cultivating the earth but also, through adequate progress in science and technology, the more modern and complex ones: machines, factories, laboratories, and computers. Thus *everything that is at the service of work,* everything that in the present state of technology constitutes its ever more highly perfected "instrument", is *the result of work.*

56   This gigantic and powerful instrument—the whole collection of means of production that in a sense are considered synonymous with "capital"—is the result of work and bears the signs of human labour. At the present stage of technological advance,

when man, who is the subject of work, wishes to make use of this collection of modern instruments, the means of production, he must first assimilate cognitively the result of the work of the people who invented those instruments, who planned them, built them and perfected them, and who continue to do so. *Capacity for work*—that is to say, for sharing efficiently in the modern production process—demands greater and greater *preparation* and, before all else, proper *training*. Obviously, it remains clear that every human being sharing in the production process, even if he or she is only doing the kind of work for which no special training or qualifications are required, is the real efficient subject in this production process, while the whole collection of instruments, no matter how perfect they may be in themselves, are only a mere instrument subordinate to human labour.

57 This truth, which is part of the abiding heritage of the Church's teaching, must always be emphasised with reference to the question of the labour system and with regard to the whole socioeconomic system. We must emphasise and give prominence to the primacy of man in the production process, *the primacy of man over things*. Everything contained in the concept of capital in the strict sense is only a collection of things. Man, as the subject of work, and independently of the work that he does—man alone is a person. This truth has important and decisive consequences.

13. *Economism and Materialism*

58 In the light of the above truth we see clearly, first of all, that capital cannot be separated from labour; in no way can labour be opposed to capital or capital to labour, and still less can the actual people behind these concepts be opposed to each other, as will be explained later. A labour system can be right, in the sense of being in conformity with the very essence of the issue, and in the sense of being intrinsically true and also morally legitimate, if in its very basis *it overcomes the opposition between labour and capital* through an effort at being shaped in accordance with the principle put forward above: the principle of the substantial and real priority of labour, of the subjectivity of human labour and its effective participation in the whole production process, independently of the nature of the services provided by the worker.

59 Opposition between labour and capital does not spring from
the structure of the production process or from the structure of
the economic process. In general the latter process demonstrates that labour and what we are accustomed to call capital
are intermingled; it shows that they are inseparably linked.
Working at any workbench, whether a relatively primitive or
an ultramodern one, a man can easily see that *through his work
he enters into two inheritances:* the inheritance of what is given to
the whole of humanity in the resources of nature, and the
inheritance of what others have already developed on the basis
of those resources, primarily by developing technology, that is
to say, by producing a whole collection of increasingly perfect
instruments for work. In working, man also "enters into the
labour of others".[21] Guided both by our intelligence and by the
faith that draws light from the word of God, we have no difficulty in accepting this image of the sphere and process of
man's labour. It is *a consistent image, one that is humanistic as well
as theological.* In it man is the master of the creatures placed at
his disposal in the visible world. If some dependence is discovered in the work process, it is dependence on the Giver of
all the resources of creation, and also on other human beings,
those to whose work and initiative we owe the perfected and
increased possibilities of our own work. All that we can say of
everything in the production process which constitutes a
whole collection of "things", the instruments, the capital, is
that it *conditions* man's work; we cannot assert that it constitutes as it were an impersonal "subject" *putting* man and man's
work *into a position of dependence.*

60 This *consistent image,* in which the principle of the primacy of the
person over things is strictly preserved, *was broken up in human
thought,* sometimes after a long period of incubation in practical living. The break occurred in such a way that labour was
separated from capital and set in opposition to it, and capital
was set in opposition to labour, as though they were two
impersonal forces, two production factors juxtaposed in the
same "economistic" perspective. This way of stating the issue
contained a fundamental error, what we can call *the error of
economism,* that of considering human labour solely according
to its economic purpose. This fundamental error of thought can
and must be called *an error of materialism,* in that economism
directly or indirectly includes a conviction of the primacy and
superiority of the material, and directly or indirectly places the

spiritual and the personal (man's activity, moral values and such matters) in a position of subordination to material reality. This is still not *theoretical materialism* in the full sense of the term, but it is certainly *practical materialism,* a materialism judged capable of satisfying man's needs, not so much on the grounds of premises derived from materialist theory, as on the grounds of a particular way of evaluating things, and so on the grounds of a certain hierarchy of goods based on the greater immediate attractiveness of what is material.

61   The error of thinking in the categories of economism went hand in hand with the formation of a materialist philosophy, as this philosophy developed from the most elementary and common phase (also called common materialism, because it professes to reduce spiritual reality to a superfluous phenomenon) to the phase of what is called dialectical materialism. However, within the framework of the present consideration, it seems that *economism had a decisive importance* for the fundamental issue of human work, in particular for the separation of labour and capital and for setting them up in opposition as two production factors viewed in the above mentioned economistic perspective; and it seems that economism influenced this non-humanistic way of stating the issue before the materialist philosophical system did. Nevertheless it is obvious that materialism, including its dialectical form, is incapable of providing sufficient and definitive bases for thinking about human work, in order that the primacy of man over the capital instrument, the primacy of the person over things, may find in it adequate and irrefutable *confirmation and support.* In dialectical materialism too man is not first and foremost the subject of work and the efficient cause of the production process, but continues to be understood and treated, in dependence on what is material, as a kind of "resultant" of the economic or production relations prevailing at a given period.

62   Obviously, the antinomy between labour and capital under consideration here—*the antinomy* in which *labour was separated from capital and set up in opposition to it,* in a certain sense on the ontic level, as if it were just an element like any other in the economic process—did not originate merely in the philosophy and economic theories of the eighteenth century; rather it originated in the whole of the *economic and social practice* of that time, the time of the birth and rapid development of industrialization, in which what was mainly seen was the possibility of

vastly increasing material wealth, means, while the end, that is to say, man, who should be served by the means, was ignored. It was this practical error that *struck a blow* first and foremost against human labour, against *the working man*, and caused the ethically just social reaction already spoken of above. The same error, which is now part of history, and which was connected with the period of primitive capitalism and liberalism, can nevertheless be repeated in other circumstances of time and place, if people's thinking starts from the same theoretical or practical premises. The only chance there seems to be for radically overcoming this error is through adequate changes both in theory and in practice, changes *in line with* the definite *conviction of the primacy* of the person over things, and of human *labour over capital* as a whole collection of means of production.

14. Work and Ownership

63 The historical process briefly presented here has certainly gone beyond its initial phase, but it is still taking place and indeed is spreading in the relationships between nations and continents. It needs to be specified further from another point of view. It is obvious that, when we speak of opposition between labour and capital, we are not dealing only with abstract concepts or "impersonal forces" operating in economic production. Behind both concepts there are people, living, actual people: on the one side are those who do the work without being the owners of the means of production, and on the other side those who act as entrepreneurs and who own these means or represent the owners. Thus *the issue of ownership or property* enters from the beginning into the whole of this difficult historical process. The Encyclical *Rerum Novarum*, which has the social question as its theme, stresses this issue also, recalling and confirming the Church's teaching on ownership, on the right to private property even when it is a question of the means of production. The Encyclical *Mater et Magistra* did the same.

64 The above principle, as it was then stated and as it is still taught by the Church, *diverges* radically from the programme of *collectivism* as proclaimed by Marxism and put into practice in various countries in the decades following the time of Leo XIII's Encyclical. At the same time it differs from the programme of *capitalism* practised by liberalism and by the political systems inspired by it. In the latter case, the difference consists in the way the right to ownership or property is

understood. Christian tradition has never upheld this right as absolute and untouchable. On the contrary, it has always understood this right within the broader context of the right common to all to use the goods of the whole of creation: *the right to private property is subordinated to the right to common use,* to the fact that goods are meant for everyone.

65 Furthermore, in the Church's teaching, ownership has never been understood in a way that could constitute grounds for social conflict in labour. As mentioned above, property is acquired first of all through work in order that it may serve work. This concerns in a special way ownership of the means of production. Isolating these means as a separate property in order to set it up in the form of "capital" in opposition to "labour"—and even to practise exploitation of labour—is contrary to the very nature of these means and their possession. They cannot be *possessed against labour,* they cannot even be *possessed for possession's sake,* because the only legitimate title to their possession—whether in the form of private ownership or in the form of public or collective ownership—is *that they should serve labour,* and thus, by serving labour, that they should make possible the achievement of the first principle of this order, namely, the universal destination of goods and the right to common use of them. From this point of view, therefore, in consideration of human labour and of common access to the goods meant for man, one cannot exclude the *socialization,* in suitable conditions, of certain means of production. In the course of the decades since the publication of the Encyclical *Rerum Novarum,* the Church's teaching has always recalled all these principles, going back to the arguments formulated in a much older tradition, for example, the well-known arguments of the *Summa Theologiae* of Saint Thomas Aquinas.[22]

66 In the present document, which has human work as its main theme, it is right to confirm all the effort with which the Church's teaching has striven and continues to strive always to ensure the priority of work and, thereby, man's character as a *subject* in social life and, especially, in the dynamic *structure of the whole economic process.* From this point of view the position of "rigid" capitalism continues to remain unacceptable, namely the position that defends the exclusive right to private ownership of the means of production as an untouchable "dogma" of economic life. The principle of respect for work

demands that this right should undergo a constructive revision, both in theory and in practice. If it is true that capital, as the whole of the means of production, is at the same time the product of the work of generations, it is equally true that capital is being unceasingly created through the work done with the help of all these means of production, and these means can be seen as a great workbench at which the present generation of workers is working day after day. Obviously we are dealing here with different kinds of work, not only so-called manual labour but also the many forms of intellectual work, including white-collar work and management.

67 In the light of the above, the many proposals put forward by experts in Catholic social teaching and by the highest Magisterium of the Church take on special significance:[23] *proposals for joint ownership of the means of work,* sharing by the workers in the management and/or profits of businesses, so-called shareholding by labour, etc. Whether these various proposals can or cannot be applied concretely, it is clear that recognition of the proper position of labour and the worker in the production process demands various adaptations in the sphere of the right to ownership of the means of production. This is so not only in view of older situations but also, first and foremost, in view of the whole of the situation and the problems in the second half of the present century with regard to the so-called Third World and the various new independent countries that have arisen, especially in Africa but elsewhere as well, in place of the colonial territories of the past.

68 Therefore, while the position of "rigid" capitalism must undergo continual revision, in order to be reformed from the point of view of human rights, both human rights in the widest sense and those linked with man's work, it must be stated that, from the same point of view, these many deeply desired reforms cannot be achieved by an *a priori elimination of private ownership of the means of production.* For it must be noted that merely taking these means of production (capital) out of the hands of their private owners is not enough to ensure their satisfactory socialization. They cease to be the property of a certain social group, namely the private owners, and become the property of organized society, coming under the administration and direct control of another group of people, namely those who, though not owning them, from the fact of exercising power in society

manage them on the level of the whole national or the local economy.

69 This group in authority may carry out its task satisfactorily from the point of view of the priority of labour; but it may also carry it out badly by claiming for itself *a monopoly of the administration and disposal* of the means of production and not refraining even from offending basic human rights. Thus, merely converting the means of production into State property in the collectivist system is by no means equivalent to "socializing" that property. We can speak of socializing only when the subject character of society is ensured, that is to say, when on the basis of his work each person is fully entitled to consider himself a part-owner of the great workbench at which he is working with every one else. A way towards that goal could be found by associating labour with the ownership of capital, as far as possible, and by producing a wide range of intermediate bodies with economic, social and cultural purposes; they would be bodies enjoying real autonomy with regard to the public powers, pursuing their specific aims in honest collaboration with each other and in subordination to the demands of the common good, and they would be living communities both in form and in substance, in the sense that the members of each body would be looked upon and treated as persons and encouraged to take an active part in the life of the body.[24]

15. The "Personalist" Argument

70 Thus, *the principle of the priority of labour* over capital is a postulate of the order of social morality. It has key importance both in the system built on the principle of private ownership of the means of production and also in the system in which private ownership of these means has been limited even in a radical way. Labour is in a sense inseparable from capital; in no way does it accept the antinomy, that is to say, the separation and opposition with regard to the means of production that has weighed upon human life in recent centuries as a result of merely economic premises. When man works, using all the means of production, he also wishes the fruit of this work to be used by himself and others, and he wishes to be able to take part in the very work process as a sharer in responsibility and creativity at the workbench to which he applies himself.

71   From this spring certain specific rights of workers, corresponding to the obligation of work. They will be discussed later. But here it must be emphasised, in general terms, that the person who works desires *not only* due *remuneration* for his work; he also wishes that, within the production process, provision be made for him to be able to *know* that in his work, even on something that is owned in common, he is working *"for himself"*. This awareness is extinguished within him in a system of excessive bureaucratic centralization, which makes the worker feel that he is just a cog in a huge machine moved from above, that he is for more reasons than one a mere production instrument rather than a true subject of work with an initiative of his own. The Church's teaching has always expressed the strong and deep conviction that man's work concerns not only the economy but also, and especially, personal values. The economic system itself and the production process benefit precisely when these personal values are fully respected. In the mind of Saint Thomas Aquinas,[25] this is the principal reason in favour of private ownership of the means of production. While we accept that for certain well founded reasons exceptions can be made to the principle of private ownership—in our own time we even see that the system of "socialized ownership" has been introduced—nevertheless the personalist *argument still holds good* both on the level of principles and *on the practical level.* If it is to be rational and fruitful, any socialization of the means of production must take this argument into consideration. Every effort must be made to ensure that in this kind of system also the human person can preserve his awareness of working "for himself". If this is not done, incalculable damage is inevitably done throughout the economic process, not only economic damage but first and foremost damage to man.

IV. Rights of Workers

16. *Within the Broad Context of Human Rights*

72   While work, in all its many senses, is an obligation, that is to say a duty, it is also a source of rights on the part of the *worker.* These rights must be examined in the broad *context of human rights as a whole,* which are connatural with man, and many of which are proclaimed by various international organizations and increasingly guaranteed by the individual States for their

citizens. Respect for this broad range of human rights constitutes the fundamental condition for peace in the modern
world: peace both within individual countries and societies
and in international relations, as the Church's Magisterium has
several times noted, especially since the Encyclical *Pacem in
Terris*. The *human rights that flow from work* are part of the
broader context of those fundamental rights of the person.

73   However, within this context they have a specific character
corresponding to the specific nature of human work as outlined above. It is in keeping with this character that we must
view them. Work is, as has been said, *an obligation*, that is to
say, a *duty, on the part of man*. This is true *in all the many meanings of the word*. Man must work, both because the Creator has
commanded it and because of his own humanity, which
requires work in order to be maintained and developed. Man
must work out of regard for others, especially his own family,
but also for the society he belongs to, the country of which he
is a child, and the whole human family of which he is a member, since he is the heir to the work of generations and at the
same time a sharer in building the future of those who will
come after him in the succession of history. All this constitutes
the moral obligation of work, understood in its wide sense.
When we have to consider the moral rights, corresponding to
this obligation, of every person with regard to work, we must
always keep before our eyes the whole vast range of points of
reference in which the labour of every working subject is
manifested.

74   For when we speak of the obligation of work and of the rights
of the worker that correspond to this obligation, we think in the
first place of the relationship between *the employer, direct or indirect, and the worker.*

75   The distinction between the direct and the indirect employer is
seen to be very important when one considers both the way in
which labour is actually organized and the possibility of the
formation of just or unjust relationships in the field of labour.

76   Since *the direct employer is* the person or institution with whom
the worker enters directly into a work contract in accordance
with definite conditions, we must understand as *the indirect*
employer many different factors, other than the direct employer, that exercise a determining influence on the shaping both of

the work contract and, consequently, of just or unjust relationships in the field of human labour.

17. *Direct and Indirect Employer*

77   The concept of indirect employer includes both persons and institutions of various kinds, and also collective labour contracts and the *principles* of conduct which are laid down by these persons and institutions and which determine the whole socioeconomic *system* or are its result. The concept of "indirect employer" thus refers to many different elements. The responsibility of the indirect employer differs from that of the direct employer—the term itself indicates that the responsibility is less direct—but it remains a true responsibility: the indirect employer substantially determines one or other facet of the labour relationship, thus conditioning the conduct of the direct employer when the latter determines in concrete terms the actual work contract and labour relations. This is not to absolve the direct employer from his own responsibility, but only to draw attention to the whole network of influences that condition his conduct. When it is a question of establishing an *ethically correct labour policy,* all these influences must be kept in mind. A policy is correct when the objective rights of the worker are fully respected.

78   The concept of indirect employer is applicable to every society, and in the first place to the State. For it is the State that must conduct a just labour policy. However, it is common knowledge that in the present system of economic relations in the world there are numerous *links between* individual *States,* links that find expression, for instance, in the import and export process, that is to say, in the mutual exchange of economic goods, whether raw materials, semi-manufactured goods, or finished industrial products. These links also create mutual *dependence,* and as a result it would be difficult to speak, in the case of any State, even the economically most powerful, of complete self-sufficiency or autarky.

79   Such a system of mutual dependence is in itself normal. However, it can easily become an occasion for various forms of exploitation or injustice and as a result influence the labour policy of individual States; and finally it can influence the individual worker, who is the proper subject of labour. For instance the *highly industrialized countries,* and even more the

businesses that direct on a large scale the means of industrial production (the companies referred to as multinational or transnational), fix the highest possible prices for their products, while trying at the same time to fix the lowest possible prices for raw materials or semi-manufactured goods. This is one of the causes of an ever increasing disproportion between national incomes. The gap between most of the richest countries and the poorest ones is not diminishing or being stabilized but is increasing more and more, to the detriment, obviously, of the poor countries. Evidently this must have an effect on local labour policy and on the worker's situation in the economically disadvantaged societies. Finding himself in a system thus conditioned, the direct employer fixes working conditions below the objective requirements of the workers, especially if he himself wishes to obtain the highest possible profits from the business which he runs (or from the businesses which he runs, in the case of a situation of "socialized" ownership of the means of production).

80 It is easy to see that this framework of forms of dependence linked with the concept of the indirect employer is enormously extensive and complicated. It is determined, in a sense, by all the elements that are decisive for economic life *within a given society and state*, but also by much wider links and forms of dependence. The attainment of the worker's rights cannot however be doomed to be merely a result of economic systems which on a larger or smaller scale are guided chiefly by the criterion of maximum profit. On the contrary, it is respect for the objective rights of the worker—every kind of worker: manual or intellectual, industrial or agricultural, etc.—that must constitute *the adequate and fundamental criterion* for shaping the whole economy, both on the level of the individual society and State and within the whole of the world economic policy and of the systems of international relationships that derive from it.

81 Influence in this direction should be exercised by all *the International Organizations* whose concern it is, beginning with the United Nations Organization. It appears that the International Labour Organization and the Food and Agriculture Organization of the United Nations and other bodies too have fresh contributions to offer on this point in particular. Within the individual States there are ministries or *public departments* and

also various *social institutions* set up for this purpose. All of this effectively indicates the importance of the indirect employer—as has been said above—in achieving full respect for the worker's rights, since the rights of the human person are the key element in the whole of the social moral order.

18. *The Employment Issue*

82   When we consider the rights of workers in relation to the "indirect employer", that is to say, all the agents at the national and international level that are responsible for the whole orientation of labour policy, we must first direct our attention to a *fundamental issue:* the question of finding work, or, in other words, the issue of *suitable employment for all who are capable of it.* The opposite of a just and right situation in this field is unemployment, that is to say the lack of work for those who are capable of it. It can be a question of general unemployment or of unemployment in certain sectors of work. The role of the agents included under the title of indirect employer is *to act against unemployment,* which in all cases is an evil, and which, when it reaches a certain level, can become a real social disaster. It is particularly painful when it especially affects young people, who after appropriate cultural, technical and professional preparation fail to find work, and see their sincere wish to work and their readiness to take on their own responsibility for the economic and social development of the community sadly frustrated. The obligation to provide unemployment benefits, that is to say, the duty to make suitable grants indispensable for the subsistence of unemployed workers and their families, is a duty springing from the fundamental principle of the moral order in this sphere, namely the principle of the common use of goods or, to put it in another and still simpler way, the right to life and subsistence.

83   In order to meet the danger of unemployment and to ensure employment for all, the agents defined here as "indirect employer" must make provision for *overall planning* with regard to the different kinds of work by which not only the economic life but also the cultural life of a given society is shaped; they must also give attention to organizing that work in a correct and rational way. In the final analysis this overall concern weighs on the shoulders of the State, but it cannot mean one-sided centralization by the public authorities. Instead, what is

in question is a just and rational *coordination,* within the framework of which the *initiative* of individuals, free groups and local work centres and complexes must be *safeguarded,* keeping in mind what has been said above with regard to the subject character of human labour.

84 The fact of the mutual dependence of societies and States and the need to collaborate in various areas mean that, while preserving the sovereign rights of each society and State in the field of planning and organizing labour in its own society, action in this important area must also be taken in the dimension of *international collaboration* by means of the necessary treaties and agreements. Here too the criterion for these pacts and agreements must more and more be the criterion of human work considered as a fundamental right of all human beings, work which gives similar rights to all those who work, in such a way that the living standard of the workers in the different societies will *less and less show those disturbing differences* which are unjust and are apt to provoke even violent reactions. The International Organizations have an enormous part to play in this area. They must let themselves be guided by an exact diagnosis of the complex situations and of the influence exercised by natural, historical, civil and other such circumstances. They must also be more highly operative with regard to plans for action jointly decided on, that is to say, they must be more effective in carrying them out.

85 In this direction it is possible to actuate a plan for universal and proportionate progress by all, in accordance with the guidelines of Paul VI's Encyclical *Populorum Progressio.* It must be stressed that the constitutive element in this *progress* and also the most adequate *way* to *verify it* in a spirit of justice and peace, which the Church proclaims and for which she does not cease to pray to the Father of all individuals and of all peoples, is *the continual reappraisal of man's work,* both in the aspect of its objective finality and in the aspect of the dignity of the subject of all work, that is to say, man. The progress in question must be made through man and for man and it must produce its fruit in man. A test of this progress will be the increasingly mature recognition of the purpose of work and increasingly universal respect for the rights inherent in work in conformity with the dignity of man, the subject of work.

86   Rational planning and the proper organization of human labour in keeping with individual societies and States should also facilitate the discovery of the right proportions between the different kinds of employment: work on the land, in industry, in the various services, white-collar work and scientific or artistic work, in accordance with the capacities of individuals and for the common good of each society and of the whole of mankind. The organization of human life in accordance with the many possibilities of labour should be matched by a suitable *system of instruction* and education, aimed first of all at developing mature human beings, but also aimed at preparing people specifically for assuming to good advantage an appropriate place in the vast and socially differentiated world of work.

87   As we view the whole human family throughout the world, we cannot fail to be struck by *a disconcerting fact* of immense proportions: the fact that, while conspicuous natural resources remain unused, there are huge numbers of people who are unemployed or under-employed and countless multitudes of people suffering from hunger. This is a fact that without any doubt demonstrates that both within the individual political communities and in their relationships on the continental and world level there is something wrong with the organization of work and employment, precisely at the most critical and socially most important points.

19. *Wages and Other Social Benefits*

88   After outlining the important role that concern for providing employment for all workers plays in safeguarding respect for the inalienable rights of man in view of his work, it is worthwhile taking a closer look at these rights, which in the final analysis are formed within the relationship *between worker and direct employer.* All that has been said above on the subject of the indirect employer is aimed at defining these relationships more exactly, by showing the many forms of conditioning within which these relationships are indirectly formed. This consideration does not however have a purely descriptive purpose; it is not a brief treatise on economics or politics. It is a matter of highlighting the *deontological and moral aspect.* The key problem of social ethics in this case is that of *just remuneration* for work done. In the context of the present there is no more important

way for securing a just relationship between the worker and the employer than that constituted by remuneration for work. Whether the work is done in a system of private ownership of the means of production or in a system where ownership has undergone a certain "socialization", the relationship between the employer (first and foremost the direct employer) and the worker is resolved on the basis of the wage, that is through just remuneration for work done.

89   It should also be noted that the justice of a socioeconomic system and, in each case, its just functioning, deserve in the final analysis to be evaluated by the way in which man's work is properly remunerated in the system. Here we return once more to the first principle of the whole ethical and social order, namely, *the principle of the common use of goods.* In every system, regardless of the fundamental relationships within it between capital and labour, wages, that is to say *remuneration for work,* are still a *practical means* whereby the vast majority of people can have access to those goods which are intended for common use: both the goods of nature and manufactured goods. Both kinds of goods become accessible to the worker through the wage which he receives as remuneration for his work. Hence, in every case, a just wage is the concrete means of *verifying the justice* of the whole socioeconomic system and, in any case, of checking that it is functioning justly. It is not the only means of checking, but it is a particularly important one and, in a sense, the key means.

90   This means of checking concerns above all the family. Just remuneration for the work of an adult who is responsible for a family means remuneration which will suffice for establishing and properly maintaining a family and for providing security for its future. Such remuneration can be given either through what is called a *family wage*—that is, a single salary given to the head of the family for his work, sufficient for the needs of the family without the other spouse having to take up gainful employment outside the home—or through *other social measures* such as family allowances or grants to mothers devoting themselves exclusively to their families. These grants should correspond to the actual needs, that is, to the number of dependents for as long as they are not in a position to assume proper responsibility for their own lives.

91 Experience confirms that there must be a *social re-evaluation of the mother's role,* of the toil connected with it, and of the need that children have for care, love and affection in order that they may develop into responsible, morally and religiously mature and psychologically stable persons. It will redound to the credit of society to make it possible for a mother—without inhibiting her freedom, without psychological or practical discrimination, and without penalizing her as compared with other women—to devote herself to taking care of her children and educating them in accordance with their needs, which vary with age. Having to abandon these tasks in order to take up paid work outside the home is wrong from the point of view of the good of society and of the family when it contradicts or hinders these primary goals of the mission of a mother.[26]

92 In this context it should be emphasised that, on a more general level, the whole labour process must be organized and adapted in such a way as to respect the requirements of the person and his or her forms of life, above all life in the home, taking into account the individual's age and sex. It is a fact that in many societies women work in nearly every sector of life. But it is fitting that they should be able to fulfil their tasks *in accordance with their own nature,* without being discriminated against and without being excluded from jobs for which they are capable, but also without lack of respect for their family aspirations and for their specific role in contributing, together with men, to the good of society. The *true advancement of women* requires that labour should be structured in such a way that women do not have to pay for their advancement by abandoning what is specific to them and at the expense of the family, in which women as mothers have an irreplaceable role.

93 Besides wages, various *social benefits* intended to ensure the life and health of workers and their families play a part here. The expenses involved in health care, especially in the case of accidents at work, demand that medical assistance should be easily available for workers, and that as far as possible it should be cheap or even free of charge. Another sector regarding benefits is the sector associated with the *right to rest.* In the first place this involves a regular weekly rest comprising at least Sunday, and also a longer period of rest, namely the holiday or vacation taken once a year or possibly in several shorter periods during the year. A third sector concerns the right to a pension and to insurance for old age and in case of accidents at

work. Within the sphere of these principal rights, there develops a whole system of particular rights which, together with remuneration for work, determine the correct relationship between worker and employer. Among these rights there should never be overlooked the right to a working environment and to manufacturing processes which are not harmful to the workers' physical health or to their moral integrity.

20. *Importance of Unions*

94   All these rights, together with the need for the workers themselves to secure them, give rise to yet another right: *the right of association,* that is to form associations for the purpose of defending the vital interests of those employed in the various professions. These associations are called *labour or trade unions.* The vital interests of the workers are to a certain extent common for all of them; at the same time however each type of work, each profession, has its own specific character which should find a particular reflection in these organizations.

95   In a sense, unions go back to the mediaeval guilds of artisans, insofar as those organizations brought together people belonging to the same craft and thus *on the basis of their work.* However, unions differ from the guilds on this essential point: the modern unions grew up from the struggle of the workers—workers in general but especially the industrial workers—to protect their *just rights* vis-a-vis the entrepreneurs and the owners of the means of production. Their task is to defend the existential interests of workers in all sectors in which their rights are concerned. The experience of history teaches that organizations of this type are an indispensable *element of social life,* especially in modern industrialized societies. Obviously, this does not mean that only industrial workers can set up associations of this type. Representatives of every profession can use them to ensure their own rights. Thus there are unions of agricultural workers and of white-collar workers; there are also employers' associations. All, as has been said above, are further divided into groups or subgroups according to particular professional specializations.

96   Catholic social teaching does not hold that unions are no more than a reflection of the "class" structure of society and that they are a mouthpiece for a class struggle which inevitably governs social life. They are indeed *a mouthpiece for the struggle for social*

justice, for the just rights of working people in accordance with their individual professions. However, this struggle should be seen as a normal endeavour "for" the just good: in the present case, for the good which corresponds to the needs and merits of working people associated by profession; but it is *not* a *struggle "against" others.* Even if in controversial questions the struggle takes on a character of opposition towards others, this is because it aims at the good of social justice, not for the sake of "struggle" or in order to eliminate the opponent. It is characteristic of work that it first and foremost unites people. In this consists its social power: the power to build a community. In the final analysis, both those who work and those who manage the means of production or who own them must in some way be united in this community. *In the light of this fundamental structure* of all work—in the light of the fact that, in the final analysis, labour and capital are indispensable components of the process of production in any social system—it is clear that, even if it is because of their work needs that people unite to secure their rights, their union remains a constructive factor of *social order* and *solidarity,* and it is impossible to ignore it.

97   Just efforts to secure the rights of workers who are united by the same profession should always take into account the limitations imposed by the general economic situation of the country. Union demands cannot be turned into a kind of *group or class "egoism",* although they can and should also aim at correcting—with a view to the common good of the whole of society—everything defective in the system of ownership of the means of production or in the way these are managed. Social and socioeconomic life is certainly like a system of "connected vessels", and every social activity directed towards safeguarding the rights of particular groups should adapt itself to this system.

98   In this sense, union activity undoubtedly enters the field of *politics,* understood as *prudent concern for the common good.* However, the role of unions is not to "play politics" in the sense that the expression is commonly understood today. Unions do not have the character of political parties struggling for power; they should not be subjected to the decision of political parties or have too close links with them. In fact, in such a situation they easily lose contact with their specific role, which is to secure the just rights of workers within the framework of the

common good of the whole of society; instead they become *an instrument used for other purposes.*

99 Speaking of the protection of the just rights of workers according to their individual professions, we must of course always keep in mind that which determines the subjective character of work in each profession, but at the same time, indeed before all else, we must keep in mind that which conditions the specific dignity of the subject of the work. The activity of union organizations opens up many possibilities in this respect, including their *efforts to instruct and educate* the workers and to *foster their self-education.* Praise is due to the work of the schools, what are known as workers' or people's universities and the training programmes and courses which have developed and are still developing this field of activity. It is always to be hoped that, thanks to the work of their unions, workers will not only *have* more, but above all *be* more: in other words, that they will realize their humanity more fully in every respect.

100 *One method* used by unions in pursuing the just rights of their members is *the strike* or work stoppage, as a kind of ultimatum to the competent bodies, especially the employers. This method is recognized by Catholic social teaching as legitimate in the proper conditions and within just limits. In this connection workers should be assured the *right to strike,* without being subjected to personal penal sanctions for taking part in a strike. While admitting that it is a legitimate means, we must at the same time emphasise that a strike remains, in a sense, an extreme means. It *must not be abused;* it must not be abused especially for "political" purposes. Furthermore it must never be forgotten that, when essential community services are in question, they must in every case be ensured, if necessary by means of appropriate legislation. Abuse of the strike weapon can lead to the paralysis of the whole of socioeconomic life, and this is contrary to the requirements of the common good of society, which also corresponds to the properly understood nature of work itself.

21. Dignity of Agricultural Work

101 All that has been said thus far on the dignity of work, on the objective and subjective dimension of human work, can be directly applied to the question of agricultural work and to the

situation of the person who cultivates the earth by toiling in the fields. This is a vast sector of work on our planet, a sector not restricted to one or other continent, nor limited to the societies which have already attained a certain level of development and progress. The world of agriculture, which provides society with the goods it needs for its daily sustenance, is of *fundamental importance*. The conditions of the rural population and of agricultural work vary from place to place, and the social position of agricultural workers differs from country to country. This depends not only on the level of development of agricultural technology but also, and perhaps more, on the recognition of the just rights of agricultural workers and, finally, on the level of awareness regarding the social ethics of work.

102 Agricultural work involves considerable difficulties, including unremitting and sometimes exhausting physical effort and a lack of appreciation on the part of society, to the point of making agricultural people feel that they are social outcasts and of speeding up the phenomenon of their mass exodus from the countryside to the cities and unfortunately to still more dehumanizing living conditions. Added to this are the lack of adequate professional training and of proper equipment, the spread of a certain individualism, and also *objectively unjust situations*. In certain developing countries, millions of people are forced to cultivate the land belonging to others and are exploited by the big landowners, without any hope of ever being able to gain possession of even a small piece of land of their own. There is a lack of forms of legal protection for the agricultural workers themselves and for their families in case of old age, sickness or unemployment. Long days of hard physical work are paid miserably. Land which could be cultivated is left abandoned by the owners. Legal titles to possession of a small portion of land that someone has personally cultivated for years are disregarded or left defenceless against the "land hunger" of more powerful individuals or groups. But even in the economically developed countries, where scientific research, technological achievements and State policy have brought agriculture to a very advanced level, the right to work can be infringed when the farm workers are denied the possibility of sharing in decisions concerning their services, or when they are denied the right to free association with a view to their just advancement socially, culturally and economically.

103 In many situations radical and urgent changes are therefore needed in order to restore to agriculture—and to rural people—their just value *as the basis for a healthy economy,* within the social community's development as a whole. Thus it is necessary to proclaim and promote the dignity of work, of all work but especially of agricultural work, in which man so eloquently "subdues" the earth he has received as a gift from God and affirms his "dominion" in the visible world.

22. *The Disabled Person and Work*

104 Recently, national communities and international organizations have turned their attention to another question connected with work, one full of implications: the question of disabled people. They too are fully human subjects with corresponding innate, sacred and inviolable rights, and, in spite of the limitations and sufferings affecting their bodies and faculties, they point up more clearly the dignity and greatness of man. Since disabled people are subjects with all their rights, they should be helped to participate in the life of society in all its aspects and at all the levels accessible to their capacities. The disabled person is one of us and participates fully in the same humanity that we possess. It would be radically unworthy of man, and a denial of our common humanity, to admit to the life of the community, and thus admit to work, only those who are fully functional. To do so would be to practise a *serious form of discrimination,* that of the strong and healthy against the weak and sick. Work in the objective sense should be subordinated, in this circumstance too, to the dignity of man, to the subject of work and not to economic advantage.

105 The various bodies involved in the world of labour, both the direct and the indirect employer, should therefore by means of effective and appropriate measures foster the right of disabled people to professional training and work, so that they can be given a productive activity suited to them. Many practical problems arise at this point, as well as legal and economic ones; but the community, that is to say, the public authorities, associations and intermediate groups, business enterprises and the disabled themselves should pool their ideas and resources so as to attain this goal that must not be shirked: *that disabled people may be offered work according to their capabilities,* for this is

demanded by their dignity as persons and as subjects of work. Each community will be able to set up suitable structures for finding or creating jobs for such people both in the usual public or private enterprises, by offering them ordinary or suitably adapted jobs, and in what are called "protected" enterprises and surroundings.

106 Careful attention must be devoted to the physical and psychological working conditions of disabled people—as for all workers—to their just remuneration, to the possibility of their promotion, and to the elimination of various obstacles. Without hiding the fact that this is a complex and difficult task, it is to be hoped that *a correct concept of labour in the subjective sense* will produce a situation which will make it possible for disabled people to feel that they are not cut off from the working world or dependent upon society, but that they are full-scale subjects of work, useful, respected for their human dignity and called to contribute to the progress and welfare of their families and of the community according to their particular capacities.

23. *Work and the Emigration Question*

107 Finally, we must say at least a few words on the subject of *emigration in search of work*. This is an age-old phenomenon which nevertheless continues to be repeated and is still today very widespread as a result of the complexities of modern life. Man has the right to leave his native land for various motives—and also the right to return—in order to seek better conditions of life in another country. This fact is certainly not without difficulties of various kinds. Above all it generally constitutes a loss for the country which is left behind. It is the departure of a person who is also a member of a great community united by history, tradition and culture; and that person must begin life in the midst of another society united by a different culture and very often by a different language. In this case, it is the loss of *a subject of work,* whose efforts of mind and body could contribute to the common good of his own country, but these efforts, this contribution, are instead offered to another society which in a sense has less right to them than the person's country of origin.

108 Nevertheless, even if emigration is in some aspects an evil, in certain circumstances it is, as the phrase goes, a necessary evil. Everything should be done—and certainly much is being done

to this end—to prevent this material evil from causing greater *moral harm;* indeed every possible effort should be made to ensure that it may bring benefit to the emigrant's personal, family and social life, both for the country to which he goes and the country which he leaves. In this area much depends on just legislation, in particular with regard to the rights of workers. It is obvious that the question of just legislation enters into the context of the present considerations, especially from the point of view of these rights.

109 The most important thing is that the person working away from his native land, whether as a permanent emigrant or as a seasonal worker, should not be *placed at a disadvantage* in comparison with the other workers in that society in the matter of working rights. Emigration in search of work must in no way become an opportunity for financial or social exploitation. As regards the work relationship, the same criteria should be applied to immigrant workers as to all other workers in the society concerned. The value of work should be measured by the same standard and not according to the difference in nationality, religion or race. For even greater reason the *situation of constraint* in which the emigrant may find himself *should not be exploited.* All these circumstances should categorically give way, after special qualifications have of course been taken into consideration, to the fundamental value of work, which is bound up with the dignity of the human person. Once more the fundamental principle must be repeated: the hierarchy of values and the profound meaning of work itself require that capital should be at the service of labour and not labour at the service of capital.

V. Elements for a Spirituality of Work

24. *A Particular Task for the Church*

110 It is right to devote the last part of these reflections about human work, on the occasion of the ninetieth anniversary of the Encyclical *Rerum Novarum,* to the spirituality of work in the Christian sense. Since work in its subjective aspect is always a personal action, an *actus personae,* it follows that *the whole person, body and spirit,* participates in it, whether it is manual or intellectual work. It is also to the whole person that the word of the living God is directed, the evangelical message of salvation,

in which we find many points which concern human work and which throw particular light on it. These points need to be properly assimilated: an inner effort on the part of the human spirit, guided by faith, hope and charity, is needed in order that through these points the *work* of the individual human being may *be given the meaning which it has in the eyes of God* and by means of which work enters into the salvation process on a par with the other ordinary yet particularly important components of its texture.

111 The Church considers it her duty to speak out on work from the viewpoint of its human value and of the moral order to which it belongs, and she sees this as one of her important tasks within the service that she renders to the evangelical message as a whole. At the same time she sees it as her particular duty *to form a spirituality of work* which will help all people to come closer, through work, to God, the Creator and Redeemer, to participate in his salvific plan for man and the world and to deepen their friendship with Christ in their lives by accepting, through faith, a living participation in his threefold mission as Priest, Prophet and King, as the Second Vatican Council so eloquently teaches.

25. *Work as a Sharing in the Activity of the Creator*

112 As the Second Vatican Council says, "throughout the course of the centuries, men have laboured to better the circumstances of their lives through a monumental amount of individual and collective effort. To believers, this point is settled: considered in itself, such human activity accords with God's will. For man, created to God's image, received a mandate to subject to himself the earth and all that it contains, and to govern the world with justice and holiness; a mandate to relate himself and the totality of things to him who was to be acknowledged as the Lord and Creator of all. Thus, by the subjection of all things to man, the name of God would be wonderful in all the earth".[27]

113 The word of God's revelation is profoundly marked by the fundamental truth that *man*, created in the image of God, *shares by his work in the activity of the Creator* and that, within the limits of his own human capabilities, man in a sense continues to develop that activity, and perfects it as he advances further and further in the discovery of the resources and values contained in the whole of creation. We find this truth at the very beginning of Sacred Scripture, in the Book of Genesis,

where the creation activity itself is presented in the form of "work" done by God during "six days",[28] "resting" on the seventh day.[29] Besides, the last book of Sacred Scripture echoes the same respect for what God has done through his creative "work" when it proclaims: "Great and wonderful are your deeds, O Lord God the Almighty";[30] this is similar to the Book of Genesis, which concludes the description of each day of creation with the statement: "And God saw that it was good".[31]

114 This description of creation, which we find in the very first chapter of the Book of Genesis, is also *in a sense the first "gospel of work"*. For it shows what the dignity of work consists of: it teaches that man ought to imitate God, his Creator, in working, because man alone has the unique characteristic of likeness to God. Man ought to imitate God both in working and also in resting, since God himself wished to present his own creative activity under the form of *work and rest*. This activity by God in the world always continues, as the words of Christ attest: "My Father is working still . . .":[32] he works with creative power by sustaining in existence the world that he called into being from nothing, and he works with salvific power in the hearts of those whom from the beginning he has destined for "rest"[33] in union with himself in his "Father's house".[34] Therefore man's work too not only requires a rest every "seventh day",[35] but also cannot consist in the mere exercise of human strength in external action; it must leave room for man to prepare himself, by becoming more and more what in the will of God he ought to be, for the *"rest" that the Lord reserves for his servants and friends.*[36]

115 Awareness that man's work is a participation in God's activity ought to permeate, as the Council teaches, even *"the most ordinary everyday activities.* For, while providing the substance of life for themselves and their families, men and women are performing their activities in a way which appropriately benefits society. They can justly consider that by their labour they are unfolding the Creator's work, consulting the advantages of their brothers and sisters, and contributing by their personal industry to the realization in history of the divine plan".[37]

116 This Christian spirituality of work should be a heritage shared by all. Especially in the modern age, the *spirituality* of work should show the *maturity* called for by the tensions and restlessness of mind and heart. "Far from thinking that works

produced by man's own talent and energy are in opposition to God's power, and that the rational creature exists as a kind of rival to the Creator, Christians are convinced that the triumphs of the human race are a sign of God's greatness and the flowering of his own mysterious design. For the greater man's power becomes, the farther his individual and community responsibility extends. . . . People are not deterred by *the Christian message* from building up the world, or impelled to neglect the welfare of their fellows. They are, rather, more stringently bound to do these very things".[38]

117 The knowledge that by means of work man shares in the work of creation constitutes the most profound *motive* for undertaking it in various sectors. "The faithful, therefore", we read in the Constitution *Lumen Gentium,* "must learn the deepest meaning and the value of all creation, and its orientation to the praise of God. Even by their secular activity they must assist one another to live holier lives. In this way the world will be permeated by the spirit of Christ and more effectively achieve its purpose in justice, charity and peace. . . . Therefore, by their competence in secular fields and by their personal activity, elevated from within by the grace of Christ, let them work vigorously so that by human labour, technical skill, and civil culture created goods may be perfected according to the design of the Creator and the light of his Word".[39]

26. Christ, the Man of Work

118 The truth that by means of work man participates in the activity of God himself, his Creator, was *given particular prominence by Jesus Christ*—the Jesus at whom many of his first listeners in Nazareth "were astonished, saying, 'Where did this man get all this? What is the wisdom given to him? . . . Is not this the carpenter?'".[40] For Jesus not only proclaimed but first and foremost fulfilled by his deeds the "gospel", the word of eternal Wisdom, that had been entrusted to him. Therefore this was also "the gospel of work", because *he who proclaimed it was himself a man of work,* a craftsman like Joseph of Nazareth.[41] And if we do not find in his words a special command to work—but rather on one occasion a prohibition against too much anxiety about work and life[42]—at the same time the eloquence of the life of Christ is unequivocal: he belongs to the "working world", he has appreciation and respect for human work. It can indeed be said that *he looks with love upon human work* and

the different forms that it takes, seeing in each one of these forms a particular facet of man's likeness with God, the Creator and Father. Is it not he who says: "My Father is the vine-dresser",[43] and in various ways puts *into his teaching* the fundamental truth about work which is already expressed in the whole tradition of the Old Testament, beginning with the Book of Genesis?

119 *The books of the Old Testament* contain many references to human work and to the individual professions exercised by man: for example, the doctor,[44] the pharmacist,[45] the craftsman or artist,[46] the blacksmith[47]—we could apply these words to today's foundry-workers—the potter,[48] the farmer,[49] the scholar,[50] the sailor,[51] the builder,[52] the musician,[53] the shepherd,[54] and the fisherman.[55] The words of praise for the work of women are well known.[56] *In his parables on the Kingdom* of God Jesus Christ constantly refers to human work: that of the shepherd,[57] the farmer[58], the doctor,[59] the sower,[60] the householder,[61] the servant,[62] the steward,[63] the fisherman,[64] the merchant,[65] the labourer.[66] He also speaks of the various form of women's work.[67] He compares the apostolate to the manual work of harvesters[68] or fishermen.[69] He refers to the work of scholars too.[70]

120 This teaching of Christ on work, based on the example of his life during his years in Nazareth, finds a particularly lively echo *in the teaching of the Apostle Paul*. Paul boasts of working at his trade (he was probably a tent-maker),[71] and thanks to that work he was able even as an Apostle to earn his own bread.[72] "With toil and labour we worked night and day, that we might not burden any of you".[73] Hence his instructions, in the form of *exhortation and command*, on the subject of work: "Now such persons we command and exhort in the Lord Jesus Christ to do their work in quietness and to earn their own living", he writes to the Thessalonians.[74] In fact, noting that some "are living in idleness . . . not doing any work",[75] the Apostle does not hesitate to say in the same context: "If any one will not work, let him not eat".[76] In another passage *he encourages* his readers: "Whatever your task, work heartily, as serving the Lord and not men, knowing that from the Lord you will receive the inheritance as your reward".[77]

121 The teachings of the Apostle of the Gentiles obviously have key importance for the morality and spirituality of human work. They are an important complement to the great though discreet

gospel of work that we find in the life and parables of Christ, in what Jesus "did and taught".[78]

122 On the basis of these illuminations emanating from the Source himself, the Church has always proclaimed what we find *expressed in modern terms* in the teaching of the Second Vatican Council: "Just as human activity proceeds from man, so it is ordered towards man. For when a man works he not only alters things and society, he develops himself as well. He learns much, he cultivates his resources, he goes outside of himself and beyond himself. Rightly understood, this kind of growth is of greater value than any external riches which can be garnered . . . Hence, the norm of human activity is this: that in accord with the divine plan and will, it should harmonize with the genuine good of the human race, and allow people as individuals and as members of society to pursue their total vocation and fulfil it".[79]

123 Such a *vision of the values of human work*, or in other words such a spirituality of work, fully explains what we read in the same section of the Council's Pastoral Constitution with regard to the right *meaning of progress:* "A person is more precious for what he is than for what he has. Similarly, all that people do to obtain greater justice, wider brotherhood, and a more humane ordering of social relationships has greater worth than technical advances. For these advances can supply the material for human progress, but of themselves alone they can never actually bring it about".[80]

124 This teaching on the question of progress and development—a subject that dominates present-day thought—can be understood only as the fruit of a tested spirituality of human work; and it is *only on the basis of such a spirituality* that it can be realized and put into practice. This is the teaching, and also the programme, that has its roots in "the gospel of work".

27. *Human Work in the Light of the Cross and the Resurrection of Christ*

125 There is yet another aspect of human work, an essential dimension of it, that is profoundly imbued with the spirituality based on the Gospel. All *work*, whether manual or intellectual, is inevitably linked with *toil*. The Book of Genesis expresses it in a truly penetrating manner: the original *blessing* of work contained in the very mystery of creation and connected with

man's elevation as the image of God is contrasted with the *curse* that *sin* brought with it: "Cursed is the ground because of you; in toil you shall eat of it all the days of your life".[81] This toil connected with work marks the way of human life on earth and constitutes *an announcement of death:* "In the sweat of your face you shall eat bread till you return to the ground, for out of it you were taken".[82] Almost as an echo of these words, the author of one of the Wisdom books says: "Then I considered all that my hands had done and the toil I had spent in doing it".[83] There is no one on earth who could not apply these words to himself.

126　In a sense, the final word of the Gospel on this matter as on others is found in the Paschal Mystery of Jesus Christ. It is here that we must seek an answer to these problems so important for the spirituality of human work. *The Paschal Mystery* contains *the Cross* of Christ and his obedience unto death, which the Apostle contrasts with the disobedience which from the beginning has burdened man's history on earth.[84] It also contains *the elevation* of Christ, who by means of death on a Cross returns to his disciples in *the Resurrection* with the power of the Holy Spirit.

127　Sweat and toil, which work necessarily involves the present condition of the human race, present the Christian and everyone who is called to follow Christ with the possibility of sharing lovingly in the work that Christ came to do.[85] This work of salvation came about through suffering and death on a Cross. By enduring the toil of work in union with Christ crucified for us, man in a way collaborates with the Son of God for the redemption of humanity. He shows himself a true disciple of Christ by carrying the cross in his turn every day[86] in the activity that he is called upon to perform.

128　Christ, "undergoing death itself for all of us sinners, taught us by example that we too must shoulder that cross which the world and the flesh inflict upon those who pursue peace and justice"; but also, at the same time, "appointed Lord by *his Resurrection* and given all authority in heaven and on earth, Christ is now at work in people's hearts through the power of his Spirit . . . He animates, purifies, and strengthens those noble longings too, by which the human family strives *to make its life more human* and to render the whole earth submissive to this goal".[87]

129 The Christian finds in human work a small part of the Cross of Christ and accepts it in the same spirit of redemption in which Christ accepted his Cross for us. In work, thanks to the light that penetrates us from the Resurrection of Christ, we always find a *glimmer* of new life, of the *new good*, as if it were an announcement of "the new heavens and the new earth"[88] in which man and the world participate precisely through the toil that goes with work. Through toil—and never without it. On the one hand this confirms the indispensability of the Cross in the spirituality of human work; on the other hand the Cross which this toil constitutes reveals a new good springing from work itself, from work understood in depth and in all its aspects and never apart from work.

130 Is this *new good*—the fruit of human work—already a small part of that "new earth" where justice dwells?[89] If it is true that the many forms of toil that go with man's work are a small part of the Cross of Christ, what is the relationship of this new good to *the Resurrection of Christ?*

131 The Council seeks to reply to this question also, drawing light from the very sources of the revealed word: "Therefore, while we are warned that it profits a man nothing if he gains the whole world and loses himself (cf. *Lk* 9: 25), the expectation of a new earth must not weaken but rather stimulate our concern for cultivating this one. For here grows the body of a new human family, a body which even now is able to give some kind of foreshadowing of the new age. Earthly progress must be carefully distinguished from the growth of Christ's kingdom. Nevertheless, to the extent that the former can contribute to the better ordering of human society, it is of vital concern to the Kingdom of God".[90]

132 In these present reflections devoted to human work we have tried to emphasise everything that seemed essential to it, since it is through man's labour that not only "the fruits of our activity" but also "human dignity, brotherhood and freedom" must increase on earth.[91] Let the Christian who listens to the word of the living God, uniting work with prayer, know the place that his work has not only in *earthly progress* but also in *the development of the Kingdom of God*, to which we are all called through the power of the Holy Spirit and through the word of the Gospel.

133 In concluding these reflections, I gladly impart the Apostolic Blessing to all of you, venerable Brothers and beloved sons and daughters.

134 I prepared this document for publication on 15 May last, on the ninetieth anniversary of the Encyclical *Rerum Novarum*, but it is only after my stay in hospital that I have been able to revise it definitively.

135

Given at Castel Gandolfo,
on the fourteenth day of September,
the Feast of the Triumph of the Cross,
in the year 1981,
the third of the Pontificate.

Notes

[1] Cf. Ps. 127(128):2; cf. also Gn. 3:17–19; Prv. 10:22; Ex. 1:8–14; Jer. 22:13.

[2] Cf. Gn. 1:26.

[3] Cf. Gn. 1:28.

[4] Encyclical *Redemptor hominis,* no. 14: AAS 71 (1979), p. 284.

[5] Cf. Ps. 127(128):2.

[6] Gn. 3:19.

[7] Cf. Mt. 13:52.

[8] Second Vatican Ecumenical Council, Pastoral Constitution on the Church in the Modern World *Gaudium et spes,* no. 38: AAS 58 (1966), p. 1055.

[9] Gn. 1:27.

[10] Gn. 1:28.

[11] Cf. Heb. 2:17; Phil. 2:5–8.

[12] Cf. Pope Pius XI, Encyclical *Quadragesimo Anno:* AAS 23 (1931), p. 221.

[13] Dt. 24:15; Jas. 5:4; and also Gn. 4:10.

[14] Cf. Gn. 1:28.

[15] Cf. Gn. 1:26–27.

[16] Gn. 3:19.

17 Heb. 6:8; cf. Gn. 3:18.

18 Cf. *Summa* Th. I–II, q. 40, a. 1, c.; I–II, q. 34, a. 2, ad 1.

19 Cf. *Summa* Th., I–II, q. 40, a. 1, c.: I–II, q. 34, a. 2 and 1.

20 Cf. Pope Pius XI, Encyclical Quadragesimo Anno: AAS 23 (1931), pp. 221–222.

21 Cf. Jn. 4:38.

22 On the right to property see *Summa Th.* II–II, q.66, arts. 2 and 6; *De Regimine Principum,* book 1, chapters 15 and 17. On the social function of property see *Summa Th.,* II–II, q. 134, art. 1, ad. 3

23 Cf. Pope Pius XI, Encyclical *Quadragesimo Anno:* AAS 23 (1931), p. 199; Second Vatican Ecumenical Council, Pastoral Constitution on the Church in the Modern World *Gaudium et spes,* no. 68: AAS 58 (1966), pp. 1089–1090.

24 Cf. Pope John XXIII, Encyclical *Mater et magistra:* AAS 53 (1961), p. 419.

25 Cf. *Summa Th.,* II–II, q. 65, a. 2

26 Second Vatican Ecumenical Council, Pastoral Constitution on the Church in the Modern World *Gaudium et spes,* no. 67: AAS 58 (1966), p. 1089.

27 Second Vatican Ecumenical Council, Pastoral Constitution on the Church in the Modern World *Gaudium et spes,* no. 34; AAS 58 (1966), pp. 1052–1053.

28 Cf. Gn. 2:2; Ex. 20:8, 11; Dt. 5:12–14.

29 Cf. Gn. 2:3.

30 Rv. 15:3.

31 Gn. 1:4, 10, 12, 18, 21, 25, 31.

32 Jn. 5:17.

33 Cf. Heb. 4:1, 9–10.

34 Jn. 14:2.

35 Cf. Dt. 5:12–14; Ex. 20:8–12.

36 Cf. Mt. 25:21.

37 Second Vatican Ecumenical Council, Pastoral Constitution on the Church in the Modern World *Gaudium et spes,* no. 34, AAS 58 (1966), pp. 1052–1053.

38 Ibid.

39 Second Vatican Ecumenical Council, Dogmatic Constitution on the Church *Lumen gentium,* no. 36: AAS 57 (1965), p. 41.

40 Mk. 6:2–3.

41 Cf. Mt. 13:55.

42 Cf. Mt. 6:25–34.

43 Jn. 15:1.

44 Cf. Sir. 38:1–3.

45 Cf. Sir. 38:4–8.

46 Cf. Ex. 31:1–5; Sir. 38:27.

47 Cf. Gn. 4:22; Is. 44:12.

48 Cf. Jer. 18:3–4; Sir. 38:29–30.

49 Cf. Gn. 9:20; Is. 5:1–2.

50 Cf. Eccl. 12:9–12; Sir. 39:1–8.

51 Cf. Ps. 107(108):23–30; Wis. 14:2–3a.

52 Cf. Gn. 11:3; 2 Kgs. 12:12–13; 22:5–6.

53 Cf. Gn. 4:21.

54 Cf. Gn. 4:2, 37:3; Ex. 3:1; 1 Sm. 16:11; et passim.

55 Cf. Ez. 47:10.

56 Cf. Prv. 31:15–27.

57 E.g. Jn. 10:1–16.

58 Cf. Mk. 12:1–12.

59 Cf. Lk. 4:23.

60 Cf. Mk. 4:1–9.

61 Cf. Mt. 13–52.

62 Cf. Mt. 24:45; Lk. 12:42–48.

63 Cf. Lk. 16:1–8.

64 Cf. Mt. 13:47–50.

65 Cf. Mt. 13:45–46.

66 Cf. Mt. 20:1–16.

67 Cf. Mt. 13:33; Lk. 15:8–9.

68 Cf. Mt. 9:37; Jn. 4:35–38.

69 Cf. Mt. 4:19.

70 Cf. Mt. 13:52.

71 Cf. Acts 18:3.

72 Cf. Acts 20:34–35.

73 2 Thes. 3:8. St. Paul recognizes that missionaries have a right to their keep; 1 Cor. 9:6–14; Gal. 6:6; 2 Thes. 3:9; cf. Lk. 10:7.

74 2 Thes. 3:12.

75 2 Thes. 3:11.

76 2 Thes. 3:10.

77 Col. 3:23–24.

78 Cf. Acts 1:1.

[79] Second Vatican Ecumenical Council, Pastoral Constitution on the Church in the Modern World *Gaudium et spes,* no. 35: AAS 58 (1966), p. 1053.

[80] Ibid.

[81] Gn. 3:17.

[82] Gn. 3:19.

[83] Eccl. 2:11.

[84] Cf. Rom. 5:19.

[85] Cf. Jn. 17:4.

[86] Cf. Lk. 9:23.

[87] Second Vatican Ecumenical Council, Pastoral Constitution on the Church in the Modern World *Gaudium et spes,* no. 38: AAS 58 (1966), pp. 1055–1056.

[88] Cf. 2 Pt. 3:13; Rv. 21:1.

[89] Cf. 2 Pt. 3:13.

[90] Second Vatican Ecumenical Council, Pastoral Constitution on the Church in the Modern World *Gaudium et spes,* no. 39: AAS 58 (1966), p. 1057.

[91] Ibid.

A Call for Unity

Clergymen of Alabama

April 12, 1963

1   We the undersigned clergymen are among those who, in January, issued "An Appeal for Law and Order and Common Sense," in dealing with racial problems in Alabama. We expressed understanding that honest convictions in racial matters could properly be pursued in the courts, but urged that decisions of those courts should in the meantime be peacefully obeyed.

2   Since that time there had been some evidence of increased forebearance and a willingness to face facts. Responsible citizens have undertaken to work on various problems which cause racial friction and unrest. In Birmingham, recent public events have given indication that we all have opportunity for a new constructive and realistic approach to racial problems.

3   However, we are now confronted by a series of demonstrations by some of our Negro citizens, directed and led in part by outsiders. We recognize the natural impatience of people who feel that their hopes are slow in being realized. But we are convinced that these demonstrations are unwise and untimely.

4   We agree rather with certain local Negro leadership which has called for honest and open negotiation of racial issues in our area. And we believe this kind of facing of issues can best be accomplished by citizens of our own metropolitan area, white and Negro, meeting with their knowledge and experience of the local situation. All of us need to face that responsibility and find proper channels for its accomplishment.

5   Just as we formerly pointed out that "hatred and violence have no sanction in our religious and political traditions," we also point out that such actions as incite to hatred and violence, however technically peaceful those actions may be, have not contributed to the resolution of our local problems. We do not believe that these days of new hope are days when extreme measures are justified in Birmingham.

6   We commend the community as a whole, and the local news media and law enforcement officials in particular, on the calm manner in which these demonstrations have been handled. We urge the public to continue to show restraint should the demonstrations continue, and the law enforcement officials to remain calm and continue to protect óur city from violence.

7   We further strongly urge our own Negro community to withdraw support from these demonstrations, and to unite locally in working peacefully for a better Birmingham. (When rights are consistently denied, a cause should be pressed in the courts and in negotiations among local leaders, and not in the streets. We appeal to both our white and Negro citizenry to observe the principles of law and order and common sense.)

8   C.C.J. Carpenter, D.D., L.L.D., Bishop of Alabama; Joseph A. Durick, D.D., Auxiliary Bishop, Diocese of Mobile-Birmingham; Rabbi Milton L. Grafman, Temple Emanu-El, Birmingham, Alabama; Bishop Paul Hardin, Bishop of the Alabama-West Florida Conference of the Methodist Church; Bishop Nolan B. Harmon, Bishop of the North Alabama Conference of the Methodist Church; George M. Murray, D.D., L.L.D., Bishop Coadjutor, Episcopal Diocese of Alabama; Edward V. Ramage, Moderator, Synod of the Alabama Presbyterian Church in the United States; Earl Stallings, Pastor, First Baptist Church, Birmingham, Alabama.

*M*artin Luther King (1929–1968), prominent American preacher who led the civil rights movement in the 1950s and 1960s, was born in Atlanta, Georgia in 1929, the son and grandson of Baptist ministers. After completing his undergraduate studies at Morehouse College in 1951, he went on to receive a Ph.D. from Boston University in 1955. Drawing on Gandhian and Christian principles of peaceful resistance to evil, he advocated nonviolent protest of the racial injustice embedded in American society. He organized and led the Southern Christian Leadership Conference which sponsored boycotts, marches and voter registration drives. In response to criticism of his activism by local clergymen in 1963, he wrote the "Letter from Birmingham Jail" which justifies and calls others to such activism. His writings and speeches, most notably his 1963 "I Have a Dream" speech delivered before the Lincoln Memorial in Washington, provided the moral vision underlying the civil rights movement. He was awarded the 1964 Nobel Peace Prize; four years later he was assassinated in Memphis, Tennessee.

Letter from Birmingham Jail

Martin Luther King, Jr.

April 16, 1963

My Dear Fellow Clergymen:

1 ·While confined here in the Birmingham city jail, I came across your recent statement calling my present activities "unwise and untimely." Seldom do I pause to answer criticism of my work and ideas. If I sought to answer all the criticisms that cross my desk, my secretaries would have little time for anything other than such correspondence in the course of the day, and I would have no time for constructive work. But since I feel that you are men of genuine good will and that your criticisms are sincerely set forth, I want to try to answer your statement in what I hope will be patient and reasonable terms.

2 I think I should indicate why I am here in Birmingham, since you have been influenced by the view which argues against "outsiders coming in." I have the honor of serving as president of the Southern Christian Leadership Conference, an organization

operating in every southern state, with headquarters in Atlanta, Georgia. We have some eighty-five affiliated organizations across the South, and one of them is the Alabama Christian Movement for Human Rights. Frequently we share staff, educational and financial resources with our affiliates. Several months ago the affiliate here in Birmingham asked us to be on call to engage in a nonviolent direct-action program if such were deemed necessary. We readily consented, and when the hour came we lived up to our promise. So I, along with several members of my staff, am here because I was invited here. I am here because I have organizational ties here.

3   But more basically, I am in Birmingham because injustice is here. Just as the prophets of the eighth century B.C. left their villages and carried their "thus saith the Lord" far beyond the boundaries of their home towns, and just as the Apostle Paul left his village of Tarsus and carried the gospel of Jesus Christ to the far corners of the Greco-Roman world, so am I compelled to carry the gospel of freedom beyond my own home town. Like Paul, I must constantly respond to the Macedonian call for aid.

[handwritten margin note: talking in his religious terms to clergymen]

4   Moreover, I am cognizant of the interrelatedness of all communities and states. I cannot sit idly by in Atlanta and not be concerned about what happens in Birmingham. Injustice anywhere is a threat to justice everywhere. We are caught in an inescapable network of mutuality, tied in a single garment of destiny. Whatever affects one directly, affects all indirectly. Never again can we afford to live with the narrow, provincial "outside agitator" idea. Anyone who lives inside the United States can never be considered an outsider anywhere within its bounds.

[handwritten margin note: appeals to patriotism]

5   You deplore the demonstrations taking place in Birmingham. But your statement, I am sorry to say, fails to express a similar concern for the conditions that brought about the demonstrations. I am sure that none of you would want to rest content with the superficial kind of social analysis that deals merely with effects and does not grapple with underlying causes. It is unfortunate that demonstrations are taking place in Birmingham, but it is even more unfortunate that the city's white power structure left the Negro community with no alternative.

[handwritten margin note: ouch. →]

6 [In any nonviolent campaign there are four basic steps: collection of the facts to determine whether injustices exist; negotiation; self-purification; and direct action.] We have gone through all these steps in Birmingham. There can be no gainsaying the fact that racial injustice engulfs this community. Birmingham is probably the most thoroughly segregated city in the United States. Its ugly record of brutality is widely known. Negroes have experienced grossly unjust treatment in the courts. There have been more unsolved bombings of Negro homes and churches in Birmingham than in any other city in the nation. These are the hard, brutal facts of the case. On the basis of these conditions, Negro leaders sought to negotiate with the city fathers. But the latter consistently refused to engage in good-faith negotiation.

7 Then, last September, came the opportunity to talk with leaders of Birmingham's economic community. In the course of the negotiations, certain promises were made by the merchants—for example, to remove the stores' humiliating racial signs. On the basis of these promises, the Reverend Fred Shuttlesworth and the leaders of the Alabama Christian Movement for Human Rights agreed to a moratorium on all demonstrations. As the weeks and months went by, we realized that we were the victims of a broken promise. A few signs, briefly removed, returned; the others remained.

8 As in so many past experiences, our hopes had been blasted, and the shadow of deep disappointment settled upon us. We had no alternative except to prepare for direct action, whereby we would present our very bodies as a means of laying our case before the conscience of the local and the national community. Mindful of the difficulties involved, we decided to undertake a process of self-purification. We began a series of workshops on nonviolence, and we repeatedly asked ourselves: "Are you able to accept blows without retaliating?" "Are you able to endure the ordeal of jail?" We decided to schedule our direct-action program for the Easter season, realizing that except for Christmas, this is the main shopping period of the year. Knowing that a strong economic-withdrawal program would be the by-product of direct action, we felt that this would be the best time to bring pressure to bear on the merchants for the needed change.

9   Then it occurred to us that Birmingham's mayoral election was coming up in March, and we speedily decided to postpone action until after election day. When we discovered that the Commissioner of Public Safety, Eugene "Bull" Connor, had piled up enough votes to be in the run-off, we decided again to postpone action until the day after the run-off so that the demonstrations could not be used to cloud the issues. Like many others, we waited to see Mr. Connor defeated, and to this end we endured postponement after postponement. Having aided in this community need, we felt that our direct-action program could be delayed no longer.

10   You may well ask: "Why direct action? Why sit-ins, marches and so forth? Isn't negotiation a better path?" You are quite right in calling for negotiation. Indeed, this is the very purpose of direct action. Nonviolent direct action seeks to create such a crisis and foster such a tension that a community which has constantly refused to negotiate is forced to confront the issue. It seeks so to dramatize the issue that it can no longer be ignored. My citing the creation of tension as part of the work of the nonviolent-resister may sound rather shocking. But I must confess that I am not afraid of the word "tension." I have earnestly opposed violent tension, but there is a type of constructive, nonviolent tension which is necessary for growth. Just as Socrates felt that it was necessary to create a tension in the mind so that individuals could rise from the bondage of myths and half-truths to the unfettered realm of creative analysis and objective appraisal, so must we see the need for nonviolent gadflies to create the kind of tension in society that will help men rise from the dark depths of prejudice and racism to the majestic heights of understanding and brotherhood.

11   The purpose of our direct-action program is to create a situation so crisis-packed that it will inevitably open the door to negotiation. I therefore concur with you in your call for negotiation. Too long has our beloved Southland been bogged down in a tragic effort to live in monologue rather than dialogue.

12   One of the basic points in your statement is that the action that I and my associates have taken in Birmingham is untimely. Some have asked: "Why didn't you give the new city administration time to act?" The only answer that I can give to this query is that the new Birmingham administration must be

prodded about as much as the outgoing one, before it will act. We are sadly mistaken if we feel that the election of Albert Boutwell as mayor will bring the millennium to Birmingham. While Mr. Boutwell is a much more gentle person than Mr. Connor, they are both segregationists, dedicated to maintenance of the status quo. I have hope that Mr. Boutwell will be reasonable enough to see the futility of massive resistance to desegregation. But he will not see this without pressure from devotees of civil rights. My friends, I must say to you that we have not made a single gain in civil rights without determined legal and nonviolent pressure. Lamentably, it is an historical fact that privileged groups seldom give up their privileges voluntarily. Individuals may see the moral light and voluntarily give up their unjust posture; but, as Reinhold Niebuhr has reminded us, groups tend to be more immoral than individuals.

13 We know through painful experience that freedom is never voluntarily given by the oppressor; it must be demanded by the oppressed. Frankly, I have yet to engage in a direct-action campaign that was "well timed" in the view of those who have not suffered unduly from the disease of segregation. For years now I have heard the word "Wait!" It rings in the ear of every Negro with piercing familiarity. This "Wait" has almost always meant "Never." We must come to see, with one of our distinguished jurists, that "justice too long delayed is justice denied."

14 We have waited for more than 340 years for our constitutional and God-given rights. The nations of Asia and Africa are moving with jetlike speed toward gaining political independence, but we still creep at horse-and-buggy pace toward gaining a cup of coffee at a lunch counter. Perhaps it is easy for those who have never felt the stinging darts of segregation to say, "Wait." But when you have seen vicious mobs lynch your mothers and fathers at will and drown your sisters and brothers at whim; when you have seen hate-filled policemen curse, kick and even kill your black brothers and sisters; when you see the vast majority of your twenty million Negro brothers smothering in an airtight cage of poverty in the midst of an affluent society; when you suddenly find your tongue twisted and your speech stammering as you seek to explain to your six-year-old daughter why she can't go to the public

amusement park that has just been advertised on television, and see tears welling up in her eyes when she is told that Funtown is closed to colored children, and see ominous clouds of inferiority beginning to form in her little mental sky, and see her beginning to distort her personality by developing an unconscious bitterness toward white people; when you have to concoct an answer for a five-year-old son who is asking: "Daddy, why do white people treat colored people so mean?"; when you take a cross-country drive and find it necessary to sleep night after night in the uncomfortable corners of your automobile because no motel will accept you; when you are humiliated day in and day out by nagging signs reading "white" and "colored"; when your first name becomes "nigger," your middle name becomes "boy" (however old you are) and your last name becomes "John," and your wife and mother are never given the respected title "Mrs."; when you are harried by day and haunted by night by the fact that you are a Negro, living constantly at tiptoe stance, never quite knowing what to expect next, and are plagued with inner fears and outer resentments; when you are forever fighting a degenerating sense of "nobodiness"—then you will understand why we find it difficult to wait. There comes a time when the cup of endurance runs over, and men are no longer willing to be plunged into the abyss of despair. I hope, sirs, you can understand our legitimate and unavoidable impatience.

15 You express a great deal of anxiety over our willingness to break laws. This is certainly a legitimate concern. Since we so diligently urge people to obey the Supreme Court's decision of 1954 outlawing segregation in the public schools, at first glance it may seem rather paradoxical for us consciously to break laws. One may well ask: "How can you advocate breaking some laws and obeying others?" The answer lies in the fact that there are two types of laws: just and unjust. I would be the first to advocate obeying just laws. One has not only a legal but a moral responsibility to obey just laws. Conversely, one has a moral responsibility to disobey unjust laws. I would agree with St. Augustine that "an unjust law is no law at all."

16 Now, what is the difference between the two? How does one determine whether a law is just or unjust? A just law is a man-made code that squares with the moral law or the law of God. An unjust law is a code that is out of harmony with the moral law. To put it in the terms of St. Thomas Aquinas: An

unjust law is a human law that is not rooted in eternal law and natural law. Any law that uplifts human personality is just. Any law that degrades human personality is unjust. All segregation statutes are unjust because segregation distorts the soul and damages the personality. It gives the segregator a false sense of superiority and the segregated a false sense of inferiority. Segregation, to use the terminology of the Jewish philosopher Martin Buber, substitutes an "I-it" relationship for an "I-thou" relationship and ends up relegating persons to the status of things. Hence segregation is not only politically, economically and sociologically unsound, it is morally wrong and sinful. Paul Tillich has said that sin is separation. Is not segregation an existential expression of man's tragic separation, his awful estrangement, his terrible sinfulness? Thus it is that I can urge men to obey the 1954 decision of the Supreme Court, for it is morally right; and I can urge them to disobey segregation ordinances, for they are morally wrong.

17   Let us consider a more concrete example of just and unjust laws. An unjust law is a code that a numerical or power majority group compels a minority group to obey but does not make binding on itself. This is *difference* made legal. By the same token, a just law is a code that a majority compels a minority to follow and that it is willing to follow itself. This is *sameness* made legal.

18   Let me give another explanation. A law is unjust if it is inflicted on a minority that, as a result of being denied the right to vote, had no part in enacting or devising the law. Who can say that the legislature of Alabama which set up that state's segregation laws was democratically elected? Throughout Alabama all sorts of devious methods are used to prevent Negroes from becoming registered voters, and there are some counties in which, even though Negroes constitute a majority of the population, not a single Negro is registered. Can any law enacted under such circumstances be considered democratically structured?

19   Sometimes a law is just on its face and unjust in its application. For instance, I have been arrested on a charge of parading without a permit. Now, there is nothing wrong in having an ordinance which requires a permit for a parade. But such an ordinance becomes unjust when it is used to maintain segregation and to deny citizens the First-Amendment privilege of peaceful assembly and protest.

20   I hope you are able to see the distinction I am trying to point out. In no sense do I advocate evading or defying the law, as would the rabid segregationist. That would lead to anarchy. One who breaks an unjust law must do so openly, lovingly, and with a willingness to accept the penalty. I submit that an individual who breaks a law that conscience tells him is unjust, and who willingly accepts the penalty of imprisonment in order to arouse the conscience of the community over its injustice, is in reality expressing the highest respect for law.

21   Of course, there is nothing new about this kind of civil disobedience. It was evidenced sublimely in the refusal of Shadrach, Meshach and Abednego to obey the laws of Nebuchadnezzar, on the ground that a higher moral law was at stake. It was practiced superbly by the early Christians, who were willing to face hungry lions and the excruciating pain of chopping blocks rather than submit to certain unjust laws of the Roman Empire. To a degree, academic freedom is a reality today because Socrates practiced civil disobedience. In our own nation, the Boston Tea Party represented a massive act of civil disobedience.

22   We should never forget that everything Adolf Hitler did in Germany was "legal" and everything the Hungarian freedom fighters did in Hungary was "illegal." It was "illegal" to aid and comfort a Jew in Hitler's Germany. Even so, I am sure that, had I lived in Germany at the time, I would have aided and comforted my Jewish brothers. If today I lived in a Communist country where certain principles dear to the Christian faith are suppressed, I would openly advocate disobeying that country's antireligious laws.

23   I must make two honest confessions to you, my Christian and Jewish brothers. First, I must confess that over the past few years I have been gravely disappointed with the white moderate. I have almost reached the regrettable conclusion that the Negro's great stumbling block in his stride toward freedom is not the White Citizen's Counciler or the Ku Klux Klanner, but the white moderate, who is more devoted to "order" than to justice; who prefers a negative peace which is the absence of tension to a positive peace which is the presence of justice; who constantly says: "I agree with you in the goal you seek, but I cannot agree with your methods of direct action"; who paternalistically believes he can set the timetable for another

man's freedom; who lives by a mythical concept of time and who constantly advises the Negro to wait for a "more convenient season." Shallow understanding from people of good will is more frustrating than absolute misunderstanding from people of ill will. Lukewarm acceptance is much more bewildering than outright rejection.

24   I had hoped that the white moderate would understand that law and order exist for the purpose of establishing justice and that when they fail in this purpose they become the dangerously structured dams that block the flow of social progress. I had hoped that the white moderate would understand that the present tension in the South is a necessary phase of the transition from an obnoxious negative peace, in which the Negro passively accepted his unjust plight, to a substantive and positive peace, in which all men will respect the dignity and worth of human personality. (Actually, we who engage in nonviolent direct action are not the creators of tension. We merely bring to the surface the hidden tension that is already alive. We bring it out in the open, where it can be seen and dealt with. Like a boil that can never be cured so long as it is covered up but must be opened with all its ugliness to the natural medicines of air and light, injustice must be exposed, with all the tension its exposure creates, to the light of human conscience and the air of national opinion before it can be cured.)

25   In your statement you assert that our actions, even though peaceful, must be condemned because they precipitate violence. But is this a logical assertion? Isn't this like condemning a robbed man because his possession of money precipitated the evil act of robbery? Isn't this like condemning Socrates because his unswerving commitment to truth and his philosophical inquiries precipitated the act by the misguided populace in which they made him drink hemlock? Isn't this like condemning Jesus because his unique God-consciousness and never-ceasing devotion to God's will precipitated the evil act of crucifixion? We must come to see that, as the federal courts have consistently affirmed, it is wrong to urge an individual to cease his efforts to gain his basic constitutional rights because the quest may precipitate violence. Society must protect the robbed and punish the robber.

26   I had also hoped that the white moderate would reject the myth concerning time in relation to the struggle for freedom. I

have just received a letter from a white brother in Texas. He writes: "All Christians know that the colored people will receive equal rights eventually, but it is possible that you are in too great a religious hurry. It has taken Christianity almost two thousand years to accomplish what it has. The teachings of Christ take time to come to earth." Such an attitude stems from a tragic misconception of time, from the strangely irrational notion that there is something in the very flow of time that will inevitably cure all ills. Actually, time itself is neutral; it can be used either destructively or constructively. More and more I feel that the people of ill will have used time much more effectively than have the people of good will. We will have to repent in this generation not merely for the hateful words and actions of the bad people but for the appalling silence of the good people. Human progress never rolls in on wheels of inevitability; it comes through the tireless efforts of men willing to be co-workers with God, and without this hard work, time itself becomes an ally of the forces of social stagnation. We must use time creatively, in the knowledge that the time is always ripe to do right. Now is the time to make real the promise of democracy and transform our pending national elegy into a creative psalm of brotherhood. Now is the time to lift our national policy from the quicksand of racial injustice to the solid rock of human dignity.

27   You speak of our activity in Birmingham as extreme. At first I was rather disappointed that fellow clergymen would see my nonviolent efforts as those of an extremist. I began thinking about the fact that I stand in the middle of two opposing forces in the Negro community. One is a force of complacency, made up in part of Negroes who, as a result of long years of oppression, are so drained of self-respect and a sense of "somebodiness" that they have adjusted to segregation; and in part of a few middle-class Negroes who, because of a degree of academic and economic security and because in some ways they profit by segregation, have become insensitive to the problems of the masses. The other force is one of bitterness and hatred, and it comes perilously close to advocating violence. It is expressed in the various black nationalist groups that are springing up across the nation, the largest and best-known being Elijah Muhammad's Muslim movement. Nourished by the Negro's frustration over the continued existence of racial discrimination, this movement is made up of people who have

lost faith in America, who have absolutely repudiated Christianity, and who have concluded that the white man is an incorrigible "devil."

28   I have tried to stand between these two forces, saying that we need emulate neither the "do-nothingism" of the complacent nor the hatred and despair of the black nationalist. For there is the more excellent way of love and nonviolent protest. I am grateful to God that, through the influence of the Negro church, the way of nonviolence became an integral part of our struggle.

29   If this philosophy had not emerged, by now many streets of the South would, I am convinced, be flowing with blood. And I am further convinced that if our white brothers dismiss as "rabble-rousers" and "outside agitators" those of us who employ nonviolent direct action, and if they refuse to support our nonviolent efforts, millions of Negroes will, out of frustration and despair, seek solace and security in black-nationalist ideologies—a development that would inevitably lead to a frightening racial nightmare.

30   Oppressed people cannot remain oppressed forever. The yearning for freedom eventually manifests itself, and that is what has happened to the American Negro. Something within has reminded him of his birthright of freedom, and something without has reminded him that it can be gained. Consciously or unconsciously, he has been caught up by the *Zeitgeist*, and with his black brothers of Africa and his brown and yellow brothers of Asia, South America and the Caribbean, the United States Negro is moving with a sense of great urgency toward the promised land of racial justice. If one recognizes this vital urge that has engulfed the Negro community, one should readily understand why public demonstrations are taking place. The Negro has many pent-up resentments and latent frustrations, and he must release them. So let him march; let him make prayer pilgrimages to the city hall; let him go on freedom rides—and try to understand why he must do so. If his repressed emotions are not released in nonviolent ways, they will seek expression through violence; this is not a threat but a fact of history. So I have not said to my people: "Get rid of your discontent." Rather, I have tried to say that this normal and healthy discontent can be channeled into the creative outlet of

get worse if something don't do it.
about it.
Actions are better and than what could happen

nonviolent direct action. And now this approach is being termed extremist.

31   But though I was initially disappointed at being categorized as an extremist, as I continued to think about the matter I gradually gained a measure of satisfaction from the label. Was not Jesus an extremist for love: "Love your enemies, bless them that curse you, do good to them that hate you, and pray for them which despitefully use you, and persecute you." Was not Amos an extremist for justice: "Let justice roll down like waters and righteousness like an ever-flowing stream." Was not Paul an extremist for the Christian gospel: "I bear in my body the marks of the Lord Jesus." Was not Martin Luther an extremist: "Here I stand; I cannot do otherwise, so help me God." And John Bunyan: "I will stay in jail to the end of my days before I make a butchery of my conscience." And Abraham Lincoln: "This nation cannot survive half slave and half free." And Thomas Jefferson: "We hold these truths to be self-evident, that all men are created equal . . ." So the question is not whether we will be extremists, but what kind of extremists we will be. Will we be extremists for hate or for love? Will we be extremists for the preservation of injustice or for the extension of justice? In that dramatic scene on Calvary's hill three men were crucified. We must never forget that all three were crucified for the same crime—the crime of extremism. Two were extremists for immorality, and thus fell below their environment. The other, Jesus Christ, was an extremist for love, truth and goodness, and thereby rose above his environment. Perhaps the South, the nation and the world are in dire need of creative extremists.

32   I had hoped that the white moderate would see this need. Perhaps I was too optimistic; perhaps I expected too much. I suppose I should have realized that few members of the oppressor race can understand the deep groans and passionate yearnings of the oppressed race, and still fewer have the vision to see that injustice must be rooted out by strong, persistent and determined action. I am thankful, however, that some of our white brothers in the South have grasped the meaning of this social revolution and committed themselves to it. They are still all too few in quantity, but they are big in quality. Some—such as Ralph McGill, Lillian Smith, Harry Golden, James McBride Dabbs, Ann Braden and Sarah Patton Boyle—have written

about our struggle in eloquent and prophetic terms. Others have marched with us down nameless streets of the South. They have languished in filthy, roach-infested jails, suffering the abuse and brutality of policemen who view them as "dirty nigger-lovers." Unlike so many of their moderate brothers and sisters, they have recognized the urgency of the moment and sensed the need for powerful "action" antidotes to combat the disease of segregation.

33 Let me take note of my other major disappointment. I have been so greatly disappointed with the white church and its leadership. Of course, there are some notable exceptions. I am not unmindful of the fact that each of you has taken some significant stands on this issue. I commend you, Reverend Stallings, for your Christian stand on this past Sunday, in welcoming Negroes to your worship service on a nonsegregated basis. I commend the Catholic leaders of this state for integrating Spring Hill College several years ago.

34 But despite these notable exceptions, I must honestly reiterate that I have been disappointed with the church. I do not say this as one of those negative critics who can always find something wrong with the church. I say this as a minister of the gospel, who loves the church; who was nurtured in its bosom; who has been sustained by its spiritual blessings and who will remain true to it as long as the cord of life shall lengthen.

35 When I was suddenly catapulted into the leadership of the bus protest in Montgomery, Alabama, a few years ago, I felt we would be supported by the white church. I felt that the white ministers, priests and rabbis of the South would be among our strongest allies. Instead, some have been outright opponents, refusing to understand the freedom movement and misrepresenting its leaders; all too many others have been more cautious than courageous and have remained silent behind the anesthetizing security of stained-glass windows.

36 In spite of my shattered dreams, I came to Birmingham with the hope that the white religious leadership of this community would see the justice of our cause and, with deep moral concern, would serve as the channel through which our just grievances could reach the power structure. I had hoped that each of you would understand. But again I have been disappointed.

37   I have heard numerous southern religious leaders admonish their worshipers to comply with a desegregation decision because it is the law, but I have longed to hear white ministers declare: "Follow this decree because integration is morally right and because the Negro is your brother." In the midst of blatant injustices inflicted upon the Negro, I have watched white churchmen stand on the sideline and mouth pious irrelevancies and sanctimonious trivialities. In the midst of a mighty struggle to rid our nation of racial and economic injustice, I have heard many ministers say: "Those are social issues, with which the gospel has no real concern." And I have watched many churches commit themselves to a completely otherworldly religion which makes a strange, un-Biblical distinction between body and soul, between the sacred and the secular.

38   I have traveled the length and breadth of Alabama, Mississippi and all the other southern states. On sweltering summer days and crisp autumn mornings I have looked at the South's beautiful churches with their lofty spires pointing heavenward. I have beheld the impressive outlines of her massive religious-education buildings. Over and over I have found myself asking: "What kind of people worship here? Who is their God? Where were their voices when the lips of Governor Barnett dripped with words of interposition and nullification? Where were they when Governor Wallace gave a clarion call for defiance and hatred? Where were their voices of support when bruised and weary Negro men and women decided to rise from the dark dungeons of complacency to the bright hills of creative protest?"

39   Yes, these questions are still in my mind. In deep disappointment I have wept over the laxity of the church. But be assured that my tears have been tears of love. There can be no deep disappointment where there is not deep love. Yes, I love the church. How could I do otherwise? I am in the rather unique position of being the son, the grandson and the great-grandson of preachers. Yes, I see the church as the body of Christ. But, oh! How we have blemished and scarred that body through social neglect and through fear of being nonconformists.

40   There was a time when the church was very powerful—in the time when the early Christians rejoiced at being deemed worthy to suffer for what they believed. In those days the church

was not merely a thermometer that recorded the ideas and principles of popular opinion; it was a thermostat that transformed the mores of society. Whenever the early Christians entered a town, the people in power became disturbed and immediately sought to convict the Christians for being "disturbers of the peace" and "outside agitators." But the Christians pressed on, in the conviction that they were "a colony of heaven," called to obey God rather than man. Small in number, they were big in commitment. They were too God-intoxicated to be "astronomically intimidated." By their effort and example they brought an end to such ancient evils as infanticide and gladiatorial contests.

41   Things are different now. So often the contemporary church is a weak, ineffectual voice with an uncertain sound. So often it is an archdefender of the status quo. Far from being disturbed by the presence of the church, the power structure of the average community is consoled by the church's silent—and often even vocal—sanction of things as they are.

42   But the judgment of God is upon the church as never before. If today's church does not recapture the sacrificial spirit of the early church, it will lose its authenticity, forfeit the loyalty of millions, and be dismissed as an irrelevant social club with no meaning for the twentieth century. Every day I meet young people whose disappointment with the church has turned into outright disgust.

43   Perhaps I have once again been too optimistic. Is organized religion too inextricably bound to the status quo to save our nation and the world? Perhaps I must turn my faith to the inner spiritual church, the church within the church, as the true *ekklesia* and the hope of the world. But again I am thankful to God that some noble souls from the ranks of organized religion have broken loose from the paralyzing chains of conformity and joined us as active partners in the struggle for freedom. They have left their secure congregations and walked the streets of Albany, Georgia, with us. They have gone down the highways of the South on tortuous rides for freedom. Yes, they have gone to jail with us. Some have been dismissed from their churches, have lost the support of their bishops and fellow ministers. But they have acted in the faith that right defeated is stronger than evil triumphant. Their witness has been the spiritual salt that has preserved the true meaning of

the gospel in these troubled times. They have carved a tunnel of hope through the dark mountain of disappointment.

44   I hope the church as a whole will meet the challenge of this decisive hour. But even if the church does not come to the aid of justice, I have no despair about the future. I have no fear about the outcome of our struggle in Birmingham, even if our motives are at present misunderstood. We will reach the goal of freedom in Birmingham and all over the nation, because the goal of America is freedom. Abused and scorned though we may be, our destiny is tied up with America's destiny. Before the pilgrims landed at Plymouth, we were here. Before the pen of Jefferson etched the majestic words of the Declaration of Independence across the pages of history, we were here. For more than two centuries our forebears labored in this country without wages; they made cotton king; they built the homes of their masters while suffering gross injustice and shameful humiliation—and yet out of a bottomless vitality they continued to thrive and develop. If the inexpressible cruelties of slavery could not stop us, the opposition we now face will surely fail. We will win our freedom because the sacred heritage of our nation and the eternal will of God are embodied in our echoing demands.

45   Before closing I feel impelled to mention one other point in your statement that has troubled me profoundly. You warmly commended the Birmingham police force for keeping "order" and "preventing violence." I doubt that you would have so warmly commended the police force if you had seen its dogs sinking their teeth into unarmed, nonviolent Negroes. I doubt that you would so quickly commend the policemen if you were to observe their ugly and inhumane treatment of Negroes here in the city jail; if you were to watch them push and curse old Negro women and young Negro girls; if you were to see them slap and kick old Negro men and young boys; if you were to observe them, as they did on two occasions, refuse to give us food because we wanted to sing our grace together. I cannot join you in your praise of the Birmingham police department.

46   It is true that the police have exercised a degree of discipline in handling the demonstrators. In this sense they have conducted themselves rather "nonviolently" in public. But for what purpose? To preserve the evil system of segregation. Over the past

few years I have consistently preached that nonviolence demands that the means we use must be as pure as the ends we seek. I have tried to make clear that it is wrong to use immoral means to attain moral ends. But now I must affirm that it is just as wrong, or perhaps even more so, to use moral means to preserve immoral ends. Perhaps Mr. Connor and his policemen have been rather nonviolent in public, as was Chief Pritchett in Albany, Georgia, but they have used the moral means of nonviolence to maintain the immoral end of racial injustice. As T. S. Eliot has said: "The last temptation is the greatest treason: To do the right deed for the wrong reason."

47   I wish you had commended the Negro sit-inners and demonstrators of Birmingham for their sublime courage, their willingness to suffer and their amazing discipline in the midst of great provocation. One day the South will recognize its real heroes. They will be the James Merediths, with the noble sense of purpose that enables them to face jeering and hostile mobs, and with the agonizing loneliness that characterizes the life of the pioneer. They will be old, oppressed, battered Negro women, symbolized in a seventy-two-year-old woman in Montgomery, Alabama, who rose up with a sense of dignity and with her people decided not to ride segregated buses, and who responded with ungrammatical profundity to one who inquired about her weariness: "My feets is tired, but my soul is at rest." They will be the young high school and college students, the young ministers of the gospel and a host of their elders, courageously and nonviolently sitting in at lunch counters and willingly going to jail for conscience' sake. One day the South will know that when these disinherited children of God sat down at lunch counters, they were in reality standing up for what is best in the American dream and for the most sacred values in our Judaeo-Christian heritage, thereby bringing our nation back to those great wells of democracy which were dug deep by the founding fathers in their formulation of the Constitution and the Declaration of Independence.

48   Never before have I written so long a letter. I'm afraid it is much too long to take your precious time. I can assure you that it would have been much shorter if I had been writing from a comfortable desk, but what else can one do when he is alone in a narrow jail cell, other than write long letters, think long thoughts and pray long prayers?

49   If I have said anything in this letter that overstates the truth and indicates an unreasonable impatience, I beg you to forgive me. If I have said anything that understates the truth and indicates my having a patience that allows me to settle for anything less than brotherhood, I beg God to forgive me.

50   I hope this letter finds you strong in the faith. I also hope that circumstances will soon make it possible for me to meet each of you, not as an integrationist or a civil-rights leader but as a fellow clergyman and a Christian brother. Let us all hope that the dark clouds of racial prejudice will soon pass away and the deep fog of misunderstanding will be lifted from our fear-drenched communities, and in some not too distant tomorrow the radiant stars of love and brotherhood will shine over our great nation with all their scintillating beauty.

Yours for the cause of Peace and Brotherhood,

Martin Luther King, Jr.

Barbara Kingsolver (1955–) has written all her life, but did not devote herself to full-time writing until 1987 with the publication of her first novel, The Bean Trees. *Before that, she held a striking variety of jobs—from artist's model to medical lab tech—as she traveled widely. She was born in Annapolis, Maryland, but was raised in Kentucky, spent several years traveling through Europe after graduating from DePauw University with a degree in biology, and then moved to Tucson, Arizona, where she stayed for over twenty-five years, completing graduate work in evolutionary biology, and eventually becoming a full-time author. King-solver has published poetry, short stories, novels, and essays. Her most recent work,* Animal, Vegetable, Miracle *(2007), chronicles her family's move from Tucson to rural Virginia and their efforts to grow and raise their own food. The two selections here, "High Tide in Tucson" and "The Spaces Between," are both from her essay collection,* High Tide in Tuc-son. *Kingsolver received the National Humanities Medal in 2000, Amer-ica's highest honor for service through the arts.*

High Tide in Tucson

Barbara Kingsolver

1   A hermit crab lives in my house. Here in the desert he's hiding out from local animal ordinances, at minimum, and maybe even the international laws of native-species transport. For sure, he's an outlaw against nature. So be it.

2   He arrived as a stowaway two Octobers ago. I had spent a week in the Bahamas, and while I was there, wishing my daughter could see those sparkling blue bays and sandy coves, I did exactly what she would have done: I collected shells. Spiky murexes, smooth purple moon shells, ancient-looking whelks sandblasted by the tide—I tucked them in the pockets of my shirt and shorts until my lumpy, suspect hemlines gave me away, like a refugee smuggling the family fortune. When it was time to go home, I rinsed my loot in the sink and packed it carefully into a plastic carton, then nested it deep in my suit-case for the journey to Arizona.

3   I got home in the middle of the night, but couldn't wait till morning to show my hand. I set the carton on the coffee table

for my daughter to open. In the dark living room her face glowed, in the way of antique stories about children and treasure. With perfect delicacy she laid the shells out on the table, counting, sorting, designating scientific categories like yellow-striped pinky, Barnacle Bill's pocketbook . . . Yeek! She let loose a sudden yelp, dropped her booty, and ran to the far end of the room. The largest, knottiest whelk had begun to move around. First it extended one long red talon of a leg, tap-tap-tapping like a blind man's cane. Then came half a dozen more red legs, plus a pair of eyes on stalks, and a purple claw that snapped open and shut in a way that could not mean We Come in Friendship.

4   Who could blame this creature? It had fallen asleep to the sound of the Caribbean tide and awakened on a coffee table in Tucson, Arizona, where the nearest standing water source of any real account was the municipal sewage-treatment plant.

5   With red stiletto legs splayed in all directions, it lunged and jerked its huge shell this way and that, reminding me of the scene I make whenever I'm moved to rearrange the living-room sofa by myself. Then, while we watched in stunned reverence, the strange beast found its bearings and began to reveal a determined, crabby grace. It felt its way to the edge of the table and eased itself over, not falling bang to the floor but hanging suspended underneath within the long grasp of its ice-tong legs, lifting any two or three at a time while many others still held in place. In this remarkable fashion it scrambled around the underside of the table's rim, swift and sure and fearless like a rock climber's dream.

6   If you ask me, when something extraordinary shows up in your life in the middle of the night, you give it a name and make it the best home you can.

7   The business of naming involved a grasp of hermit-crab gender that was way out of our league. But our household had a deficit of males, so my daughter and I chose Buster, for balance. We gave him a terrarium with clean gravel and a small cactus plant dug out of the yard and a big cockleshell full of tap water. All this seemed to suit him fine. To my astonishment our local pet store carried a product called Vitaminized Hermit Crab Cakes. Tempting enough (till you read the ingredients) but we passed, since our household leans more toward the recycling ethic. We

give him leftovers. Buster's rapture is the day I drag the unidentifiable things in cottage cheese containers out of the back of the fridge.

8   We've also learned to give him a continually changing assortment of seashells, which he tries on and casts off like Cinderella's stepsisters preening for the ball. He'll sometimes try to squeeze into ludicrous outfits too small to contain him (who can't relate?). In other moods, he will disappear into a conch the size of my two fists and sit for a day, immobilized by the weight of upward mobility. He is in every way the perfect housemate: quiet, entertaining, and willing to eat up the trash. He went to school for first-grade show-and-tell, and was such a hit the principal called up to congratulate me (I think) for being a broad-minded mother.

9   It was a long time, though before we began to understand the content of Buster's character. He required more patient observation than we were in the habit of giving to a small, cold-blooded life. As months went by, we would periodically notice with great disappointment that Buster seemed to be dead. Or not entirely dead, but ill, or maybe suffering the crab equivalent, of the blues. He would burrow into a gravelly corner, shrink deep into his shell, and not move, for days and days. We'd take him out to play, dunk him in water, offer him a new frock—nothing. He wanted to be still.

10   Life being what it is, we'd eventually quit prodding our sick friend to cheer up, and would move on to the next stage of a difficult friendship: neglect. We'd ignore him wholesale, only to realize at some point later on that he'd lapsed into hyperactivity. We'd find him ceaselessly patrolling the four corners of his world, turning over rocks, rooting out and dragging around truly disgusting pork-chop bones, digging up his cactus and replanting it on its head. At night when the household fell silent I would lie in bed listening to his methodical pebbly racket from the opposite end of the house. Buster was manic-depressive.

11   I wondered if he might be responding to the moon. I'm partial to lunar cycles, ever since I learned as a teenager that human females in their natural state—which is to say, sleeping outdoors—arrive at menses in synchrony and ovulate with the full moon. My imagination remains captive to that primordial village: the comradely grumpiness of new-moon days, when the

entire world at once would go on PMS alert. And the compensation that would turn up two weeks later on a wild wind, under that great round headlamp, driving both men and women to distraction with the overt prospect of conception. The surface of the land literally rises and falls—as much as fifty centimeters!—as the moon passes over, and we clay-footed mortals fall like dominoes before the swell. It's no surprise at all if a full moon inspires lyricists to corny love songs, or inmates to slamming themselves against barred windows. A hermit crab hardly seems this impetuous, but animals are notoriously responsive to the full moon: wolves howl; roosters announce daybreak all night. Luna moths, Arctic loons, and lunatics have a sole inspiration in common. Buster's insomniac restlessness seemed likely to be part of the worldwide full-moon fellowship.

12   But it wasn't, exactly. The full moon didn't shine on either end of his cycle, the high or the low. We tried to keep track, but it soon became clear: Buster marched to his own drum. The cyclic force that moved him remained as mysterious to us as his true gender and the workings of his crustacean soul.

13   Buster's aquarium occupies a spot on our kitchen counter right next to the coffeepot, and so it became my habit to begin mornings with chin in hands, pondering the oceanic mysteries while awaiting percolation. Finally, I remembered something. Years ago when I was a graduate student of animal behavior, I passed my days reading about the likes of animals' internal clocks. Temperature, photoperiod, the rise and fall of hormones—all these influences have been teased apart like so many threads from the rope that pulls every creature to its regulated destiny. But one story takes the cake. F. A. Brown, a researcher who is more or less the grandfather of the biological clock, set about in 1954 to track the cycles of intertidal oysters. He scooped his subjects from the clammy coast of Connecticut and moved them into the basement of a laboratory in landlocked Illinois. For the first fifteen days in their new aquariums, the oysters kept right up with their normal intertidal behavior: they spent time shut away in their shells, and time with their mouths wide open, siphoning their briny bath for the plankton that sustained them, as the tides ebbed and flowed on the distant Connecticut shore. In the next two weeks, they made a mystifying shift. They still carried out their cycles in unison,

and were regular as the tides, but their high-tide behavior did-n't coincide with high tide in Connecticut, or for that matter California, or any other tidal charts known to science. It dawned on the researchers after some calculations that the oysters were responding to high tide in Chicago. Never mind that the gentle mollusks lived in glass boxes in the basement of a steel-and-cement building. Nor that Chicago has no ocean. In the circumstances, the oysters were doing their best.

14   When Buster is running around for all he's worth, I can presume it's high tide in Tucson. With or without evidence, I'm romantic enough to believe it. This is the lesson of Buster, the poetry that camps outside the halls of science: Jump for joy, hallelujah. Even a desert has tides.

15   When I was twenty-two, I donned the shell of a tiny yellow Renault and drove with all I owned from Kentucky to Tucson. I was a typical young American, striking out. I had no earthly notion that I was bringing on myself a calamity of the magnitude of the one that befell poor Buster. I am the commonest kind of North American refugee: I believe I like it here, far-flung from my original home. I've come to love the desert that bristles and breathes and sleeps outside my windows. In the course of seventeen years I've embedded myself in a family here—neighbors, colleagues, friends I can't foresee living without, and a child who is native to this ground, with loves of her own. I'm here for good, it seems.

16   And yet I never cease to long in my bones for what I left behind. I open my eyes on every new day expecting that a creek will run through my backyard under broad-leafed maples, and that my mother will be whistling in the kitchen. Behind the howl of coyotes, I'm listening for meadowlarks. I sometimes ache to be rocked in the bosom of the blood relations and busybodies of my childhood. Particularly in my years as a mother without a mate, I have deeply missed the safety net of extended family.

17   In a city of half a million I still really look at every face, anticipating recognition, because I grew up in a town where every face meant something to me. I have trouble remembering to lock the doors. Wariness of strangers I learned the hard way.

When I was new to the city I let a man into my house one hot afternoon because he seemed in dire need of a drink of water; when I turned from the kitchen sink I found sharpened steel shoved against my belly. And so I know, I know. But I cultivate suspicion with as much difficulty as I force tomatoes to grow in the drought-stricken hardpan of my strange backyard. No creek runs here, but I'm still listening to secret tides, living as if I belonged to an earlier place: not Kentucky, necessarily, but a welcoming earth and a human family. A forest. A species.

18   In my life I've had frightening losses and unfathomable gifts: A knife in my stomach. The death of an unborn child. Sunrise in a rain forest. A stupendous column of blue butterflies rising from a Greek monastery. A car that spontaneously caught fire while I was driving it. The end of a marriage, followed by a year in which I could barely understand how to keep living. The discovery, just weeks ago when I rose from my desk and walked into the kitchen, of three strangers industriously relieving my house of its contents.

19   I persuaded the strangers to put down the things they were holding (what a bizarre tableau of anti-Magi they made, these three unwise men, bearing a camera, an electric guitar, and a Singer sewing machine), and to leave my home, pronto. My daughter asked excitedly when she got home from school, "Mom, did you say bad words?" (I told her this was the very occasion that bad words exist for.) The police said, variously, that I was lucky, foolhardy, and "a brave lady." But it's not good luck to be invaded, and neither foolish nor brave to stand your ground. It's only the way life goes, and I did it, just as years ago I fought off the knife; mourned the lost child; bore witness to the rain forest; claimed the blue butterflies as Holy Spirit in my private pantheon; got out of the burning car; survived the divorce by putting one foot in front of the other and taking good care of my child. On most important occasions, I cannot think how to respond, I simply do. What does it mean, anyway, to be an animal in human clothing? We carry around these big brains of ours like the crown jewels, but mostly I find that millions of years of evolution have prepared me for one thing only: to follow internal rhythms. To walk upright, to protect my loved ones, to cooperate with my family group—however broadly I care to define it—to do whatever will help us thrive. Obviously, some habits that saw us through the millennia are proving hazardous in a modern context: for example,

the yen to consume carbohydrates and fat whenever they cross our path, or the proclivity for unchecked reproduction. But it's surely worth forgiving ourselves these tendencies a little, in light of the fact that they are what got us here. Like Buster, we are creatures of inexplicable cravings. Thinking isn't every-thing. The way I stock my refrigerator would amuse a level-headed interplanetary observer, who would see I'm respond-ing not to real necessity but to the dread of famine honed in the African savannah. I can laugh at my Rhodesian Ridgeback as she furtively sniffs the houseplants for a place to bury bones, and circles to beat down the grass before lying on my kitchen floor. But she and I are exactly the same kind of hairpin.

20   We humans have to grant the presence of some past adapta-tions, even in their unforgivable extremes, if only to admit they are permanent rocks in the stream we're obliged to navigate. It's easy to speculate and hard to prove, ever, that genes control our behaviors. Yet we are persistently, excruciatingly adept at many things that seem no more useful to modern life than the tracking of tides in a desert. At recognizing insider/outsider status, for example, starting with white vs. black and grading straight into distinctions so fine as to baffle the bystander—Serb and Bosnian, Hutu and Tutsi, Crip and Blood. We hold that children learn discrimination from their parents, but they learn it fiercely and well, world without end. Recite it by rote like a multiplication table. Take it to heart, though it's neither helpful nor appropriate, any more than it is to hire the taller of two men applying for a position as bank clerk, though statisti-cally we're likely to do that too. Deference to the physical superlative, a preference for the scent of our own clan: a thou-sand anachronisms dance down the strands of our DNA from a hidebound tribal past, guiding us toward the glories of sur-vival, and some vainglories as well. If we resent being bound by these ropes, the best hope is to seize them out like snakes, by the throat, look them in the eye and own up to their venom.

21   But we rarely do, silly egghead of a species that we are. We invent the most outlandish intellectual grounds to justify dis-crimination. We tap our toes to chaste love songs about the sil-very moon without recognizing them as hymns to copulation. We can dress up our drives, put them in three-piece suits or ballet slippers, but still they drive us. The wonder of it is that our culture attaches almost unequivocal shame to our animal

nature, believing brute urges must be hurtful, violent things. But it's no less an animal instinct that leads us to marry (species that benefit from monogamy tend to practice it); to organize a neighborhood cleanup campaign (rare and doomed is the creature that fouls its nest); to improvise and enforce morality (many primates socialize their young to be cooperative and ostracize adults who won't share food).

22   It's starting to look as if the most shameful tradition of Western civilization is our need to deny we are animals. In just a few centuries of setting ourselves apart as landlords of the Garden of Eden, exempt from the natural order and entitled to hold dominion, we have managed to behave like so-called animals anyway, and on top of it to wreck most of what took three billion years to assemble. Air, water, earth, and fire—so much of our own element so vastly contaminated, we endanger our own future. Apparently we never owned the place after all. Like every other animal, we're locked into our niche: the mercury in the ocean, the pesticides on the soybean fields, all come home to our breastfed babies. In the silent spring we are learning it's easier to escape from a chain gang than a food chain. Possibly we will have the sense to begin a new century by renewing our membership in the Animal Kingdom.

23   Not long ago I went backpacking in the Eagle Tail Mountains. This range is a trackless wilderness in western Arizona that most people would call Godforsaken, taking for granted God's preference for loamy topsoil and regular precipitation. Whoever created the Eagle Tails had dry heat on the agenda, and a thing for volcanic rock. Also cactus, twisted mesquites, and five-alarm sunsets. The hiker's program in a desert like this is dire and blunt: carry in enough water to keep you alive till you can find a water source; then fill your bottles and head for the next one, or straight back out. Experts warn adventurers in this region, without irony, to drink their water while they're still alive, as it won't help later.

24   Several canyons looked promising for springs on our topographical map, but turned up dry. Finally, at the top of a narrow, overgrown gorge we found a blessed tinaja, a deep, shaded hollow in the rock about the size of four or five clawfoot tubs, holding water. After we drank our fill, my friends struck out again, but I opted to stay and spend the day in the

hospitable place that had slaked our thirst. On either side of the natural water tank, two shallow caves in the canyon wall faced each other, only a few dozen steps apart. By crossing from one to the other at noon, a person could spend the whole day here in shady comfort—or in colder weather, follow the winter sun. Anticipating a morning of reading, I pulled *Angle of Repose* out of my pack and looked for a place to settle on the flat, dusty floor of the west-facing shelter. Instead, my eyes were startled by a smooth corn-grinding stone. It sat in the exact center of its rock bowl, as if the Hohokam woman or man who used this mortar and pestle had walked off and left them there an hour ago. The Hohokam disappeared from the earth in A.D. 1450. It was inconceivable to me that no one had been here since then, but that may have been the case—that is the point of trackless wilderness. I picked up the grinding stone. The size and weight and smooth, balanced perfection of it in my hand filled me at once with a longing to possess it. In its time, this excellent stone was the most treasured thing in a life, a family, maybe the whole neighborhood. To whom it still belonged. I replaced it in the rock depression, which also felt smooth to my touch. Because my eyes now understood how to look at it, the ground under my feet came alive with worked flint chips and pottery shards. I walked across to the other cave and found its floor just as lively with historic debris. Hidden under brittlebush and cat-claw I found another grinding stone, this one some distance from the depression in the cave floor that once answered its pressure daily, for the grinding of corn or mesquite beans.

25   For a whole day I marveled at this place, running my fingers over the knife edges of dark flint chips, trying to fit together thick red pieces of shattered clay jars, biting my lower lip like a child concentrating on a puzzle. I tried to guess the size of whole pots from the curve of the broken pieces: some seemed as small as my two cupped hands, and some maybe as big as a bucket. The sun scorched my neck, reminding me to follow the shade across to the other shelter. Bees hummed at the edge of the water hole, nosing up to the water, their abdomens pulsing like tiny hydraulic pumps; by late afternoon they rimmed the pool completely, a collar of busy lace. Off and on, the lazy hand of a hot breeze shuffled the white leaves of the brittlebush. Once I looked up to see a screaming pair of red-tailed hawks mating in midair, and once a clatter of hooves warned me to

hold still. A bighorn ram emerged through the brush, his head
bent low under his hefty cornice, and ambled by me with nothing on his mind so much as a cool drink.

26   How long can a pestle stone lie still in the center of its mortar?
That long ago—that recently—people lived here. *Here*, exactly,
and not one valley over, or two, or twelve, because this place
had all a person needs: shelter, food, and permanent water.
They organized their lives around a catchment basin in a gran-
ite boulder, conforming their desires to the earth's charities;
they never expected the opposite. The stories I grew up with
lauded Moses for striking the rock and bringing forth the bub-
bling stream. But the stories of the Hohokam—oh, how they
must have praised that good rock.

27   At dusk my friends returned with wonderful tales of the
ground they had covered. We camped for the night, refilled our
canteens, and hiked back to the land of plumbing and a fair
guarantee of longevity. But I treasure my memory of the day I
lingered near water and covered no ground. I can't think of a
day in my life in which I've had such a clear fix on what it
means to be human.

28   *Want* is a thing that unfurls unbidden like fungus, opening
large upon itself, stopless, filling the sky. But *needs*, from one
day to the next, are few enough to fit in a bucket, with room
enough left to rattle like brittlebush in a dry wind.

29   For each of us—furred, feathered, or skinned alive—the whole
earth balances on the single precarious point of our own survival. In the best of times I hold in mind the need to care for
things beyond the self: poetry, humanity, grace. In other times,
when it seems difficult merely to survive and be happy about
it, the condition of my thought tastes as simple as this: let me
be a good animal today. I've spent months at a stretch, even
years, with that taste in my mouth, and have found that it
serves.

30   But it seems a wide gulf to cross, from the raw, green passion
for survival to the dispassionate, considered state of human
grace. How does the animal mind construct a poetry for the
modern artifice in which we now reside? Often I feel as dis-
oriented as poor Buster, unprepared for the life that zooms

headlong past my line of sight. This clutter of human para-
phernalia and counterfeit necessities—what does it have to do
with the genuine business of life on earth? It feels strange to
me to be living in a box, hiding from the steadying influence
of the moon; wearing the hide of a cow, which is supposed to
be dyed to match God-knows-what, on my feet; making
promises over the telephone about things I will do at a precise
hour next *year*. (I always feel the urge to add, as my grandmother does, "Lord willing and the creeks don't rise!") I find
it impossible to think, with a straight face, about what colors
ought not to be worn after Labor Day. I can become hysterical
over the fact that someone, somewhere, invented a thing
called the mushroom scrubber, and that many other people
undoubtedly feel they *need* to possess one. It's completely
usual for me to get up in the morning, take a look around, and
laugh out loud.

31   Strangest of all, I am carrying on with all of this in a desert, two
thousand miles from my verdant childhood home. I am disembodied. No one here remembers how I was before I grew to my
present height. I'm called upon to reinvent my own childhood
time and again; in the process, I wonder how I can ever know
the truth about who I am. If someone had told me what I was
headed for in that little Renault—that I was stowing away in a
shell, bound to wake up to an alien life on a persistently foreign
shore—I surely would not have done it. But no one warned me.
My culture, as I understand it, values independence above all
things—in part to ensure a mobile labor force, grease for the
machine of a capitalist economy. Our fairy tale commands: Little Pig, go out and seek your fortune! So I did.

32   Many years ago I read that the Tohono O'odham, who dwell in
the deserts near here, traditionally bury the umbilicus of a
newborn son or daughter somewhere close to home and plant
a tree over it, to hold the child in place. In a sentimental frame
of mind, I did the same when my own baby's cord fell off. I'm
staring at the tree right now, as I write—a lovely thing grown
huge outside my window, home to woodpeckers, its boughs
overarching the house, as dissimilar from the sapling I planted
seven years ago as my present life is from the tidy future I'd
mapped out for us all when my baby was born. She will roam
light-years from the base of that tree. I have no doubt of it. I can
only hope she's growing as the tree is, absorbing strength and

rhythms and a trust in the seasons, so she will always be able
to listen for home.

33   I feel remorse about Buster's monumental relocation; it's a
weighty responsibility to have thrown someone else's life into
permanent chaos. But as for my own, I can't be sorry I made
the trip. Most of what I learned in the old place seems to suffice for the new: if the seasons like Chicago tides come at
ridiculous times and I have to plant in September instead of
May, and if I have to make up family from scratch, what matters is that I do have sisters and tomato plants, the essential
things. Like Buster, I'm inclined to see the material backdrop of
my life as mostly immaterial, compared with what moves
inside of me. I hold on to my adopted shore, chanting private
vows: wherever I am let me never forget to distinguish *want*
from *need*. Let me be a good animal today. Let me dance in the
waves of my private tide, the habits of survival and love.

34   Every one of us is called upon, probably many times, to start a
new life. A frightening diagnosis, a marriage, a move, loss of a
job or a limb or a loved one, a graduation, bringing a new baby
home: it's impossible to think at first how this all will be possible. Eventually, what moves it all forward is the subterranean
ebb and flow of being alive among the living.

35   In my own worst seasons I've come back from the colorless
world of despair by forcing myself to look hard for a long time
at a single glorious thing: a flame of red geranium outside my
bedroom window. And then another: my daughter in a yellow
dress. And another: the perfect outline of a full, dark sphere
behind the crescent moon. Until I learned to be in love with my
life again. Like a stroke victim retraining new parts of the brain
to grasp lost skills, I have taught myself joy, over and over
again.

36   It's not such a wide gulf to cross, then, from survival to poetry.
We hold fast to the old passions of endurance that buckle and
creak beneath us, dovetailed, tight as a good wooden boat to
carry us onward. And onward full tilt we go, pitched and
wrecked and absurdly resolute, driven in spite of everything
to make good on a new shore. To be hopeful, to embrace one
possibility after another—that is surely the basic instinct.
Baser even than hate, the thing with teeth, which can be stilled
with a tone of voice or stunned by beauty. If the whole world
of the living has to turn on the single point of remaining alive,

that pointed endurance is the poetry of hope. The thing with feathers.

37   What a stroke of luck. What a singular brute feat of outrageous fortune: to be born to citizenship in the Animal Kingdom. We love and we lose, go back to the start and do it right over again. For every heavy forebrain solemnly cataloging the facts of a harsh landscape, there's a rush of intuition behind it crying out: High tide! Time to move out into the glorious debris. Time to take this life for what it is.

The Spaces Between

Barbara Kingsolver

1   The drive from Tucson to Phoenix is a trip through merciless desert, where tall saguaros throw up their arms in apparent surrender to the encroaching cotton fields. Some of the land belongs to farmers holding tight to a parched midwestern dream; some belongs to the state of Arizona, mainly because nobody in particular ever bothered to want it. And a big chunk of what we were passing through belongs to the Gila River Reserve, the state's oldest Indian reservation, though nothing I could see from the highway set those particular cacti and irrigated farmlands apart from the rest, as Indian country.

2   Because Camille was five, and liked to know what to expect at all times, I reminded her that we were on our way to visit the Heard Museum, which was all about Native Americans. "Indians," I clarified. "You know who Indians are, right?"

3   "Sure," she said. "People that lived a long time ago."

4   I felt between my shoulder blades the weight of this familiar frustration. We were driving past fields being tended this very morning, presumably, by Maricopa and Pima Indians. My daughter played routinely with children from other nations including the Tohono O'odham and Yaqui. She had been a guest at their dances and passed almost daily through the Yaqui village that lies between our house and town. But five-year-olds will hear what you tell them, and merrily go right on believing what they *see*. Movies and storybooks say that Indians lived long ago, period, and there's so little else for a modern child to go on.

5   As a woman with some Cherokee ancestors on my father's side and a blonde, blue-eyed daughter, I find it impossible to pin down the meaning of ethnicity. It's an especially delicate business here in the Southwest, where so many of us boil in one pot without much melting. We're never allowed to forget we are foreign bodies in the eyes of our neighbors. The annual Winter Holiday Concert at Camille's school features a bright patchwork of languages and rituals, each of which must be learned

198

by a different subset of kids, the others having known it since they could talk. It sounds idyllic, but then spend half an hour on the playground and you're also likely to come away with a whole new vocabulary of racial slurs. On the playground no one's counting the strengths of your character, nor the woman your great-grandfather married, unless her genes have dyed your hair and fixed your features. It's the face on your passport that gets you in. Faces that set us apart, in separate houses.

6   When I pack up my child and head off to a place like the Heard Museum, it's not to claim some piece of our own lost heritage. I have only an inkling of my forebears, and they represent more worlds than I could claim: Scottish stonemasons; Portuguese sailors; farmers from the Eastern Band of Cherokee; planters and sharecroppers and hapless conscripts to both sides of the Civil War. They died without passing on to me the secrets of constructing a limestone chimney flue, navigating by the stars, or planting by the moon. Half the living souls in the southeastern U.S., it seems, claim to be descended from Sacajawea, and that is their business, but I'm not so interested in bloodlines as motivation for multicultural appreciation. I appreciate because I'm interested, just as I can admire tropical fish without being part fish. (And if I *am* part fish, that is *my* business.) We go to the Heard out of love for the great elaborate world, and also to feel more at home in our own neighborhood. I want my child to be so completely familiar with differences that she'll ignore *difference* per se and really see what she's looking at. When she looks at an Acoma water jar, I don't want her to think less of it because it was made by hand in a nonelectrified village high on a mesa. Neither do I want her to think it is the rarefied relic of saints. It seems odd to have to add the latter, but lately we've been besieged with a new, bizarre form of racism that sets apart all things Native American as object of either worship or commerce, depending on your proclivities. It's scary enough to see Kokopelli on a keychain—God for sale, under five dollars—but I'm not much more comfortable with the other angle, the sweat-lodge suburbanites who borrow the material trappings of native ceremonies as a spiritual quickie to offset the stresses of corporate life. What began as anthropology has escalated to fad, and it strikes me that assigning magical power to a culture's every belief and by-product is simply another way of setting those people apart. It's more benign than burning crosses on lawns, for sure, but ultimately not much more humane.

7   An equal in our time and place is someone with an address and
     friends, who works and plays and buys groceries in packages
     with brand names, who is capable of both nobility and mis-
     takes. People who are picture perfect, magical, untouchable, or
     worse yet, only historic, do not need equal opportunity or edu-
     cational grants.

8   An Acoma water jar is just a useful thing, really. Like a soda
     pop can, only beautiful.

9   The Heard Museum stands today because of a hobby that grew
     out of hand. Dwight and Maie Bartlett Heard settled in the pio-
     neer town of Phoenix in 1895, and long before it was fashion-
     able or provident, they found an absorbing interest in the cul-
     ture of Arizona's Native peoples. By the 1920s, their collection
     of artifacts had grown too large and valuable as a community
     resource to keep on the parlor shelves. Steadily and gently,
     over more than half a century, the Heard has grown to be one
     of the world's great centers of Native American heritage.

10   The entry courtyard welcomed us with the grace of white-
     washed arches, orange trees, and weathered *metates*—corn-
     grinding stones—hunched on the basket-weave brick floor.
     Mary Brennan, communications coordinator for the museum,
     met us there, and explained the museum's mission of appreci-
     ation for Native people and their culture, especially those of
     the Southwest. This is not a museum only of artifacts, she
     pointed out, but of modern Native American life, expressed
     through both traditional and fine arts. Museum programs
     bring Native American artists and dancers into schools, for
     example. Later today there would be a dance performance in
     the museum auditorium.

11   I was glad the museum's directors undertook this as part of
     their mission: to counter the prevailing notion that Indians
     made nice pots and shot buffalo and now are dead. I silently
     wished them luck.

12   Camille and I were immediately drawn to the wing called "Old
     Ways, New Ways," a permanent interactive exhibit where kids
     (and adults, if they're game) can learn to play a drum under the
     videotaped tutelage of a Kiowa elder, and use a computer to
     design a Navajo rug, and find enough other adventures to fill

an afternoon, easily. I stood with a crew of teenagers at a display showing how the ancient Anasazi fashioned little willow-twig animals that archaeologists frequently find tucked into high crevices in the Grand Canyon. Earnestly we all followed instructions, wrapping and looping our twigs to make horses. Mine looked like a giraffe. I stuffed it deep down in my pocket, wondering if maybe the Anasazi stuck *their* failures into those out-of-the-way crevices for the same reason, and kept the good ones around for the kids to play with.

13   Camille had better luck fitting wooden forms together to make a Tlingit mural. I stood behind her, watching how two simple shapes—a blunt oval and a curly U-shape—repeat over and over in all the familiar totem-pole aggregations of owl and raven and whale, adding up to that instantly recognizable gestalt of the art of Inuit and other northern tribes. If I hadn't seen it taken apart and reassembled, I would never have understood this amazing principle.

14   I've always felt half-blind in places where I couldn't touch anything. I find I need to assess textures, and pick things up to see how they're put together; I am far more likely than my child to get in trouble for doing so. Camille has escorted me out of many a china shop. Once, in a Japanese park, I reached out and touched a palace wall because I couldn't identify its material by sight, and wanted to know whether it was stucco or stone; my finger set off great honking alarms and brought a police car up the gravel path. (The lovely signs in Japanese, which I'd taken for part of the decor, apparently said TOUCH THIS AND DIE, HUMBLE TOURIST!) It's true we're a sight-biased species, but still it seems odd that museums that aim to instruct us about a multisensory world tend to convey their information entirely through sight, and maybe a little sound. In such places I generally feel like a child, not quite worthy of the material I'm meant to admire; in the children's wing of the Heard, oddly enough, I felt more respected.

15   Every part of the museum begged for our attention. The main gallery's permanent collection of ancient and modern Native arts are displayed as a living continuum. The entry is a spare, dark auditorium; in a continuous audiovisual loop, Hopi and Tohono O'odham and Dine people talk directly to the camera about their children and grandparents, their villages, their history, their funerals and blessing ceremonies. Their verbal

portraits fall against shifting images of their lives' dramatic backgrounds: the Grand Canyon, Taos Pueblo, saguaros with their arms in the air.

16   The words of an unidentified Taos Pueblo man are inscribed on the wall of the gallery's entrance: "We have lived upon this land from days beyond history's record, far past any living memory, deep into the time of legend. The story of my people and the story of this place are one single story."

17   Who else could make this claim? In North America, no one. All American tribes other than the Pueblo have been forced off their home ground, and everyone else migrated here from another hemisphere. The gallery is designed, I think, to stop in our tracks those of us who take transience for granted. It tells an extraordinary tale of human landscapes cradled and shaped by physical ones. Tall photographic murals show the lay of the land, and the exhibits explain life, history, and survival in these beautiful, severe places. The objects of art in the collection are exquisite, but that is not the point, for all of us have surely seen disembodied pots and baskets in a glass case. Here, those objects lie together with the matrix of their origins: the colors of Colorado mud and stone, the need for transporting water, the human passion for both survival and beauty. Baskets that celebrate the whispering colors of grass and the designs of the human heart. Wool blankets, woven from a pastoral life supported by sheep and a reverence for Spider Woman, the mother of weaving. Blankets so beautiful they are coveted by people a world away, who can hardly imagine the sound of bleating sheep in a bone-dry canyon.

18   The spaghetti-western caricature of "Indian" had been slipping away from us all day, but it was erased once and for all for Camille, I think, by the houses. We got to walk into fastidious replicas of a Zuni pueblo adobe, a Northwest Coast long house, and a Dine hogan. I've driven many times through the Navajo reservation in northeastern Arizona and looked longingly at these low, eight-sided, cozy-looking log hogans, whose chimneys poke through the center of the roofs to trail thin, blue-gray signals into the desert sky. I have even stopped by these homes to ask directions, but was never invited in. And now I found one here, dismantled and reassembled in the middle of a gallery. Camille and I went in and sat on a plank bench with our backs to the hewn logs, letting our eyes adjust to dimmer

light, admiring the way the home's roundness accommodates both function and the human need to feel hugged. On the woodstove in the center sat an iron kettle, waiting (a long time) to cook the next mutton stew. Camille poked through the assortment of bare necessities arranged in an open shelf, and touched the traditional velvet shirts and gathered skirts on coat hangers hung from nails in the wall. She talked as she went, and I was surprised to hear her taking up her own hogan fantasy. "If I meet a Navajo girl in school, maybe she'll invite me home with her and we can sleep on the floor on sheepskins like these."

19 I got it: my daughter is beginning to believe, truly, that Navajos are people who still walk the earth. They are potential school pals.

20 Just then, a woman in a sequined sweatshirt ducked in through the doorway, glanced up at the low roof, and remarked before ducking out again, "Boy, they must have been *short* back then."

21 To write novels, to design a museum, to teach fourth-graders about history—all these enterprises require the interpretation of other lives. And all of them, historically, have been corrupted by privileges of race, class, and gender. The Heard, and places like it, are paddling upstream from the get-go simply by calling themselves "museum." We go there expecting dead things, explained in flat, condescending voices.

22 "Books," as a category of papery things with the scent of mildew, are paddling up the same stream. I spent plenty of my young womanhood resenting the fact that nearly all the fictional women I'd ever read about were the inventions of men (and that I'd learned about female sexuality from D. H. Lawrence!). But I'm old enough now to stand in the shadow of my former brilliance and face incertitude: would the world really be a better place if Mr. Tolstoy had not invented Anna Karenina, or Mr. Flaubert his Emma Bovary?

23 More to the point: who, exactly, is entitled to write about the *relationships* between women and men? Hermaphrodites? This is the dilemma upon whose horns I've built my house: I want to know, and to write, about the places where disparate points of view rub together—the spaces between. Not just between man and woman but also North and South; white

and not-white; communal and individual; spiritual and car-
nal. I can think of no genetic or cultural credentials that could
entitle a writer to do this—only a keen ear, empathy, caution,
willingness to be criticized, and a passionate attraction to the
subject.

24 Of these I can claim in adequate measure only the last; I'm
drawn like a kid to mud into the sticky terrain of cultural difference. How wondrous, it seems to me, that someone else can
live on the same round egg of a world that I do but explain it
differently—how it got here, and what's to be done with it.
How remarkable that other people's stories often sound more
true to me than my own.

25 I've been advised from all quarters about my obligations as a
writer in the multicultural domain. I have been told explicitly,
in fact, both that I should write *more* and *less* (or even *not at all*)
about nearly every category of persons imaginable, including
men, women, people with disabilities, Asians, Armenians,
Native Americans. Fortunately I'm not a short-order cook,
because whenever I get lobbed rapid-fire with commands my
tendency is to go find a quieter place.

26 What seems right to me from my quieter place is to represent
the world I can see and touch as honestly as I know how, and
when writing fiction, to use that variegated world as a matrix
for the characters and conflicts I need to fathom. I can't speak
in tongues I don't understand, and so there are a thousand
tales I'll never tell: the waging of war; coming of age as a man;
childhood on an Indian reservation. But when the wounded
veteran, the masculine disposition, and the reservation child
come into the place where I live, they enter my story. I will
watch closely and report on the conversation. A magnificent
literary tool is the dramatic point of view; one of its great vir-
tuosos was John Steinbeck. Without ever pretending to know
"female" or "Mexican laborer" or "mentally retarded" from
the inside, he rendered those characters perfectly from the outside. Through reading Steinbeck I first realized this precious
truth: bearing witness is not the same as possession.

27 Godspeed the right of each of us to speak for ourselves and
not be spoken for, but I cannot suffer a possessiveness of stories. When I was nine years old, our town librarian wore
broad black picture hats and deeply disliked the idea of children rummaging through her books. I drove her to palsy by

checking out every book and dusty pamphlet she had on
Cherokee lore, even those she felt God had intended for the
Boy Scouts. She told me I would ruin my eyes with so much
reading, and hinted my character was headed down the tubes
as well. Too late; long before I discovered Cherokee lore, I felt
in a certain light that animals could talk. I believed in trees,
and that heaven had something to do with how dead trees
gentle themselves into long, mossy columns of bright-
smelling, crumbling earth, lively inside with sprouting seeds
and black beetles. I could not make myself believe in a loud-
voiced, bearded God on his throne in the clouds, but I was
moved to tears by the compost pile.

28   No wonder I perturbed the librarian. But her fearful assess-
ment of my soul was inexact. I wasn't studying up to be Cherokee; this would hardly have occurred to me. I loved stories
about Wild Boy and the waterbug who discovered the world,
not because I wanted to become a different kind of person, but
because these stories delighted the heart of the person I already
was. And they do still. For my particular brand of pantheism I
don't need to affect beads and feathers. I can go to the woods
in my jeans and sweatshirt and find grace, without a sweat
lodge. I can also fling myself on the floor and spend whole
afternoons with my volumes of Joseph Campbell, by accident,
when I only meant to be passing by the bookshelf on my way
to something productive. I'm not studying up to be Neolithic,
I just need those cave paintings and creation stories. I could
live without electricity if I had to, but not without stories.

29   *Other people's* stories—those are the ones I crave. Not Adam
and Eve, designated owners of the garden who get to plunder
it and spit it out as they please. Not Noah with his precarious
ark, who has set upon us the wrongheaded notion that preserving two specimens of something in a zoo somewhere is all
we need of biodiversity. Not the stories I already know, but the
ones I haven't heard yet: the ones that will show me a way out
of here. The point is not to emulate other lives, or usurp their
wardrobes. The point is to find sense. How is a child to find the
way to her own beliefs, unless she can stuff her pockets with all
the truths she can find—whether she finds them on a library
shelf or in a friend's warm, strange-smelling kitchen. The point
is for playground slurs to fall dead on her ears, meaningless as
locks on an open door. I want to imagine those doors not just

open but gone, lying in the dirt, thrown off their hinges by the force of accord in a house of open passage.

30   Eddie Swimmer stood before us in the auditorium, dressed in moccasins and beaded clothes and a porcupine-hair headdress, explaining the songs and dances. "These songs might all sound to you like 'Hey-ya, hey-ya,' but they're not. Listen. These are words in our languages." Camille and I sat licking our fingers, which were sticky with honey from the Indian fry bread we bought from the concession table at the back. We listened to the singers and watched Eddie do a grass dance, which, in the old days on the plains, had the polite function of stomping down the tall grass before a powwow. Then we watched Derek Davis do the fancy-dance—a fast, difficult type of dancing popular on the modern powwow circuit. Derek's elaborate costume had a beaded breastplate and headdress and showy feather bustles, all put together by members of his family. He pointed out the modern additions: metal bells instead of deer hooves; breechcloths made bright with commercial dyes instead of berries and roots. He was pleased with these improvements, unconcerned about a collector's notion of authenticity. He is a living dancer, a young man in wire-rim glasses and a lot of muscles, definitely not a museum piece. The kids selling fry bread and soft drinks hooted their approval as he began to dance, and when he finished we were all out of breath.

31   On the way home I asked Camille again, "So, okay, tell me. Who are the Native Americans?"

32   We'd stayed until closing time, seven hours, a possible world record for museum-going five-year-olds. She spoke sleepily from a horizontal position in the backseat. "They're people who love the earth, and like to sing and dance, and make a lot of pretty stuff to use."

33   She was quiet for a while, then added, "And I think they like soda pop. Those guys selling the fry bread were drinking a lot of Cokes."

34   Heaven and earth rejoice. Good enough for now.

*M*artin Malone (1950–) is a professor and former chair of the Department of Sociology at Mount Saint Mary's University. He received
a B.A. (New York University) and an M.A. (Southern Illinois University)
in anthropology, and a Ph.D. (Indiana University) in sociology. He has
taught at Mount Saint Mary's since 1985. Malone has published books
and scholarly articles on cultural anthropology, sociology, and linguistics,
including Toward Explaining Human Culture, with David Levinson
(1980), and Worlds of Talk: The Presentation of Self in Everyday
Conversation (1997). His most recent research involves a long-term
interview project on body image and the sociology of appearance. This project explores how ideas of beauty are tied to ideas about character. He lives
in Gettysburg, Pennsylvania, with his wife, Jane.

A World without Borders: The Curse of Living in Interesting Times

Martin J. Malone

1. Introduction

1   Mount Saint Mary's is a place that prizes interdisciplinary
thinking, and I have always valued the opportunity it provides
to talk to people outside of my own intellectual territory. I
think we may be a model for the world we need to create: one
in which we can comfortably talk to and understand people
who do not share our own backgrounds or assumptions and
beliefs.

2   This essay goes beyond the boundaries of my own academic
specialty, sociology, and perhaps poaches a bit on the territory
of my neighbors in economics and political science. I hope my
colleagues in those fields will excuse my trespassing and also
be a bit understanding if I demonstrate my outsider's lack of
expertise. While I am an immigrant to these regions, I am not
without papers.

This essay was originally delivered as the Distinguished Faculty Address
at the Honors Convocation on April 30, 2006.

3   We are living at a time when the nature of work, family, com-
     munity, religion, and politics are all being profoundly changed,
     and no one fully understands what is happening. The world's
     markets never sleep. Computers, the Worldwide Web, email,
     and cell phones mean that we may be on call 24 hours a day.
     Families, increasingly broken and blended, compete with work
     and organized leisure for time to share a meal or just a conver-
     sation. Some scholars have claimed that these changes have
     meant that voluntary organizations, whether bowling leagues,
     book clubs, or the Elks, or Rotary, or Kiwanis, are slowly dis-
     appearing, and in their absence, communities are losing their
     sense of a local identity (Putnam 2000). Churches are going
     begging for priests, nuns, and ministers, and it is becoming
     increasingly expensive to run for political office.

4   Nations are too small to solve the big problems and too big to
     solve the small ones. Some have said we may be witnessing
     "the withering away of nation-states" and this has produced a
     "new world disorder" (Bauman 1998, 57), in which no one is
     any longer in control. The revival of local and ethnic identi-
     ties—long suppressed by the Cold War—has reshaped the
     world in unanticipated ways—from Bosnia to Chechnya to
     Eritrea and Kurdistan (Giddens 2000, 31). These changes are
     often lumped together under the term **globalization.**

2. A World without Borders—Money

5   Computers and communication technology have made the
     world significantly smaller and economies are more tightly
     intertwined than ever before. Instantaneous electronic commu-
     nication means that government regulation of the movement of
     capital has become almost impossible. One author describes
     globalization with the evocative image of:

> A wondrous new machine that reaps as it destroys. . . . Huge and
> mobile, like modern agricultural machinery. It runs over open ter-
> rain ignoring familiar boundaries. As it goes it throws off enor-
> mous mows of wealth and bounty while it leaves behind great
> furrows of wreckage. (Greider 1997: 11)

6   He says that while there are skillful hands on board, **no one is
     at the wheel.** In fact there is no wheel or any internal governor
     to control speed or direction. It is sustained by its own forward
     motion, guided by its own appetites, **and it is accelerating.**

7   In this context, *New York Times* foreign affairs correspondent
     Thomas Freidman has coined the term "the electronic herd," to
     refer to the "anonymous stock, bond and currency traders, and
     multinational investors" who move trillions of dollars a day
     around the planet at the click of a mouse (2000, 112). Currency
     traders alone move between $1 and $3 trillion per day (Pro-
     Forex.com). In the Asian economic crisis of 1997 and 1998, the
     governments of Thailand, and Indonesia, and later Russia and
     Brazil, discovered that unhappy investors could pull billions
     out of their economies in an instant.

8   The arguments about the costs and benefits of globalization
     are complex. The reports of absolute numbers of people raised
     out of poverty by globalization are often misleading. The last
     twenty years have witnessed economic miracles in China and
     India, but the same successes have not been repeated in much
     of the rest of the world. Because China and India make up
     more than a third of the world's six and a half billion people,
     their successes tend to obscure less positive news from other
     parts of the world. While extreme poverty (less than $1.00 per
     capita per day) has dropped precipitously in China (from 58
     percent to 15 percent) and significantly in India (from 52 per-
     cent to 31 percent), it has actually gone up in Eastern Europe,
     Central Asia, and Sub-Saharan Africa (where it is now almost
     50 percent) and has remained constant (at about 10 percent) in
     Latin America (Sachs 2005, 20–25).

9   Overall, the world's wealth is becoming increasingly unevenly
     distributed. Thirty years ago, the people of the so-called devel-
     oped world (North America, Western Europe, Japan, and Aus-
     tralia), who comprised the wealthiest 20 percent of the popula-
     tion, were 30 times better off than the poorest 20 percent. Today
     we are 82 times better off. The wealthiest countries control 86
     cents of every dollar of the world's wealth. The poorest 20 per-
     cent have about 1 cent. The combined wealth of the world's
     three richest people—Bill Gates (Microsoft), Carlos Slim Helú
     (Mexican wireless telephone company Movil), and Warren Buf-
     fet (Berkshire Hathaway, investments), (roughly $161.5 billion
     as of February 2007)—is greater than the 48 poorest countries
     in the world (a quarter of the world's countries) (Shah 2006).
     This widening gap is a specter that will haunt our lives and
     make political stability impossible.

10   But this poverty is not an inevitable or even an intractable
      problem. We also live in a world in which it is realistic to
      imagine that poverty can be eradicated—and in a relatively
      short time span. If the developed countries doubled their
      financial assistance to poor countries, **we could halve pover-
      ty and hunger in eight years—by 2015, and eliminate
      extreme poverty by 2025,** according to the Columbia Univer-
      sity economist, Jeffrey Sachs, whose book, *The End of Poverty,*
      lays out the necessary, and not especially difficult, steps that
      can remake the face of the world (347–368).

11   But he reminds us that we still live in a world where more
      than a billion people live on less than one dollar a day, where
      hundreds of thousands die of starvation, malnutrition, and
      treatable diseases like malaria, and where tens of millions of
      children die in infancy. In this context, the United States gives
      about $15 billion a year in foreign aid, about one-eighth of
      one percent of our Gross Domestic Product,[1] and about one-
      thirtieth of the Pentagon budget.

3.   A World without Border—People and Politics

12   Globalization is not only about the money. These economic
      changes have had interesting and unanticipated political
      effects. As nation-states lose political power, they are less able
      to control their own multi-ethnic populations. We are more and
      more living in a world that historian Eric Hobsbawm says is
      soon likely to consist of the twenty-first century equivalents of
      Saxe-Coburg-Gotha and Schwarzburg-Sonderhausen, the tiny
      principalities that were later incorporated into the German
      nation (Bauman 1998, 64).

13   If you think this sounds unlikely, think about how many new
      countries have been born since 1989 or how likely the many
      struggling and civil-war-torn African republics are to stay
      united. And finally, at your most optimistic, think about
      whether you really believe that Iraq will continue as a single
      nation-state.

14   Thirteen years ago, Harvard political scientist Samuel Hunt-
      ington published his influential essay, "The Clash of Civiliza-
      tions" (1993) in which he said that the post-Cold War conflicts
      would be cultural, instead of political. Given today's war on
      Islamist terror, many, especially cultural conservatives, find

his analysis prophetic, while many on the cultural and political left find his sweeping claims inaccurate since they have not in fact predicted what has happened. For example, when the U.S. and NATO intervened in Bosnia, it was on the side of Muslim Bosnians against Serbian Christians, exactly the opposite of what Huntington predicted. Similarly, secular but Muslim Turkey is more likely to soon become part of the European Union (EU), rather than part of the Islamist movement (Lechner and Boli 2005, 200*ff.*). But it is also true, as Huntington predicted, that we are now living in a world in which, to everyone's great surprise, ethnicity and religion are playing a much larger role than they have for the last 500 years.

15 Not only are international borders disappearing, as in the EU, where travel is now similar to interstate travel in the U.S., but even the borders that still exist and are heavily policed are no longer very secure, as in our own southern border. And more guards and more fences and more punishment will have no effect on making that border any less porous. In the last twenty years we have increased the number of border patrol officers from 2,500 to 12,000 and have increased that agency's budget from $200 million to $1.6 billion, but the number of undocumented immigrants (adjusted for population growth) has remained relatively constant (Massey 2006).

16 In 2001, there were more than 160 million people (2.5 percent of the world's population) living and working outside of the country of their birth. That was up from 120 million in just 1990 (Eitzen 2006, 45). We can pass all the laws we like, but the economic realities of Latin America and the United States mean that people will come because there is work here and not there. Economists refer to these forces as "push and pull factors." People are both pushed out of their homes because there are no jobs nearby, and pulled north where there are jobs. Mexican migrant workers send $20 billion a year home to their families. That fact alone is more powerful than fences or laws. The same is true in Western Europe, where African, Middle Eastern and Eastern European immigrants are arriving in record numbers.

4. So How Are We to Live and Work in this World?

17 We used to think that only blue-collar manufacturing jobs were disappearing. You probably know that most of the clothes you are wearing were made in Bangladesh or Honduras or the

Philippines or somewhere else in the developing world. We also thought white-collar jobs that involved "knowledge work," the work done by the highly trained graduates of our colleges and universities, were safe (Reich 1991). But much of that work is now being done in India and Thailand and South Korea. Computer engineers working in Bangalore, India, who make $10,000, are inevitably going to replace Silicon Valley engineers, who make $150,000. In 2003, Indian accountants prepared 25,000 tax returns for Americans. In 2005, they did 400,000. CAT scans and MRIs are already in digital form so it is a simple matter to send them halfway around the world (to India or Australia) where they can be read by radiologists paid one-tenth of what Americans get, and the time difference means we will get overnight results (Friedman 2005, 13–16). Any work that can be routinized and broken down into small parts will be outsourced.

18 So what are we to do to prepare for a future that is not just close, but here right now? The simple answer—though it is important to remember that simple and easy are not the same thing—is that we all, not just eighteen-year-olds, but those of us in our thirties, forties, fifties, and older, need to learn to live in a world surrounded by difference, surrounded by new and unfamiliar ways of doing things. It is not just about realizing that for most people college is not the end of their education; that most will almost certainly be back in school in not too many years. It is also about the realization that we no longer make the rules for the rest of the world. In our lifetimes, China and India will be immensely more powerful and more important and more central to our lives than they already are. At today's growth rates (2006: 3.1 percent for the U.S., 9.0 percent for China), the size of China's economy will surpass ours in 2014, just seven years from now. And in 2050, India will be the largest country in the world, with an estimated 1.6 billion people (CIA 2005).

5. Suggestions for Work

19 We are moving back to an era of large numbers of immigrants—much like the early twentieth century. This is unavoidable. The wealthiest countries all have aging populations and there is demographic pressure from poorer countries. Immigrants are pushed out of their jobless homelands and pulled

into the wealthy countries that need labor. The developed world is rapidly becoming more multicultural. Not only does globalization mean that McDonalds and MTV are found throughout the world. It also means that in many American cities English may be the minority language and pale skin the minority appearance. Immigrants are not just working on farms in California or driving taxicabs in New York City. They are opening shops and running motels in small towns. They are practicing medicine in rural counties and working as research scientists in universities. They are studying in large and small universities and teaching in grade schools and high schools and colleges. Globalization means that everyone faces more competition. If we want to preserve a high standard of living, certain things are necessary. I would like to suggest that the following issues must be kept in mind:

20 • **Languages.** Sixty-six percent of the world's children are bilingual (Eitzen 2006, 47). Learning languages is not a strong point for Americans. We assume wherever we go people will speak English. But whenever the people you are dealing with know more than you do, guess who has the advantage. As America becomes more multicultural, monolingual Americans will be at an increasing disadvantage.

21 • **Math and Science.** Globally, advanced knowledge is widespread and low-cost labor is readily available. If our standard of living is going to continue to remain high, math and science are necessary for continued innovation (Augustine 2006).

22 • **Job Choice.** What kinds of jobs won't be outsourced? Jobs that are **not routine,** that can't be automated or broken down into repeatable steps with little variation. If you want job security, look for a job that involves high interaction, people skills, flexibility (*Business Week* 2004), abstract reasoning, problem solving, and communication (*RAND* 2004). Two recent surveys (Farr, "Best Jobs for the 21st Century" and Quinn, "The Top 25 Jobs for 2005–2009") recommend work in the following areas as the most promising for the near future: jobs in computer software, management, education, biomedical research, medical practice (including nursing), and sales. Similarly, the U.S. Bureau of Labor Statistics' "Tomorrow's Jobs" projects the

greatest growth in "education and health services," followed by "professional and business services," and
"leisure and hospitality" (U.S. Department of Labor 2005).
While those are general categories, what they have in common is that they all involve the requirements listed above:
high interaction, people skills, flexibility, abstract reasoning, problem solving, and communication.

23 • **Lifelong learning.** There is no more lifetime employment.
Work for someone who will help you get ready for your
next job (Friedman 2005, 284*ff.*).

24 • **Portable benefits.** We are in the midst of a set of serious,
severe **healthcare and pension crises** that will need to be
solved soon if our economy is to continue to provide good
work. Both sets of benefits must become reliable, afford-
able, and portable, not tied to employers. That means the
government needs to wake up (Friedman 2005, 285*ff.*).
That means you need to vote.

25 • **Social activism.** You can't be apathetic. When you buy, you
vote. Think about whom your money is going to. Globalization has made the world more transparent. Before you
buy a product, find out how a company treats its employees and whether its products are well or shoddily made
(Friedman 2005, 297*ff.*).

26 • **Work.** A good paycheck is important, but once basic needs
are met, money alone won't make you happier. Look for
jobs with creativity, relationships, fun, challenge, recognition, and a sense of meaning, a sense of purpose larger
than yourself (T. Malone 2004).

6. Finally

27 The Mount's mission statement says: "We seek to graduate
men and women who . . . see and seek to resolve the problems
facing humanity, and who commit themselves to live as
responsible citizens." I am proud of how many Mount graduates take that statement seriously. That is not only done by
those who go into the Peace Corps and Jesuit Corps and
AmeriCorps, but also those who go on to graduate and professional schools, those who go into the military, and those
who are going to work. All graduates have the same opportunity to remake this world, to realize things are changing

rapidly and to know that their education has not only given them the skills to do that work, it has also given them the responsibility to do it.

28   I hope you will never stop being activists. A speaker at a diversity conference that I went to a few years ago said, "If you don't make the world you live in, you will have to live in a world someone else has made." Whenever I want to give up; when I feel like my efforts don't matter; when I think that I should just let somebody else do it; I think of that phrase, and I realize that I do not really have a choice. If we do not work to make a livable world for ourselves, we are going to be stuck in one we may not like.

Note

[1]   Gross Domestic Product or GDP is defined as the total market value of all goods and services produced in a country in a given year.

References

Augustine, Norm. 2006. Rising above the gathering storm, 2005. National Academies of Science. http://nationalacademies.org.

Bauman, Zygmunt. 1998. *Globalization: The Human Consequences.* New York: Columbia University Press.

Business Week. 2004. The future of work. *Business Week,* March 20, 2004.

Central Intelligence Agency. 2005. *The World Factbook.*

Eitzen, D. Stanley. 2006. Dimensions of Globalization. In Eitzen and Zinn, pp. 45–49.

Eitzen, D. Stanley, and Maxine Baca Zinn. 2006. *Globalization: The Transformation of Social Worlds.* Belmont, CA: Thomson-Wadsworth.

Farr, Michael. 2006. Best jobs for the 21st century. JIST Publishing. www.jist.com/bestlists/overall.htm.

Forbes Magazine. 2003. The world's richest people. February 27, 2003. www.forbes.com/lists/2003.

Friedman, Thomas. 2000. *The Lexus and the Olive Tree.* New York: Anchor Books.

Friedman, Thomas. 2005. *The World Is Flat: A Brief History of the Twenty-first Century.* New York: Farrar, Strauss, Giroux.

Giddens, Anthony. 2000. *Runaway World: How Globalization Is Reshaping Our Lives.* New York: Routledge.

Greider, William. 1997. *One World, Ready or Not: The Manic Logic of Global Capitalism.* New York: Simon & Schuster.

Huntington, Samuel. 1993. The clash of civilizations. *Foreign Affairs.* 72:22–49.

Lechner, Frank J., and John Boli. 2005. *World Culture: Origins and Consequences.* Malden, MA: Blackwell Publishing.

Malone, Thomas. 2004. Competing in the marketplace for values. *Leader to Leader.* No. 33, Summer 2004.

Massey, Douglas. 2006. The wall that keeps illegal workers in. *The New York Times.* Op-Ed. April 4, 2006.

Pro-Forex. Foreign exchange markets. http://www.proforex.com/en/markets.php.

Putnam, Robert D. 2000. *Bowling Alone: The Collapse and Revival of American Community.* New York: Simon & Schuster.

Quinn, Matt. 2005. The top 25 jobs for 2005–2009. *FastCompany.com.* www.fastcompany.com.

RAND. 2004. The future at work—Trends and implications. *RAND Labor and Population Research Brief.* Santa Monica, CA: RAND Corporation.

Reich, Robert. 1991. *The Work of Nations: Preparing Ourselves for Twenty-first Century Capitalism.* New York: Vintage.

Sachs, Jeffrey. 2005. *The End of Poverty: Economic Possibilities for Our Time.* New York: Penguin.

Shah, Anup. 2006. Causes of poverty. www.globalissues.org/Trade Related/Facts.asp

United States Department of Labor. 2005. Tomorrow's jobs. *Occupational Outlook Handbook.* 12/20/2005. www.bls.gov/oco/oco2003.htm.

*D*avid M. McCarthy has been teaching at Mount St. Mary's University since 1998. His training is in moral theology and social ethics, and at the Mount, he has taken on responsibility in teaching Catholic Social Teaching. Catholic Social Teaching reaches back to Scripture, but its modern significance is marked in 1891, by Pope Leo XIII's encyclical on the plight of the laborer in the industrial revolution. In "Work in Catholic Social Thought," McCarthy attempts to present the perspective on work that develops from Leo XIII's "On the Condition of Labor." He also integrates ongoing discussions at the Mount about career, work, and one's calling in life. McCarthy has taught Freshman Seminar since the fall semester of 2000, and his essay on work brings together Catholic Social Teaching with many conversations among students in Freshman Seminar.

Work in Catholic Social Thought

David M. McCarthy

1   It is common in contemporary life to make a distinction between spirituality and religion. In its medieval (Latin) use, religion is something that applies to a person. It is a quality of character; someone who is religious prays and worships as part of a community. In modern times, religion continues to identify something that is visible, but it has come to refer primarily to traditions and institutions, to bodies of faith like Christianity, Judaism, and Islam. Spirituality is the term we moderns tend to use for the individual person, referring primarily to one's perspectives and attitudes. Spirituality refers to inner feelings. Religion, on the other hand, refers to a structure or way of life. Religions are concerned with the whole of life, with spirituality in the inner, affective sense as well as basic questions of social life—including how we make money and what we do with it. Religions, in short, are concerned not only with spiritual feelings and sensibilities, but also with outward acts of love and an order of justice.

2   This essay offers a religious view of work—an examination of work within the Catholic faith. Within Christianity, attention to economic affairs is unavoidable because of Jesus' teachings and message of salvation. Jesus draws upon the long line of

Hebrew prophets before him. He criticizes those who hoard their riches, and he gives hope to the poor and downtrodden. Throughout the Bible, particularly in the prophets and the Gospels, there is a consistent connection between just dealings with money and the kingdom of God. Let one example suffice. When Zaccheaus, a tax collector, pledges to reform his ways and give compensation to those whom he has defrauded, Jesus declares, "Today salvation has come to this house" (Lk. 19:19). This biblical inheritance has shaped the Catholic tradition on matters of property, work, and money, from the beginnings of the Church until today.[1]

3   This essay on work attends to what is called modern Catholic social teaching. The inaugural document for this modern stream of thought is Pope Leo XIII's *The Condition of Labor* (*Rerum novarum*) in 1891.[2] Drawing on the work of nineteenth century Catholic economists, *The Condition of Labor* offers a framework to deal with the "new things" that are in encountered with the rise of the industrial economy, specifically the problem of inhumane working conditions for laborers, the dominance of a new class of capitalists, and the emergence of socialist doctrines. *The Condition of Labor* argues against a principle common to both capitalists and socialists—the principle that the economy works by means of impersonal or mechanical forces (the invisible hand). In the document, Pope Leo calls factory owners, investors, managers, laborers, government officials, and Catholics to personal responsibility for economic and social life. Each is asked to take a role in contributing to the good of others and to the common good of all.

4   A long line of documents (an intellectual tradition) follows Leo XIII's *Rerum novarum* (the "new things" or *The Condition of Labor*). This essay will highlight two documents that provide a good perspective on this wide-ranging tradition. The first document, *The Church in the Modern World* (1965), is a pastoral constitution of the second Vatican Counsel (Vatican II) which gathers from 1962 to 1965. The Latin title is *Gaudium et spes*— "joy and hope." The second, *On Human Work* or *Laborem Exercens* (1981), is issued by John Paul II on the ninetieth anniversary of Leo's *The Condition of Labor*. *The Church in the Modern World* and *On Human Work* provide useful sources for a discussion of work because they focus on issues of justice in the context of a theological anthropology—in the context of

understanding of the human being (anthropos) in reference to God and the goodness of God's creation.

5　The first part of this essay will present the theological anthropology, and the second attends to "the priority of labor" in questions of justice. *On Human Work* and *The Church in the Modern World* will direct our attention to a few main points. In Catholic social thought, the meaning of work is understood in terms of the dignity of human beings as we are made in the image of God and in terms of our fulfillment in the goods of creation, including good work and the good we make through our labor. In part one of the essay, we will see that work is regarded as a fundamentally personal and spiritual matter. Precisely because work is believed to be eminently important to a person's dignity, it is a matter of justice. Giving work and the worker justice is the topic of part two, and this task is also a personal matter. Employers, employees, government officials, and citizens are called to take responsibility for justice in economic life. Catholic social teaching does not propose or defend any specific economic system—capitalism or socialism. Rather, it judges the worth of any given system according to its ability to sustain the dignity of the worker and the practices of meaningful, just, and fulfilling work.

The Personal Meaning of Work

6　At the beginning of *On Human Work*, John Paul II considers work in terms of its objective and subjective significance, and he regards the subjective sense as most important (*Laborem* 6).[3] The Pope's use of "subjective" and "objective" does not reflect common American usage, so that some explanation is in order. The objective and subjective meanings of work do not correspond to a division between what we do (the external) and how we feel about it subjectively. Rather, each refers to a different goal or outcome of what we do. Work in its objective sense results in an object, a product or service. Work in its subjective sense has the fulfillment of the subject (the worker) as its goal. We have an object of work (a thing to get done), but work always effects the doer (the acting subject). John Paul II proposes that whatever objective value a type of work might have, the ultimate standard of good work is "the measure of dignity" that it affords "the person, the individual who carries it out."

He holds that "in the final analysis it is man who is the purpose of the work" (*Laborem* 6).

7   John Paul II makes his case for the dignity of work by offering a theological portrayal of human beings as created in the image of God. The "image of God" is a basic theme of the biblical account of creation (Gen. 1:27). On this point, Vatican II's *The Church in the Modern World* is in the background (mainly sections 12–39) and is cited at key points in *On Human Work*. The image of God marks us as "social beings" in our "innermost nature," fulfilled in companionship with one another and ultimately by the offer of God's friendship (*Gaudium* 12). God's image in us binds body and soul; we are the nexus of material creation and God's spirit (*Gaudium* 14). For this reason, fulfillment of bodily and spiritual desires cannot run free of each other, and our expectation of heavenly life with God ought to inspire our concern for justice and peace on earth (*Gaudium* 39). The image of God signifies that we human beings have a self-conscious intellect and freedom to act and to make our mark upon the world (*Gaudium* 15). We are able to act freely according to our good and the good of creation. We can love freely, and we can measure and bring justice. We are fulfilled as human beings when we act for the good of the world.

8   When human beings, man and woman, are created in the image of God, they are given a command to "fill the earth and subdue it" and to "have dominion" (Gen. 1:28). Some have taken this command as license to exploit and abuse—to lord over the earth. However, within the Catholic frame of reference, God's creativity and lordship are seen through the ministry of Jesus Christ, who empties himself and takes the form of a servant (Phil. 2:6–11). In this context, lordship or dominion is not a "lording over" but a "joining together" and a "lifting up." Likewise, in the Jewish frame, lordship is understood in reference to the liberation of the people from slavery in Egypt and God's covenant at Mount Sinai. The defeat of Pharaoh and the liberation of the Hebrews from Egypt show that God is greater than Pharaoh. The Lord has the power to subjugate even Pharaoh, but unlike Pharaoh, God does not enslave the newly liberated people but binds himself to Israel in a covenant. God loves. Likewise, the mandate of "dominion" in Genesis is not warrant for tyranny over the earth, but situates us with God, as God's ambassadors and stewards, at the same time that we are part of (joined with) earthly creation.

9   The image of God is the basis for a call, a vocation, to fulfill-
      ment in God and the good of creation. In the image of God,
      the Lord gives us an insignia and seal of divine life. We are not
      slaves or indentured servants to God (and therefore the sub-
      jugation of a person is inhumane and unjust). The command
      to have dominion over the earth is a mandate to be creative as
      God creates, to order life, exercise authentic authority, give
      liberty, search for the truth, make peace, offer ourselves, and
      otherwise seek the good of creation. In *On Human Work*, John
      Paul II explains that "in carrying out this mandate, man, every
      human being, reflects the very action of the creator of the uni-
      verse" (*Laborem* 4). On this point, the Pope cites *The Church in
      the Modern World*, "For when a man works, he not only alters
      things and society, he develops himself as well. . . . [Human
      activity] should harmonize with the genuine good of the human
      race, and allow men as individuals and as members of society to
      pursue their total vocation and fulfill it" (*Gaudium* 35).

10   This reference to "total vocation" needs further explanation,
      for the idea of vocation will enhance our grasp of the personal
      meaning of work in the Catholic tradition. *On Human Work* and
      The Church in the Modern World follow the Catholic tradition in
      understanding the vocation of human beings as seeking fulfill-
      ment as *human beings,* that is, as striving to make actual and
      visible the image of God in us—freely and creatively doing and
      being good. This is our "total" or entire vocation, but within
      this general framework of human life, there are countless par-
      ticular callings and individual vocations, some which empha-
      size a profession or paid labor and others unpaid service to
      family and society. The Catholic tradition calls this relationship
      between the general truth of the human vocation and the par-
      ticular reality a sacramental relationship. In a sacrament, ordi-
      nary things of the earth, like bread and wine, become media of
      the presence of God. Likewise, the mundane realities of life,
      our day to day roles and responsibilities are the "stuff" of the
      human vocation, the image of God, and our sharing in God's
      love for the world. The love of God, for example, is known and
      experienced in the love of a particular person. For humans as a
      whole, there is whole (total) vocation, but for people in partic-
      ular, our callings are particular.

11   When a person asks "What should I do with my life?" she is
      likely to be thinking about a specific decision and pathway.

Should I major in communications or biology? What career or area of work should I pursue? Should I take a job with a firm in Arlington or one in Philadelphia? These questions are the "stuff" of our callings in life, and the more seriously we consider them, they more difficult they are to answer. There are two typical mistakes when thinking about what we are meant to do in life, and both make asking about our calling even more confusing. One error is to seek confirmation by waiting anxiously for a "lightning bolt" experience, and another is to look for the single thing we are meant to do, the "perfect" calling (or magic bullet) that will put the rest of our lives in order. On one hand, we wait for a voice from heaven to tell us what to do, and on the other, we seek a definitive answer that will be true for the rest of our lives. Dealing with these mistakes may help us to better understand vocation and the personal meaning of work. Both short-circuit careful self-evaluation and discernment.

12 About the first error, it is true that a person might have a lightning bolt experience and a clear confirmation that a particular line of work is her calling. This kind of lightning bolt is subjective in the sense that it provides powerful feelings and inner assurance. We know without a doubt what to do. But most questions about one's calling in life will not be answered in this subjective sense. The assurance of the lightning bolt is unusual. When an immediate experience of God's call does strike, it will not necessarily produce inner certainty. In the Bible, Moses is typical. When he hears God's voice in the burning bush, he tells God that he is not qualified for the task of leading the people out of Egypt (Exod. 4). For Moses the lightning bolt does not settle questions, but unsettles his life. Even if we do experience inner assurance (unlike Moses), the emotions may not be trustworthy because we often misinterpret our own inner desires (like confusing infatuation with abiding love). Sometimes we are too distracted to notice the lightning bolt when it strikes or we are looking in the wrong place. Sometimes looking for the lightning bolt is the distraction. When Elijah hears God in the wilderness, it is not in a great wind, earthquake or fire, but in a quiet voice (I Kings 19). While searching the heavens for the lightning bolt, we may overlook the Spirit in our lives.

13 How do we deal with the questions like, "What ought I do with my life?" According to *On Human Work*, the subjective sense of

work applies not to inner feelings but to worker as the acting subject. When a person views her calling in this "subjective" sense, she does not look only for lightning bolts but attempts to discern the role of work in her life. She spends long hours in self-examination, asking a series of questions that may not have immediate answers. What will my career or job do *to* me? What will it do to and for people with whom I live and work? How will my work reflect God's image and goodness? What are my deep desires for fulfillment? Will my work contribute to that fulfillment? What are my gifts and talents? Where can my talents flourish? Where am I needed? Where can my desires and talents meet the needs of the world?

14　These questions are seldom answered definitively. This is the second difficulty; we want final answers. In the Catholic tradition of spiritual discernment and self-examination, questions about one's calling do not lead to final answers but to day to day growth in holiness. The point of questions about vocation is not to fill in the blanks (I will major in _____ and get a job doing _____). The point of asking about my calling is to give an answer over the course of my life. The answer is not comprised of words in a sentence, but with the kind of person that I become and the good that I do with my work. My calling is understood, not before I make choices, but *while* I am struggling with important decisions. It is understood, not before I choose a path, but *while* I am taking the journey. Seldom do we get answers before we take the risk and leap of faith. If a person becomes a nurse, he is not free from asking about his calling. Questions about his desire for fulfillment, the good of his work, and the kind of person he is becoming will guide him in how he does his job. The questions ask him to throw himself into his work.

15　In the Catholic tradition, "the good that we can do" and "what we are meant to be" are discovered by an examination of our desires. Many of us assume that the basic questions of work and vocation are "to be or not to be an accountant" or "to be or not to be stockbroker." Certainly, some "walks of life" will have dishonest or self-serving intentions built into them, and these are not legitimate vocations. However, most types of work are made honest or dishonest by the worker. We pursue a line of work because we desire something good. The process of asking questions about "who we are" and "what we are meant to do" is a means to examine our deep desires. Before we attend to the question of becoming an accountant or a stockbroker, therefore, we should take a careful look at our hopes and expectations for fulfillment.

16   The deeper that we dare to look at our desires, the more life-giving our understanding may be. "I want a big house" is a surface desire (and not a bad one), but what I want from life inside and around the house and in the neighborhood is a deeper much more difficult set of questions. "I want money" is a surface (and still important) desire; "What good will I do with my money and for whom?" and "What kind of life will I make?" are deeper questions. The big house can be purchased in a day; what goes on inside requires our attention everyday. The question of income is answered by a contract and settled in a day; the question of what we do with our income is answered by our lives. In this way, the question of a calling is not answered and then cast aside. It is an ongoing process. In the process, our sense of vocation is likely to become more profound. I should assume that I could have become a lawyer rather than a teacher. The decision to become a teacher is important, but it is, in a sense, an "external" decision. It only gets me in the door. Once inside, the question is, "Who am I called to become as a teacher?" Discontent with teaching may lead me to go leave my job and go to law school. But even then, I will not have a final answer. By switching from teaching to law, I have not changed the deep questions. I will have to ask what I desire while practicing law and who I will become.

17   A few additional points follow from thinking about vocation as a personal, life-long process. If the meaning of work has its foundation in the dignity of the person, then the meaning of work does not hinge on the social status or title provided by a line of work. Further, one's vocation is not likely to be represented or represented fully by a job description or profession. Vocation is about the person rather than the job. There is no reason to assume that standard career tracks or job descriptions will correspond to what will become our callings. The standard job description (for a nurse, accountant, or police officer) might not represent the aspect of the job where I find the heart of my vocation. It may be that being a nurse or police officer, accountant or teacher is my vocation, but this coherence between "profession" and "calling" is possible when my vocation gives shape to the work (rather than vice versa). I should see my job

description or profession, not as the precise definition of my calling, but as a set of opportunities and situations where a deeper call can be heard and heeded.

18   How does my job as an electrician or accountant put me in situations where I am fulfilled and meet the needs of others? In other words, being an electrician does not define my calling; rather, my calling has come to define how I am an electrician. Pushing this point further, a job may simply contribute to broader sense of vocation—of being a wife, father, caregiver, neighbor, and friend, Christian or Jew. If my calling is grounded in these roles, I will have to ask how my career or job fits or disrupts, enhances or detracts from these higher callings. The subjective approach to work asks, not how the person serves the work, but how the work serves the calling of the person.

19   "Work is 'for man' and not man 'for work'" (John Paul, *Laborem* 6). This turn of phrase points to the central theme of John Paul II's *On Human Work* and brings us back to the beginning of this section. Human dignity (based in the image of God) and the fulfillment of the person in creative activity are fundamental purposes of work. This subjective approach focuses upon the role of work in meeting human needs and in enhancing personal and social development. It is not concerned, primarily, with subjective feelings. Certainly, some people will object. Some argue that we will not be able to do good for the long term if we do not first of all take pleasure in our work. In contrast, a theological approach first asks about the purpose of work. The Catholic tradition proposes that if our labors can be put to a good purpose, if we make and do good things, and if the work fosters our talents and sustains our dignity, then joy in our work will follow.

20   Joy (or enjoyment) is far deeper and includes pleasure at work. Pleasure occurs when our desires are heightened and satisfied, but it is sustained only as long as the object of our pleasure is meeting our desires. The pleasure of eating cake eventually exhausts itself. We push the food away; yet, later we will be hungry again. When we attempt to extend temporary and limited pleasures (like eating) beyond their limits, we fall into self-destructiveness—like gluttony, lust, and greed. Our desires are frustrated because a lower pleasure takes the place of a more comprehensive one. By analogy, if I look for

work that simply gives me pleasure, I am not likely to enjoy the work for long. Even so, I may become obsessed with the work like a glutton who tries to make food a comprehensive good. The work will not contribute to the whole of my life, but detract from it. It will be a way to escape the deeper questions of life: I will be a workaholic.

21   Joy is attained when our desires meet something that outlasts the desires. Recall that Jesus offers a Samaritan woman living water and tells her that she will never be thirsty again (Jn. 6). Our joy on earth will never be perfect; however, when we are drawn to things that have a higher purpose, we will have greater pleasure and satisfaction. We will take on difficulties willingly and accept struggles and trials. Like an athlete who pushes through physical pain, we will take pleasure in hard work. We will be able to have great passion and energy while on the job. Joy is found in reaching toward what is good in human life, and in the process we will take great pleasure in our work.

22   The relationship between joy and pleasure provides an apt conclusion to this section. In Catholic social teaching, the subjective meaning of work is primary, but it attends first, not to subjective feelings, but to how the work serves the human subject. By attending to comprehensive ideas of the personal and spiritual significance of labor, Catholic social teaching is able to attend to the material conditions of the work place and other questions of justice. An emphasis on the personal and spiritual (as a comprehensive set of questions) requires a concern that the worker is given dignity and does not become merely a part of the machinery of production.

The Priority of Labor

23   The Catholic Church's concern for the dignity of the laborer has been consistent for millennia. The fourth century, for example, is an interesting reference point because, at the beginning of that century, Christianity gains legal status in the Roman Empire and is beginning to gain social influence. At that time, Bishops like Ambrose of Milan take it upon themselves to call wealthy land owners to give restitution to the poor, particularly those who labor on their lands. The poor are going hungry while they are struggling in the fields, and by their labor the rich are getting richer (Avila 66–69). The rich

increase their wealth by not giving to the worker what is his or her due. This same concern for the poor develops in the reference to the "new things" of the industrial age—the new situation of mass production and the industrial laborer. From ancient to modern times, there is a consistent defense of the laborer, what John Paul II calls the priority of labor.

24 The "priority of labor" means that work and the working person are the source of the goods of life and all wealth (John Paul, *Laborem* 12). Goods and profits that come from investment and ownership depend, ultimately, upon people who work. Industry depends upon industrious persons. Likewise, the good of the person and the common good of all are the final goals of industry and investment. According to *The Church in the Modern World*, the fundamental purpose of work should be the whole person, "viewed in terms of his material needs and the demands of his intellectual, moral, spiritual, and religious life" (*Gaudium* 64). In other words, "man is the source, the center, and the purpose of all socioeconomic life" (*Gaudium* 63). This statement is a re-statement in social and economic terms of the theme of the previous section on "the personal meaning" or the "subjective meaning" of work. Safe, healthy and rewarding work is a basic calling of human life—basic to human development, and as such, good work is both an obligation and a human right (John Paul, *Laborem* 16).[4]

25 In the industrial age, there has been a tendency to reduce human welfare to material wealth and to see the fundamental purpose of economic activity as "the mere multiplication of products" (*Gaudium* 64). A danger of capitalism is that it creates incentives for treating the worker as merely a tool or an instrument for mass production. When laborers are paid little for long hours, profits are enhanced. When the worker becomes merely a part of the machinery of production, corporations can easily move production to other parts of the world where labor is cheap. One tool of production is simply discarded for another. The danger of capitalism is the anonymity—the namelessness and facelessness—of labor (John Paul, *Laborem* 7).

26 The "face" and "name" of labor are found in the connections between the worker and the product. It is natural to have a desire to "stand by" and "stand behind" one's work. Recall the subjective view of work: the thing done or made (the object of

work) plays a role in the life of the worker (the subject of work) and who she is becoming. The inverse is also the case. The worker leaves a mark upon the product, and the product an "expression" of our role in the world. If our Creator's image is a seal upon us, we fulfill that image when we put our imprint upon the resources of the earth and human community. *The Church in the Modern World* makes this point clear. "Far from thinking that work's produced by man's own talent and energy are in opposition to God's power . . . Christians are convinced that the triumphs of the human race are a sign of God's greatness and the flowering of his own mysterious design" (*Gaudium* 34). In this sense, the priority of labor includes a responsibility to do good work, and the responsibility implies a right to take "ownership" and "stand behind" the good things that we do and make.

27   However, the anonymity of the worker in the global economy too often separates the good of production from the good of the worker. The two are separated to such a degree that I might know where my shirt has been sewn or my television assembled, but I will have no knowledge of who did the work or what the workers' lives are like. I know only the brand name or merchandiser, whether the Gap or Walmart, and the store or brand name identifies corporate managers and shareholders, not laborers. Amid mass production, the worker is not only anonymous but often entirely forgotten. In developing countries, working conditions can be cruel, and some trends suggest that the situation for workers, world-wide, is not improving (Diamond; Rosen). Even in the U.S. where the economy has mushroomed in the last few decades, the gap between the lowest wage earners and the wealthy has been widening since 1980 and especially since 1995 ("The Rich"). When profits go up and wages do not, it is clear that the "priority of labor" is being undermined.[5] The goods of production are doing the worker very little good.

28   When faced with these trends, Catholic Social teaching calls us to personal responsibility. Like work, we are called to take the economy personally and to resist the idea that we are ruled by a system and can do nothing to change things. According to *The Church in the Modern World*, economic development "must not be left to the sole judgment of a few men or groups possessing excessive power . . . [and] must not be allowed to follow a kind

of automatic course" (*Gaudium* 65). All citizens "have the right and responsibility . . . to contribute according to their ability to the true progress of their own community" (*Gaudium* 65). Along with this call to responsibility is an attempt to resist a view of economic life that appeals only to individual self-interest. The Catholic tradition rejects the view that one's pursuit of individual self-interest *is* one's contribution to common life. The traditional conception of the common good requires that we work for the good of others—for conditions in society where persons have opportunity to be fulfilled in common life (*Gaudium* 26). *The Church in the Modern World* calls us to respect the dignity of others, and to love our neighbors, which in this sense means not an emotion, but the resolve to work for each other's good (*Gaudium* 27–8).

29   John Paul II, in *On Human Work*, takes a traditional approach to the question of responsibility by addressing the Church, individual Christians, government officials, employers, employees, and labor unions. What follows in this section will attend to these different groups and their roles and responsibilities. First, we will attend to the roles of the Church and civil government. The next step will be to focus on the tasks of individuals and local communities, and finally, we will deal with the central topic when treating questions of "the priority of labor" in the Catholic tradition—the relationship between employer and employees, including organized labor.

30   The task of the Church, according to its mission as the Church, is to care for those in need by maintaining social service institutions that express God's love and our love of neighbor, attending to the needs of families, the poor, sick, and so on. This concern is not the main topic of John Paul II's *On Human Work*, but the task is emphasized by Pope Benedict XVI in his *Deus Caritas Est* (God is Love). John Paul's concern is the role of the Church in relationship to economic "systems." The task of the Church is not to propose or defend one economic system or another, but "to speak out on work from the viewpoint of its human value and of the moral order to which it belongs" and "to form a spirituality of work which will help all people come closer, through work, to God" (John Paul, *Laborem* 24). The spirituality of work is outlined in the previous section of this essay: "by means of work man participates in the activity of God" (John Paul, *Laborem* 26). The task of speaking out on the human

value of work includes a persistent concern within the Catholic tradition for justice, particularly in the treatment of laborers, wages, and the use of wealth and private property.

31   Since the "new things" of the industrial revolution, the Church has called upon the state to protect workers who are vulnerable in the modern economy. According to Leo XII's *The Condition of Labor* (1891), government officials "should make sure that the laws and institutions, the general character and administration of the common wealth, shall be such as to produce of themselves public well-being and private prosperity" (26). Because it is responsible for the just ordering of society, Leo XIII argues that a special task of government is to safeguard the rights of workers who (in 1891 and still in some parts of the world today) have little protection (Leo 29; John Paul, *Laborem* 17). Among these protections are rights to healthy working conditions, laws against child labor in industry, provisions for just wages, the protection of private property, and the right to form trade and labor unions. Further, special attention is given to the rights and prerogatives of family, which is considered a social institution that is more fundamental than the state.

32   While civil government is called to these duties, the Catholic tradition also outlines the limits of what the state can and should do. State socialism, for example, is rejected outright because it denies the rights not only of family, but of private property and freedom of religion. In Communist states, the central government dominates all of life. In response to *laissez faire* capitalism, worry begins to arise in the late nineteenth century that the state will begin to dominate social life in an age of individualism. In an economy and politics of self-interest, individuals may become passive in relationship to the needs of their neighbors and the common good. It has been documented in twentieth century America, that economic and political individualism weakens local communities and connections of care and responsibility for our neighbors (Bellah).

33   While governments have specific responsibilities to the common good and to laborers, contemporary Catholic thought focuses, not on the task of government, but on the responsibilities of communities and individuals, particularly Catholic organizations and parishes. This responsibility is expressed through the developments of two concepts, "subsidiarity" and "solidarity." Subsidiarity refers to the role of communities and

institutions that are local and have specific responsibilities, like families, parishes, community and neighborhood organizations, charitable institutions, trade associations, and the like. The principle of subsidiarity holds that the central government ought not to take the place of these local groups. Society is constituted by a multiplicity of local groupings which provide a rich sense of social life and personal identities (Pius 78–80). Service to one's neighbor and efforts to enhance the common good are the responsibility mainly of these local groups rather than a distant bureaucracy of the state or federal government. Through the concept of subsidiarity, we are called to act in and through our local communities.

34 Solidarity is John Paul II's term for personal and communal relationships that are now possible at an international level. Because of modern developments in travel, trade, and communication, churches and civic organizations can build relationships with communities in other countries. Solidarity is an awareness of interdependence, even at a global level. "[M]en and women in various parts of the world feel personally affected by the injustices and violations of human rights committed in distant countries," and solidarity is a disposition to take action (John Paul, *Sollicitudo* 38). It "is a *firm and persevering determination* to commit oneself to the common good . . . to the good of all and of each individual, because we are *all* really responsible for *all*" (John Paul, *Sollicitudo* 38). Like subsidiary institutions at the local level, the awareness of solidarity at the international level provides a resolve for local communities and individuals to make connections with those in need abroad. In terms of workers across the world, various churches have been involved in the Fair Trade movement, which connects farmers and crafts-people in Central America, for instance, directly with consumers in the United States (Catholic Relief Services).

35 Our final topic (or sphere of responsibility) is the relationship between employers and employees. The Catholic tradition of economic thought sees the relationship between capital (investors and owners of the means of production) and labor as a complementary one. The subjective (theological) meaning of work begins with the point that we human beings share God's creativity in putting our hands to the resources of creation and take part in forming the world in which we live. If

this is the case, then those who own more than they can put to use on their own (capital) and those who need work are dependent upon each other. They ought to form a community of work, and their cooperation ought to contribute to the common good. Likewise, labor organizations are conceived, in the Catholic tradition, not as groups that are narrowly focused on self-interest, but as a community of laborers who look out for each other's good, seek to develop the trade or profession in positive ways, and make common efforts to contribute to the good of society.

36 While Catholic social thought puts labor in the context of a "community of work," it rejects communism. The Catholic tradition rejects Marxism because it assumes a fundamental opposition between capital and labor. On the other hand, it also criticizes forms of capitalism that create situations where capital interests are opposed to the good of laborers. Because capitalism usually privileges investors and owners at the expense of workers, John Paul II prefers not to use the term "capitalism" to refer to the best forms of what is typically named by that term. While socialism points to corporate ownership and Marxism is a kind of "worker-class-ism," capitalism often functions as an "ism" that points to the priority of capital interests rather than the priority of labor. John Paul II prefers the terms "business economy, market economy, or simply free economy" (*Centesimus annus* 42). The priority of labor means that managers and owners, employees and trade associations see their task as forming a community of good work.

37 According to John Paul II, the key issue in the relationship between employer and worker "is that of just remuneration for work done" (*Laborem* 19). Pushing the issue further, he holds that a just wage "is the concrete means of verifying the justice of the whole economic system" (John Paul, *Laborem* 19). The test of just payment is whether or not a single income "will suffice for establishing and properly maintaining a family and for providing security for its future" (John Paul, *Laborem* 19). The just wage includes concerns for the cost and availability of health care, time for rest and recuperation (Sundays and holidays), and some kind of plan for retirement. The U.S. Census Bureau puts the poverty level for a family of four at $19,972 ("Census Data"). This number represents a bare minimum, which does not account for what many people consider basics,

such as life insurance, Christmas presents, recreation or vacations ("Poverty USA"). It hardly covers the necessities of life, since the "average yearly rent paid in 2005 was $8,328" ("Census Data"). It is not surprising that 46.6 million people in the U.S. have no health insurance. If a wage earner were to work forty hours a week for fifty-two weeks, she would have to make $9.60 per hour to reach the minimum level for a family. By federal law, the current (2006) minimum wage at $5.15 per hour is not a just family wage. A person working forty hours a week with no vacation will make $10,712 in a year.

38 Obviously the federal minimum wage does little to protect the fulltime worker, but the moral imperative in Catholic social teaching is set primarily in the relationship of employer and employee (not between the federal government and the worker). In Catholic thought, the employer is called to be open to a worker's talents and needs within the overall context of human development—to give attention, in other words, to the person as the subject of work, not just to the material products or profits of labor. The Catholic tradition defends private property as an indispensable good, but it gives individual ownership a communal purpose. Private property is not unconditional, but relative to human welfare and the common good. For instance, I ought not waste my extra food, but give it to those who are hungry. Waste is a moral wrong because it keeps food from its proper purpose, human nourishment. Likewise, my privately owned business or factory has a purpose beyond my personal needs or mere profit, although profits are good. My business ought to provide the context for a community of work, where persons are able to develop as workers, earn a decent wage, and make a contribution to society.

39 In the modern era, Catholic social teaching has defended labor unions vigorously. In the tradition, the theoretical model for a union is the medieval guild, "insofar as those organizations brought together people belonging to the same craft and thus on the basis of their work" (John Paul, *Laborem* 20). Modern unions, emerging in the industrial age, have the purpose of protecting the rights of workers in relationship to factory owners and corporate executives. The need for such representation is recognized, but Catholic thought has resisted a conception of class struggle. Strikes are an acceptable tool, for example; yet,

they should not be used to advance ideologies or class struggle. "Union demands cannot be turned into a kind of group or class 'egoism,' although they can and should also aim at correcting—with a view to the common good of the whole society— everything defective in the system of ownership of the means of production or in the way these are managed" (John Paul, *Laborem* 20). Like employers, workers should always keep in mind the dignity of the worker (offer education and assistance) and the good of the business as a whole. In their efforts to insure a just wage, for example, workers ought to seek justice for the business (the managers and employers) and consider the effect of wages upon the good of the company and the market as a whole.

Conclusion

40   In Catholic social thought, labor unions—precisely because they are associations of workers (subsidiary institutions)—are called to contribute to wider society and economy of good work. The same responsibility is given to individual workers, as well as employers and managers. In effect, the theme of "the priority of labor" is a call to us to sustain communities of good work amid the "mere multiplication of products" and the anonymity of the modern economy. Where the economy divides the good of the worker from the goods of production, where the good of the laborer is divided from the good of owners and investors, we are called to bring them back together. Likewise, the personal meaning of work, as reviewed in the first part of the essay, puts our careers, jobs, and roles in community in reference to the "total" vocation of the human being—to live into the image of God, to put our intelligence, freedom, and persistent efforts to the task of making and doing good in the world. Each of us is called to cultivate our special talents and to find our place in the communities where we live.

41   One likely response to this call to community and good work is that it is not realistic, that the world and especially the economy actually operate by means of narrower conceptions of self-interest and individual happiness. By and large, this counter-argument is true. We are not going to change the world. However, what is the point of a call, a profession, a vocation, and good work if we aspire only to leave the world as it is? Work, in the Catholic traditions, is understood as a basic human activity through which we give form to society,

culture, and the things of the earth. The Catholic conception of the human being assumes that it is natural for us to want to make our mark by contributing to the goodness of creation. While we will not change whole world, we are called to take responsibility for what we can do. The Catholic conception of work requires that we live with hope. It begins with the goodness of God's creation and asks us to start a journey with our neighbors, so that we might begin to know the joy for which we were made.

Notes

[1] Catholic Charities USA is the largest network (other than the federal government) of social services in the United States (www.catholic charitiesusa.org).

[2] The Latin title of Church documents is constituted by the first words of the document, here for *Rerum novarum*, "new things."

[3] Church documents are numbered according to sections, and section numbers are consistent wherever the documents are published. The citations in this essay refer to section numbers. The essay uses the collection of documents edited by David O'Brien and Thomas Shannon, listed in the Works Cited. The same documents can be found (with the same section numbering) on the Vatican website, http://www.vatican.va/phome_en.htm.

[4] John Paul II makes reference to John XXIII's *Pacem in terris: Peace on Earth* (1963). Pope John's outline of rights and duties is found in Part I of the document, nos. 8–38.

[5] John F. Kavanaugh, in "Labor's Love Lost," notes that "[incomes of] the richest 300,000 Americans . . . have more than tripled since 1970, while the real, inflation-adjusted income of the working poor actually fell . . . the bottom 270 million Americans, 90 percent of us, have had basically flat incomes over the last three decades. The richest 14,000 tax payers have had their income quadruple since 1980" (9).

References

Avila, Charles. *Ownership: Early Christian Teaching*. Eugene, OR: Wipf and Stock, 1983.

Bellah, Robert, et al. *Habits of the Heart: Individualism and Commitment in American Life*. Updated Edition. Berkeley: University of California Press, 1996.

Benedict XVI, *Deus Caritas Est*. Libreria Editrice Vaticana, 2005, http://www.vatican.va/holy_father/benedict_xvi/encyclicals/documents/hf_ben-xvi_enc_20051225_deus-caritas-est_en.html.

Catholic Relief Services. "Welcome to CRS Fair Trade." http://www.crsfairtrade.org/index.cfm.

"Census Data and the Poor." *America: The International Catholic Weekly.* Vol. 195, no. 9 (October 2, 2006): 4.

Diamond, Stephen F. "The PetroChina Syndrome: Regulating Capital Martkets in the Anti-Globalization Era." *Iowa Journal of Corporate Law,* Vol. 29, no. 41 (2003): 39–102.

Gaudium et spes: Pastoral Constitution on the Church in the Modern World. In O'Brien and Shannon (eds.), *Catholic Social Thought.* 166–237.

John XXIII, *Pacem in terris: Peace on Earth.* In O'Brien and Shannon (eds.), *Catholic Social Thought.* 131–62.

John Paul II, *Centesimus annus: On the Hundredth Anniversary of Rerum Novarum.* In O'Brien and Shannon (eds.), *Catholic Social Thought.* 439–88.

John Paul II, *Laborem exercens: On Human Work.* In O'Brien and Shannon (eds.), *Catholic Social Thought.* 352–92.

John Paul II, *Sollicitudo rei socialis: On Social Concern.* In O'Brien and Shannon (eds.), *Catholic Social Thought.* 395–436.

Kavanaugh, John F., S.J. "Labor's Love Lost." *America* (Aug 28–Sept 4, 2006): 9.

Leo XIII, *Rerum novarum: The Condition of Labor.* In O'Brien and Shannon (eds.), *Catholic Social Thought.* 14–39.

O'Brien, David J. and Thomas A. Shannon (eds.). *Catholic Social Thought: The Documentary Heritage.* MaryKnoll, NY: Orbis Books, 1992.

Pius XI, *Quadragesimo anno: After Forty Years.* In O'Brien and Shannon (eds.), *Catholic Social Thought.* 42–80.

"Poverty USA: The State of Poverty in America." United State Conference of Catholic Bishops: Catholic Campaign for Human Development. http://www.usccb.org/cchd/povertyusa/povfacts.shtml.

"The Rich, the poor and the growing gap between them." *Economist.* Vol. 379, Issue 8482 (June 17, 2006): 28–30.

Rosen, Ellen Israel, "The Wal-Mart Effect: The World Trade Organization and the Race to the Bottom." *Chapman Law Review.* Vol. 8 (Spring 2005): 261–282.

*A*ndrew Mills (1968–) teaches philosophy and religion at Otterbein College in Ohio. He specializes in the philosophy of language and mind, and has published several articles. The one below, "What's So Good about a College Education?" (2001), is taken from his Web site. It examines what he sees as the typical answers to his title question, and why those aren't always the most important or accurate ones.

What's So Good about a College Education?

Andrew P. Mills

1   Why is it good to go to college? What is so valuable about a college education? College is expensive, and you wouldn't spend all that money on something that wasn't valuable. Moreover, college requires a great deal of work, and it requires that you spend time reading and writing and studying and going to class and taking tests—time that you could spend doing other things—and you wouldn't spend your time on all those college-related tasks unless you thought you were getting something valuable for all your effort. You are in college, and so you think that getting a college education is a good thing—that it is valuable in some way or other—but what sort of value does it have? It's worthwhile to spend some time thinking about the answer to this question, for it will affect the way you spend your time at college, and it will affect the sort of education that you get there. If you don't know why college is valuable, you're very likely wasting your time and money and effort during your college years.

2   Most people give what I will call the simple "Can Opener Answer" to this question. I think there are two serious problems with that answer, and that is what I want to convince you of. Once we see what is wrong with the simple Can Opener Answer, we can talk about some of the differences between high school and college, and the right way to approach your college education.

237

The Can Opener Answer

3   Why is it good to have a can opener? People pay money for can openers, and people spend time with can openers, so they must think that can openers are valuable in some way or other, but how are they valuable? The answer here is easy: can openers are valuable because they allow you to open cans. There's tasty stuff inside of cans, and you can't get at the tasty stuff unless the can is open, and you can't open the can unless you've got a can opener. If you could open cans by snapping your fingers, then you wouldn't need a can opener. Can openers are *tools*: they are valuable, but only as tools or instruments are valuable. That is, they are valuable because of what you can get with them. Once we acquire the ability to open cans by snapping our fingers, or once they stop hiding the tasty stuff inside of cans, then can openers will be useless. They will cease to have the sort of value they now have.[1]

4   So what's the Can Opener Answer to the question about the value of college? It's this: a college education is valuable because of what you can do with it. In particular, it's valuable because you can trade it for a job. Crudely put, you can take your diploma, show it to an employer, and then you'll get a job. Of course the job interview process is not that easy, but in rough outline that's how many people (maybe even you!) think about the value of a college education. I hope you can see the analogy with the can opener case. The job is the analogue of the tasty stuff in the can. If you could get a job without a college education, then, it would seem, it's silly and wasteful and foolish to spend all that time and money and effort at college. Just as it would be silly to spend money on a can opener if you could open the can by snapping your fingers.

5   People who ask the question, "So, what are you going to do with an English major?", or "How much money do Sociology majors make?" are thinking in can opener terms. They think that the only thing valuable about a college education is what sort of job (and how high-paying a job) you can get with that college education. And they also think that people who major in Classics or Philosophy or Women's Studies won't get very good jobs. So, they think, since you're spending all that time and money and effort on college, you should get yourself the sort of education that is *useful* for getting a good job. So, they might say, you should major in Nursing or

Education or Business or Journalism or Computer Science because those are the sort of majors that you can trade for good jobs.

6　Now I think there is something right about the Can Opener Answer, but there are two serious problems with it.

The First Problem with the Can Opener Answer

7　What the Can Opener Answer has right is that a college education is useful for getting a job. After all, college graduates, in general, have better, higher paying, more interesting, potentially more fulfilling jobs than those without college degrees. But that is not the only thing a college education is useful for. A college education—in particular, a broad-based, multidisciplinary, liberal arts education—is useful for so much more. The problem with the simple Can Opener Answer is that it misses this "so much more" when it focuses merely on the job-getting features of a college degree. Here are just some of the other things that college educated people are able to do.

8　• College can equip us for our leisure time just as much, if not more so, than it can equip us for our working lives. College educated people are able to appreciate and enjoy literature, art, music, essays, movies, and other products of the culture. Or, to put it better, the sort of appreciation and enjoyment that they have is deeper because of their education: those with a liberal arts education see things in movies and music and literature that those without the education don't. And, as a consequence, their experience is richer.

9　• We live in a democracy, the success of which requires that each of us participates actively and intelligently in the democratic institutions. Such participation includes not simply voting, but critically examining the candidates' positions, speaking out as an advocate for policy change, perhaps even serving in a leadership role on a governmental body. Moreover, it requires being critical of the institutions themselves, and seeing what needs changing and why. The appreciation of history, the ability to formulate a persuasive argument, an analytic skill with budgets and statistics and polling data—these are all skills you get as a college educated person and they are skills necessary for successful participation as a citizen in a democracy.

10 • The developments in technology and the advances in science (especially medical science) are an ever-present, and ever-more-important part of our lives. The growing presence of medications in the treatment of psychological maladies, the possibilities opened up by study and manipulation of DNA, and the prospects for artificial intelligence (just to name a few) are developments that require an intelligent response. Which of the many possibilities opened up to us by science should be pursued? How reliable is DNA testing? Should we treat depression with a drug or with traditional therapy? College graduates are well-positioned to answer these questions because they know some science, and can distinguish quackery from good scientific practice. Moreover, they are accustomed to asking questions about *value*[2] and these are the sorts of questions which very much need to be asked about technological developments.

11 • This last point applies not simply to the advances in science and technology, but to the information that comes to us via the media. We need to be able to distinguish the foolish fad from the important trend; we need to be able to determine which news outlets are reliable and which are overly biased; we need to be able to figure out where to turn for information and how to navigate between the twin vices of gullibility (believing everything you read in the newspaper, or see on the internet, or hear from a TV anchor) and skepticism (believing nothing that anybody else tells you). Because during your college education you will spend a significant amount of time doing research and evaluating sources, you will be, once you finish college, perfectly situated to be intelligent consumers of information.

12 • Finally, a college education equips people with the tools for self-examination that renders them able to make informed and intelligent choices about the direction of their own lives. College may equip you for a career, but you have to decide *which* career to pursue, and how to balance the competing demands of work and family. At what point do you leave the comfort of a safe but boring job for the excitement of a new, but insecure job? How important a role should your religious or political beliefs play in the life you lead? Should you work for (or buy the products of) a company that exploits child laborers? Should you buy your groceries

from a large national chain or from the local, but perhaps more expensive, market? At what point should you put a moral principle ahead of economic interest? These are decisions that we all must make; if we don't, someone else will make them for us. And by providing the experience and guidance at thinking th___ __ ___ _____ (and other _____ _____ _____ will turn _____

13 The point _____ _____ _____ _____ tion isn't valu____ _____ _____ ke a Swiss arm___ ___ is valuable. Or like a compu___ ____ble. People who focus simply on the job-getting feature of a college education are like people who think that the belt-punch is the only useful feature of a Swiss army knife.

14 I would go even further and argue that the benefits of a college education that I just listed are actually *more valuable* than the fact that you can get a good job with a college diploma. First, it is becoming increasingly unlikely you will spend the 40 years following college in one career, let alone in one job. To devote your college years to preparing for life as a lab assistant will turn out to be a waste when you leave the biomedical industry for a job in book publishing. But the features I listed above will be of use no matter what job you have. Secondly, and I think more importantly, the job you have is but one element in what I would hope is a complex and multi-layered life. Living your life involves so much more than working at a job. It involves being a citizen, a spouse, a friend, a parent, a decision-maker, and someone who has leisure time to fill, and a college education contributes toward improving these aspects of your life.

The Second Problem with the Can Opener Answer

15 That's the first problem with the simple Can Opener Answer: it mistakes something that has many uses for something that performs merely one task. But even when we do focus on the way in which a college education translates into a job, I think many people fail fully to grasp precisely why employers value employees who are college educated. And this failure is the second problem with the simple Can Opener Answer.

16 The reason that college degrees translate into high-end salaries and good jobs has, I would argue, more to do with the *skills* one

acquires in college than with the discipline-specific *knowledge* of the individual courses. No one is going to give you a better job because of your knowledge of Shakespeare or Plato or the Napoleonic Wars. But students who are successful in their English, Philosophy, and History classes are independent and creative thinkers who can write and speak clearly, who can juggle many responsibilities, who can conduct research, and who can take steps to educate themselves. And employers will be falling all over themselves to hire people with these skills. Consequently, it doesn't matter so much what your major is as much as it does that you acquire these more general skills. So select a major that you find interesting, which will challenge you, which will make you smarter, and don't worry exclusively about "what you can do" with a degree in, say, religious studies.

17   Even when it comes to the more vocationally-related majors like nursing or business or education or biology, it is sure to be the case that the knowledge you will need in your job will far outstrip what you will learn in your college classes. This is not a failing of the college classes, it is just a fact that specific industries and jobs require highly specific knowledge. It is also a fact that what you need to know to be an accountant or a teacher or a nurse or a biologist will change in response to advances in those fields. (Think, for example, about how much more today's middle school teachers need to know about computers compared to their predecessors 30 years ago.) One of the goals of a college education is to give you the general knowledge into which you can fit the more specific knowledge required by your particular job. And, more importantly, a college education will give you the ability to teach yourself, so that when you need a new job skill, you'll be prepared.

18   When you get a job, the employer very likely will train you to do whatever it is that needs to be done. Large corporations have entire human resources departments and internal "universities" the sole purpose of which is to train the new employees to perform the necessary tasks. The Widget Corporation will understand if you can't come in on the first day of the job and start making the widgets; their trainers will show you how to do that. But what they won't show you is how to write clearly, how to organize your time, how to give a presentation to the Board of Directors, how to ask questions, and how to make decisions. What an employer wants above all is an employee who can

think, and that is what they expect from people with a college education. Once you understand that it is these more generally intellectual skills which employers desire, you'll realize that they can be acquired in just about any major.

19   The second problem, then, with the simple Can Opener Answer is that it fails to recognize that it is the general skills and not simply the domain-specific content knowledge which turns college graduates into desirable employees. I think I can put the point this way. A college education does not, as most people believe, prepare you do to *something*. Rather, it prepares you to do *anything*.[3]

How to Get the Most Out of College

20   Now that we understand the value of a college education, we can think about what you should do in college, and how you can make the most of your college years. Given that college is valuable not simply because it gets you a job, but because it prepares you to be a complete person, *and* given that what you want from college in the way of job-related skills are general intellectual abilities more than particular, task-specific knowledge, what should you do? I don't have all the answers, but here are some about which I'm fairly confident.

21   1.   Write as much as you can. Then write some more. The written word is the medium of academic communication. Academics talk to one another through books and published articles. Students talk to their professors through exams and term papers. If you cannot write well, you will not succeed in college, it's as simple as that. I once spoke to a group of college juniors, and I asked them what they wish they knew about college when they were entering freshmen. One of them[4] said that he wished he had known how much writing he would have to do, and to how high a standard his writing would be held. So now you know: writing is crucially important.

22   And since writing is a skill like juggling or playing the guitar, the only way to get better at it is to practice. Write at every opportunity. Keep a class journal. Take notes when you read (and don't simply underline or highlight your books. This is next to worthless.). Write drafts of your assigned papers. Demand feedback on your writing from

your professors. The more you write, the better a writer you will become. And, you will find, the better a *thinker* you will become, because more than anything else, writing is just thinking out loud. Write for yourself, to clarify your own thinking, not simply because you have a paper due at the end of the term. Because writing is the medium of academic communication, you need to treat it that way—as a form of communication. Don't think of your papers as something that you turn in for a grade, but as an opportunity to talk to your professors and to tell them what you have been thinking about. I hardly need say that if you are a talented writer, you will succeed in the workplace. You won't have to write essays on Jane Austen or the Protestant Reformation once you leave college, but you will have to write memos and reports and presentations and speeches, and honing this skill in college will serve you well once you leave.

23   2.   Talk. And not just about your weekend plans or about the details of your friends' love lives. Talk about ideas that fascinate you. Talk about politics and religion and racism and abortion and all the other issues that are important but which are not usually talked about in "polite society." It is through talking about these issues that you may very well come to turn confusion into clarity. Many of these questions can only be solved when a number of minds come together at once, and gathering in a group and talking is the best way to bring minds together. How will you know if there is a flaw in your position if you don't show it to someone else? Moreover, you can use your talking about these issues as practice for the talking that you will have to do with your spouse, your children, your co-workers, your boss, and the members of your town council. Speaking to others in private and to groups in public is one of those life and job skills that I was talking about above, and if you can treat college as an opportunity for honing that skill, you will be ready to talk in these other sorts of situations. Finally, as you will soon learn, talking about ideas is valuable for its own sake. The late-night conversations at coffee houses or in dorm rooms about the meaning of life and the way to fix the world are just plain fun. Do it as often as you can.

24   3.   Take responsibility for your education. Here's the part where college distinguishes itself from high school. High

school students are there because they have to be. College students are in college because they want to be. (And make sure you really *want* to be in college before you go. It is a sizeable investment of time and money, and if there's something else you'd rather be doing, you should take some time and re-assess your situation. Taking a year off to figure out what you want, and entering college with a clear plan in mind can make all the difference in the world.) You are paying dearly for your college education, so you should go out and *get* it. Don't wait for someone else to hand it to you; it won't come. Taking responsibility for your own education manifests itself in small ways, and in larger ways. On the small side it means going to the dictionary when you run across a word you don't know. It also means asking your professor to read a draft of your essay, or raising your hand in class to ask for a difficult point to be repeated. But taking responsibility for your education means more than this. It means seeking out challenging courses and inspiring professors, for only if you push yourself by taking hard courses will you improve your academic and intellectual skills. It means having the courage to change your major if you find your current one uninteresting. It means engaging your friends in the dormitories and coffee shops about what you are learning in the classroom. It means speaking up and agitating for change if things aren't going the way you want. If you sit passively through your classes, skipping the readings, and taking only the easy courses, you will fail to gain the very education to which you are committing so much time and money.

25   It might help to think of college as a sort of health club— a health club for the mind.[5] There are all sorts of machines in the health club: these are your professors, your classes, and the many extra-curricular activity opportunities. The machines at this intellectual health club can improve your mind in the way that the weights and stair-climbers at your gym can improve your body. But, just as at the gym, the machines are useless if you don't use them. Merely buying a health club membership won't turn flab into muscle; you have to lift weights and do sit-ups. And merely enrolling in college won't turn an uneducated person into an educated one. Doing the reading, talking in class,

visiting your professors in office hours, pursuing research topics outside of class—this is the sort of "machine using" behavior that will turn the gray matter inside your head into a well-toned mental muscle.

26 4. Do something completely different. I see so many students who take the same menu of courses they took in high school: history, English, math, science, and a foreign language. All of those are important classes, but a quick glance at any college's course catalog will show that there are dozens if not hundreds of comparatively exotic courses. Religious studies, communication, anthropology, economics, psychology, film theory—the list goes on. Take a course that is completely different from anything you have taken before. Explore the unknown. Not only might the strange and exotic be something you like (and have a talent for!), but the challenge of these new courses will push you to develop the intellectual skills I have been talking about. This injunction to do something completely different shouldn't stop at the course catalog, however. Find the person on campus most different from you and take them out to coffee. Try out for a play, join the debate team, write for the newspaper, join a campus service organization. Try your hand at some of those activities that you would never have done in high school. Of course you will meet new people, but the primary reason for engaging in these pursuits is to discover something about yourself. Maybe you would enjoy the theatre or find that you have a talent for organizing fund-drives (and can translate that into a career!). It is foolish to commit yourself to a life-plan before you have discovered what you like and what talents you have. And after you get a "real job" and "settle down" you will find precious little time for these extra-curricular pursuits.

27 5. Become curious. The late Canadian novelist Robertson Davies has hit upon the essence of college. "Energy and curiosity are the lifeblood of universities," Davies had one of his characters say. "The desire to find out, to uncover, to dig deeper, to puzzle out obscurities, is the spirit of the university and it is a channelling of that unresting curiosity that holds mankind together."[6] Since this 'unresting curiosity' is the essence of any college, succeeding during the next four years requires that you tap into this energy, and that you

become an unrestingly curious person yourself. Feed your curiosity by taking courses that interest you, rather than the courses which might look good on a law school application. Find those issues and problems that interest you and pursue them doggedly. Become curious about everything—about medieval history, about the structure of the cell, about what your roommates are learning in their classes, about the research interests of your professors—and you will find not only that you are getting better grades, but that you are becoming a smarter, more intellectually independent person. And that is, at the end, the goal of a college education.[7]

Notes

[1] Of course in such a situation can openers may have value as antiques, or as objects of art. And that is a real sort of value, but it is not (at least not standardly) why we think can openers are valuable now.

[2] Like this very essay: it's an examination of the value of a college education.

[3] I learned of this way of putting the point from Ami Berger, though I don't think she was the originator of this thought.

[4] His name is Caleb Bell.

[5] For this health club analogy I am indebted to Craig Froehle.

[6] This is from Davies' novel, *The Rebel Angels*.

[7] An earlier, abbreviated, version of this essay was published under the title "College is more than job training" in *The Blade* (Toledo, Ohio) on September 30, 2000. For helpful conversation on this essay, I would like to thank Lori Aronson, Ami Berger, Brad Cohen, Craig Froehle, Glenna Jackson, Brain Lindeman, Kristine LaLonde, Mary MacLeod, Lisa Pollak, Charles Salter, and the audiences at Otterbein College to whom I have presented the main ideas contained above. I would like to dedicate this essay to Jack Meiland, who ignited my thinking on the question of why a college education is valuable. His little book, *College Thinking*, is as valuable a guide to college as I can think of.

Kent Nerburn (1946–) holds a Ph.D. in both theology and art, and lives in northern Minnesota. He is an author, a sculptor, and an educator, committed to Native American issues and education, and has published many books, including two oral histories and three collections of Native American writings and wisdom. The selection below is taken from his 1993 book, Letters to My Son, *a collection of essays written as a gift to his son. This essay focuses on the role of work in one's life. (The book includes an introduction by Richard Carlson, author of* Don't Sweat the Small Stuff, *among other works.)*

Work

Kent Nerburn

1   I often hear people say, "I have to find myself." What they really mean is, "I have to make myself." Life is an endlessly creative experience, and we are making ourselves every moment by every decision we make.

2   That is why the work you choose for yourself is so crucial to your sense of value and well-being. No matter how much you might believe that your work is nothing more than what you do to make money, your work makes you who you are, because it is where you put your time.

3   I remember several years ago when I was intent upon building my reputation as a sculptor. I took a job driving a cab, because, as I told people, "I want some job that I will never confuse with a profession." Yet within six months I was talking like a cab driver, thinking like a cab driver, looking at the world through the eyes of a cab driver. My anecdotes came from my job, as did my observations about life. I became embroiled in the personalities and politics of the company for which I worked and developed the habits and rhythms of life that went along with my all-night driving shift. On the days when I did not drive and instead worked on my sculpture, I still carried the consciousness of a cab driver with me.

4   Whether I liked it or not, I was a cab driver.

5   This happens to anyone who takes a job. Even if you hate the job and keep a distance from it, you are defining yourself in opposition to the job by resisting it. By giving the job your time, you are giving it your consciousness. And it will, in turn, fill your life with the reality that it presents.

6   Many people ignore this fact. They choose a profession because it seems exciting, or because they can make a lot of money, or because it has some prestige in their minds. They commit themselves to their work, but slowly find themselves feeling restless and empty. The time they have to spend on their work begins to hang heavy on their hands, and soon they feel constricted and trapped.

7   They join the legions of humanity who Thoreau said lead lives of quiet desperation—unfulfilled, unhappy, and uncertain of what to do. Yet the lure of financial security and the fear of the unknown keep them from acting to change their lives, and their best energies are spent creating justifications for staying where they are or inventing activities outside of work that they hope will provide them with a sense of meaning.

8   But these efforts can never be totally successful. We are what we do, and the more we do it, the more we become it. The only way out is to change our lives or to change our expectations for our lives. And if we lower our expectations we are killing our dreams, and a man without dreams is already half dead.

9   So you need to choose your work carefully. You need to look beyond the external measurements of prestige and money and glamour to see what you will be doing on a day-to-day, hour-to-hour, minute-to-minute basis to see if that is how you want to spend your time. Time may not be the way you measure the value of your work, but it is the way you experience it.

10 What you need to do is think of work as "vocation." This word may seem stilted in its tone, but it has a wisdom within it. It comes from the Latin word for calling, which comes from the word for voice. In those meanings it touches on what work really should be. It should be something that calls to you as something you want to do, and it should be something that gives voice to who you are and what you want to say to the world.

11   So a true vocation calls to you to perform it and it allows your life to speak. This is very different from work, which is just an exchange of labor for money. It is even very different from a profession, which is an area of expertise you have been sanctioned to represent.

12   A vocation is something you feel compelled to do, or at least something that fills you with a sense of meaning. It is something you choose because of what it allows you to say with your life, not because of the money it pays you or the way it will make you appear to others. It is, above all else, something that lets you love.

13   When you find a vocation, embrace it with your whole heart. Few people are so lucky. They begin their search for work with an eye to the wrong prize, so when they win they win something of little value. They gain money or prestige, but they lose their hearts. Eventually their days become nothing more than a commodity that they exchange for money, and they begin to shrivel and die.

14   I often think of a man I met on the streets of Cleveland. He was an assembly-line worker in an automobile plant. He said his work was so hateful that he could barely stand to get up in the morning. I asked him why he didn't quit. "I've only got thirteen more years to retirement," he answered. And he meant it. His life had so gotten away from him that he was willing to accept a thirteen-year death sentence for his spirit rather than give up the security he had earned.

15   When I spoke with him I was about twenty. I was young and free; I didn't understand what he was saying at all. It seemed incomprehensible to me that a man could have becomes so defeated by life that he was willing to let his life die as he held it in his hands.

16   Now I understand too well. Lured by what had seemed like big money at the time, he had chosen a job that didn't offer him any inner satisfaction. He lived a good life, rolling from paycheck to paycheck and getting the car or the boat that he had always dreamed of having. Year by year he advanced, because businesses reward perseverance.

17   His salary went up, his options for other types of employment went down, and he settled into a routine that financed his life.

He married, bought a house, had children, and grew into middle age. The job that had seemed like freedom when he was young became a deadening routine. Year by year he began to hate it. It choked him, but he had no means of escape. He needed its money to live; no job he might change to would pay him as much as he was currently making. His fear for the health and security of his family kept him from breaking free into a world where all things were possible but no things were paid for, and so he gave in.

18   "I've only got thirteen more years to retirement" was a prisoner's way of counting the days until the job would release him and pay him for his freedom.

19   Most people's lives are a variation on that theme. So few take the time when they are young to explore the real meaning of the jobs they are taking or to consider the real implications of the occupations to which they are committing their lives.

20   Some have no choice. Without money, without training, with the pressures of life building around them, they choose the best alternative that offers itself. But many others just fail to see clearly. They chase false dreams, and fall into traps they could have avoided if they had listened more closely to their hearts when choosing their life's work.

21   But even if you listen closely to your heart, making the right choice is difficult. You can't really know what it is you want to do by thinking about it. You have to do it and see how it fits. You have to let the work take you over until it becomes you and you become it; then you have to decide whether to embrace it or to abandon it. And few have the courage to abandon something that defines their security and prosperity.

22   Yet there is no reason why a person cannot have two, three, or more careers in the course of a life. There is no reason why a person can't abandon a job that does not fit anymore and strike out into the unknown for something that lies closer to the heart. There is risk, there is loss, and there likely will be privation. If you have allowed your job to define your sense of self-worth, there may even be a crisis of identity. But no amount of security is worth the suffering of a life lived chained to a routine that has killed all your dreams.

23   You must never forget that to those who hire you, your labor is a commodity. You are paid because you provide a service that is useful. If the service you provide is no longer needed, it doesn't matter how honorable, how diligent, how committed you have been in your work. If what you can contribute is no longer needed, you are no longer needed and you will be let go. Even if you've committed your life to the job, you are, at heart, a part of a commercial exchange, and you are valuable only so long as you are a significant contributor to that commercial exchange. It is nothing personal; it's just the nature of economic transaction.

24   So it does not pay to tie yourself to a job that kills your love of life. The job will abandon you if it has to. You can abandon the job if you have to. The man I met in Cleveland may have been laid off the year before he was due to retire. He may have lost his pension because of a legal detail he never knew existed. He may have died on the assembly line while waiting to put a bolt in a fender.

25   I once had a professor who dreamed of being a concert pianist. Fearing the possibility of failure, he went into academics where the work was secure and the money was predictable. One day, when I was talking to him about my unhappiness in my graduate studies, he walked over and sat down at his piano. He played a beautiful glissando and then, abruptly, stopped. "Do what is in your heart," he said. "I really only wanted to be a concert pianist. Now I spend every day wondering how good I might have been."

26   Don't let this be your epitaph at the end of your working life. Find what it is that burns in your heart and do it. Choose a vocation, not a job, and you will be at peace. Take a job instead of finding a vocation, and eventually you will find yourself saying, "I've only got thirteen more years to retirement," or "I spend every day wondering how good I might have been."

27   We all owe ourselves better than that.

John Henry Newman (1801–1890), an English theologian and philosopher, was raised in the Church of England and ordained an Anglican priest in 1825. As a Fellow of Oriel College and then vicar of St. Mary's, Oxford, he became a major figure in the "Oxford Movement," which sought to restore Catholic elements in the Church of England. Work on his book, An Essay on the Development of Christian Doctrine *(1845), led to his conviction that the Christian Church of the early centuries was continued in the Roman Catholic Church. Newman became a Roman Catholic in 1845 and was ordained priest in 1847. From 1854 to 1858 he was Rector of a new Catholic university in Dublin, Ireland, an endeavor which occasioned* The Idea of a University *(1858), which set out an ideal of the university as an environment for the development of the mind. This work and his* Apologia *(the story of his conversion) rank among the classics of nineteenth-century English prose. Newman is noteworthy for his efforts to introduce the emerging historical consciousness of the nineteenth century into Catholic theology. He was named a Cardinal in 1878.*

Knowledge Viewed in Relation to Professional Skill

John Henry Newman

1.

1   I have been insisting, in my two preceding Discourses, first, on the cultivation of the intellect, as an end which may reasonably be pursued for its own sake; and next, on the nature of that cultivation, or what that cultivation consists in. Truth of whatever kind is the proper object of the intellect; its cultivation then lies in fitting it to apprehend and contemplate truth. Now the intellect in its present state, with exceptions, which need not here be specified, does not discern truth intuitively, or as a whole. We know, not by a direct and simple vision, not at a glance, but, as it were, by piecemeal and accumulation, by a mental process, by going round an object, by the comparison, the combination, the mutual correction, the continual adaptation, of many partial notions, by the employment, concentration, and joint action of many faculties and exercises of mind.

Such a union and concert of the intellectual powers, such an enlargement and development, such a comprehensiveness, is necessarily a matter of training. And again, such a training is a matter of rule; it is not mere application, however exemplary, which introduces the mind to truth, nor the reading many books, nor the getting up many subjects, nor the witnessing many experiments, nor the attending many lectures. All this is short of enough; a man may have done it all, yet be lingering in the vestibule of knowledge:—he may not realize what his mouth utters; he may not see with his mental eye what confronts him; he may have no grasp of things as they are; or at least he may have no power at all of advancing one step forward of himself, in consequence of what he has already acquired, no power of discriminating between truth and falsehood, of sifting out the grains of truth from the mass, of arranging things according to their real value, and, if I may use the phrase, of building up ideas. Such a power is the result of a scientific formation of mind; it is an acquired faculty of judgment, of clear-sightedness, of sagacity, of wisdom, of philosophical reach of mind, and of intellectual self-possession and repose,—qualities which do not come of mere acquirement. The bodily eye, the organ for apprehending material objects, is provided by nature; the eye of the mind, of which the object is truth, is the work of discipline and habit.

2   This process of training, by which the intellect, instead of being formed or sacrificed to some particular or accidental purpose, some specific trade or profession, or study or science, is disciplined for its own sake, for the perception of its own proper object, and for its own highest culture, is called Liberal Education; and though there is no one in whom it is carried as far as is conceivable, or whose intellect would be a pattern of what intellects should be made, yet there is scarcely any one but may gain an idea of what real training is, and at least look towards it, and make its true scope and result, not something else, his standard of excellence; and numbers there are who may submit themselves to it, and secure it to themselves in good measure. And to set forth the right standard, and to train according to it, and to help forward all students towards it according to their various capacities, this I conceive to be the business of a University.

2.

3   Now this is what some great men are very slow to allow; they insist that Education should be confined to some particular and narrow end, and should issue in some definite work, which can be weighed and measured. They argue as if every thing, as well as every person, had its price; and that where there has been a great outlay, they have a right to expect a return in kind. This they call making Education and Instruction "useful," and "Utility" becomes their watchword. With a fundamental principle of this nature, they very naturally go on to ask, what there is to show for the expense of a University; what is the real worth in the market of the article called "a Liberal Education," on the supposition that it does not teach us definitely how to advance our manufactures, or to improve our lands, or to better our civil economy; or again, if it does not at once make this man a lawyer, that an engineer, and that a surgeon; or at least if it does not lead to discoveries in chemistry, astronomy, geology, magnetism, and science of every kind.

4   This question, as might have been expected, has been keenly debated in the present age, and formed one main subject of the controversy, to which I referred in the Introduction to the present Discourses, as having been sustained in the first decade of this century by a celebrated Northern Review on the one hand, and defenders of the University of Oxford on the other. Hardly had the authorities of that ancient seat of learning, waking from their long neglect, set on foot a plan for the education of the youth committed to them, than the representatives of science and literature in the city, which has sometimes been called the Northern Athens, remonstrated, with their gravest arguments and their most brilliant satire, against the direction and shape which the reform was taking. Nothing would content them, but that the University should be set to rights on the basis of the philosophy of Utility; a philosophy, as they seem to have thought, which needed but to be proclaimed in order to be embraced. In truth, they were little aware of the depth and force of the principles on which the academical authorities were proceeding, and, this being so, it was not to be expected that they would be allowed to walk at leisure over the field of controversy which they had selected. Accordingly they were encountered in behalf of the University by two men of great name and influence in their day, of very different minds, but united, as by Collegiate ties, so in the clear-sighted and large

view which they took of the whole subject of Liberal Education; and the defence thus provided for the Oxford studies
has kept its ground to this day.

3.

5   Let me be allowed to devote a few words to the memory of distinguished persons, under the shadow of whose name I once
lived, and by whose doctrine I am now profiting. In the heart
of Oxford there is a small plot of ground, hemmed in by public thoroughfares, which has been the possession and the home
of one Society for above five hundred years. In the old time of
Boniface the Eighth and John the Twenty-second, in the age of
Scotus and Occam and Dante, before Wiclif or Huss had kin-
dled those miserable fires which are still raging to the ruin of
the highest interests of man, an unfortunate king of England,
Edward the Second, flying from the field of Bannockburn, is
said to have made a vow to the Blessed Virgin to found a religious house in her honour, if he got back in safety. Prompted
and aided by his Almoner, he decided on placing this house in
the city of Alfred; and the Image of our Lady, which is opposite its entrance-gate, is to this day the token of the vow and its
fulfillment. King and Almoner have long been in the dust, and
strangers have entered into their inheritance, and their creed
has been forgotten, and their holy rites disowned; but day by
day a memento is still made in the holy Sacrifice by at least one
Catholic Priest, once a member of that College, for the souls of
those Catholic benefactors who fed him there for so many
years. The visitor, whose curiosity has been excited by its present fame, gazes perhaps with something of disappointment
on a collection of buildings which have with them so few of
the circumstances of dignity or wealth. Broad quadrangles,
high halls and chambers, ornamented cloisters, stately walks,
or umbrageous gardens, a throng of students, ample revenues,
or a glorious history, none of these things were the portion of
that old Catholic foundation; nothing in short which to the
common eye sixty years ago would have given tokens of what
it was to be. But it had at that time a spirit working within it,
which enabled its inmates to do, amid its seeming insignifi-
cance, what no other body in the place could equal; not a very
abstruse gift or extraordinary boast, but a rare one, the honest
purpose to administer the trust committed to them in such a
way as their conscience pointed out as best. So, whereas the
Colleges of Oxford are self-electing bodies, the fellows in each

perpetually filling up for themselves the vacancies which occur in their number, the members of this foundation determined, at a time when, either from evil custom or from ancient statute, such a thing was not known elsewhere, to throw open their fellowships to the competition of all comers, and, in the choice of associates henceforth, to cast to the winds every personal motive and feeling, family connexion, and friendship, and patronage, and political interest, and local claim, and prejudice, and party jealousy, and to elect solely on public and patriotic grounds. Nay, with a remarkable independence of mind, they resolved that even the table of honours, awarded to literary merit by the University in its new system of examination for degrees, should not fetter their judgment as electors; but that at all risks, and whatever criticism it might cause, and whatever odium they might incur, they would select the men, whoever they were, to be children of their Founder, whom they thought in their consciences to be most likely from their intellectual and moral qualities to please him, if (as they expressed it) he were still upon earth, most likely to do honour to his College, most likely to promote the objects which they believed he had at heart. Such persons did not promise to be the disciples of a low Utilitarianism; and consequently, as their collegiate reform synchronized with that reform of the Academical body, in which they bore a principal part, it was not unnatural that, when the storm broke upon the University from the North, their Alma Mater, whom they loved, should have found her first defenders within the walls of that small College, which had first put itself into a condition to be her champion.

6   These defenders, I have said, were two, of whom the more distinguished was the late Dr. Copleston, then a Fellow of the College, successively its Provost, and Protestant Bishop of Llandaff. In that Society, which owes so much to him, his name lives, and ever will live, for the distinction which his talents bestowed on it, for the academical importance to which he raised it, for the generosity of spirit, the liberality of sentiment, and the kindness of heart, with which he adorned it, and which even those who had least sympathy with some aspects of his mind and character could not but admire and love. Men come to their meridian at various periods of their lives; the last years of the eminent person I am speaking of were given to duties which, I am told, have been the means of endearing him

to numbers, but which afforded no scope for that peculiar vigour and keenness of mind which enabled him, when a young man, single-handed, with easy gallantry, to encounter and overthrow the charge of three giants of the North combined against him. I believe I am right in saying that, in the progress of the controversy, the most scientific, the most critical, and the most witty, of that literary company, all of them now, as he himself, removed from this visible scene, Professor Playfair, Lord Jeffrey, and the Rev. Sydney Smith, threw together their several efforts into one article of their Review, in order to crush and pound to dust the audacious controvertist who had come out against them in defence of his own Institutions. To have even contended with such men was a sufficient voucher for his ability, even before we open his pamphlets, and have actual evidence of the good sense, the spirit, the scholar-like taste, and the purity of style, by which they are distinguished.

7   He was supported in the controversy, on the same general principles, but with more of method and distinctness, and, I will add, with greater force and beauty and perfection, both of thought and of language, by the other distinguished writer, to whom I have already referred, Mr. Davison; who, though not so well known to the world in his day, has left more behind him than the Provost of Oriel, to make his name remembered by posterity. This thoughtful man, who was the admired and intimate friend of a very remarkable person, whom, whether he wish it or not, numbers revere and love as the first author of the subsequent movement in the Protestant Church towards Catholicism,[1] this grave and philosophical writer, whose works I can never look into without sighing that such a man was lost to the Catholic Church, as Dr. Butler before him, by some early bias or some fault of self-education—he, in a review of a work by Mr. Edgeworth on Professional Education, which attracted a good deal of attention in its day, goes leisurely over the same ground, which had already been rapidly traversed by Dr. Copleston, and, though professedly employed upon Mr. Edgeworth, is really replying to the northern critic who had brought that writer's work into notice, and to a far greater author than either of them, who in a past age had argued on the same side.

4.

8 The author to whom I allude is no other than Locke. That celebrated philosopher has preceded the Edinburgh Reviewers in condemning the ordinary subjects in which boys are instructed at school, on the ground that they are not needed by them in after life; and before quoting what his disciples have said in the present century, I will refer to a few passages of the master. "'Tis matter of astonishment," he says in his work on Education, "that men of quality and parts should suffer themselves to be so far misled by custom and implicit faith. Reason, if consulted with, would advise, that their children's time should be spent in acquiring what might be useful to them, when they come to be men, rather than that their heads should be stuffed with a deal of trash, a great part whereof they usually never do ('tis certain they never need to) think on again as long as they live; and so much of it as does stick by them they are only the worse for."

9 And so again, speaking, of verse-making, he says, "I know not what reason a father can have to wish his son a poet, who does not desire him to *bid defiance to all other callings and business;* which is not yet the worst of the case; for, if he proves a successful rhymer, and gets once the reputation of a wit, I desire it to be considered, what company and places he is likely to spend his time in, nay, and estate too; for it is very seldom seen that any one discovers *mines of gold or silver in Parnassus.* 'Tis a pleasant air, but a barren soil."

10 In another passage he distinctly limits utility in education to its bearing on the future profession or trade of the pupil, that is, he scorns the idea of any education of the intellect, simply as such. "Can there be any thing more ridiculous," he asks, "than that a father should waste his own money, and his son's time, in setting him to *learn the Roman language,* when at the same time he *designs him for a trade,* wherein he, having no use of Latin, fails not to forget that little which he brought from school, and which 'tis ten to one he abhors for the ill-usage it procured him? Could it be believed, unless we have every where amongst us examples of it, that a child should be forced to learn the rudiments of a language, which *he is never to use in the course of life that he is designed to,* and neglect all the while

the writing a good hand, and casting accounts, which are of great advantage in all conditions of life, and to most trades indispensably necessary?" Nothing of course can be more absurd than to neglect in education those matters which are necessary for a boy's future calling; but the tone of Locke's remarks evidently implies more than this, and is condemnatory of any teaching which tends to the general cultivation of the mind.

11   Now to turn to his modern disciples. The study of the Classics had been made the basis of the Oxford education, in the reforms which I have spoken of, and the Edinburgh Reviewers protested, after the manner of Locke, that no good could come of a system which was not based upon the principle of Utility.

12   "Classical Literature," they said, "is the great object at Oxford. Many minds, so employed, have produced many works and much fame in that department; but if all liberal arts and sciences, *useful to human life,* had been taught there, if *some* had dedicated themselves to *chemistry, some* to *mathematics, some* to *experimental philosophy,* and if *every* attainment had been honoured in the mixt ratio of its difficulty and *utility,* the system of such a University would have been much more valuable, but the splendour of its name something less."

13   Utility may be made the end of education, in two respects: either as regards the individual educated, or the community at large. In which light do these writers regard it ? in the latter. So far they differ from Locke, for they consider the advancement of science as the supreme and real end of a University. This is brought into view in the sentences which follow.

14   "When a University has been doing *useless* things for a long time, it appears at first degrading to them to be *useful.* A set of Lectures on Political Economy would be discouraged in Oxford, probably despised, probably not permitted. To discuss the inclosure of commons, and to dwell upon imports and exports, to come so near to common life, would seem to be undignified and contemptible. In the same manner, the Parr or the Bentley of the day would be scandalized, in a University, to be put on a level with the discoverer of a neutral salt; and yet, *what other measure is there of dignity in intellectual labour but usefulness?* And what ought the term University to mean, but a place where every science is taught which is liberal, and at the

same time useful to mankind? Nothing would so much tend to bring classical literature within proper bounds as *a steady and invariable appeal to utility* in our appreciation of all human knowledge. . . . *Looking always to real utility as our guide,* we should see, with equal pleasure, a studious and inquisitive mind arranging the productions of nature, investigating the qualities of bodies, or mastering the difficulties of the learned languages. We should not care whether he was chemist, naturalist, or scholar, because we know it to be as *necessary* that matter should be studied and subdued *to the use of man,* as that taste should be gratified, and imagination inflamed."

15 Such then is the enunciation, as far as words go, of the theory of Utility in Education; and both on its own account, and for the sake of the able men who have advocated it, it has a claim on the attention of those whose principles I am here representing. Certainly it is specious to contend that nothing is worth pursuing but what is useful; and that life is not long enough to expend upon interesting, or curious, or brilliant trifles. Nay, in one sense, I will grant it is more than specious, it is true; but, if so, how do I propose directly to meet the objection? Why, Gentlemen, I have really met it already, viz., in laying down, that intellectual culture is its own end; for what has its *end* in itself, has its *use* in itself also. I say, if a Liberal Education consists in the culture of the intellect, and if that culture be in itself a good, here, without going further, is an answer to Locke's question; for if a healthy body is a good in itself, why is not a healthy intellect? and if a College of Physicians is a useful institution, because it contemplates bodily health, why is not an Academical Body, though it were simply and solely engaged in imparting vigour and beauty and grasp to the intellectual portion of our nature? And the Reviewers I am quoting seem to allow this in their better moments, in a passage which putting aside the question of its justice in fact, is sound and true in the principles to which it appeals:—

16 "The present state of classical education," they say, "cultivates the *imagination* a great deal too much, and other *habits of mind* a great deal too little, and trains up many young men in a style of elegant imbecility, utterly unworthy of the talents with which nature has endowed them. . . . The matter of fact is, that a classical scholar of twenty-three or twenty-four is a man principally conversant with works of imagination. His feelings

are quick, his fancy lively, and his taste good. Talents for *speculation* and *original inquiry* he has none, nor has he formed the invaluable *habit of pushing things up to their first principles*, or of collecting dry and unamusing facts as the materials for reasoning. All the solid and masculine parts of his *understanding* are left wholly without *cultivation*; he hates the pain of thinking, and suspects every man whose boldness and originality call upon him to defend his opinions and prove his assertions."

5.

17   Now, I am not at present concerned with the specific question of classical education; else, I might reasonably question the justice of calling an intellectual discipline, which embraces the study of Aristotle, Thucydides, and Tacitus, which involves Scholarship and Antiquities, *imaginative;* still so far I readily grant, that the cultivation of the "understanding," of a "talent for speculation and original inquiry," and of "the habit of pushing things up to their first principles," is a principal portion of a *good* or *liberal* education. If then the Reviewers consider such cultivation the characteristic of a *useful* education, as they seem to do in the foregoing passage, it follows, that what they mean by "useful" is just what I mean by "good" or "liberal:" and Locke's question becomes a verbal one. Whether youths are to be taught Latin or verse-making will depend on the *fact*, whether these studies tend to mental culture; but, however this is determined, so far is clear, that in that mental culture consists what I have called a liberal or non-professional, and what the Reviewers call a useful education.

18   This is the obvious answer which may be made to those who urge upon us the claims of Utility in our plans of Education; but I am not going to leave the subject here: I mean to take a wider view of it. Let us take "useful," as Locke takes it, in its proper and popular sense, and then we enter upon a large field of thought, to which I cannot do justice in one Discourse, though to-day's is all the space that I can give to it. I say, let us take "useful" to mean, not what is simply good, but what *tends* to good, or is the *instrument* of good; and in this sense also, Gentlemen, I will show you how a liberal education is truly and fully a useful, though it be not a professional, education. "Good" indeed means one thing, and "useful" means another; but I lay it down as a principle, which will save us a great deal

of anxiety, that, though the useful is not always good, the good is always useful. Good is not only good, but reproductive of good; this is one of its attributes; nothing is excellent, beautiful, perfect, desirable for its own sake, but it overflows, and spreads the likeness of itself all around it. Good is prolific; it is not only good to the eye, but to the taste; it not only attracts us, but it communicates itself; it excites first our admiration and love, then our desire and our gratitude, and that, in proportion to its intenseness and fulness in particular instances. A great good will impart great good. If then the intellect is so excellent a portion of us, and its cultivation so excellent, it is not only beautiful, perfect, admirable, and noble in itself, but in a true and high sense it must be useful to the possessor and to all around him; not useful in any low, mechanical, mercantile sense, but as diffusing good, or as a blessing, or a gift, or power, or a treasure, first to the owner, then through him to the world. I say then, if a liberal education be good, it must necessarily be useful too.

6.

19 You will see what I mean by the parallel of bodily health. Health is a good in itself, though nothing came of it, and is especially worth seeking and cherishing; yet, after all, the blessings which attend its presence are so great, while they are so close to it and so redound back upon it and encircle it, that we never think of it except as useful as well as good, and praise and prize it for what it does, as well as for what it is, though at the same time we cannot point out any definite and distinct work or production which it can be said to effect. And so as regards intellectual culture, I am far from denying utility in this large sense as the end of Education, when I lay it down, that the culture of the intellect is a good in itself and its own end; I do not exclude from the idea of intellectual culture what it cannot but be, from the very nature of things; I only deny that we must be able to point out, before we have any right to call it useful, some art, or business, or profession, or trade, or work, as resulting from it, and as its real and complete end. The parallel is exact:—As the body may be sacrificed to some manual or other toil, whether moderate or oppressive, so may the intellect be devoted to some specific profession; and I do not call *this* the culture of the intellect. Again, as some member or organ of the body may be inordinately used and developed,

so may memory, or imagination, or the reasoning faculty; and *this* again is not intellectual culture. On the other hand, as the body may be tended, cherished, and exercised with a simple view to its general health, so may the intellect also be generally exercised in order to its perfect state; and this *is* its cultivation.

20 Again, as health ought to precede labour of the body, and as a man in health can do what an unhealthy man cannot do, and as of this health the properties are strength, energy, agility, graceful carriage and action, manual dexterity, and endurance of fatigue, so in like manner general culture of mind is the best aid to professional and scientific study, and educated men can do what illiterate cannot; and the man who has learned to think and to reason and to compare and to discriminate and to analyze, who has refined his taste, and formed his judgment, and sharpened his mental vision, will not indeed at once be a lawyer, or a pleader, or an orator, or a statesman, or a physician, or a good landlord, or a man of business, or a soldier, or an engineer, or a chemist, or a geologist, or an antiquarian, but he will be placed in that state of intellect in which he can take up any one of the sciences or callings I have referred to, or any other for which he has a taste or special talent, with an ease, a grace, a versatility, and a success, to which another is a stranger. In this sense then, and as yet I have said but a very few words on a large subject, mental culture is emphatically *useful*.

21 If then I am arguing, and shall argue, against Professional or Scientific knowledge as the sufficient end of a University Education, let me not be supposed, Gentlemen, to be disrespectful towards particular studies, or arts, or vocations, and those who are engaged in them. In saying that Law or Medicine is not the end of a University course, I do not mean to imply that the University does not teach Law or Medicine. What indeed can it teach at all, if it does not teach something particular? It teaches *all* knowledge by teaching all branches of knowledge, and in no other way. I do but say that there will be this distinction as regards a Professor of Law, or of Medicine, or of Geology, or of Political Economy, in a University and out of it, that out of a University he is in danger of being absorbed and narrowed by his pursuit, and of giving Lectures which are the Lectures of nothing more than a lawyer, physician, geologist,

or political economist; whereas in a University he will just know where he and his science stand, he has come to it, as it were, from a height, he has taken a survey of all knowledge, he is kept from extravagance by the very rivalry of other studies, he has gained from them a special illumination and largeness of mind and freedom and self-possession, and he treats his own in consequence with a philosophy and a resource, which belongs not to the study itself, but to his liberal education.

22 This then is how I should solve the fallacy, for so I must call it, by which Locke and his disciples would frighten us from cultivating the intellect, under the notion that no education is useful which does not teach us some temporal calling, or some mechanical art, or some physical secret. I say that a cultivated intellect, because it is a good in itself, brings with it a power and a grace to every work and occupation which it undertakes, and enables us to be more useful, and to a greater number. There is a duty we owe to human society as such, to the state to which we belong, to the sphere in which we move, to the individuals towards whom we are variously related, and whom we successively encounter in life; and that philosophical or liberal education, as I have called it, which is the proper function of a University, if it refuses the foremost place to professional interests, does but postpone them to the formation of the citizen, and, while it subserves the larger interests of philanthropy, prepares also for the successful prosecution of those merely personal objects, which at first sight it seems to disparage.

7.

23 And now, Gentlemen, I wish to be allowed to enforce in detail what I have been saying, by some extracts from the writings to which I have already alluded, and to which I am so greatly indebted.

24 "It is an undisputed maxim in Political Economy," says Dr. Copleston, "that the separation of professions and the division of labour tend to the perfection of every art, to the wealth of nations, to the general comfort and well-being of the community. This principle of division is in some instances pursued so far as to excite the wonder of people to whose notice it is for the first time pointed out. There is no saying to what extent it may not be carried; and the more the powers of each individual are concentrated in one employment, the greater skill and

quickness will he naturally display in performing it. But, while he thus contributes more effectually to the accumulation of national wealth, he becomes himself more and more degraded as a rational being. In proportion as his sphere of action is narrowed his mental powers and habits become contracted; and he resembles a subordinate part of some powerful machinery, useful in its place, but insignificant and worthless out of it. If it be necessary, as it is beyond all question necessary, that society should be split into divisions and subdivisions, in order that its several duties may be well performed, yet we must be careful not to yield up ourselves wholly and exclusively to the guidance of this system; we must observe what its evils are, and we should modify and restrain it, by bringing into action other principles, which may serve as a check and counterpoise to the main force.

25   "There can be no doubt that every art is improved by confining the professor of it to that single study. But, *although the art itself is advanced by this concentration of mind in its service, the individual who is confined to it goes back.* The advantage of the community is nearly in an inverse ratio with his own.

26   "Society itself requires some other contribution from each individual, besides the particular duties of his profession. And, if no such liberal intercourse be established, it is the common failing of human nature, to be engrossed with petty views and interests, to underrate the importance of all in which we are not concerned, and to carry our partial notions into cases where they are inapplicable, to act, in short, as so many unconnected units, displacing and repelling one another.

27   "In the cultivation of literature is found that common link, which, among the higher and middling departments of life, unites the jarring sects and subdivisions into one interest, which supplies common topics, and kindles common feelings, unmixed with those narrow prejudices with which all professions are more or less infected. The knowledge, too, which is thus acquired, expands and enlarges the mind, excites its faculties, and calls those limbs and muscles into freer exercise which, by too constant use in one direction, not only acquire an illiberal air, but are apt also to lose somewhat of their native play and energy. And thus, without directly qualifying a man for any of the employments of life, it enriches and ennobles all. Without teaching him the peculiar business of any one office or

calling, it enables him to act his part in each of them with better grace and more elevated carriage; and, if happily planned and conducted, is a main ingredient in that complete and generous education which fits a man 'to perform justly, skilfully, and magnanimously, all the offices, both private and public, of peace and war.'"[2]

8.

28 The view of Liberal Education, advocated in these extracts, is expanded by Mr. Davison in the Essay to which I have already referred. He lays more stress on the "usefulness" of Liberal Education in the larger sense of the word than his predecessor in the controversy. Instead of arguing that the Utility of knowledge to the individual varies inversely with its Utility to the public, he chiefly employs himself on the suggestions contained in Dr. Copleston's last sentences. He shows, first, that a Liberal Education is something far higher, even in the scale of Utility, than what is commonly called a Useful Education, and next, that it is necessary or useful for the purposes even of that Professional Education which commonly engrosses the title of Useful. The former of these two theses he recommends to us in an argument from which the following passages are selected:—

29 "It is to take a very contracted view of life," he says, "to think with great anxiety how persons may be educated to superior skill in their department, comparatively neglecting, or excluding the more liberal and enlarged cultivation. In his (Mr. Edgeworth's) system, the value of every attainment is to be measured by its subserviency to a calling. The specific duties of that calling are exalted at the cost of those free and independent tastes and virtues which come in to sustain the common relations of society, and raise the individual in them. In short, a man is to be usurped by his profession. He is to be clothed in its garb from head to foot. His virtues, his science, and his ideas are all to be put into a gown or uniform, and the whole man to be shaped, pressed, and stiffened, in the exact mould of his technical character. Any interloping accomplishments, or a faculty which cannot be taken into public pay, if they are to be indulged in him at all, must creep along, under the cloak of his more serviceable privileged merits. Such is the state of perfection to which the spirit and general tendency of this system would lead us.

30   "But the professional character is not the only one which a person engaged in a profession has to support. He is not always upon duty. There are services he owes, which are neither parochial, nor forensic, nor military, nor to be described by any such epithet of civil regulation, and yet are in no wise inferior to those that bear these authoritative titles; inferior neither in their intrinsic value, nor their moral import, nor their impression upon society. As a friend, as a companion, as a citizen at large; in the connections of domestic life; in the improvement and embellishment of his leisure, he has a sphere of action, revolving, if you please, within the sphere of his profession, but not clashing with it; in which if he can show none of the advantages of an improved understanding, whatever may be his skill or proficiency in the other, he is no more than an ill-educated man.

31   "There is a certain faculty in which all nations of any refinement are great practitioners. It is not taught at school or college as a distinct science; though it deserves that what is taught there should be made to have some reference to it; nor is it endowed at all by the public; everybody being obliged to exercise it for himself in person, which he does to the best of his skill. But in nothing is there a greater difference than in the manner of doing it. The advocates of professional learning will smile when we tell them that this same faculty which we would have encouraged, is simply that of speaking good sense in English, without fee or reward, in common conversation. They will smile when we lay some stress upon it; but in reality it is no such trifle as they imagine. Look into the huts of savages, and see, for there is nothing to listen to, the dismal blank of their stupid hours of silence; their professional avocations of war and hunting are over; and, having nothing to do, they have nothing to say. Turn to improved life, and you find conversation in all its forms the medium of something more than an idle pleasure; indeed, a very active agent in circulating and forming the opinions, tastes, and feelings of a whole people. It makes of itself a considerable affair. Its topics are the most promiscuous— all those which do not belong to any particular province. As for its power and influence, we may fairly say that it is of just the same consequence to a man's immediate society, how he talks, as how he acts. Now of all those who furnish their share to rational conversation, a mere adept in his own art is universally admitted to be the worst. The sterility

and uninstructiveness of such a person's social hours are quite proverbial. Or if he escape being dull, it is only by launching into ill-timed, learned loquacity. We do not desire of him lectures or speeches; and he has nothing else to give. Among benches he may be powerful; but seated on a chair he is quite another person. On the other hand, we may affirm, that one of the best companions is a man who, to the accuracy and research of a profession, has joined a free excursive acquaintance with various learning, and caught from it the spirit of general observation."

9.

32   Having thus shown that a liberal education is a real benefit to the subjects of it, as members of society, in the various duties and circumstances and accidents of life, he goes on, in the next place, to show that, over and above those direct services which might fairly be expected of it, it actually subserves the discharge of those particular functions, and the pursuit of those particular advantages, which are connected with professional exertion, and to which Professional Education is directed.

33   "We admit," he observes, "that when a person makes a business of one pursuit, he is in the right way to eminence in it; and that divided attention will rarely give excellence in many. But our assent will go no further. For, to think that the way to prepare a person for excelling in any one pursuit (and that is the only point in hand), is to fetter his early studies, and cramp the first development of his mind, by a reference to the exigencies of that pursuit barely, is a very different notion, and one which, we apprehend, deserves to be exploded rather than received. Possibly a few of the abstract, insulated kinds of learning might be approached in that way The exceptions to be made are very few, and need not be recited. But for the acquisition of professional and practical ability such maxims are death to it. The main ingredients of that ability are requisite knowledge and cultivated faculties; but, of the two, the latter is by far the chief. A man of well improved faculties has the command of another's knowledge. A man without them, has not the command of his own.

34   "Of the intellectual powers, the judgment is that which takes the foremost lead in life. How to form it to the two habits it ought to possess, of exactness and vigour, is the problem. It

would be ignorant presumption so much as to hint at any routine of method by which these qualities may with certainty be
imparted to every or any understanding. Still, however, we
may safely lay it down that they are not to be got 'by a gather-
er of simples,' but are the combined essence and extracts of
many different things, drawn from much varied reading and
discipline, first, and observation afterwards. For if there be a
single intelligible point on this head, it is that a man who has
been trained to think upon one subject or for one subject only,
will never be a good judge even in that one: whereas the
enlargement of his circle gives him increased knowledge and
power in a rapidly increasing ratio. So much do ideas act, not
as solitary units, but by grouping and combination; and so
clearly do all the things that fall within the proper province of
the same faculty of the mind, intertwine with and support
each other. Judgment lives as it were by comparison and discrimination. Can it be doubted, then, whether the range and
extent of that assemblage of things upon which in is practiced
in its first essays are of use to its power?

35   "To open our way a little further on this matter, we will define
what we mean by the power of judgment; and then try to
ascertain among what kind of studies the improvement of it
may be expected at all.

36   "Judgment does not stand here for a certain homely, useful quality of intellect, that guards a person from committing mistakes to
the injury of his fortunes or common reputation; but for that
master-principle of business, literature, and talent, which gives
him strength in any subject he chooses to grapple with, and
enables him to *seize the strong point in it*. Whether this definition
be metaphysically correct or not, it comes home to the substance
of our inquiry. It describes the power that every one desires to
possess when he comes to act in a profession, or elsewhere; and
corresponds with our best idea of a cultivated mind.

37   "Next, it will not be denied, that in order to do any good to the
judgment, the mind must be employed upon such subjects as
come within the cognizance of that faculty, and give some real
exercise to its perceptions. Here we have a rule of selection by
which the different parts of learning may be classed for our
purpose. Those which belong to the province of the judgment
are religion (in its evidences and interpretation), ethics, history, eloquence, poetry, theories of general speculation, the fine

arts, and works of wit. Great as the variety of these large divisions of learning may appear, they are all held in union by two capital principles of connexion. First, they are all quarried out of one and the same great subject of man's moral, social, and feeling nature. And secondly, they are all under the control (more or less strict) of the same power of moral reason."

38 "If these studies," he continues, "be such as give a direct play and exercise to the faculty of the judgment, then they are the true basis of education for the active and inventive powers, whether destined for a profession or any other use. Miscellaneous as the assemblage may appear, of history, eloquence, poetry, ethics, etc., blended together, they will all conspire in an union of effect. They are necessary mutually to explain and interpret each other. The knowledge derived from them all will amalgamate, and the habits of a mind versed and practiced in them by turns will join to produce a richer vein of thought and of more general and practical application than could be obtained of any single one, as the fusion of the metals into Corinthian brass gave the artist his most ductile and perfect material. Might we venture to imitate an author (whom indeed it is much safer to take as an authority than to attempt to copy), Lord Bacon, in some of his concise illustrations of the comparative utility of the different studies, we should say that history would give fulness, moral philosophy strength, and poetry elevation to the understanding. Such in reality is the natural force and tendency of the studies; but there are few minds susceptible enough to derive from them any sort of virtue adequate to those high expressions. We must be contented therefore to lower our panegyric to this, that a person cannot avoid receiving some infusion and tincture, at least, of those several qualities, from that course of diversified reading. One thing is unquestionable, that the elements of general reason are not to be found fully and truly expressed in any one kind of study; and that he who would wish to know her idiom, must read it in many books.

39 "If different studies are useful for aiding, they are still more useful for correcting each other; for as they have their particular merits severally, so they have their defects, and the most extensive acquaintance with one can produce only an intellect either too flashy or too jejune, or infected with some other fault of confined reading. History, for example, shows things as they

are, that is, the morals and interests of men disfigured and perverted by all their imperfections of passion, folly, and ambition; philosophy strips the picture too much; poetry adorns it too much; the concentrated lights of the three correct the false peculiar colouring of each, and show us the truth. The right mode of thinking upon it is to be had from them taken all together, as every one must know who has seen their united contributions of thought and feeling expressed in the masculine sentiment of our immortal statesman, Mr. Burke, whose eloquence is inferior only to his more admirable wisdom. If any mind improved like his, is to be our instructor, we must go to the fountain head of things as he did, and study not his works but his method; by the one we may become feeble imitators, by the other arrive at some ability of our own. But, as all biography assures us, he, and every other able thinker, has been formed, not by a parsimonious admeasurement of studies to some definite future object (which is Mr. Edgeworth's maxim) but by taking a wide and liberal compass, and thinking a great deal on many subjects with no better end in view than because the exercise was one which made them more rational and intelligent beings."

10.

40   But I must bring these extracts to an end. To-day I have confined myself to saying that that training of the intellect, which is best for the individual himself, best enables him to discharge his duties to society. The Philosopher, indeed, and the man of the world differ in their very notion, but the methods, by which they are respectively formed, are pretty much the same. The Philosopher has the same command of matters of thought, which the true citizen and gentleman has of matters of business and conduct. If then a practical end must be assigned to a University course, I say it is that of training good members of society. Its art is the art of social life, and its end is fitness for the world. It neither confines its views to particular professions on the one hand, nor creates heroes or inspires genius on the other. Works indeed of genius fall under no art; heroic minds come under no rule; a University is not a birthplace of poets or of immortal authors, of founders of schools, leaders of colonies, or conquerors of nations. It does not promise a generation of Aristotles or Newtons, of Napoleons or Washingtons, of Raphaels or Shakespeares, though such miracles of nature it has before now contained within its precincts. Nor is it content on the other hand with forming

the critic or the experimentalist, the economist or the engineer, though such too it includes within its scope. But a University training is the great ordinary means to a great but ordinary end; it aims at raising the intellectual tone of society, at cultivating the public mind, at purifying the national taste, at supplying true principles to popular enthusiasm and fixed aims to popular aspiration, at giving enlargement and sobriety to the ideas of the age, at facilitating the exercise of political power, and refining the intercourse of private life. It is the education which gives a man a clear conscious view of his own opinions and judgments, a truth in developing them, an eloquence in expressing them, and a force in urging them. It teaches him to see things as they are, to go right to the point, to disentangle a skein of thought, to detect what is sophistical, and to discard what is irrelevant. It prepares him to fill any post with credit, and to master any subject with facility. It shows him how to accommodate himself to others, how to throw himself into their state of mind, how to bring before them his own, how to influence them, how to come to an understanding with them, how to bear with them. He is at home in any society, he has common ground with every class; he knows when to speak and when to be silent; he is able to converse, he is able to listen; he can ask a question pertinently, and gain a lesson seasonably, when he has nothing to impart himself; he is ever ready, yet never in the way; he is a pleasant companion, and a comrade you can depend upon; he knows when to be serious and when to trifle, and he has a sure tact which enables him to trifle with gracefulness and to be serious with effect. He has the repose of a mind which lives in itself, while it lives in the world, and which has resources for its happiness at home when it cannot go abroad. He has a gift which serves him in public, and supports him in retirement, without which good fortune is but vulgar, and with which failure and disappointment have a charm. The art which tends to make a man all this, is in the object which it pursues as useful as the art of wealth or the art of health, though it is less susceptible of method, and less tangible, less certain, less complete in its result.

Notes

[1] Mr. Keble, Vicar of Hursley, late Fellow of Oriel, and Professor of Poetry in the University of Oxford.

[2] Vid. Milton on Education.

What Is a University?

John Henry Newman

1   If I were asked to describe as briefly and popularly as I could, what a University was, I should draw my answer from its ancient designation of a *Studium Generale,* or "School of Universal Learning." This description implies the assemblage of strangers from all parts in one spot;—*from all parts;* else, how will you find professors and students for every department of knowledge? and *in one spot;* else, how can there be any school at all? Accordingly, in its simple and rudimental form, it is a school of knowledge of every kind, consisting of teacher and learners from every quarter. Many things are requisite to complete and satisfy the idea embodied in this description; but such as this a University seems to be in its essence, a place for the communication and circulation of thought, by means of personal intercourse, through a wide extent of country.

2   There is nothing far-fetched or unreasonable in the idea thus presented to us; and if this be a University, then a University does but contemplate a necessity of our nature, and is but one specimen in a particular medium, out of many which might be adduced in others, of a provision for that necessity. Mutual education, in a large sense of the word, is one of the great and incessant occupations of human society, carried on partly with set purpose, and partly not. One generation forms another; and the existing generation is ever acting and reacting upon itself in the persons of its individual members. Now, in this process, books, I need scarcely say, that is, the *litera scripta,* are one special instrument. It is true; and emphatically so in this age. Considering the prodigious powers of the press, and how they are developed at this time in the never-intermitting issue of periodicals, tracts, pamphlets, works in series, and light literature, we must allow there never was a time which promised fairer for dispensing with every other means of information and instruction. What can we want more, you will say, for the intellectual education of the whole man, and for every man, than so exuberant and diversified and persistent a promulgation of all kinds of knowledge? Why, you will ask, need we go up to knowledge, when knowledge comes down to us? The

Sibyl wrote her prophecies upon the leaves of the forest, and wasted them; but here such careless profusion might be prudently indulged, for it can be afforded without loss, in consequence of the almost fabulous fecundity of the instrument which these latter ages have invented. We have sermons in stones, and books in the running brooks; works larger and more comprehensive than those which have gained for ancients an immortality, issue forth every morning, and are projected onwards to the ends of the earth at the rate of hundreds of miles a day. Our seats are strewed, our pavements are powdered, with swarms of little tracts; and the very bricks of our city walls preach wisdom, by informing us by their placards where we can at once cheaply purchase it.

3   I allow all this, and much more; such certainly is our popular education, and its effects are remarkable. Nevertheless, after all, even in this age, whenever men are really serious about getting what, in the language of trade, is called "a good article," when they aim at something precise, something refined, something really luminous, something really large, something choice, they go to another market; they avail themselves, in some shape or other, of the rival method, the ancient method, of oral instruction, of present communication between man and man, of teachers instead of learning, of the personal influence of a master, and the humble initiation of a disciple, and, in consequence, of great centres of pilgrimage and throng, which such a method of education necessarily involves. This, I think, will be found to hold good in all those departments or aspects of society, which possess an interest sufficient to bind men together, or to constitute what is called "a world." It holds in the political world, and in the high world, and in the religious world; and it holds also in the literary and scientific world.

4   If the actions of men may be taken as any test of their convictions, then we have reason for saying this, viz.:—that the province and the inestimable benefit of the *litera scripta* is that of being a record of truth, and an authority of appeal, and an instrument of teaching in the hands of a teacher; but that, if we wish to become exact and fully furnished in any branch of knowledge which is diversified and complicated, we must consult the living man and listen to his living voice. I am not bound to investigate the cause of this, and anything I may say

will, I am conscious, be short of its full analysis;—perhaps we
may suggest, that no books can get through the number of
minute questions which it is possible to ask on any extended
subject, or can hit upon the very difficulties which are severally felt by each reader in succession. Or again, that no book can
convey the special spirit and delicate peculiarities of its subject
with that rapidity and certainty which attend on the sympathy
of mind with mind, through the eyes, the look, the accent, and
the manner, in casual expressions thrown off at the moment,
and the unstudied turns of familiar conversation. But I am
already dwelling too long on what is but an incidental portion
of my main subject. Whatever be the cause, the fact is undeni-
able. The general principles of any study you may learn by
books at home; but the detail, the colour, the tone, the air, the
life which makes it live in us, you must catch all these from
those in whom it lives already. You must imitate the student in
French or German, who is not content with his grammar, but
goes to Paris or Dresden: you must take example from the
young artist, who aspires to visit the great Masters in Florence
and in Rome. Till we have discovered some intellectual da-
guerreotype, which takes off the course of thought, and the
form, lineaments, and features of truth, as completely and
minutely, as the optical instrument reproduces the sensible
object, we must come to the teachers of wisdom to learn wisdom, we must repair to the fountain, and drink there. Portions
of it may go from thence to the ends of the earth by means of
books; but the fulness is in one place alone. It is in such assem-
blages and congregations of intellect that books themselves,
the masterpieces of human genius, are written, or at least originated.

5   The principle on which I have been insisting is so obvious, and
instances in point are so ready, that I should think it tiresome
to proceed with the subject, except that one or two illustrations
may serve to explain my own language about it, which may
not have done justice to the doctrine which it has been intended to enforce.

6   For instance, the polished manners and high-bred bearing
which are so difficult of attainment, and so strictly personal
when attained,—which are so much admired in society, from
society are acquired. All that goes to constitute a gentleman,—the carriage, gait, address, gestures, voice; the ease,
the self-possession, the courtesy, the power of conversing, the

talent of not offending; the lofty principle, the delicacy of thought, the happiness of expression, the taste and propriety, the generosity and forbearance, the candour and consideration, the openness of hand;—these qualities, some of them come by nature, some of them may be found in any rank, some of them are a direct precept of Christianity; but the full assemblage of them, bound up in the unity of an individual character, do we expect they can be learned from books? are they not necessarily acquired, where they are to be found, in high society? The very nature of the case leads us to say so; you cannot fence without an antagonist, nor challenge all comers in disputation before you have supported a thesis; and in like manner, it stands to reason, you cannot learn to converse till you have the world to converse with; you cannot unlearn your natural bashfulness, or awkwardness, or stiffness, or other besetting deformity, till you serve your time in some school of manners. Well, and is it not so in matter of fact? The metropolis, the court, the great houses of the land, are the centres to which at stated times the country comes up, as to shrines of refinement and good taste; and then in due time the country goes back again home, enriched with a portion of the social accomplishments, which those very visits serve to call out and heighten in the gracious dispensers of them. We are unable to conceive how the "gentlemanlike" can otherwise be maintained; and maintained in this way it is.

7 And now a second instance: and here too I am going to speak without personal experience of the subject I am introducing. I admit I have not been in Parliament, any more than I have figured in the *beau monde;* yet I cannot but think that statesmanship, as well as high breeding, is learned, not by books, but in certain centres of education. If it be not presumption to say so, Parliament puts a clever man *au courant* with politics and affairs of state in a way surprising to himself. A member of the Legislature, if tolerably observant, begins to see things with new eyes, even though his views undergo no change. Words have a meaning now, and ideas a reality, such as they had not before. He hears a vast deal in public speeches and private conversation, which is never put into print. The bearings of measures and events, the action of parties, and the persons of friends and enemies, are brought out to the man who is in the midst of them with a distinctness, which the most diligent perusal of newspapers will fail to impart to them. It is access

to the fountain-heads of political wisdom and experience, it is daily intercourse, of one kind or another, with the multitude who go up to them, it is familiarity with business, it is access to the contributions of feet and opinion thrown together by many witnesses from many quarters, which does this for him. However, I need not account for a fact, to which it is sufficient to appeal; that the Houses of Parliament and the atmosphere around them are a sort of University of politics.

8   As regards the world of science, we find a remarkable instance of the principle which I am illustrating, in the periodical meetings for its advance, which have arisen in the course of the last twenty years, such as the British Association. Such gatherings would to many persons appear at first sight simply preposterous. Above all subjects of study, Science is conveyed, is propagated, by books, or by private teaching; experiments and investigations are conducted in silence; discoveries are made in solitude. What have philosophers to do with festive celebrities, and panegyrical solemnities with mathematical and physical truth? Yet on a closer attention to the subject, it is found that not even scientific thought can dispense with the suggestions, the instruction, the stimulus, the sympathy, the intercourse with mankind on a large scale, which such meetings secure. A fine time of year is chosen, when days are long, skies are bright, the earth smiles, and all nature rejoices; a city or town is taken by turns, of ancient name or modern opulence, where buildings are spacious and hospitality hearty. The novelty of place and circumstance, the excitement of strange, or the refreshment of well-known faces, the majesty of rank or of genius, the amiable charities of men pleased both with themselves and with each other; the elevated spirits, the circulation of thought, the curiosity; the morning sections, the outdoor exercise, the well-furnished, well-earned board, the not ungraceful hilarity, the evening circle; the brilliant lecture, the discussions or collisions or guesses of great men one with another, the narratives of scientific processes, of hopes, disappointments, conflicts, and successes, the splendid eulogistic orations; these and the like constituents of the annual celebration, are considered to do something real and substantial for the advance of knowledge which can be done in no other way. Of course they can but be occasional; they answer to the annual Act, or Commemoration of a University, not to its ordinary condition; but they are of a University nature; and I can well believe in their utility. They issue

in the promotion of a certain living and, as it were, bodily communication of knowledge from one to another, of a general interchange of ideas, and a comparison and adjustment of science with science, of an enlargement of mind, intellectual and social, of an ardent love of the particular study, which may be chosen by each individual, and a noble devotion to its interests.

9   Such meetings, I repeat, are but periodical, and only partially represent the idea of a University. The bustle and whirl which are their usual concomitants, are in ill keeping with the order and gravity of earnest intellectual education. We desiderate means of instruction which involve no interruption of our ordinary habits; nor need we seek it long, for the natural course of things brings it about, while we debate over it. In every great country, the metropolis itself becomes a sort of necessary University, whether we will or no. As the chief city is the seat of the court, of high society, of politics, and of law, so as a matter of course is it the seat of letters also; and at this time, for a long term of years, London and Paris are in fact and in operation Universities, though in Paris its famous University is no more, and in London a University scarcely exists except as a board of administration. The newspapers, magazines, reviews, journals, and periodicals of all kinds, the publishing trade, the libraries, museums, and academies there found, the learned and scientific societies, necessarily invest it with the functions of a University; and that atmosphere of intellect, which in a former age hung over Oxford or Bologna or Salamanca, has, with the change of times, moved away to the centre of civil government. Thither come up youths from all parts of the country, the students of law, medicine, and the fine arts, and the *employés* and *attachés* of literature. There they live, as chance determines; and they are satisfied with their temporary home, for they find in it all that we promised to them there. They have not come in vain, as far as their own object in coming is concerned. They have not learned any particular religion, but they have learned their own particular profession well. They have, moreover, become acquainted with the habits, manner, and opinions of their place of sojourn, and done their part in maintaining the tradition of them. We cannot then be without virtual Universities; a metropolis is such: the simple question is, whether the education sought and given should be based on principle, formed upon rule, directed to the highest ends, or left to the random succession

of masters and schools, one after another, with a melancholy waste of thought and an extreme hazard of truth.

10   Religious teaching itself affords us an illustration of our subject to a certain point. It does not indeed seat itself merely in centres of the world; this is impossible from the nature of the case. It is intended for the many not the few; its subject matter is truth necessary for us, not truth recondite and rare; but it concurs in the principle of a University so far as this, that its great instrument, or rather organ, has ever been that which nature prescribes in all education, the personal presence of a teacher, or, in theological language, Oral Tradition. It is the living voice, the breathing form, the expressive countenance, which preaches, which catechises. Truth, a subtle, invisible, manifold spirit, is poured into the mind of the scholar by his eyes and ears, through his affections, imagination, and reason; it is poured into his mind and is sealed up there in perpetuity, by propounding and repeating it, by questioning and requestioning, by correcting and explaining, by progressing and then recurring to first principles, by all those ways which are implied in the word "catechising." In the first ages, it was a work of a long time; months, sometimes years, were devoted to the arduous task of disabusing the mind of the incipient Christian of its pagan errors, and of moulding it upon the Christian faith. The Scriptures indeed were at hand for the study of those who could avail themselves of them; but St. Irenaeus does not hesitate to speak of whole races, who had been converted to Christianity, without being able to read them. To be unable to read or write was in those times no evidence of want of learning: the hermits of the deserts were, in this sense of the word, illiterate; yet the great St. Anthony, though he knew not letter, was a match in disputation for the learned philosophers who came to try him. Didymus again, the great Alexandrian theologian, was blind. The ancient discipline, called the *Disciplina Arcani,* involved the same principle. The more sacred doctrines of Revelation were not committed to books but passed on by successive tradition. The teaching on the Blessed Trinity and the Eucharist appears to have been so handed down for some hundred years; and when at length reduced to writing, it has filled many folios, yet has not been exhausted.

11   But I have said more than enough in illustration; I end as I began;—a University is a place of concourse, whither students

come from every quarter for every kind of knowledge. You cannot have the best of every kind everywhere; you must go to some great city or emporium for it. There you have all the choicest productions of nature and art all together, which you find each in its own separate place elsewhere. All the riches of the land, and of the earth, are carried up thither; there are the best markets, and there the best workmen. It is the centre of trade, the supreme court of fashion, the umpire of rival talents, and the standard of things rare and precious. It is the place for seeing: galleries of first-rate pictures, and for hearing wonderful voices and performers of transcendent skill. It is the place for great preachers, great orators, great nobles, great statesmen. In the nature of things, greatness and unity go together; excellence implies a centre. And such, for the third or fourth time, is a University; I hope I do not weary out the reader by repeating it. It is the place to which a thousand schools make contributions; in which the intellect may safely range and speculate, sure to find its equal in some antagonist activity, and its judge in the tribunal of truth. It is a place where inquiry is pushed forward, and discoveries verified and perfected, and rashness rendered innocuous, and error exposed, by the collision of mind with mind, and knowledge with knowledge. It is the place where the professor becomes eloquent, and is a missionary and a preacher, displaying his science in its most complete and most winning form, pouring it forth with the zeal of enthusiasm, and lighting up his own love of it in the breasts of his hearers. It is the place where the catechist makes good his ground as he goes, treading in the truth day by day into the ready memory, and wedging and tightening it into the expanding reason. It is a place which wins the admiration of the young by its celebrity, kindles the affections of the middle-aged by its beauty, and rivets the fidelity of the old by its associations. It is a seat of wisdom, a light of the world, a minister of the faith, an Alma Mater of the rising generation. It is this and a great deal more, and demands a somewhat better head and hand than mine to describe it well.

12 Such is a University in its idea and in its purpose; such in good measure has it before now been in fact. Shall it ever be again? We are going forward in the strength of the Cross, under the patronage of the Blessed Virgin, in the name of St Patrick, to attempt it.

Mary Flannery O'Connor was born in Savannah, Georgia in 1925, her family moving to Milledgeville, Georgia thirteen years later. In this small, southern town, O'Connor attended Georgia State College for Women, now Georgia College and State University. After graduating, O'Connor began the Program in Creative Writing at the University of Iowa, better known as the Iowa Writers' Workshop, then and now one of the best creative writing programs in the country. O'Connor next spent time in New York and Connecticut working on her writing, until she was stricken with systemic lupus erythematosus in 1950. This disease had taken her father's life nine years earlier, so O'Connor returned to Milledgeville to live with her mother on the family farm, Andalusia. Here she published her first novel, Wise Blood *(1952); a collection of short stories,* A Good Man Is Hard to Find And Other Stories *(1955); and her second novel,* The Violent Bear It Away *(1960). Her second collection of short stories,* Everything That Rises Must Converge, *was published posthumously one year after her death in 1964 of complications from lupus.*

Total Effect and the Eighth Grade

Flannery O'Connor

1   In two recent instances in Georgia, parents have objected to their eighth- and ninth-grade children's reading assignments in modern fiction. This seems to happen with some regularity in cases throughout the country. The unwitting parent picks up his child's book, glances through it, comes upon passages of erotic detail or profanity, and takes off at once to complain to the school board. Sometimes, as in one of the Georgia cases, the teacher is dismissed and hackles rise in liberal circles everywhere.

2   The two cases in Georgia, which involved Steinbeck's *East of Eden* and John Hersey's *A Bell for Adano*, provoked considerable newspaper comment. One columnist, in commending the enterprise of the teachers, announced that students do not like to read the fusty works of the nineteenth century, that their attention can best be held by novels dealing with the realities of our own time, and that the Bible, too, is full of racy stories.

282

3   Mr. Hersey himself addressed a letter to the State School Super-
     intendent in behalf of the teacher who had been dismissed. He
     pointed out that his book is not scandalous, that it attempts to
     convey an earnest message about the nature of democracy, and
     that it falls well within the limits of the principle of "total
     effect," that principle followed in legal cases by which a book
     is judged not for isolated parts but by the final effect of the
     whole book upon the general reader.

4   I do not want to comment on the merits of these particular
     cases. What concerns me is what novels ought to be assigned
     in the eighth and ninth grades as a matter of course, for if these
     cases indicate anything, they indicate the haphazard way in
     which fiction is approached in our high schools. Presumably
     there is a state reading list which contains "safe" books for
     teachers to assign; after that it is up to the teacher.

5   English teachers come in Good, Bad, and Indifferent, but too
     frequently in high schools anyone who can speak English is
     allowed to teach it. Since several novels can't easily be gathered
     into one textbook, the fiction that students are assigned
     depends upon their teacher's knowledge, ability, and taste:
     variable factors at best. More often than not, the teacher assigns
     what he thinks will hold the attention and interest of the stu-
     dents. Modern fiction will certainly hold it.

6   Ours is the first age in history which has asked the child what
     he would tolerate learning, but that is a part of the problem
     with which I am not equipped to deal. The devil of Education-
     ism that possesses us is the kind that can be "cast out only by
     prayer and fasting." No one has yet come along strong enough
     to do it. In other ages the attention of children was held by
     Homer and Virgil, among others, but, by the reverse evolu-
     tionary process, that is no longer possible; our children are too
     stupid now to enter the past imaginatively. No one asks the
     student if algebra pleases him or if he finds it satisfactory that
     some French verbs are irregular, but if he prefers Hersey to
     Hawthorne, his taste must prevail.

7   I would like to put forward the proposition, repugnant to most
     English teachers, that fiction, if it is going to be taught in the high
     schools, should be taught as a subject and as a subject with a his-
     tory. The total effect of a novel depends not only on its innate
     impact, but upon the experience, literary and otherwise, with
     which it is approached. No child needs to be assigned Hersey or

Steinbeck until he is familiar with a certain amount of the best work of Cooper, Hawthorne, Melville, the early James, and Crane, and he does not need to be assigned these until he has been introduced to some of the better English novelists of the eighteenth and nineteenth centuries.

8   The fact that these works do not present him with the realities of his own time is all to the good. He is surrounded by the realities of his own time, and he has no perspective whatever from which to view them. Like the college student who wrote in her paper on Lincoln that he went to the movies and got shot, many students go to college unaware that the world was not made yesterday; their studies began with the present and dipped backward occasionally when it seemed necessary or unavoidable.

9   There is much to be enjoyed in the great British novels of the nineteenth century, much that a good teacher can open up in them for the young student. There is no reason why these novels should be either too simple or too difficult for the eighth grade. For the simple, they offer simple pleasures; for the more precocious, they can be made to yield subtler ones if the teacher is up to it. Let the student discover, after reading the nineteenth-century British novel, that the nineteenth-century American novel is quite different as to its literary characteristics, and he will thereby learn something not only about these individual works but about the sea-change which a new historical situation can effect in a literary form. Let him come to modern fiction with this experience behind him, and he will be better able to see and to deal with the more complicated demands of the best twentieth century fiction.

10   Modern fiction often looks simpler than the fiction that preceded it, but in reality it is more complex. A natural evolution has taken place. The author has for the most part absented himself from direct participation in the work and has left the reader to make his own way amid experiences dramatically rendered and symbolically ordered. The modern novelist merges the reader in the experience; he tends to raise the passions he touches upon. If he is a good novelist, he raises them to effect by their order and clarity a new experience—the total effect—which is not in itself sensuous or simply of the moment. Unless the child has had some literary experience before, he is not going to be able to resolve the immediate passions the book arouses into any true, total picture.

11 It is here the moral problem will arise. It is one thing for a child to read about adultery in the Bible or in *Anna Karenina*, and quite another for him to read about it in most modern fiction. This is not only because in both the former instances adultery is considered a sin, and in the latter, at most, an inconvenience, but because modern writing involves the reader in the action with a new degree of intensity, and literary mores now permit him to be involved in any action a human being can perform.

12 In our fractured culture, we cannot agree on morals; we cannot even agree that moral matters should come before literary ones when there is a conflict between them. All this is another reason why the high schools would do well to return to their proper business of preparing foundations. Whether in the senior year students should be assigned modern novelists should depend both on their parents' consent and on what they have already read and understood.

13 The high-school English teacher will be fulfilling his responsibility if he furnishes the student a guided opportunity, through the best writing of the past, to come, in time, to an understanding of the best writing of the present. He will teach literature, not social studies or little lessons in democracy or the customs of many lands.

14 And if the student finds that this is not to his taste? Well, that is regrettable. Most regrettable. His taste should not be consulted; it is being formed.

*R*obert Pirsig (1928–) was born in Minneapolis, Minnesota. His father was professor and dean of the University of Minnesota Law School. Pirsig began his university studies at the age of seventeen, but after two years he withdrew to join the army. He returned to complete his B.A. degree in 1950 at the University of Minnesota. Upon graduation he traveled to India, a trip that influenced his thought and subsequent writing of Zen and the Art of Motorcycle Maintenance. In 1958 he married and earned his M.A. degree in journalism from the University of Minnesota. The following year he began to teach English composition at Montana State College in Bozeman, where he felt overworked with no time for quiet reflection. He moved to Chicago in order to enroll in the Ph.D. program at the University of Chicago (1961–1962). It was during this time that Pirsig suffered a nervous breakdown which landed him in a state mental institution. In 1968 he motorcycled cross country with his twelve-year-old son Chris. The trip provided needed time to sort out his thoughts. The autobiographical book, Zen and the Art of Motorcycle Maintenance, was published in 1974.

from Zen and the Art of Motorcycle Maintenance

Robert M. Pirsig

16

1   Chris and I have had a good night's sleep and this morning have packed the backpacks carefully, and now have been going up the mountainside for about an hour. The forest here at the bottom of the canyon is mostly pine, with a few aspen and broad leafed shrubs. Steep canyon walls rise way above us on both sides. Occasionally the trail opens into a patch of sunlight and grass that edges the canyon stream, but soon it reenters the deep shade of the pines. The earth of the trail is covered with a soft springy duff of pine needles. It is very quiet here.

2   Mountains like these and travelers in the mountains and events that happen to them here are found not only in Zen literature but in the tales of every major religion. The allegory of

a physical mountain for the spiritual one that stands between each soul and its goal is an easy and natural one to make. Like those in the valley behind us, most people stand in sight of the spiritual mountains all their lives and never enter them, being content to listen to others who have been there and thus avoid the hardships. Some travel into the mountains accompanied by experienced guides who know the best and least dangerous routes by which they arrive at their destination. Still others, inexperienced and untrusting, attempt to make their own routes. Few of these are successful, but occasionally some, by sheer will and luck and grace, do make it. Once there they become more aware than any of the others that there's no single or fixed number of routes. There are as many routes as there are individual souls.

3   I want to talk now about Phaedrus' exploration into the meaning of the term *Quality*, an exploration which he saw as a route through the mountains of the spirit. As best I can puzzle it out, there were two distinct phases.

4   In the first phase he made no attempt at a rigid, systematic definition of what he was talking about. This was a happy, fulfilling and creative phase. It lasted most of the time he taught at the school back in the valley behind us.

5   The second phase emerged as a result of normal intellectual criticism of his lack of definition of what he was talking about. In this phase he made systematic, rigid statements about what Quality is, and worked out an enormous hierarchic structure of thought to support them. He literally had to move heaven and earth to arrive at this systematic understanding and when he was done felt he'd achieved an explanation of existence and our consciousness of it better than any that had existed before.

6   If it was truly a new route over the mountain it's certainly a needed one. For more than three centuries now the old routes common in this hemisphere have been undercut and almost washed out by the natural erosion and change of the shape of the mountain wrought by scientific truth. The early climbers established paths that were on firm ground with an accessibility that appealed to all, but today the Western routes are all but closed because of dogmatic inflexibility in the face of change.

To doubt the literal meaning of the words of Jesus or Moses incurs hostility from most people, but it's just a fact that if Jesus or Moses were to appear today, unidentified, with the same message he spoke many years ago, his mental stability would be challenged. This isn't because what Jesus or Moses said was untrue or because modern society is in error but simply because the route they chose to reveal to others has lost relevance and comprehensibility. "Heaven above" fades from meaning when space-age consciousness asks, Where is "above"? But the fact that the old routes have tended, because of language rigidity, to lose their everyday meaning and become almost closed doesn't mean that the mountain is no longer there. It's there and will be there as long as consciousness exists.

7   Phaedrus' second metaphysical phase was a total disaster. Before the electrodes were attached to his head he'd lost everything tangible: money, property, children; even his rights as a citizen had been taken away from him by order of the court. All he had left was his one crazy lone dream of Quality, a map of a route across the mountain, for which he had sacrificed everything. Then, after the electrodes were attached, he lost that.

8   I will never know all that was in his head at that time, nor will anyone else. What's left now is just fragments: debris, scattered notes, which can be pieced together but which leave huge areas unexplained.

9   When I first discovered this debris I felt like some agricultural peasant near the outskirts of, say, Athens, who occasionally and without much surprise plows up stones that have strange designs on them. I knew that these were part of some larger overall design that had existed in the past, but it was far beyond my comprehension. At first I deliberately avoided them, paid no attention to them because I knew these stones had caused some kind of trouble I should avoid. But I could see even then that they were a part of a huge structure of thought and I was curious about it in a secret sort of way.

10 Later, when I developed more confidence in my immunity to his affliction, I became interested in this debris in a more positive way and began to jot down the fragments amorphically, that is, without regard to form, in the order in which they

occurred to me. Many of these amorphic statements have been supplied by friends. There are thousands of them now, and although only a small portion of them can fit into this Chautauqua, this Chautauqua is clearly based on them.

11 It is probably a long way from what he thought. When trying to recreate a whole pattern by deduction from fragments I am bound to commit errors and put down inconsistencies, for which I must ask some indulgence. In many cases the fragments are ambiguous; a number of different conclusions could be drawn. If something is wrong there's a good chance that the error isn't in what he thought but in my reconstruction of it, and a better reconstruction can later be found.

12 A whirr sounds and a partridge disappears through the trees.

13 "Did you see it?" says Chris.

14 "Yes," I say back.

15 "What was it?"

16 "A partridge."

17 "How do you know?"

18 "They rock back and forth like that when they fly," I say. I'm not sure of this but it sounds right. "They stay close to the ground too."

19 "Oh," says Chris and we continue hiking. The rays of the sun create a cathedral effect through the pines.

20 Today now I want to take up the first phase of his journey into Quality, the nonmetaphysical phase, and this will be pleasant. It's nice to start journeys pleasantly, even when you know they won't end that way. Using his class notes as reference material I want to reconstruct the way in which Quality became a working concept for him in the teaching of rhetoric. His second phase, the metaphysical one, was tenuous and speculative, but this first phase, in which he simply taught rhetoric, was by all accounts solid and pragmatic and probably deserves to be judged on its own merits, independently of the second phase.

21 He'd been innovating extensively. He'd been having trouble with students who had nothing to say. At first he thought it as laziness but later it became apparent that it wasn't. They just couldn't think of anything to say.

22 One of them, a girl with strong-lensed glasses, wanted to write a five-hundred-word essay about the United States. He was used to the sinking feeling that comes from statements like this, and suggested without disparagement that she narrow it down to just Bozeman.

23 When the paper came due she didn't have it and was quite upset. She had tried and tried but she just couldn't think of anything to say.

24 He had already discussed her with her previous instructors and they'd confirmed his impressions of her. She was very serious, disciplined and hardworking, but extremely dull. Not a spark of creativity in her anywhere. Her eyes, behind the thick-lensed glasses, were the eyes of a drudge. She wasn't bluffing him, she really couldn't think of anything to say, and was upset by her inability to do as she was told.

25 It just stumped him. Now *he* couldn't think of anything to say. A silence occurred, and then a peculiar answer: "Narrow it down to the *main street* of Bozeman." It was a stroke of insight.

26 She nodded dutifully and went out. But just before her next class she came back in *real* distress, tears this time, distress that had obviously been there for a long time. She still couldn't think of anything to say, and couldn't understand why, if she couldn't think of anything about *all* of Bozeman, she should be able to think of something about just one street.

27 He was furious. "You're not *looking*!" he said. A memory came back of his own dismissal from the University for having *too much* to say. For every fact there is an *infinity* of hypotheses. The more you *look* the more you *see*. She really wasn't looking and yet somehow didn't understand this.

28 He told her angrily, "Narrow it down to the *front* of *one* building on the main street of Bozeman. The Opera House. Start with the upper left-hand brick."

29 Her eyes, behind the thick-lensed glasses, opened wide.

She came in the next class with a puzzled look and handed him a five-thousand-word essay on the front of the Opera House on the main street of Bozeman, Montana. "I sat in the hamburger stand across the street," she said, "and started writing about the first brick, and the second brick, and then by the third brick it all started to come and I couldn't stop. They thought I was crazy, and they kept kidding me, but here it all is. I don't understand it."

31 Neither did he, but on long walks through the streets of town he thought about it and concluded she was evidently stopped with the same kind of blockage that had paralyzed him on his first day of teaching. She was blocked because she was trying to repeat, in her writing, things she had already heard, just as on the first day he had tried to repeat things he had already decided to say. She couldn't think of anything to write about Bozeman because she couldn't recall anything she had heard worth repeating. She was strangely unaware that she could look and see freshly for herself, as she wrote, without primary regard for what had been said before. The narrowing down to one brick destroyed the blockage because it was so obvious she *had* to do some original and direct seeing.

32 He experimented further. In one class he had everyone write all hour about the back of his thumb. Everyone gave him funny looks at the beginning of the hour, but everyone did it, and there wasn't a single complaint about "nothing to say."

33 In another class he changed the subject from the thumb to a coin, and got a full hour's writing from every student. In other classes it was the same. Some asked, "Do you have to write about both sides?" Once they got into the idea of seeing directly for themselves they also saw there was no limit to the amount they could say. It was a confidence-building assignment too, because what they wrote, even though seemingly trivial, was nevertheless their own thing, not a mimicking of someone else's. Classes where he used that coin exercise were always less balky and more interested.

34 As a result of his experiments he concluded that imitation was a real evil that had to be broken before real rhetoric teaching could begin. This imitation seemed to be an external compulsion. Little children didn't have it. It seemed to come later on, possibly as a result of school itself.

35   That sounded right, and the more he thought about it the more right it sounded. Schools teach you to imitate. If you don't imitate what the teacher wants you get a bad grade. Here, in college, it was more sophisticated, of course; you were supposed to imitate the teacher in such a way as to convince the teacher you were not imitating, but taking the essence of the instruction and going ahead with it on your own. That got you A's. Originality on the other hand could get you any-thing—from A to F. The whole grading system cautioned against it.

36   He discussed this with a professor of psychology who lived next door to him, an extremely imaginative teacher, who said, "Right. Eliminate the whole degree-and-grading system and then you'll get real education."

37   Phaedrus thought about this, and when weeks later a very bright student couldn't think of a subject for a term paper, it was still on his mind, so he gave it to her as a topic. She didn't like the topic at first, but agreed to take it anyway.

38   Within a week she was talking about it to everyone, and with-in two weeks had worked up a superb paper. The class she delivered it to didn't have the advantage of two weeks to think about the subject, however, and was quite hostile to the whole idea of eliminating grades and degrees. This didn't slow her down at all. Her tone took on an old-time religious fervor. She begged the other students to *listen*, to understand this was really *right*. "I'm not saying this for *him*," she said and glanced at Phaedrus. "It's for *you*."

39   Her pleading tone, her religious fervor, greatly impressed him, along with the fact that her college entrance examinations had placed her in the upper one percent of the class. During the next quarter, when teaching "persuasive writing," he chose this topic as a "demonstrator," a piece of persuasive writing he worked up by himself, day by day, in front of and with the help of the class.

40   He used the demonstrator to avoid talking in terms of princi-ples of composition, all of which he had deep doubts about. He felt that by exposing classes to his own sentences as he made them, with all the misgivings and hang-ups and era-sures, he would give a more honest picture of what writing

was like than by spending class time picking nits in completed student work or holding up the completed work of masters for emulation. This time he developed the argument that the whole grading system and degree should be eliminated, and to make it something that truly involved the students in what they were hearing, he withheld all grades during the quarter.

41   Just up above the top of the ridge the snow can be seen now. On foot it's many days away though. The rocks below it are too steep for a direct hiking climb, particularly with the heavy loads we are carrying, and Chris is way too young for any kind of ropes-and-pitons stuff. We must cross over the forested ridge we are now approaching, enter another canyon, follow it to its end and then come back at an upward angle along to the ridge. Three days hard to the snow. Four days easy. If we don't show up in nine, DeWeese will start looking for us.

42   We stop for a rest, sit down and brace against a tree so that we don't topple over backward from the packs. After a while I reach around over my shoulder, take the machete from the top of my pack and hand it to Chris.

43   "See those two aspens over there? The straight ones? At the edge?" I point to them. "Cut those down about a foot from the ground."

44   "Why?"

45   "We'll need them later for hiking sticks and tent poles."

46   Chris takes the machete, starts to rise but then settles back again. "You cut them," he says.

47   So I take the machete and go over and cut the poles. They both cut neatly in one swing, except for the final strip of bark, which I sever with the back hook of the machete. Up in the rocks you need the poles for balancing and the pine up above is no good for poles, and this is about the last of the aspen here. It bothers me a little though that Chris is turning down work. Not a good sign in the mountains.

48   A short rest and then on we go. It'll take a while to get used to this load. There's a negative reaction to all the weight. As we go on though, it'll become more natural. . . .

49   Phaedrus' argument for the abolition of the degree-and-grading system produced a nonplussed or negative reaction in all but a few students at first, since it seemed, on first judgment, to destroy the whole University system. One student laid it wide open when she said with complete candor, "Of course you can't eliminate the degree and grading system. After all, that's what we're here for."

50   She spoke the complete truth. The idea that the majority of students attend a university for an education independent of the degree and grades is a little hypocrisy everyone is happier not to expose. Occasionally some students do arrive for an education but rote and the mechanical nature of the institution soon converts them to a less idealistic attitude.

51   The demonstrator was an argument that elimination of grades and degrees would destroy this hypocrisy. Rather than deal with generalities it dealt with the specific career of an imaginary student who more or less typified what was found in the classroom, a student completely conditioned to work for a grade rather than for the knowledge the grade was supposed to represent.

52   Such a student, the demonstrator hypothesized, would go to his first class, get his first assignment and probably do it out of habit. He might go to his second and third as well. But eventually the novelty of the course would wear off and, because his academic life was not his only life, the pressure of other obligations or desires would create circumstances where he just would not be able to get an assignment in.

53   Since there was no degree or grading system he would incur no penalty for this. Subsequent lectures which presumed he'd completed the assignment might be a little more difficult to understand, however, and this difficulty, in turn, might weaken his interest to a point where the next assignment, which he would find quite hard, would also be dropped. Again no penalty.

54   In time his weaker and weaker understanding of what the lectures were about would make it more and more difficult for him to pay attention in class. Eventually he would see he wasn't learning much; and facing the continual pressure of outside obligations, he would stop studying, feel guilty about this and stop attending class. Again, no penalty would be attached.

55   But what had happened? The student, with no hard feelings on anybody's part, would have flunked himself out. Good! This is what should have happened. He wasn't there for a real education in the first place and had no real business there at all. A large amount of money and effort had been saved and there would be no stigma of failure and ruin to haunt him the rest of his life. No bridges had been burned.

56   The student's biggest problem was a slave mentality which had been built into him by years of carrot-and-whip grading, a mule mentality which said, "If you don't whip me, I won't work." He didn't get whipped. He didn't work. And the cart of civilization, which he supposedly was being trained to pull, was just going to have to creak along a little slower without him.

57   This is a tragedy, however, only if you presume that the cart of civilization, "the system," is pulled by mules. This is a common, vocational, "location" point of view, but it's not the Church attitude.

58   The Church attitude is that civilization, or "the system" or "society" or whatever you want to call it, is best served not by mules but by free men. The purpose of abolishing grades and degrees is not to punish mules or to get rid of them but to provide an environment in which that mule can turn into a free man.

59   The hypothetical student, still a mule, would drift around for a while. He would get another kind of education quite as valuable as the one he'd abandoned, in what used to be called the "school of hard knocks." Instead of wasting money and time as a high-status mule, he would now have to get a job as a low-status mule, maybe as a mechanic. Actually his *real* status would go up. He would be making a contribution for a change. Maybe that's what he would do for the rest of his life. Maybe he'd found his level. But don't count on it.

60   In time—six months; five years, perhaps—a change could easily begin to take place. He would become less and less satisfied with a kind of dumb, day-to-day shopwork. His creative intelligence, stifled by too much theory and too many grades in college, would now become reawakened by the boredom of the shop. Thousands of hours of frustrating mechanical problems would have made him more interested in machine design. He

would like to design machinery himself. He'd think he could do a better job. He would try modifying a few engines, meet with success, look for more success, but feel blocked because he didn't have the theoretical information. He would discover that when before he felt stupid because of his lack of interest in theoretical information, he'd now find a brand of theoretical information which he'd have a lot of respect for, namely, mechanical engineering.

61   So he would come back to our degreeless and gradeless school, but with a difference. He'd no longer be a grade-motivated person. He'd be a knowledge-motivated person. He would need no external pushing to learn. His push would come from inside. He'd be a free man. He wouldn't need a lot of discipline to shape him up. In fact, if the instructors assigned him were slacking on the job he would be likely to shape *them* up by asking rude questions. He'd be there to learn something, would be paying to learn something and they'd better come up with it.

62   Motivation of this sort, once it catches hold, is a ferocious force, and in the gradeless, degreeless institution where our student would find himself, he wouldn't stop with rote engineering information. Physics and mathematics were going to come within his sphere of interest because he'd see he needed them. Metallurgy and electrical engineering would come up for attention. And, in the process of intellectual maturing that these abstract studies gave him, he would be likely to branch out into other theoretical areas that weren't directly related to machines but had become a part of a newer larger goal. This larger goal wouldn't be the imitation of education in Universities today, glossed over and concealed by grades and degrees that give the appearance of something happening when, in fact, almost nothing is going on. It would be the real thing.

63   Such was Phaedrus' demonstrator, his unpopular argument, and he worked on it all quarter long, building it up and modifying it, arguing for it, defending it. All quarter long papers would go back to the students with comments but no grades, although the grades were entered in a book.

64   As I said before, at first almost everyone was sort of nonplussed. The majority probably figured they were stuck with some idealist who thought removal of grades would make them happier and thus work harder, when it was obvious that without grades everyone would just loaf. Many of the students

with A records in previous quarters were contemptuous and angry at first, but because of their acquired self-discipline went ahead and did the work anyway. The B students and high-C students missed some of the early assignments or turned in sloppy work. Many of the low-C and D students didn't even show up for class. At this time another teacher asked him what he was going to do about this lack of response.

65   "Outwait them," he said.

66   His lack of harshness puzzled the students at first, then made them suspicious. Some began to ask sarcastic questions. These received soft answers and the lectures and speeches proceeded as usual, except with no grades.

67   Then a hoped-for phenomenon began. During the third or fourth week some of the A students began to get nervous and started to turn in superb work and hang around after class with questions that fished for some indication as to how they were doing. The B and high-C students began to notice this and work a little and bring up the quality of their papers to a more usual level. The low C, D and future F's began to show up for class just to see what was going on.

68   After midquarter an even more hoped-for phenomenon took place. The A-rated students lost their nervousness and became active participants in everything that went on with a friendliness that was uncommon in a grade-getting class. At this point the B and C students were in a panic, and turned in stuff that looked as though they'd spent hours of painstaking work on it. The D's and F's turned in satisfactory assignments.

69   In the final weeks of the quarter, a time when normally everyone knows what his grade will be and just sits back half asleep, Phaedrus was getting a kind of class participation that made other teachers take notice. The B's and C's had joined the A's in friendly free-for-all discussion that made the class seem like a successful party. Only the D's and F's sat frozen in their chairs, in a complete internal panic.

70   The phenomenon of relaxation and friendliness was explained later by a couple of students who told him, "A lot of us got together outside of class to try to figure out how to beat this system. Everyone decided the best way was just to figure you were going to fail and then go ahead and do what you could

anyway. Then you start to relax. Otherwise you go out of your mind!"

71   The students added that once you got used to it it wasn't so bad, you were more interested in the subject matter, but repeated that it wasn't easy to get used to.

72   At the end of the quarter the students were asked to write an essay evaluating the system. None of them knew at the time of writing what his or her grade would be. Fifty-four percent opposed it. Thirty-seven percent favored it. Nine percent were neutral.

73   On the basis of one man, one vote, the system was very unpopular. The majority of students definitely wanted their grades as they went along. But when Phaedrus broke down the returns according to the grades that were in his book—and the grades were not out of line with grades predicted by previous classes and entrance evaluations—another story was told. The A students were 2 to 1 in favor of the system. The B and C students were evenly divided. And the D's and F's were *unanimously* opposed!

74   This surprising result supported a hunch he had had for a long time: that the brighter, more serious students were the *least* desirous of grades, possibly because they were more interested in the subject matter of the course, whereas the dull or lazy students were the *most* desirous of grades, possibly because grades told them if they were getting by.

75   As DeWeese said, from here straight south you can go seventy-five miles through nothing but forests and snow without ever encountering a road, although there are roads to the east and the west. I've arranged it so that if things work out badly at the end of the second day we'll be near a road that can get us back fast. Chris doesn't know about this, and it would hurt his YMCA-camp sense of adventure to tell him, but after enough trips into the high country, the YMCA desire for adventure diminishes and the more substantial benefits of cutting down risks appear. This country can be dangerous. You take one bad step in a million, sprain an ankle, and then you find out how far from civilization you really are.

This is apparently a seldom-entered canyon this far up. After another hour of hiking we see that the trail is about gone.

77 Phaedrus thought withholding grades was good, according to his notes, but he didn't give it scientific value. In a true experiment you keep constant every cause you can think of except one, and then see what the effects are of varying that one cause. In the classroom you can never do this. Student knowledge, student attitude, teacher attitude, all change from all kinds of causes which are uncontrollable and mostly unknowable. Also, the observer in this case is himself one of the causes and can never judge his effects without altering his effects. So he didn't attempt to draw any hard conclusions from all this, he just went ahead and did what he liked.

78 The movement from this to his enquiry into Quality took place because of a sinister aspect of grading that the withholding of grades exposed. Grades really cover up failure to teach. A bad instructor can go through an entire quarter leaving absolutely nothing memorable in the minds of his class, curve out the scores on an irrelevant test, and leave the impression that some have learned and some have not. But if the grades are removed the class is forced to wonder each day what it's *really* learning. The questions, What's being taught? What's the goal? How do the lectures and assignments accomplish the goal? become ominous. The removal of grades exposes a huge and frightening vacuum.

79 What was Phaedrus trying to do, anyway? This question became more and more imperative as he went on. The answer that had seemed right when he started now made less and less sense. He had wanted his students to become creative by deciding for themselves what was good writing instead of asking him all the time. The real purpose of withholding the grades was to force them to look within themselves, the only place they would ever get a really right answer.

80 But now this made no sense. If they already knew what was good and bad, there was no reason for them to take the course in the first place. The fact that they were there as students presumed they did *not* know what was good or bad. That was his

job as instructor—to tell them what was good or bad. The whole idea of individual creativity and expression in the classroom was really basically opposed to the whole idea of the University.

81   For many of the students, this withholding created a Kafkaesque situation in which they saw they were to be punished for failure to do something but no one would tell them what they were supposed to do. They looked within themselves and saw nothing and looked at Phaedrus and saw nothing and just sat there helpless, not knowing what to do. The vacuum was deadly. One girl suffered a nervous breakdown. You cannot withhold grades and sit there and create a goalless vacuum. You have to provide some goal for a class to work toward that will fill that vacuum. This he wasn't doing.

82   He couldn't. He could think of no possible way he could tell them what they should work toward without falling back into the trap of authoritarian, didactic teaching. But how can you put on the blackboard the mysterious internal goal of each creative person?

83   The next quarter he dropped the whole idea and went back to regular grading, discouraged, confused, feeling he was right but somehow it had come out all wrong. When spontaneity and individuality and really good original stuff occurred in a classroom it was in spite of the instruction, not because of it. This seemed to make sense. He was ready to resign. Teaching dull conformity to hateful students wasn't what he wanted to do.

84   He'd heard that Reed College in Oregon withheld grades until graduation, and during the summer vacation he went there but was told the faculty was divided on the value of withholding grades and that no one was tremendously happy about the system. During the rest of the summer his mood became depressed and lazy. He and his wife camped a lot in those mountains. She asked why he was so silent all the time but he couldn't say why. He was just stopped. Waiting. For that missing seed crystal of thought that would suddenly solidify everything.

17

85   It's looking bad for Chris. For a while he was way ahead of me and now he sits under a tree and rests. He doesn't look at me, and that's how I know it's bad.

86   I sit down next to him and his expression is distant. His face is flushed and I can see he's exhausted. We sit and listen to the wind through the pines.

87   I know eventually he'll get up and keep going but *he* doesn't know this, and is afraid to face the possibility that his fear creates: that he may not be able to climb the mountain at all. I remember something Phaedrus had written about these mountains and tell it to Chris now.

88   "Years ago," I tell him, "your mother and I were at the timberline not so far from here and we camped near a lake with a marsh on one side."

89   He doesn't look up but he's listening.

90   "At about dawn we heard falling rocks and we thought it must be an animal, except that animals don't usually clatter around. Then I heard a squishing sound in the marsh and we were really wide-awake. I got out of the sleeping bag slowly and got our revolver from my jacket and crouched by a tree."

91   Now Chris's attention is distracted from his own problems.

92   "There was another squish," I say. "I thought it could be horses with dudes packing in, but not at this hour. Another *squish*! And a loud *galoomph*! That's no horse! And a *Galoomph*! and a *GALOOMPH*! And there, in the dim grey light of dawn coming straight for me through the muck of the marsh, was the biggest bull moose I ever saw. Horns as wide as a man is tall. Next to the grizzly the most dangerous animal in the mountains. Some say the worst."

93   Chris's eyes are bright again.

94   "*GALOOMPH*! I cocked the hammer on the revolver, thinking a thirty-eight Special wasn't very much for a moose. *GALOOMPH*! He didn't SEE me! *GALOOMPH*! I couldn't get out of his way. Your mother was in the sleeping bag right in his path. *GALOOMPH*! What a GIANT! *GALOOMPH*! He's ten yards away! *GALOOMPH*! I stand up and take aim. *GALOOMPH*! . . . *GALOOMPH*! . . . *GALOOMPH*! . . . He stops, THREE YARDS AWAY, and sees me. . . . The gunsights lie right between his eyes. . . . We're motionless."

95   I reach around into my pack and get out some cheese.

96   "Then what happened?" Chris asks.

97   "Wait until I cut off some of this cheese."

98   I remove my hunting knife and hold the cheese wrapper so that my fingers don't get on it. I slice out a quarter-inch hunk and hold it out for him.

99   He takes it. "Then what happened?"

100   I watch until he takes his first bite. "That bull moose looked at me for what must have been five seconds. Then he looked down at your mother. Then he looked at me again, and at the revolver which was practically lying on top of his big round nose. And then he smiled and slowly walked away."

101   "Oh," says Chris. He looks disappointed.

102   "Normally when they're confronted like that they'll charge," I say, "but he just thought it was a nice morning, and we were there first, so why make trouble? And that's why he smiled."

103   "Can they *smile?*"

104   "No, but it looked that way."

105   I put the cheese away and add, "Later on that day we were jumping from boulder to boulder down the side of a slope. I was about to land on a great big brown boulder when all of a sudden the great big brown boulder jumped into the air and ran off into the woods. It was the same moose. . . . I think that moose must have been pretty sick of us that day."

106   I help Chris get to his feet. "You were going a little too fast," I say. "Now the mountainside's becoming steep and we have to go slowly. If you go too fast you get winded and when you get winded you get dizzy and that weakens your spirit and you think, I can't do it. So go slow for a while."

107   "I'll stay behind you," he says.

108   "Okay."

109   We walk now away from the stream we were following, up the canyon side at the shallowest angle I can find.

110   Mountains should be climbed with as little effort as possible and without desire. The reality of your own nature should determine the speed. If you become restless, speed up. If you become winded, slow down. You climb the mountain in an

equilibrium between restlessness and exhaustion. Then, when you're no longer thinking ahead, each footstep isn't just a means to an end but a unique event in itself. *This* leaf has jagged edges. *This* rock looks loose. From *this* place the snow is less visible, even though closer. These are things you should notice anyway. To live only for some future goal is shallow. It's the sides of the mountain which sustain life, not the top. Here's where things grow.

111 But of course, without the top you can't have any sides. It's the top that *defines* the sides. So on we go . . . we have a long way . . . no hurry . . . just one step after the next . . . with a little Chautauqua for entertainment. . . . Mental reflection is so much more interesting than TV it's a shame more people don't switch over to it. They probably think what they hear is unimportant but it never is.

112 There's a large fragment concerning Phaedrus' first class after he gave that assignment on "What is quality in thought and statement?" The atmosphere was explosive. Almost everyone seemed as frustrated and angered as he had been by the question.

113 "How are *we* supposed to know what quality is?" they said. "You're supposed to tell *us!*"

114 Then he told them he couldn't figure it out either and really wanted to know. He had assigned it in the hope that somebody would come up with a good answer.

115 That ignited it. A roar of indignation shook the room. Before the commotion had settled down another teacher had stuck his head in the door to see what the trouble was.

116 "It's all right," Phaedrus said. "We just accidentally stumbled over a genuine question, and the shock is hard to recover from." Some students looked curious at this, and the noise simmered down.

117 He then used the occasion for a short return to his theme of "Corruption and Decay in the Church of Reason." It was a measure of this corruption, he said, that students should be outraged by someone trying to *use* them to seek the truth. You were supposed to *fake* this search for the truth, to *imitate* it. To actually *search* for it was a damned imposition.

118 The truth was, he said, that he genuinely did want to know what they thought, not so that he could put a grade on it, but because he really wanted to know.

119 They looked puzzled.

120 "I sat there all night long," one said.

121 "I was ready to cry, I was so mad," a girl next to the window said.

122 "You should warn us," a third said.

123 "How could I warn you," he said, "when I had no idea how you'd react?"

124 Some of the puzzled ones looked at him with a first dawning. He wasn't playing games. He really wanted to know.

125 A most peculiar person.

126 Then someone said, "What do *you* think?"

127 "I don't *know*," he answered.

128 "But what do you *think*?"

129 He paused for a long time. "I think there is such a thing as Quality, but that as soon as you try to define it, something goes haywire. You can't do it."

130 Murmurs of agreement.

131 He continued, "Why this is, I don't know. I thought maybe I'd get some ideas from your papers. I just don't know."

132 This time the class was silent.

133 In subsequent classes that day there was some of the same commotion, but a number of students in each class volunteered friendly answers that told him the first class had been discussed during lunch.

134 A few days later he worked up a definition of his own and put it on the blackboard to be copied for posterity. The definition was: "Quality is a characteristic of thought and statement that is recognized by a nonthinking process. Because definitions are a product of rigid, formal thinking, quality cannot be defined."

The fact that this "definition" was actually a refusal to define did not draw comment. The students had no formal training that would have told them his statement was, in a formal sense, completely irrational. If you can't define something you have no formal rational way of knowing that it exists. Neither can you *really* tell anyone else what it is. There is, in fact, no formal difference between inability to define and stupidity. When I say, "Quality cannot be defined," I'm really saying formally, "I'm stupid about Quality."

136 Fortunately the students didn't know this. If they'd come up with these objections he wouldn't have been able to answer them at the time.

137 But then, below the definition on the blackboard, he wrote, "But even though Quality cannot be defined, *you know what Quality is!*" and the storm started all over again.

138 "Oh, no, we don't!"

139 "Oh, yes, you do."

140 "Oh, *no,* we *don't!*"

141 "Oh, *yes,* you *do!*" he said and he had some material ready to demonstrate it to them.

142 He had selected two examples of student composition. The first was a rambling, disconnected thing with interesting ideas that never built into anything. The second was a magnificent piece by a student who was mystified himself about why it had come out so well. Phaedrus read both, then asked for a show of hands on who thought the first was best. Two hands went up. He asked how many liked the second better. Twenty-eight hands went up.

143 "Whatever it is," he said, "that caused the overwhelming majority to raise their hands for the second one is what I mean by Quality. So *you* know what it is."

144 There was a long reflective silence after this, and he just let it last.

145 This was just intellectually outrageous, and he knew it. He wasn't teaching anymore, he was indoctrinating. He had erected an imaginary entity, defined it as incapable of definition, told

the students over their own protests that they knew what it was, and demonstrated this by a technique that was as confusing logically as the term itself. He was able to get away with this because logical refutation required more talent than any of the students had. In subsequent days he continually invited their refutations, but none came. He improvised further.

146   To reinforce the idea that they already knew what Quality was he developed a routine in which he read four student papers in class and had everyone rank them in estimated order of Quality on a slip of paper. He did the same himself. He collected the slips, tallied them on the blackboard and averaged the rankings for an overall class opinion. Then he would reveal his own rankings, and this would almost always be close to, if not identical with the class average. Where there were differences it was usually because two papers were close in quality.

147   At first the classes were excited by this exercise, but as time went on they became bored. What he meant by Quality was obvious. They obviously knew what it was too, and so they lost interest in listening. Their question now was "All right, we know what Quality is. How do we get it?"

148   Now, at last, the standard rhetoric texts came into their own. The principles expounded in them were no longer rules to rebel against, not ultimates in themselves, but just techniques, gimmicks, for producing what really counted and stood independently of the techniques—Quality. What had started out as a heresy from traditional rhetoric turned into a beautiful introduction to it.

149   He singled out aspects of Quality such as unity, vividness, authority, economy, sensitivity, clarity, emphasis, flow, suspense, brilliance, precision, proportion, depth and so on; kept each of these as poorly defined as Quality itself, but demonstrated them by the same class reading techniques. He showed how the aspect of Quality called unity, the hanging-togetherness of a story, could be improved with a technique called an outline. The authority of an argument could be jacked up with a technique called footnotes, which gives authoritative reference. Outlines and footnotes are standard things taught in all freshman composition classes, but now as devices for improving Quality they had a purpose. And if a student turned in a bunch of dumb references or a sloppy outline that showed he was just fulfilling an assignment by rote, he could be told that

while his paper may have fulfilled the letter of the assignment it obviously didn't fulfill the goal of Quality, and was therefore worthless.

150 Now, in answer to that eternal student question, How do I *do* this? that had frustrated him to the point of resignation, he could reply, "It doesn't make a bit of difference *how* you do it! Just so it's good." The reluctant student might ask in class, "But how do we know what's good?" but almost before the question was out of his mouth he would realize the answer had already been supplied. Some other student would usually tell him, "You just *see* it." If he said, "No, I don't," he'd be told, "Yes, you do. He proved it." The student was finally and completely trapped into making quality judgments for himself. And it was just exactly this and nothing else that taught him to write.

151 Up to now Phaedrus had been compelled by the academic system to say what he wanted, even though he knew that this forced students to conform to artificial forms that destroyed their own creativity. Students who went along with his rules were then condemned for their inability to be creative or produce a piece of work that reflected their own personal standards of what is good.

152 Now that was over with. By reversing a basic rule that all things which are to be taught must first be defined, he had found a way out of all this. He was pointing to no principle, no rule of good writing, no theory—but he was pointing to something, nevertheless, that was very real, whose reality they couldn't deny. The vacuum that had been created by the withholding of grades was suddenly filled with the positive goal of Quality, and the whole thing fit together. Students, astonished, came by his office and said, "I used to just *hate* English. Now I spend more time on it than anything else." Not just one or two. Many. The whole Quality concept was beautiful. It worked. It was that mysterious, individual, internal goal of each creative person, on the blackboard at last.

153 I turn to see how Chris is doing. His face looks tired.

154 I ask, "How do you feel?"

155 "Okay," he says, but his tone is defiant.

156 "We can stop anywhere and camp," I say.

157   He flashes a fierce look at me, and so I say nothing more. Soon I see he's working his way around me on the slope. With what must be great effort he pulls ahead. We go on.

158   Phaedrus got this far with his concept of Quality because he deliberately refused to look outside the immediate classroom experience. Cromwell's statement, "No one ever travels so high as he who knows not where he is going," applied at this point. He didn't know where he was going. All he knew was that it worked.

159   In time, however, he wondered *why* it worked, especially when he already knew it was irrational. Why should an irrational method work when rational methods were all so rotten? He had an intuitive feeling, growing rapidly, that what he had stumbled on was no small gimmick. It went far beyond. How far, he didn't know.

160   This was the beginning of the crystallization that I talked about before. Others wondered at the time, "Why should he get so excited about 'quality'?" But they saw only the word and its rhetoric context. They didn't see his past despair over abstract questions of existence itself that he had abandoned in defeat.

161   If anyone else had asked, What is Quality? it *would* have been just another question. But when *he* asked it, because of his past, it spread out for him like waves in all directions simultaneously, not in a hierarchic structure, but in a concentric one. At the center, generating the waves, was Quality. As these waves of thought expanded for him I'm sure he fully expected each wave to reach some shore of existing patterns of thought so that he had a kind of unified relationship with these thought structures. But the shore was never reached until the end, if it appeared at all. For him there was nothing but ever expanding waves of crystallization. I'll now try to follow these waves of crystallization, the second phase of his exploration into quality, as best I can.

162   Up ahead all of Chris's movements seem tired and angry. He stumbles on things, lets branches tear at him, instead of pulling them to one side.

163 I'm sorry to see this. Some blame can be put on the YMCA camp he attended for two weeks just before we started. From what he's told me, they made a big ego thing out of the whole outdoor experience. A proof-of-manhood thing. He began in a lowly class they were careful to point out was rather disgraceful to be in . . . original sin. Then he was allowed to prove himself with a long series of accomplishments—swimming, rope tying . . . he mentioned a dozen of them, but I've forgotten them.

164 It made the kids at camp much more enthusiastic and cooperative when they had ego goals to fulfill, I'm sure, but ultimately that kind of motivation is destructive. Any effort that has self-glorification as its final endpoint is bound to end in disaster. Now we're paying the price. When you try to climb a mountain to prove how big you are, you almost never make it. And even if you do it's a hollow victory. In order to sustain the victory you have to prove yourself again and again in some other way, and again and again and again, driven forever to fill a false image, haunted by the fear that the image is not true and someone will find out. That's never the way.

165 Phaedrus wrote a letter from India about a pilgrimage to holy Mount Kailas, the source of the Ganges and the abode of Shiva, high in the Himalayas, in the company of a holy man and his adherents.

166 He never reached the mountain. After the third day he gave up, exhausted, and the pilgrimage went on without him. He said he had the physical strength but that physical strength wasn't enough. He had the intellectual motivation but that wasn't enough either. He didn't think he had been arrogant but thought that he was undertaking the pilgrimage to broaden *his* experience, to gain understanding for *himself*. He was trying to use the mountain for his own purposes and the pilgrimage too. He regarded himself as the fixed entity, not the pilgrimage or the mountain, and thus wasn't ready for it. He speculated that the other pilgrims, the ones who reached the mountain, probably sensed the holiness of the mountain so intensely that each footstep was an act of devotion, an act of submission to this holiness. The holiness of the mountain infused into their own spirits enabled them to endure far more than anything he, with his greater physical strength, could take.

167 To the untrained eye ego-climbing and selfless climbing may appear identical. Both kinds of climbers place one foot in front of the other. Both breathe in and out at the same rate. Both stop when tired. Both go forward when rested. But what a difference! The ego-climber is like an instrument that's out of adjustment. He puts his foot down an instant too soon or too late. He's likely to miss a beautiful passage of sunlight through the trees. He goes on when the sloppiness of his step shows he's tired. He rests at odd times. He looks up the trail trying to see what's ahead even when he knows what's ahead because he just looked a second before. He goes too fast or too slow for the conditions and when he talks his talk is forever about somewhere else, something else. He's here but he's not here. He rejects the here, is unhappy with it, wants to be farther up the trail but when he gets there will be just as unhappy because then *it* will be "here." What he's looking for, what he wants, is all around him, but he doesn't want that because it *is* all around him. Every step's an effort, both physically and spiritually, because he imagines his goal to be external and distant.

168 That seems to be Chris's problem now.

*T*eresa Rupp (1958–) was born in New York City and raised in San Jose, California. She graduated in 1980 from Santa Clara University with a B.A. in history and received a master's degree and Ph.D., both in medieval history, from Cornell University. She is an associate professor of history and director of the Western Civilization program at Mount St. Mary's University, where she has taught since 1988. In addition to the core curriculum courses Origins of the West, History of the West: Renaissance to Revolutions ("Ren-Rev") and Freshman Seminar, she also teaches elective courses in ancient and medieval history. Her research focuses on Italian medieval political thought. She is working on a book on the treatises and sermons of Remigio dei Girolami, a thirteenth-century Florentine Dominican preacher and teacher. Rupp is a member of an amateur chamber music group, the Monocacy String Quartet. She lives in Frederick, Maryland, with her husband Randy and her sons Gilbert and Simon. This essay was written in 2005 for a Mount St. Mary's faculty summer seminar on Vocation.

Origins of the Calling

Teresa Rupp

1   When asked the question, "what do you want to be when you grow up, little girl?" I can guarantee you that I never answered, "I want to teach Origins of the West, Ren-Rev, and Freshman Seminar at a small Catholic liberal arts college." At various stages of my life, the answer to that question was "nurse," "music teacher," "astronomer," and "museum curator." Although I eventually became none of these things, I now realize that that elements of those earlier dreams pointed the way to my eventual calling.

2   The earliest career dream I can remember having, from around the age of four, was to be a nurse. Maybe it was because I had my tonsils out at about that time; maybe it was just the cool uniform with the hat and cape.[1] This one didn't last long, although I do remember my mother saying I shouldn't be a nurse, I should be a doctor.

Whatever happened to those nurses' uniforms?

3   My mother also influenced my next choice. When I was seven, she got a job teaching stringed instruments in elementary school. Although she had studied all the orchestral instruments as a music major in college, piano was her main instrument, and she had never taught the violin before. So she took a class the summer before her job started in the Suzuki method, taught by its founder, Shinichi Suzuki himself, in what I believe was his first trip to the U.S. She came back all fired up about the potential of his ideas, starting with the conviction that making music was possible for everyone, not just a talented few. This coincided with her sense of her own calling to "bring music to the masses." Since she needed someone to practice teaching on, I became her first pupil. I advanced easily through the early Suzuki materials, playing at school and in various orchestras and chamber groups my mother formed throughout my elementary school years. At this point, I imagined myself as a music teacher one day.[2]

4   In fourth grade, I had the first of several inspiring teachers whom I still model myself after—Mrs. Chamberlain. It was the late Sixties, time of the Cold War and the Space Race, and elementary school teachers, especially in gifted classrooms, were putting a lot of emphasis on learning science using lots of hands-on experiments. I even remember the textbook we used: *Concepts in Science*, which explicitly used the "discovery method" in place of memorization of facts—problem-posing instead of banking, in Freire's terms.[3]

My mother's after-school string orchestra, ca. 1967. I'm playing second violin; my brother (in the bow tie) is playing cello.

I couldn't find an image of the fourth-grade textbook; I think it had a picture of a prism and a ray of light. This is the first grade volume.

5   I loved doing the experiments, but the science I was most interested in was astronomy. It was the Sixties, after all, and we *knew* we were going into space. One of the picture books I remember from early childhood was called *You Will Go to the Moon*, and I believed that absolutely. But my friend David Shaw and I noticed that the astronomy chapter was the last one in our *Concepts in Science* book, and we were afraid we would

never get to it,[4] so we launched a campaign to get Mrs. Chamberlain to skip ahead to that chapter. We did ask her directly, but we also noted the page number the chapter started on, and whenever a page number was mentioned in class ("boys and girls, please open your math books to page . . ."), we would shout out, "page 255!" Amazingly, it worked, and we spent several weeks studying astronomy.

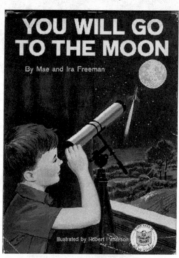

I never doubted it!

6   At this point, I developed a lasting habit—reading every book in the library on whatever topic I was interested in at the time.[5] I read all the astronomy books from the 500s section of the library, but what I really enjoyed were biographies of scientists like Galileo and Newton. I thought all this reading would be good preparation for my planned career as an astronomer. These career plans faded after fifth grade, when my teacher Mr. Munger actually had a 6-inch reflecting telescope, bought with money from the gifted program, that he passed from student to student throughout the year. In those days, it was very difficult to aim a telescope at a particular spot, especially for a beginner. Better-made telescopes, including our class model, came with something called setting circles that let you set the coordinates for whatever you wanted to look at, but they were confusing and frustrating to use.[6] This, combined with the fact that we were attempting to do stargazing in the dense suburbia of the Santa Clara Valley, where light pollution made it impossible to

see anything fainter than a first-magnitude star, eventually cooled my enthusiasm for astronomy as a career.

7 I entered Presentation High School in 1972, still vaguely planning on a career in science. I did the standard Biology and Chemistry in tenth and eleventh grades, but Presentation didn't offer Physics in those days. They had an arrangement with Bellarmine, the all-boys' Jesuit school in town, but you had to get there on your own and then make it back to Presentation in time for second period, and that just sounded like too much hassle to me.[7] Besides, by twelfth grade I had a new ambition.

8 Back in ninth grade, I'd gone on one of those school-sponsored spring break trips to Washington, D.C. We toured the monuments as a group, of course, but we also had free time for exploring. I don't know what the other girls did on the free days, but I dragged Kathy Sosnowski, the girl I was rooming with, to all the Smithsonian museums we could fit in. As I viewed the exhibits, seeing how they used objects to teach, make a point, or tell a story, I thought, "I'd like to do that." I'd found my dream job: museum curator at the Smithsonian.

9 So when I entered the University of Santa Clara in the fall of 1976, I had it all figured out. They had a design-your-own interdisciplinary major called General Humanities. I went through the catalog and circled all the courses that I thought would be useful for a future museum curator. I realized that actually working at the Smithsonian was too narrowly impractical a dream; it was more likely that I'd end up at a small local institution where everybody did some of everything. So I planned to take courses in history, art history, and anthropology (the broad subjects covered by most museums); I also noted courses like the Theatre department's Set Design, which I thought would translate to designing exhibits. You had to wait until your sophomore year to propose a General Humanities major, so I entered as an undeclared.

10 In the meantime, early in my freshman year, I walked into the University museum, the De Saisset, and volunteered my services. I ended up working there until graduation,[8] first as a volunteer, and then, when a paid position opened up, as a student worker earning minimum wage (then $2.50/hour). The De Saisset is the type of institution I imagine I would have worked in if I had stayed in the field. It was founded as an art museum

showcasing the work of the original donor, local artist Ernest
De Saisset; by the 1970s they had a small permanent collection
of other artworks, both historic and contemporary. It also func-
tioned as the historical museum for the University, with a
gallery known as the Mission Room displaying historical arti-
facts. Our temporary exhibits were mostly of modern and contemporary art; one of the most memorable was an exhibit of
rocker Graham Nash's collection of photography.[9] I really did
do some of everything at that museum—clerical tasks, working
in the shop, repainting gallery walls, making exhibit labels,[10]
even helping to catalog the collection.

The De Saisset Museum, Santa Clara University

11 My senior year, Santa Clara art history professor Brigid Barton
    was brought in as interim director while the permanent direc-
    tor was on medical leave. Dr. Barton decided that the student
    workers ought to be engaged in educational activities, not just
    typing and filing. She mounted an exhibit of German Expres-
    sionist Woodcuts (her scholarly specialty) and involved sever-
    al of us in the research and execution of the exhibit. My respon-
    sibility was the group known as *Die Brücke*—I decided what
    would be hung where in the gallery, wrote all the label text for
    that gallery, and wrote commentary on the *Brücke* plates for the
    catalog. Working on this exhibit, as well as others, showed me
    that I enjoyed researching and writing about objects more than
    handling them, and I realized a museum career was not what I
    was called to do.

Page from the exhibition catalog *German Expressionist Woodcuts from the Robert Gore Rifkind Foundation*, De Saisset Museum, 1980

12   I'd already scrapped the idea of the General Humanities major by sophomore year. I envied the sense of community I saw that my friends had in their majors—the clubs, the departmental picnics, the small group of professors whose courses you took over and over—and I decided that I also needed a departmental home. I chose a History major, still planning to take most of the museum-related courses on the side.[11] But in the fall quarter of my sophomore year, I had what I now realize was a ten-week long "core moment." I signed up for the first term of the Honors section of European history and the first term of the Honors philosophy survey (both required for Santa Clara's core curriculum) as well as the first of the Art History survey (part of my personal museum curriculum, taught by my future boss Dr. Barton). All three of these courses covered the ancient and medieval periods—I didn't know it at the time, but it was an unofficial three-course cluster. I had the time of my life, and started reading everything I could find on the Middle Ages (just like astronomy, years before). I found myself signing up for all the courses on medieval subjects that I could fit in and hanging out in the professors' offices just to chat.

13   That summer, my advisor, Dr. Thomas Turley, recommended that I take the paper I had just written in his medieval history course and expand it into an article-length work. I did it, producing "The Relationship between Papacy and Episcopacy

during the Reign of Gregory VII."[12] I didn't get credit for it; it didn't fulfill any requirement; I was just, in the words of Dorothy Sayers, "doing well a thing that is well worth doing."[13]

14   I found myself drawn more and more to the academic life—I wanted to be like the professors I was hanging around with. One day, maybe in my junior year, I thought to myself, "Too bad I'm going to become a museum curator, because I'd really like to go to graduate school and become a medieval history professor." No sooner were the words formed in my mind than I thought, "You don't have to be a museum curator just because that was your ambition when you were 14! If you want to be professor, be a professor!" It was the most freeing thought I'd ever had. From then on I prepared openly for an academic career, ending up at Cornell, studying medieval history with Brian Tierney, who had also been Tom Turley's dissertation director.

15   The rest, of course, is history. I wrote my dissertation and got hired by the Mount. And though I ended up in a place I never dreamed of being, doing a job I never dreamed of doing, living a life I never dreamed of living,[14] I find numerous connections to my original dreams. I'm not a music teacher, but I play in an amateur string quartet. I'm not a scientist, but when I teach Ren-Rev, and especially the unclustered Ren-Rev course for science majors, I cover history of astronomy topics that I first read about in fourth grade. I'm not a museum curator, but when I teach Origins I model myself on Dr. Barton's art history classes, and when I make PowerPoints I imagine that I'm creating virtual museum exhibits. And I'm not a nurse, but maybe I can find one of those cool capes on EBay!

Notes

[1] The cultural meaning of the shift in nurses' wear away from the white uniform, including a hat whose configuration proclaimed your nursing school, would be an interesting topic for research.

[2] Interestingly, never as a virtuoso soloist or even an orchestral musician; probably because I knew even then that I didn't have the single-minded commitment that would take.

[3] I just discovered that *Concepts in Science* was developed by an acknowledged pioneer in science and gifted education, Paul Brandwein (I love the internet).

⁴ Think about it—did you ever get to the last chapter of a textbook in school?

⁵ I read enough astronomy books that when I took Intro. to Astronomy in college to fulfill a science requirement, I could have taught the class myself for about the first three weeks. After that, we got to stuff that either hadn't been discovered yet when I was reading about it, or at least hadn't made it into the children's section of the library.

⁶ Now, I understand, they use computers; you just type the coordinates in and the telescope goes there automatically.

⁷ An example of the kind of obstacle that keeps girls out of the sciences.

⁸ At which point, because of staff turnover, I had the most seniority of anyone on the staff, student or professional.

⁹ To this day, the only celebrity I've ever had lunch with.

¹⁰ This became my specialty. I typed the text on an IBM Selectric. It wasn't easy; the text had to be perfect, and our Selectric wasn't a self-correcting model. Finally, I mounted them on mat board and cut them to size.

¹¹ And I did take most of them, although not Set Design.

¹² How stuffy-sounding; I'm much better at writing titles now.

¹³ Although I did eventually win the departmental essay prize for it, worth all of $25.

¹⁴ My vision for my personal life was never to be a wife and mother; it was to be Mary Tyler Moore. But I think I've made it after all.

*D*orothy Sayers (1893–1957), Oxford-educated detective novelist, dramatist, translator, and philosopher of aesthetics, explored the sacramental value of work in a wide array of genres. Sayers's mysteries are considered true classics of detective fiction. However, after 1943 she devoted her life almost exclusively to writing essays that expressed her devotion to her faith. Commissioned by the dean of Canterbury Cathedral to write an original play on a specifically Christian theme, Sayers created The Zeal of Thy House, which opened to rave reviews. Sayers went on to write a number of stage and radio plays that combined her Christian orthodoxy with her dramatic flair. Throughout her works, she stressed the importance of work well done.

Why Work?

Dorothy L. Sayers

1   I have already, on a previous occasion, spoken at some length on the subject of Work and Vocation.[1] What I urged then was a thoroughgoing revolution in our whole attitude to work. I asked that it should be looked upon—not as a necessary drudgery to be undergone for the purpose of making money, but as a way of life in which the nature of man should find its proper exercise and delight and so fulfill itself to the glory of God. That it should, in fact, be thought of as a creative activity undertaken for the love of the work itself; and that man, made in God's image, should make things, as God makes them, for the sake of doing well a thing that is well worth doing.

2   It may well seem to you—as it does to some of my acquaintances—that I have a sort of obsession about this business of the right attitude to work. But I do insist upon it, because it seems to me that what becomes of civilization after this war is going to depend enormously on our being able to effect this revolution in our ideas about work. Unless we do change our whole way of thought about work. I do not think we shall ever escape from the appalling squirrel cage of economic confusion in which we have been madly turning for the last three centuries or so, the cage in which we landed ourselves by acquiescing in a social system based upon Envy and Avarice.

3   A society in which consumption has to be artificially stimulated in order to keep production going is a society founded on trash and waste, and such a society is a house built upon sand.

4   It is interesting to consider for a moment how our outlook has been forcibly changed for us in the last twelve months by the brutal presence of war. War is a judgment that overtakes societies when they have been living upon ideas that conflict too violently with the laws governing the universe. People who would not revise their ideas voluntarily find themselves compelled to do so by the sheer pressure of the events which these very ideas have served to bring about.

5   Never think that wars are irrational catastrophes: they happen when wrong ways of thinking and living bring about intolerable situations; and whichever side may be the more outrageous in its aims and the more brutal in its methods, the root causes of conflict are usually to be found in some wrong way of life in which all parties have acquiesced, and for which everybody must, to some extent, bear the blame.

6   It is quite true that false Economics is one of the root causes of the present war; and one of the false ideas we had about Economics was a false attitude both to Work and to the goods produced by Work. This attitude we are now being obliged to alter, under the compulsion of war—and a very strange and painful process it is in some ways. It is always strange and painful to have to change a habit of mind: though, when we have made the effort, we may find a great relief, even a sense of adventure and delight, in getting rid of the false and returning to the true.

7   Can you remember—it is already getting difficult to remember—what things were like before the war? The stockings we bought cheap and threw away to save the trouble of mending? The cars we scrapped every year to keep up with the latest fashion in engine design and streamlining? The bread and bones and scraps of fat that littered the dustbins—not only of the rich, but of the poor? The empty bottles that even the dustman scorned to collect, because the manufacturers found it cheaper to make new ones than to clean the old? The mountains of empty tins that nobody found it worthwhile to salvage, rusting and stinking on the refuse dumps? The food that was burnt or buried because it did not pay to distribute it? The land

choked and impoverished with thistle and ragwort, because it did not pay to farm it? The handkerchiefs used for paint rags and kettleholders? The electric lights left blazing because it was too much trouble to switch them off? The fresh peas we could not be bothered to shell, and threw aside for something out of a tin? The paper that cumbered the shelves, and lay knee-deep in the parks, and littered the seats of railway trains? The scattered hairpins and smashed crockery, the cheap knickknacks of steel and wood and rubber and glass and tin that we bought to fill in an odd half hour at Woolworth's and forgot as soon as we had bought them? The advertisements imploring and exhorting and cajoling and menacing and bullying us to glut ourselves with things we did not want, in the name of snobbery and idleness and sex appeal? And the fierce international scramble to find in helpless and backward nations a market on which to fob off all the superfluous rubbish which the inexorable machines ground out hour by hour, to create money and to create employment?

8   Do you realize how we have had to alter our whole scale of values, now that we are no longer being urged to consume but to conserve? We have been forced back to the social morals of our great-grandparents. When a piece of lingerie costs three precious coupons, we have to consider, not merely its glamour value, but how long it will wear. When fats are rationed, we must not throw away scraps, but jealously use to advantage what it cost so much time and trouble to breed and rear. When paper is scarce we must—or we should—think whether what we have to say is worth saying before writing or printing it. When our life depends on the land, we have to pay in short commons for destroying its fertility by neglect or overcropping. When a haul of herrings takes valuable manpower from the forces, and is gathered in at the peril of men's lives by bomb and mine and machine gun, we read a new significance into those gloomy words which appear so often in the fishmonger's shop: NO FISH TODAY. . . . We have had to learn the bitter lesson that in all the world there are only two sources of real wealth: the fruit of the earth and the labor of men; and to estimate work not by the money it brings to the producer, but by the worth of the thing that is made.

9   The question that I will ask you to consider today is this: When the war is over, are we likely, and *do we want* to keep this

attitude to work and the results of work? Or are we preparing and *do we want* to go back to our old habits of thought? Because I believe that on our answer to this question the whole economic future of society will depend.

10   Sooner or later the moment will come when we have to make a decision about this. At the moment, we are not making it— don't let as flatter ourselves that we are. It is being made for us. And don't let us imagine that a wartime economy has stopped waste. It has not. It has only transferred it elsewhere. The glut and waste that used to clutter our own dustbins have been removed to the field of battle. That is where all the surplus consumption is going. The factories are roaring more loudly than ever, turning out night and day goods that are of no conceivable value for the maintenance of life; on the contrary, their sole object is to destroy life, and instead of being thrown away they are being blown away—in Russia, in North Africa, over Occupied France, in Burma, China, and the Spice Islands, and on the Seven Seas.

11   What is going to happen when the factories stop turning out armaments? No nation has yet found a way to keep the machines running and whole nations employed under modern industrial conditions without wasteful consumption. For a time, a few nations could contrive to keep going by securing a monopoly of production and forcing their waste products onto new and untapped markets. When there are no new markets and all nations are industrial producers, the only choice we have been able to envisage so far has been that between armaments and unemployment. This is the problem that some time or other will stare us in the face again, and this time we must have our minds ready to tackle it. It may not come at once—for it is quite likely that after the war we shall have to go through a further period of managed consumption while the shortages caused by the war are being made good. But sooner or later we shall have to grapple with this difficulty, and everything will depend on our attitude of mind about it.

12   Shall we be prepared to take the same attitude to the arts of peace as to the arts of war? I see no reason why we should not sacrifice our convenience and our individual standard of living just as readily for the building of great public works as for the building of ships and tanks—but when the stimulus of fear and anger is removed, shall we be prepared to do any such thing?

Or shall we want to go back to that civilization of greed and waste which we dignify by the name of a "high standard of living"? I am getting very much afraid of that phrase about the standard of living. And I am also frightened by the phrase "after the war"—it is so often pronounced in a tone that suggests: "After the war, we want to relax, and go back, and live as we did before." And that means going back to the time when labor was valued in terms of its cash returns, and not in terms of the work.

13   Now the answer to this question, if we are resolute to know what we are about, will not be left to rich men—to manufacturers and financiers. If these people have governed the world of late years it is only because we ourselves put the power into their hands. The question can and should be answered by the worker and the consumer.

14   It is extremely important that the worker should really understand where the problem lies. It is a matter of brutal fact that in these days labor, more than any other section of the community has a vested interest in war. Some rich employers make profit out of war—that is true; but what is infinitely more important is that for all working people war means full employment and high wages.

15   When war ceases, then the problem of employing labor at the machines begins again. The relentless pressure of hungry labor is behind the drive toward wasteful consumption, whether in the destruction of war or in the trumpery of peace.

16   The problem is far too much simplified when it is presented as a mere conflict between labor and capital, between employed and employer. The basic difficulty remains, even when you make the State the sole employer, even when you make Labor into the employer. It is not simply a question of profits and wages or living conditions—but of what is to be done with the work of the machines, and what work the machines are to do.

17   If we do not deal with this question now, while we have time to think about it, then the whirligig of wasteful production and wasteful consumption will start again and will again end in war. And the driving power of labor will be thrusting to turn the wheels, because it is to the financial interest of labor to keep the whirligig going faster and faster till the inevitable catastrophe comes.

18　And so that those wheels may turn, the consumer—that is you and I, including the workers, who are consumers also—will again be urged to consume and waste; and unless we change our attitude—or rather unless we keep hold of the new attitude forced upon us by the logic of war—we shall again be bamboozled by our vanity, indolence, and greed into keeping the squirrel cage of wasteful economy turning. We could—you and I—bring the whole fantastic economy of profitable waste down to the ground overnight, without legislation and without revolution, merely by refusing to cooperate with it. I say, we could—as a matter of fact, we have; or rather, it has been done for us. If we do not want it to rise up again after the war, we can prevent it—simply by preserving the wartime habit of valuing work instead of money. The point is: do we *want* to? . . .

19　Whatever we do, we shall be faced with grave difficulties. That cannot be disguised. But it will make a great difference to the result if we are genuinely aiming at a real change in economic thinking. And by that I mean a radical change from top to bottom—a new system; not a mere adjustment of the old system to favor a different set of people.

20　The habit of thinking about work as something one does to make money is so ingrained in us that we can scarcely imagine what a revolutionary change it would be to think about it instead in terms of the work done. To do so would mean taking the attitude of mind we reserve for our unpaid work—our hobbies, our leisure interests, the things we make and do for pleasure—and making *that* the standard of all our judgments about things and people. We should ask of an enterprise, not "will it pay?" but "is it good?"; of a man, not "what does he make?" but "what is his work worth?"; of goods, not "can we induce people to buy them?" but "are they useful things well made?"; of employment, not "how much a week?" but "will it exercise my faculties to the utmost?" And shareholders in—let us say—brewing companies, would astonish the directorate by arising at shareholders' meetings and demanding to know, not merely where the profits go or what dividends are to be paid, not even merely whether the workers' wages are sufficient and the conditions of labor satisfactory, but loudly, and with a proper sense of personal responsibility: "What goes into the beer?"

21   You will probably ask at once: How is this altered attitude going to make any difference to the question of employment? Because it sounds as though it would result in not more employment, but less. I am not an economist, and I can only point to a peculiarity of war economy that usually goes without notice in economic textbooks. In war, production for wasteful consumption still goes on: but there is one great difference in the goods produced. None of them is valued for what it will fetch, but only for what it is worth in itself. The gun and the tank, the airplane and the warship have to be the best of their kind. A war consumer does not buy shoddy. He does not buy to sell again. He buys the thing that is good for its purpose, asking nothing of it but that it shall do the job it has to do. Once again, war forces the consumer into a right attitude to the work. And, whether by strange coincidence, or whether because of some universal law, as soon as nothing is demanded of the thing made but its own integral perfection, its own absolute value, the skill and labor of the worker are fully employed and likewise acquire an absolute value.

22   This is probably not the kind of answer that you will find in any theory of economics. But the professional economist is not really trained to answer, or even to ask himself questions about absolute values. The economist is inside the squirrel cage and turning with it. Any question about absolute values belongs to the sphere, not of economics, but of religion.

23   And it is very possible that we cannot deal with economics at all, unless we can see economy from outside the cage; that we cannot begin to settle the relative values without considering absolute values. And if so, this may give a very precise and practical meaning to the words: "Seek ye first the kingdom of God, and his righteousness: and all these things shall be added unto you."[2] . . . I am persuaded that the reason why the Churches are in so much difficulty about giving a lead in the economic sphere is because they are trying to fit a Christian standard of economics to a wholly false and pagan understanding of work.

24   What is the Christian understanding of work? . . . I should like to put before you two or three propositions arising out of the doctrinal position which I stated at the beginning: namely, that work is the natural exercise and function of man—the creature who is made in the image of his Creator. You will find that any

one of them, if given in effect everyday practice, is so revolutionary (as compared with the habits of thinking into which we have fallen), as to make all political revolutions look like conformity.

25 The first, stated quite briefly, is that work is not, primarily, a thing one does to live, but the thing one lives to do. It is, or it should be, the full expression of the worker's faculties, the thing in which he finds spiritual, mental, and bodily satisfaction, and the medium in which he offers himself to God.

26 Now the consequences of this are not merely that the work should he performed under decent living and working conditions. That is a point we have begun to grasp, and it is a perfectly sound point. But we have tended to concentrate on it to the exclusion of other considerations far more revolutionary.

27 (a) There is, for instance, the question of profits and remuneration. We have all got it fixed in our heads that the proper end of work is to be paid for—to produce a return in profits or payment to the worker which fully or more than compensates the effort he puts into it. But if our proposition is true, this does not follow at all. So long as Society provides the worker with a sufficient return in real wealth to enable him to carry on the work properly, then he has his reward. For his work is the measure of his life, and his satisfaction is found in the fulfillment of his own nature, and in contemplation of the perfection of his work.

28 That, in practice, there is this satisfaction, is shown by the mere fact that a man will put loving labor into some hobby which can never bring him any economically adequate return. His satisfaction comes, in the godlike manner, from looking upon what he has made and finding it very good. He is no longer bargaining with his work, but serving it. It is only when work has to be looked on as a means to gain that it becomes hateful; for then, instead of a friend, it becomes an enemy from whom tolls and contributions have to be extracted. What most of us demand from society is that we should always get out of it a little *more* than the value of the labor we give to it. By this process, we persuade ourselves that society is always in our debt—a conviction that not only piles up actual financial burdens, but leaves us with a grudge against society.

29   (b) Here is the second consequence. At present we have no
clear grasp of the principle that every man should do the work
for which he is fitted by nature. The employer is obsessed by
the notion that he must find cheap labor, and the worker by the
notion that the best-paid job is the job for him. Only feebly,
inadequately, and spasmodically do we ever attempt to tackle
the problem from the other end, and inquire: What type of
worker is suited to this type of work? People engaged in education see clearly that this is the right end to start from, but
they are frustrated by economic pressure, and by the failure of
parents on the one hand and employers on the other to grasp
the fundamental importance of this approach. And that the
trouble results far more from a failure of intelligence than from
economic necessity is seen clearly under war conditions, when,
although competitive economics is no longer a governing factor, the right men and women are still persistently thrust into
the wrong jobs, through sheer inability on everybody's part to
imagine a purely vocational approach to the business of fitting
together the worker and his work.

30   (c) A third consequence is that, if we really believed this proposition and arranged our work and our standard of values
accordingly, we should no longer think of work as something
that we hastened to get through in order to enjoy our leisure;
we should look on our leisure as the period of changed rhythm
that refreshed us for the delightful purpose of getting on with
our work. And, this being so, we should tolerate no regulations
of any sort that prevented us from working as long and as well
as our enjoyment of work demanded. We should resent any
such restrictions as a monstrous interference with the liberty of
the subject. How great an upheaval of our ideas that would
mean I leave you to imagine. It would turn topsy-turvy all our
notions about hours of work, rates of work, unfair competition,
and all the rest of it. We should all find ourselves fighting, as
now only artists and the members of certain professions fight,
for precious time in which to get on with the job—instead of
fighting for precious hours saved from the job.

31   (d) A fourth consequence is that we should fight tooth and
nail, not for mere employment, but for the quality of the work
that we had to do. We should clamor to be engaged in work
that was worth doing, and in which we could take pride. The
worker would demand that the stuff he helped to turn out
should be good stuff—he would no longer be content to take

the cash and let the credit go. Like the shareholders in the brewery, he would feel a sense of personal responsibility and clamor to know, and to control, what went into the beer he brewed. There would be protests and strikes—not only about pay and conditions, but about the quality of the work demanded and the honesty, beauty, and usefulness of the goods produced. The greatest insult which a commercial age has offered to the worker has been to rob him of all interest in the end product of the work and to force him to dedicate his life to making badly things which were not worth making.

32 This first proposition chiefly concerns the worker as such. My second proposition directly concerns Christians as such, and is this: it is the business of the Church to recognize that the secular vocation, as such, is sacred. Christian peoples and particularly perhaps the Christian clergy, must get it firmly into their heads that when a man or woman is called to a particular job of secular work, that is as true vocation as though he or she were called to specifically religious work. The Church must concern Herself not only with such questions as the just price and proper working conditions: She must concern Herself with seeing that the work itself is such as a human being can perform without degradation—that no one is required by economic or any other considerations to devote himself to work that is contemptible, soul destroying, or harmful. It is not right for Her to acquiesce in the notion that a man's life is divided into the time he spends on his work and the time he spends in serving God. He must he able to serve God *in* his work, and the work itself must be accepted and respected as the medium of divine creation.

33 In nothing has the Church so lost Her hold on reality as in Her failure to understand and respect the secular vocation. She has allowed work and religion to become separate departments, and is astonished to find that, as a result, the secular work of the world is turned to purely selfish and destructive ends, and that the greater part of the world's intelligent workers have become irreligious, or at least, uninterested in religion.

34 But is it astonishing? How can anyone remain interested in a religion which seems to have no concern with nine-tenths of his life? The Church's approach to an intelligent carpenter is usually confined to exhorting him not to be drunk and disorderly in his leisure hours, and to come to church on Sundays. What

the Church *should* be telling him is this: that the very first demand that his religion makes upon him is that he should make good tables.

35   Church by all means, and decent forms of amusement, certainly—but what use is all that if in the very center of his life and occupation he is insulting God with bad carpentry? No crooked table legs or ill-fitting drawers ever, I dare swear, came out of the carpenter's shop at Nazareth. Nor, if they did, could anyone believe that they were made by the same hand that made Heaven and earth. No piety in the worker will compensate for work that is not true to itself; for any work that is untrue to its own technique is a living lie.

36   Yet in Her own buildings, in Her own ecclesiastical art and music, in Her hymns and prayers, in Her sermons and in Her little hooks of devotion, the Church will tolerate, or permit a pious intention to excuse work so ugly, so pretentious, so tawdry and twaddling, so insincere and insipid, so *bad* as to shock and horrify any decent draftsman.

37   And why? Simply because She has lost all sense of the fact that the living and eternal truth is expressed in work only so far as that work is true in itself, to itself, to the standards of its own technique. She has forgotten that the secular vocation is sacred. Forgotten that a building must be good architecture before it can be a good church; that a painting must be well painted before it can be a good sacred picture; that work must be good work before it can call itself God's work.

38   Let the Church remember this: that every maker and worker is to serve God *in* his profession or trade—not outside it. The Apostles complained rightly when they said it was not meet they should leave the word of God and serve tables; their vocations was to preach the word.[3] But the person whose vocation it is to prepare the meals beautifully might with equal justice protest: It is not meet for us to leave the service of our tables to preach the word.

39   The official Church wastes time and energy, and, moreover, commits sacrilege, in demanding that secular workers should neglect their proper vocation in order to do Christian work— by which She means ecclesiastical work. The only Christian work is good work well done. Let the Church see to it that the workers are Christian people and do their work well, as to

God: then all the work will be Christian work, whether it is church embroidery, or sewage farming. As Jacques Maritain says: "If you want to produce Christian work, be a Christian, and to make a work of beauty into which you have put your heart; do not adopt a Christian pose."[4] He is right.

40 And let the Church remember that the beauty of the work will be judged [...]astical standards.

41 Let me giv[...] mean. When my play *The Zeal o[...]*n London, a dear old pious lady [...]auty of the four great archangels[...]lay in their heavy, gold robes, elev[...] sandal-tip. She asked with great i[...] the actors who played the angels [...]ral character?"

42 I replied that the angels were selected, to begin with, not by me but by the producer, who had the technical qualifications for selecting suitable actors—for that was part of his vocation. And that he selected, in the first place, young men who were six feet tall so that they would match properly together. Secondly angels had to be of good physique, so as to be able to stand stiff on the stage for two and a half hours, carrying the weight of their wings and costumes, without wobbling, or fidgeting, or fainting. Thirdly, they had to be able to speak verse well, in an agreeable voice and audibly. Fourthly, they had to be reasonably good actors. When all these technical conditions had been fulfilled, we might come to the moral qualities, of which the first would be the ability to arrive on the stage punctually and in a sober condition, since the curtain must go up on time, and a drunken angel would be indecorous.

43 After that, and only after that, one might take character into consideration, but that, provided his behavior was not so scandalous as to cause dissension among the company, the right kind of actor with no morals would give a far more reverent and seemly performance than a saintly actor with the wrong technical qualifications. The worst religious films I ever saw were produced by a company which chose its staff exclusively for their piety. Bad photography, bad acting, and bad dialogue produced a result so grotesquely irreverent that the pictures could not have been shown in churches without bringing Christianity into contempt.

44 God is not served by technical incompetence; and incompetence and untruth always result when the secular vocation is treated as a thing alien to religion. . . .

45 And conversely: when you find a man who is a Christian praising God by the excellence of his work—do not distract him and take him away from his proper vocation to address religious meetings and open church bazaars. Let him serve God in the way to which God has called him. If you take him away from that, he will exhaust himself in an alien technique and lose his capacity to do his dedicated work. It is your business, you churchmen, to get what good you can from observing his work—not to take him away from it, so that he may do ecclesiastical work for you. But, if you have any power, see that he is set free to do his own work as well as it may be done. He is not there to serve you; he is there to serve God by serving his work.

46 This brings me to my third proposition; and this may sound to you the most revolutionary of all. It is this: the worker's first duty is to *serve the work*. The popular catchphrase of today is that it is everybody's duty to serve the community. It is a well-sounding phrase, but there *is* a catch in it. It is the old catch about the two great commandments. "Love God and your neighbor: on those two commandments hang all the Law and the Prophets."[5]

47 The catch in it, which nowadays the world has largely forgotten, is that the second commandment depends upon the first, and that without the first, it is a delusion and a snare. Much of our present trouble and disillusionment have come from putting the second commandment before the first.

48 If we put our neighbor first, we are putting man above God, and that is what we have been doing ever since we began to worship humanity and make man the measure of all things. Whenever man is made the center of things, he becomes the storm center of trouble—and that is precisely the catch about serving the community. It ought perhaps to make us suspicious of that phrase when we consider that it is the slogan of every commercial scoundrel and swindler who wants to make sharp business practice pass muster as social improvement.

49 "Service" is the motto of the advertiser, of big business, and of fraudulent finance. And of others, too. Listen to this. "I expect

the judiciary to understand that the nation does not exist for their convenience, but that justice exists to serve the nation." That was Hitler yesterday—and that is what becomes of "service," when the community, and not the work, becomes its idol. There is, in fact, a paradox about working to serve the community, and it is this: that to aim directly at serving the community is to falsify the work; the only way to serve the community is to forget the community and serve the work. There are three very good reasons for this:

50 The first is that you cannot do good work if you take your mind off the work to see how the community is taking it—any more than you can make a good drive from the tee if you take your eye off the ball. "Blessed are the singlehearted" (for that is the real meaning of the word we translate "the pure in heart"[6]). If your heart is not wholly in the work, the work will not be good—and work that is not good serves neither God nor the community; it only serves mammon.

51 The second reason is that the moment you think of serving other people, you begin to have a notion that other people owe you something for your pains; you begin to think that you have a claim on the community. You will begin to bargain for reward, to angle for applause, and to harbor a grievance if you are not appreciated. But if your mind is set upon serving the work, then you know you have nothing to look for; the only reward the *work* can give you is the satisfaction of beholding its perfection. The work takes all and gives nothing but itself; and to serve the work is a labor of pure love.

52 And thirdly, if you set out to serve the community, you will probably end by merely fulfilling a public demand—and you may not even do that. A public demand is a changeable thing. Nine-tenths of the bad plays put on in theaters owe their badness to the fact that the playwright has aimed at pleasing the audience, instead of at producing a good and satisfactory play. Instead of doing the work as its own integrity demands that it should be done, he has falsified the play by putting in this or that which he thinks will appeal to the groundlings[7] (who by that time have probably come to want something else), and the play fails by its insincerity. The work has been falsified to please the public, and in the end even the public is not pleased. As it is with works of art, so it is with all work.

53   We are coming to the end of an era of civilization which began
      by pandering to public demand, and ended by frantically try-
      ing to create public demand for an output so false and mean-
      ingless that even a doped public revolted from the trash
      offered to it and plunged into war rather than swallow any
      more of it. The danger of "serving the community" is that one
      is part of the community; and that in serving it one may only
      be serving a kind of communal egotism. The only true way of
      serving the community is to be truly in sympathy with the
      community, to be oneself part of the community, and then to
      serve the work, without giving the community another
      thought. Then the work will endure, because it will be true to
      itself. It is the work that serves the community; the business of
      the worker is to serve the work.

54   Where we have become confused is in mixing up the ends to
      which our work is put with the *way* in which the work is done.
      The end of the work will be decided by our religious outlook:
      as we *are* so we *make*. It is the business of religion to make us
      Christian people, and then our work will naturally be turned to
      Christian ends, because our work is the expression of our-
      selves. But the *way* in which the work is done is governed by
      no sanction except the good of the work itself, and religion has
      no direct connection with that, except to insist that the work-
      man should be free to do his work well according to its own
      integrity. Jacques Maritain, one of the very few religious writ-
      ers of our time who really understands the nature of creative
      work, has summed the matter up in a sentence:

          What is required is the perfect practical discrimination
          between the end pursued by the workman (*finis operantis,*
          said the Schoolmen) and the end to be served by the work
          (*finis operas*), so that the workman may work for his wages
          but the work be controlled and set in being only in relation
          to its own proper good and nowise in relation to the wages
          earned; so that the artist may work for any and every human
          intention he likes, but the work taken by itself be performed
          and constructed for its own proper beauty alone.[8]

55   Or perhaps we may put it more shortly still: If work is to find its
      right place in the world, it is the duty of the Church to see to it
      that the work serves God, and that the worker serves the work.

Notes

1   These topics were covered in a speech at Brighton in March 1941. The major part of that speech was published in *A Christian Basis for the Post-War World* (S.C.M. Press). "Why Work?" was first presented as a speech at Eastbourne, England, April 23, 1942.

2   Matt. 6:33.

3   Acts 6:2.

4   Ch. 8, "Christian Art." sect. 2, in Jacques Maritain, *Art and Scholasticism with Other Essays,* trans. J. F. Scanlon (New York: Charles Scribner's Sons, 1930), 70.

5   Cf. Matt. 22:37–40.

6   Matt. 5:8.

7   An English slang term that originally referred to spectators in the cheapest seats in a theater. It came to refer to "those of ordinary or unsophisticated taste or critical judgment."

8   Ch. 9. "Art and Morality," sect. 2, in Maritain, *Art and Scholasticism.* 77–78.

*E*arl Shorris *is the founder and chairman of the advisory board of the Clemente Course in the Humanities, based at Bard College, a college level course designed for people living in poverty. He has had a successful career as a critic, journalist, and novelist. He has published in* Harper's Magazine, The Atlantic Monthly, *and* The Nation *among other publications. His books include* The Death of the Great Spirit, Latinos: A Biography of a People, New American Blues: A Journey Through Poverty to Democracy, *and* Riches for the Poor: The Clemente Course in the Humanities. *The following essay was published in the September 1997* Harpers.

On the Uses of a Liberal Education

As a Weapon in the Hands of the Restless Poor

Earl Shorris

1   Next month I will publish a book about poverty in America, but not the book I intended. The world took me by surprise— not once, but again and again. The poor themselves led me in directions I could not have imagined, especially the one that came out of a conversation in a maximum-security prison for women that is set, incongruously, in a lush Westchester suburb fifty miles north of New York City.

2   I had been working on the book for about three years when I went to the Bedford Hills Correctional Facility for the first time. The staff and inmates had developed a program to deal with family violence, and I wanted to see how their ideas fit with what I had learned about poverty.

3   Numerous forces—hunger, isolation, illness, landlords, police, abuse, neighbors, drugs, criminals, and racism, among many others—exert themselves on the poor at all times and enclose them, making up a "surround of force" from which, it seems, they cannot escape. I had come to understand that this was what kept the poor from being political and that the absence of politics in their lives was what kept them poor. I don't mean

"political" in the sense of voting in an election but in the way
Thucydides used the word: to mean activity with other people
at every level, from the family to the neighborhood to the
broader community to the city-state.

4   By the time I got to Bedford Hills, I had listened to more than
six hundred people, some of them over the course of two or
three years. Although my method is that of the bricoleur, the
tinkerer who assembles a thesis of the bric-a-brac he finds in
the world, I did not think there would be any more surprises.
But I had not counted on what Viniece Walker was to say.

5   It is considered bad form in prison to speak of a person's crime,
and I will follow that precise etiquette here. I can tell you that
Viniece Walker came to Bedford Hills when she was twenty
years old, a high school dropout who read at the level of a college sophomore, a graduate of crackhouses, the streets of
Harlem, and a long alliance with a brutal man. On the surface
Viniece has remained as tough as she was on the street. She
speaks bluntly, and even though she is HIV positive and the
virus has progressed during her time in prison, she still swag-
gers as she walks down the long prison corridors. While in
prison, Niecie, as she is known to her friends, completed her
high school requirements and began to pursue a college degree
(psychology is the only major offered at Bedford Hills, but
Niecie also took a special interest in philosophy). She became a
counselor to women with a history of family violence and a
comforter to those with AIDS.

6   Only the deaths of other women cause her to stumble in the
midst of her swaggering step, to spend days alone with the
remorse that drives her to seek redemption. She goes through
life as if she had been imagined by Dostoevsky, but even more
complex than his fictions, alive, a person, a fair-skinned and
freckled African-American woman, and in prison. It was she
who responded to my sudden question, "Why do you think
people are poor?"

7   We had never met before. The conversation around us focused
on the abuse of women. Niecie's eyes were perfectly opaque—
hostile, prison eyes. Her mouth was set in the beginning of a
sneer.

8   "You got to begin with the children," she said, speaking rapidly, clipping out the street sounds as they came into her speech.

9   She paused long enough to let the change of direction take effect, then resumed the rapid, rhythmless speech. "You've got to teach the moral life of downtown to the children. And the way you do that, Earl, is by taking them downtown to plays, museums, concerts, lectures, where they can learn the moral life of downtown."

10 I smiled at her, misunderstanding, thinking I was indulging her. "And then they won't be poor anymore?"

11 She read every nuance of my response, and answered angrily, "And they won't be poor no more."

12 "What you mean is—"

13 "What I mean is what I said—a moral alternative to the street."

14 She didn't speak of jobs or money. In that, she was like the others I had listened to. No one had spoken of jobs or money. But how could the "moral life of downtown" lead anyone out from the surround of force? How could a museum push poverty away? Who can dress in statues or eat the past? And what of the political life? Had Niecie skipped a step or failed to take a step? The way out of poverty was politics, not the "moral life of downtown." But to enter the public world, to practice the political life, the poor had first to learn to reflect. That was what Niecie meant by the "moral life of downtown." She did not make the error of divorcing ethics from politics. Niecie had simply said, in a kind of shorthand, that no one could step out of the panicking circumstance of poverty directly into the public world.

15 Although she did not say so, I was sure that when she spoke of the "moral life of downtown" she meant something that had happened to her. With no job and no money, a prisoner, she had undergone a radical transformation. She had followed the same path that led to the invention of politics in ancient Greece. She had learned to reflect. In further conversation it became clear that when she spoke of "the moral life of downtown" she meant the humanities, the study of human constructs and concerns, which has been the source of reflection for the secular world since the Greeks first stepped back from

nature to experience wonder at what they beheld. If the political life was the way out of poverty, the humanities provided an entrance to reflection and the political life. The poor did not need anyone to release them; an escape route existed. But to open this avenue to reflection and politics a major distinction between the preparation for the life of the rich and the life of the poor had to be eliminated.

16   Once Niecie had challenged me with her theory, the comforts of tinkering came to an end; I could no longer make an homage to the happenstance world and rest. To test Niecie's theory, students, faculty, and facilities were required. Quantitative measures would have to be developed; anecdotal information would also be useful. And the ethics of the experiment had to be considered: I resolved to do no harm. There was no need for the course to have a "sink or swim" character; it could aim to keep as many afloat as possible.

17   When the idea for an experimental course became clear in my mind, I discussed it with Dr. Jaime Inclan, director of the Roberto Clemente Family Guidance Center in lower Manhattan, a facility that provides counseling to poor people, mainly Latinos, in their own language and in their own community. Dr. Inclan offered the center's conference room for a classroom. We would put three metal tables end to end to approximate the boat-shaped tables used in discussion sections at the University of Chicago of the Hutchins era,[1] which I used as a model for the course. A card table in the back of the room would hold a coffeemaker and a few cookies. The setting was not elegant, but it would do. And the front wall was covered by a floor-to-ceiling blackboard.

18   Now the course lacked only students and teachers. With no funds and a budget that grew every time a new idea for the course crossed my mind, I would have to ask the faculty to donate its time and effort. Moreover, when Hutchins said, "The best education for the best is the best education for us all," he meant it: he insisted that full professors teach discussion sections in the college. If the Clemente Course in the Humanities was to follow the same pattern, it would require a faculty with the knowledge and prestige that students might encounter in their first year at Harvard, Yale, Princeton, or Chicago.

19   I turned first to the novelist Charles Simmons. He had been assistant editor of the *New York Times Book Review* and had

taught at Columbia University. He volunteered to teach poetry, beginning with simple poems, Housman, and ending with Latin poetry. Grace Glueck, who writes art news and criticism for the *New York Times,* planned a course that began with cave paintings and ended in the late twentieth century. Timothy Koranda, who did his graduate work at MIT, had published journal articles on mathematical logic, but he had been away from his field for some years and looked forward to getting back to it. I planned to teach the American history course through documents, beginning with the Magna Carta, moving on to the second of Locke's *Two Treatises of Government,* the Declaration of Independence, and so on through the documents of the Civil War. I would also teach the political philosophy class.

20 Since I was a *naïf* in this endeavor, it did not immediately occur to me that recruiting students would present a problem. I didn't know how many I needed. All I had were criteria for selection:

21 Age: 18-35.

22 Household income: Less than 150 percent of the Census Bureau's Official Poverty Threshold (though this was to change slightly).

23 Educational level: Ability to read a tabloid newspaper.

24 Educational goals: An expression of intent to complete the course.

25 Dr. Inclan arranged a meeting of community activists who could help recruit students. Lynette Lauretig of The Door, a program that provides medical and educational services to adolescents, and Angel Roman of the Grand Street Settlement, which offers work and training and GED programs, were both willing to give us access to prospective students. They also pointed out some practical considerations. The course had to provide bus and subway tokens, use fares ranged between three and six dollars per class per student, and the students could not afford sixty or even thirty dollars a month for transportation. We also had to offer dinner or a snack, because the classes were to be held from 6:00 to 7:30 p.m.

26 The first recruiting session came only a few days later. Nancy Mamis-King, associate executive director of the Neighborhood Youth & Family Services program in the South Bronx,

had identified some Clemente Course candidates and had assembled about twenty of her clients and their supervisors in a circle of chairs in a conference room. Everyone in the room was black or Latino, with the exception of one social worker and me.

27   After I explained the idea of the course, the white social worker was the first to ask a question: "Are you going to teach African history?"

28   "No. We'll be teaching a section on American history, based on documents, as I said. We want to teach the ideas of history so that—"

29   "You have to teach African history."

30   "This is America, so we'll teach American history. If we were in Africa, I would teach African history, and if we were in China, I would teach Chinese history."

31   "You're indoctrinating people in Western culture."

32   I tried to get beyond her. "We'll study African art," I said, "as it affects art in America. We'll study American history and literature; you can't do that without studying African-American culture, because culturally all Americans are black as well as white, Native American, Asian, and so on." It was no use; not one of them applied for admission to the course.

33   A few days later Lynette Lauretig arranged a meeting with some of her staff at The Door. We disagreed about the course. They thought it should be taught at a much lower level. Although I could not change their views, they agreed to assemble a group of Door members who might be interested in the humanities.

34   On an early evening that same week, about twenty prospective students were scheduled to meet in a classroom at The Door. Most of them came late. Those who arrived first slumped in their chairs, staring at the floor or greeting me with sullen glances. A few ate candy or what appeared to be the remnants of a meal. The students were mostly black and Latino, one was Asian, and five were white; two of the whites were immigrants who had severe problems with English. When I introduced myself, several of the students would not shake my hand, two or three refused even to look at me, one

girl giggled, and the last person to volunteer his name, a young man dressed in a Tommy Hilfiger sweatshirt and wearing a cap turned sideways, drawled, "Henry Jones, but they call me Sleepy, because I got these sleepy eyes—"

35 "In our class, we'll call you Mr. Jones."

36 He smiled and slid down in his chair so that his back was parallel to the floor.

37 Before I finished attempting to shake hands with the prospective students, a waiflike Asian girl with her mouth half-full of cake said, "Can we get on with it? I'm bored."

38 I liked the group immediately.

39 Having failed in the South Bronx, I resolved to approach these prospective students differently. "You've been cheated," I said. "Rich people learn the humanities; you didn't. The humanities are a foundation for getting along in the world, for thinking, for learning to reflect on the world instead of just reacting to whatever force is turned against you. I think the humanities are one of the ways to become political, and I don't mean political in the sense of voting in an election but in the broad sense." I told them Thucydides' definition of politics.

40 "Rich people know politics in that sense. They know how to negotiate instead of using force. They know how to use politics to get along, to get power. It doesn't mean that rich people are good and poor people are bad. It simply means that rich people know a more effective method for living in this society.

41 "Do all rich people, or people who are in the middle, know the humanities? Not a chance. But some do. And it helps. It helps to live better and enjoy life more. Will the humanities make you rich? Yes. Absolutely. But not in terms of money. In terms of life.

42 "Rich people learn the humanities in private schools and expensive universities. And that's one of the ways in which they learn the political life. I think that is the real difference between the haves and have-nots in this country. If you want real power, legitimate power, the kind that comes from the people and belongs to the people, you must understand politics. The humanities will help.

43 "Here's how it works: We'll pay your subway fare; take care of your children, if you have them; give you a snack or a sandwich; provide you with books and any other materials you need. But we'll make you think harder, use your mind more fully, than you ever have before. You'll have to read and think about the same kinds of ideas you would encounter in a first-year course at Harvard or Yale or Oxford.

44 "You'll have to come to class in the snow and the rain and the cold and the dark. No one will coddle you, no one will slow down for you. There will be tests to take, papers to write. And I can't promise you anything but a certificate of completion at the end of the course. I'll be talking to colleges about giving credit for the course, but I can't promise anything. If you come to the Clemente Course, you must do it because you want to study the humanities, because you want a certain kind of life, a richness of mind and spirit. That's all I offer you: philosophy, poetry, art history, logic, rhetoric, and American history.

45 "Your teachers will all be people of accomplishment in their fields," I said, and I spoke a little about each teacher. That's the course. October through May, with a two-week break at Christmas. It is generally accepted in America that the liberal arts and the humanities in particular belong to the elites. I think you're the elites."

46 The young Asian woman said, "What are you getting out of this?"

47 "This is a demonstration project. I'm writing a book. This will be proof, I hope, of my idea about the humanities. Whether it succeeds or fails will be up to the teachers and you."

48 All but one of the prospective students applied for admission to the course.

49 I repeated the new presentation at the Grand Street Settlement and at other places around the city. There were about fifty candidates for the thirty positions in the course. Personal interviews began in early September.

50 Meanwhile, almost all of my attempts to raise money had failed. Only the novelist Starling Lawrence, who is also editor in chief of W. W. Norton, which had contracted to publish the book; the publishing house itself; and a small, private family

foundation supported the experiment. We were far short of our budgeted expenses, but my wife, Sylvia, and I agreed that the cost was still very low, and we decided to go ahead.

51   Of the fifty prospective students who showed up at the Clemente Center for personal interviews, a few were too rich (a postal supervisor's son, a fellow who claimed his father owned a factory in Nigeria that employed sixty people) and more than a few could not read. Two home-care workers from Local 1199 could not arrange their hours to enable them to take the course. Some of the applicants were too young: a thirteen-year-old and two who had just turned sixteen.

52   Lucia Medina, a woman with five children who told me that she often answered the door at the single-room occupancy hotel where she lived with a butcher knife in her hand, was the oldest person accepted into the course. Carmen Quinones, a recovering addict who had spent time in prison, was the next eldest. Both were in their early thirties. The interviews went on for days.

53   Abel Lomas[2] shared an apartment and worked part-time wrapping packages at Macy's. His father had abandoned the family when Abel was born. His mother was murdered by his stepfather when Abel was thirteen. With no one to turn to and no place to stay, he lived on the streets, first in Florida, then back in New York City. He used the tiny stipend from his mother's Social Security to keep himself alive.

54   After the recruiting session at The Door, I drove up Sixth Avenue from Canal Street with Abel, and we talked about ethics. He had a street tough's delivery, spitting out his ideas in crudely formed sentences of four, five, eight words, strings of blunt declarations, with never a dependent clause to qualify his thoughts. He did not clear his throat with badinage, as timidity teaches us to do, nor did he waste his breath with tact.

55   "What do you think about drugs?" he asked, the strangely breathless delivery further coarsened by his Dominican accent. "My cousin is a dealer."

56   "I've seen a lot of people hurt by drugs."

57   "Your family has nothing to eat. You sell drugs. What's worse? Let your family starve or sell drugs?"

58   "Starvation and drug addiction are both bad, aren't they?"

59   "Yes," he said, not "yeah" or "uh-huh" but a precise, almost formal "yes."

60   "So it's a question of the worse of two evils? How shall we decide?"

61   The question came up near Thirty-fourth Street, where Sixth Avenue remains hellishly traffic-jammed well into the night. Horns honked, people flooded into the street against the light. Buses and trucks and taxicabs threatened their way from one lane to the next where the overcrowded avenue crosses the equally crowded Broadway. As we passed Herald Square and made our way north again, I said, "There are a couple of ways to look at it. One comes from Immanuel Kant, who said that you should not do anything unless you want it to become a universal law; that is, unless you think it's what everybody should do. So Kant wouldn't agree to selling drugs or letting your family starve."

62   Again he answered with a formal "Yes."

63   "There's another way to look at it, which is to ask what is the greatest good for the greatest number: in this case, keeping your family from starvation or keeping tens, perhaps hundreds of people from losing their lives to drugs. So which is the greatest good for the greatest number?"

64   "That's what I think," he said.

65   "What?"

66   "You shouldn't sell drugs. You can always get food to eat. Welfare. Something."

67   "You're a Kantian."

68   "Yes."

69   "You know who Kant is?"

70   "I think so."

71   We had arrived at Seventy-seventh Street, where he got out of the car to catch the subway before I turned east. As he opened the car door and the light came on, the almost military neatness of him struck me. He had the newly cropped hair of a cadet.

His clothes were clean, without a wrinkle. He was an orphan, a street kid, an immaculate urchin. Within a few weeks he would be nineteen years old, the Social Security payments would end, and he would have to move into a shelter.

72   Some of those who came for interviews were too poor. I did not think that was possible when we began, and I would like not to believe it now, but it was true. There is a point at which the level of forces that surround the poor can become insurmountable, when there is no time or energy left to be anything but poor. Most often I could not recruit such people for the course; when I did, they soon dropped out.

73   Over the days of interviewing, a class slowly assembled. I could not then imagine who would last the year and who would not. One young woman submitted a neatly typed essay that said, "I was homeless once, then I lived for some time in a shelter. Right now, I have got my own space granted by the Partnership for the Homeless. Right now, I am living alone, with very limited means. Financially I am overwhelmed by debts. I cannot afford all the food I need. . . ."

74   A brother and sister, refugees from Tashkent, lived with their parents in the farthest reaches of Queens, far beyond the end of the subway line. They had no money, and they had been refused admission by every school to which they had applied. I had not intended to accept immigrants or people who had difficulty with the English language, but I took them into the class.

75   I also took four who had been in prison, three who were homeless, three who were pregnant, one who lived in a drugged dream-state in which she was abused, and one whom I had known for a long time and who was dying of AIDS. As I listened to them, I wondered how the course would affect them. They had no public life, no place; they lived within the surround of force, moving as fast as they could, driven by necessity, without a moment to reflect. Why should they care about fourteenth-century Italian painting or truth tables or the death of Socrates?

76   Between the end of recruiting and the orientation session that would open the course, I made a visit to Bedford Hills to talk with Niecie Walker. It was hot, and the drive up from the city had been unpleasant. I didn't yet know Niecie very well. She

didn't trust me, and I didn't know what to make of her. While we talked, she held a huge white pill in her hand. "For AIDS," she said.

77 "Are you sick?"

78 "My T-cell count is down. But that's neither here nor there. Tell me about the course, Earl. What are you going to teach?"

79 "Moral philosophy."

80 "And what does that include?"

81 She had turned the visit into an interrogation. I didn't mind. At the end of the conversation I would be going out into "the free world"; if she wanted our meeting to be an interrogation, I was not about to argue. I said, "We'll begin with Plato: the *Apology*, a little of the *Crito*, a few pages of the *Phaedo* so that they'll know what happened to Socrates. Then we'll read Aristotle's *Nicomachean Ethics.* I also want them to read Thucydides, particularly Pericles' Funeral Oration in order to make the connection between ethics and politics, to lead them in the direction I hope the course will take them. Then we'll end with *Antigone*, but read as moral and political philosophy as well as drama."

82 "There's something missing," she said, leaning back in her chair, taking on an air of superiority.

83 The drive had been long, the day was hot, the air in the room was dead and damp. "Oh, yeah," I said, "and what's that?"

84 "Plato's Allegory of the Cave. How can you teach philosophy to poor people without the Allegory of the Cave? The ghetto is the cave. Education is the light. Poor people can understand that."

85 At the beginning of the orientation at the Clemente Center a week later, each teacher spoke for a minute or two. Dr. Inclan and his research assistant, Patricia Vargas, administered the questionnaire he had devised to measure, as best he could, the role of force and the amount of reflection in the lives of the students. I explained that each class was going to be videotaped as another way of documenting the project. Then I gave out the first assignment: "In preparation for our next meeting, I would like you to read a brief selection from Plato's *Republic*: the Allegory of the Cave."

86   I tried to guess how many students would return for the first class. I hoped for twenty, expected fifteen, and feared ten. Sylvia, who had agreed to share the administrative tasks of the course, and I prepared coffee and cookies for twenty-five. We had a plastic container filled with subway tokens. Thanks to Starling Lawrence, we had thirty copies of Bernard Knox's *Norton Book of Classical Literature*, which contained all of the texts for the philosophy section except the *Republic* and the *Nicomachean Ethics.*

87   At six o'clock there were only ten students seated around the long table, but by six-fifteen the number had doubled, and a few minutes later two more straggled in out of the dusk. I had written a time line on the blackboard, showing them the temporal progress of thinking—from the role of myth in Neolithic societies to The Gilgamesh Epic and forward to the Old Testament, Confucius, the Greeks, the New Testament, the Koran, the Epic of Son-Jara, and ending with Nahuatl and Maya poems, which took us up to the contact between Europe and America, where the history course began. The time line served as context and geography as well as history: no race, no major culture was ignored. "Let's agree," I told them, "that we are all human, whatever our origins. And now let's go into Plato's cave."

88   I told them that there would be no lectures in the philosophy section of the course; we would use the Socratic method, which is called maieutic dialogue. "'Maieutic' comes from the Greek word for midwifery. I'll take the role of midwife in our dialogue. Now, what do I mean by that? What does a midwife do?"

89   It was the beginning of a love affair, the first moment of their infatuation with Socrates. Later, Abel Lomas would characterize that moment in his no-nonsense fashion, saying that it was the first time anyone had ever paid attention to their opinions.

90   Grace Glueck began the art history class in a darkened room lit with slides of the Lascaux caves and next turned the students' attention to Egypt, arranging for them to visit the Metropolitan Museum of Art to see the Temple of Dendur and the Egyptian Galleries. They arrived at the museum on a Friday evening. Darlene Codd brought her two-year-old son. Pearl Lau was late, as usual. One of the students, who had told me how much he was looking forward to the museum visit, didn't show up,

which surprised me. Later I learned that he had been arrested for jumping a turnstile in a subway station on his way to the museum and was being held in a prison cell under the Brooklyn criminal courthouse. In the Temple of Dendur, Samantha Smoot asked questions of Felicia Blum, a museum lecturer. Samantha was the student who had burst out with the news, in one of the first sessions of the course, that people in her neighborhood believed it "wasn't no use goin' to school because the white man wouldn't let you up no matter what." But in a hall where the statuary was of half-human, half-animal female figures, it was Samantha who asked what the glyphs meant, encouraging Felicia Blum to read them aloud, to translate them into English. Toward the end of the evening, Grace led the students out of the halls of antiquities into the Rockefeller Wing, where she told them of the connections of culture and art in Mali, Benin, and the Pacific Islands. When the students had collected their coats and stood together near the entrance to the museum, preparing to leave, Samantha stood apart, a tall, slim young woman, dressed in a deerstalker cap and a dark blue peacoat. She made an exaggerated farewell wave at us and returned to Egypt—her ancient mirror.

91   Charles Simmons began the poetry class with poems as puzzles and laughs. His plan was to surprise the class, and he did. At first he read the poems aloud to them, interrupting himself with footnotes to bring them along. He showed them poems of love and of seduction, and satiric commentaries on those poems by later poets. "Let us read," the students demanded, but Charles refused. He tantalized them with the opportunity to read poems aloud. A tug-of-war began between him and the students, and the standoff was ended not by Charles directly but by Hector Anderson. When Charles asked if anyone in the class wrote poetry, Hector raised his hand.

92   "Can you recite one of your poems for us?" Charles said.

93   Until that moment, Hector had never volunteered a comment, though he had spoken well and intelligently when asked. He preferred to slouch in his chair, dressed in full camouflage gear, wearing a nylon stocking over his hair and eating slices of fresh cantaloupe or honeydew melon.

94   In response to Charles's question, Hector slid up to a sitting position. "If you turn that camera off," he said. "I don't want anybody using my lyrics." When he was sure the red light of

the video camera was off, Hector stood and recited verse after verse of a poem that belonged somewhere in the triangle formed by Ginsberg's *Howl*, the Book of Lamentations, and hip-hop. When Charles and the students finished applauding, they asked Hector to say the poem again, and he did. Later Charles told me, "That kid is the real thing." Hector's discomfort with Sylvia and me turned to ease. He came to our house for a small Christmas party and at other times. We talked on the telephone about a scholarship program and about what steps he should take next in his education. I came to know his parents. As a student, he began quietly, almost secretly, to surpass many of his classmates.

95   Timothy Koranda was the most professorial of the professors. He arrived precisely on time, wearing a hat of many styles— part fedora, part Borsalino, part Stetson, and at least one-half World War I campaign hat. He taught logic during class hours, filling the blackboard from floor to ceiling, wall to wall, drawing the intersections of sets here and truth tables there and a great square of oppositions in the middle of it all. After class, he walked with students to the subway, chatting about Zen or logic or Heisenberg.

96   On one of the coldest nights of the winter, he introduced the students to logic problems stated in ordinary language that they could solve by reducing the phrases to symbols. He passed out copies of a problem, two pages long, then wrote out some of the key phrases on the blackboard. "Take this home with you," he said, "and at our next meeting we shall see who has solved it. I shall also attempt to find the answer."

97   By the time he finished writing out the key phrases, however, David Iskhakov raised his hand. Although they listened attentively, neither David nor his sister Susana spoke often in class. She was shy, and he was embarrassed at his inability to speak perfect English.

98   "May I go to blackboard?" David said. "And will see if I have found correct answer to zis problem."

99   Together Tim and David erased the black-board, then David began covering it with signs and symbols. "If first man is earning this money, and second man is closer to this town . . . ," he said, carefully laying out the conditions. After five minutes or so, he said, "And the answer is: B will get first to Cleveland!"

100 Samantha Smoot shouted, "That's not the answer. The mistake you made is in the first part there, where it says who earns more money."

101 Tim folded his arms across his chest, happy. "I shall let you all take the problem home," he said.

102 When Sylvia and I left the Clemente Center that night, a knot of students was gathered outside, huddled against the wind. Snow had begun to fall, a slippery powder on the gray ice that covered all but a narrow space down the center of the sidewalk. Samantha and David stood in the middle of the group, still arguing over the answer to the problem. I leaned in for a moment to catch the character of the argument. It was even more polite than it had been in the classroom, because now they govern themselves.

103 One Saturday morning in January, David Howell telephoned me at home. "Mr. Shores," he said, Anglicizing my name, as many of the students did.

104 "Mr. Howell," I responded, recognizing his voice.

105 "How you doin', Mr. Shores?"

106 "I'm fine. How are you?"

107 "I had a little problem at work."

108 Uh-oh, I thought, bad news was coming. David is a big man, generally good-humored but with a quick temper. According to his mother, he had a history of violent behavior. In the classroom he had been one of the best students, a steady man, twenty-four years old, who always did the reading assignments and who often made interesting connections between the humanities and daily life. "What happened?"

109 "Mr. Shores, there's a woman at my job, she said some things to me and I said some things to her. And she told my supervisor I had said things to her, and he called me in about it. She's forty years old and she don't have no social life, and I have a good social life, and she's jealous of me."

110 "And then what happened?" The tone of his voice and the timing of the call did not portend good news.

111 "Mr. Shores, she made me so mad, I wanted to smack her up against the wall. I tried to talk to some friends to calm myself down a little, but nobody was around."

112 "And what did you do?" I asked, fearing this was his one telephone call from the city jail.

113 "Mr. Shores, I asked myself, 'What would Socrates do?'"

114 David Howell had reasoned that his co-worker's envy was not his problem after all, and he had dropped his rage.

115 One evening, in the American history section, I was telling the students about Gordon Wood's ideas in *The Radicalism of the American Revolution*. We were talking about the revolt by some intellectuals against classical learning at the turn of the eighteenth century, including Benjamin Franklin's late-life change of heart, when Henry Jones raised his hand.

116 "If the Founders loved the humanities so much, how come they treated the natives so badly?"

117 I didn't know how to answer this question. There were confounding explanations to offer about changing attitudes toward Native Americans, vaguely useful references to views of Rousseau and James Fenimore Cooper. For a moment I wondered if I should tell them about Heidegger's Nazi past. Then I saw Abel Lomas's raised hand at the far end of the table. "Mr. Lomas," I said.

118 Abel said, "That's what Aristotle means by incontinence, when you know what's morally right but you don't do it, because you're overcome by your passions."

119 The other students nodded. They were all inheritors of wounds caused by the incontinence of educated men; now they had an ally in Aristotle, who had given them a way to analyze the actions of their antagonists.

120 Those who appreciate ancient history understand the radical character of the humanities. They know that politics did not begin in a perfect world but in a society even more flawed than ours: one that embraced slavery, denied the rights of women, practiced a form of homosexuality that verged on pedophilia, and endured the intrigues and corruption of its leaders. The genius of that society originated in man's re-creation of himself through the recognition of his humanness as expressed in art,

literature, rhetoric, philosophy, and the unique notion of freedom. At that moment, the isolation of the private life ended and politics began.

121 The winners in the game of modern society, and even those whose fortune falls in the middle, have other means to power: they are included at birth. They know this. And they know exactly what to do to protect their place in the economic and social hierarchy. As Allan Bloom, author of the nationally best-selling tract in defense of elitism, *The Closing of the American Mind,* put it, they direct the study of the humanities exclusively at those young people who "have been raised in comfort and with the expectation of ever increasing comfort."

122 In the last meeting before graduation, the Clemente students answered the same set of questions they'd answered at orientation. Between October and May, students had fallen to AIDS, pregnancy, job opportunities, pernicious anemia, clinical depression, a schizophrenic child, and other forces, but of the thirty students admitted to the course, sixteen had completed it, and fourteen had earned credit from Bard College. Dr. Inclan found that the students' self-esteem and their abilities to divine and solve problems had significantly increased; their use of verbal aggression as a tactic for resolving conflicts had significantly decreased. And they all had notably more appreciation for the concepts of benevolence, spirituality, universalism, and collectivism.

123 It cost about $2,000 for a student to attend the Clemente Course. Compared with unemployment, welfare, or prison, the humanities are a bargain. But coming into possession of the faculty of reflection and the skills of politics leads to a choice for the poor—and whatever they choose, they will be dangerous: they may use politics to get along in a society based on the game, to escape from the surround of force into a gentler life, to behave as citizens, and nothing more; or they may choose to oppose the game itself. No one can predict the effect of politics, although we all would like to think that wisdom goes our way. That is why the poor are so often mobilized and so rarely politicized. The possibility that they will adopt a moral view other than that of their mentors can never be discounted. And who wants to run that risk?

124 On the night of the first Clemente Course graduation, the students and their families filled the eighty-five chairs we crammed into the conference room where classes had been held. Robert Martin, associate dean of Bard College, read the graduates' names. David Dinkins, the former mayor of New York City, handed out the diplomas. There were speeches and presentations. The students gave me a plaque on which they had misspelled my name. I offered a few words about each student, congratulated them, and said finally, "This is what I wish for you: May you never be more active than when you are doing nothing. . . ." I saw their smiles of recognition at the words of Cato, which I had written on the blackboard early in the course. They could recall again too the moment when we had come to the denouement of Aristotle's brilliantly constructed thriller, the *Nicomachean Ethics*—the idea that in the contemplative life man was most like God. One or two, perhaps more of the students, closed their eyes. In the momentary stillness of the room it was possible to think.

125 The Clemente Course in the Humanities ended a second year in June 1997. Twenty-eight new students had enrolled; fourteen graduated. Another version of the course will begin this fall in Yucatan, Mexico, using classical Maya literature in Maya.

126 On May 14, 1997, Viniece Walker came up for parole for the second time. She had served more than ten years of her sentence, and she had been the best of prisoners. In a version of the Clemente Course held at the prison, she had been my teaching assistant. After a brief hearing, her request for parole was denied. She will serve two more years before the parole board will reconsider her case.

127 A year after graduation, ten of the first sixteen Clemente Course graduates were attending four-year colleges or going to nursing school; four of them had received full scholarships to Bard College. The other graduates were attending community college or working full-time. Except for one: she had been fired from her job in a fast-food restaurant for trying to start a union.

Notes

[1] Under the guidance of Robert Maynard Hutchins (1929–1951), the University of Chicago required year-long courses in the humanities, social sciences, and natural sciences for the Bachelor of Arts degree. Hutchins developed the curriculum with the help of Mortimer Adler, among others; the Hutchins courses later influenced Adler's Great Books program.

[2] Not his real name.

Barbara Dafoe Whitehead is known for speaking and writing about fam-ily and child well-being. She is best known for her 1993 article, "Dan Quayle Was Right," in which she supported the then vice president's com-ments regarding single television-mother Murphy Brown. Her work has appeared in the Wall Street Journal, Reader's Digest, *the* Washington Post, *the* Los Angeles Times, *and the* Boston Globe. *Born and raised in Minnesota, Whitehead now lives in Amherst, Massachusetts, with her hus-band and three children. She serves on the Massachusetts Commission for Responsible Fatherhood and the Religion and Public Values Task Force of the National Campaign to Prevent Teen Pregnancy.*

Lost in Work

Barbara Dafoe Whitehead

1   It's little wonder that *E.R.* has become America's favorite tele-vision show. An emergency room is the perfect metaphor for today's culture of work: a 24-hour work day; a workplace loaded with dazzling technology; a buzz induced by adrena-line and fueled by caffeine; and an overwhelming sense of urgency and importance. For the medical team in the E.R., no other domain offers comparable attractions.

2   For a growing number of Americans, work is gobbling up not only our time but also our loyalties. Especially for the most well-educated and successfully employed Americans, work identities are overtaking other identities. Work itself is crowd-ing out other life pursuits. Partly because of the personal and portable technologies, partly because of our acquiescence to its claims, work has become an imperial presence—setting up out-posts everywhere.

3   *Take family life:* The technology that makes it possible for par-ents to work at home also turns home into a 24-hour work-place. Just when it's time to put the kids to bed, the fax spurts an urgent communication, the pager beeps, the e-mail dings. Along with home as workplace, we are getting workplace as home. Businesses now offer emergency childcare so their employees can work overtime or on weekends; others provide temporary childcare for children who are sick or on school

vacations. I know a mother whose boss so valued her services that when she threatened to quit to spend more time with her children, he offered to provide a chauffeured limousine to take her kids to Little League and music lessons. Most employees, as well as advocates for family-friendly workplaces, find these efforts praiseworthy, and they do accomplish the goal of making parents more reliable employees. But we should not be fooled about what is going on here. The workplace is bidding for and acquiring time once pledged to children, and children have no way to make a reasonable counteroffer.

4   *Take neighborhood and community life:* Membership in community organizations is declining. Some people attribute this trend to increases in women's workforce participation and this is a factor. However, there has also been a 25 percent drop in men's participation in community groups over roughly the past decade. One reason to suspect that work plays a role in the disengagement from civic life is that membership in professional associations has not suffered a similar decline but in fact has been rising. (I suspect the same might be said for memberships in private health clubs.)

5   *Take vacations:* The "getting-away-from-it-all" vacation is disappearing as more Americans tote lap-tops, cellular phones, and portable faxes to the cottage and the beach. Not only is this practice spreading from senior executives to mid- and lower-level managers, but it is establishing a new work norm: never leave the office.

6   *Take Sundays:* Sunday has become another work day. Once dedicated to churchgoing and late sleeping, Sunday mornings are increasingly devoted to work or work disguised as leisure. According to a recent biography, Senator Robert Dole watches political talk shows on Sunday morning while he rides an exercycle. He goes to church only when his wife drags him there. In Massachusetts, businesses are challenging the blue laws on the grounds that opening stores on Sunday mornings is friendly to families, providing jobs and expanded hours for grocery shopping. Similarly, work is taking over Sunday evenings. According to one unscientific study, home technologies begin to hum on Sundays around four P.M. People start calling on Sunday night to set up the next day's meetings, assignments, appointments.

7   *Take marriage:* According to divorce researcher Judith Waller-
     stein, the institution of marriage and the institution of work
     may be on a collision course. In particular, the marriages of two-
     career couples who have children are "frighteningly fragile."
     The demands and pressures of building a career, often coincid-
     ing with the peak childrearing years, can introduce tension and
     conflict between spouses, particularly when the strain of hold-
     ing it all together seems to fall on one parent more than the
     other.

8   *Take last but certainly not least, love and sex:* Our intimate lives are
     increasingly described not in the language of love and
     romance, but in the language of work. We are encouraged to
     "work" on our relationships, to develop new "skills" in our
     love lives, to use computerized technologies to locate potential
     partners, even to engage in sex as a form of aerobic exercise.
     (Moderate intensity sex, says one woman's magazine, can burn
     off 40 calories an hour.) Too, there is the exhaustion factor. One
     working mother confesses: I don't crave sex. I crave sleep.

9   If pursuit of our work lives has crowded out pursuit of our
     lives as husbands and wives, mothers and fathers, neighbors,
     friends, and citizens, does it matter? It may matter a lot. To
     begin, it makes for a more atomized and disconnected society,
     where workers jostle and contend in the marketplace, leaving
     empty chairs at the PTA meetings and volunteer fire depart-
     ments and church suppers. The result is a weakened and
     impoverished civil society, a reduced sense of social trust and
     responsibility, and a decline in the nation's social capital.

10   The incursions of work into family and community life may
     prove especially detrimental to children. Children are the last
     American provincials, bound to a particular family and local
     geography, dependent on the richness and resources of a social
     world created by adults. That social world is growing more
     meager and fragile as the work world claims the loyalties and
     investments of the grownups.

11   From time to time, I read an obituary that describes the recent-
     ly deceased not as an executive for a pharmaceutical firm or a
     successful lobbyist, but as a church member or a Red Cross vol-
     unteer. Yet it is increasingly difficult to imagine a successful life
     in these terms—because we cannot imagine ourselves defined
     by anything but our work.

*W*illiam Zinsser wrote this essay, "College Pressures," out of his experiences as master of Branford College at Yale University in the 1970s, where he also taught humor writing and nonfiction writing. Zinsser began his professional career in 1947, joining the New York Herald Tribune. *In his time there, he worked variously as a newswriter, editor, and critic. He left in 1959 to become a freelance writer. He has since been a frequent contributor to such publications as* Life *and* The New Yorker. *From 1979 to 1986, Zinsser was the general editor of the Book-of-the-Month Club. He is also the author of twelve books, including* On Writing Well *and* Writing to Learn.

College Pressures

William Zinsser

1   Dear Carlos: I desperately need a dean's excuse for my chem midterm which will begin in about 1 hour. All I can say is that I totally blew it this week. I've fallen incredibly, inconceivably behind.

2   Carlos: Help! I'm anxious to hear from you. I'll be in my room and won't leave it until I hear from you. Tomorrow is the last day for . . .

3   Carlos: I left town because I started bugging out again. I stayed up all night to finish a take-home makeup exam & am typing it to hand in on the 10th. It was due on the 5th. P.S. I'm going to the dentist. Pain is pretty bad.

4   Carlos: Probably by Friday I'll be able to get back to my studies. Right now I'm going to take a long walk. This whole thing has taken a lot out of me.

5   Carlos: I'm really up the proverbial creek. The problem is I really *bombed* the history final. Since I need that course for my major I . . .

6   Carlos: Here follows a tale of woe. I went home this weekend, had to help my Mom, & caught a fever so didn't have much time to study. My professor . . .

7   Carlos: Aargh! Trouble. Nothing original but everything's piling up at once. To be brief, my job interview. . .

8   Hey Carlos, good news! I've got mononucleosis.

9   Who are these wretched supplicants, scribbling notes so laden with anxiety, seeking such miracles of postponement and balm? They are men and women who belong to Branford College, one of the twelve residential colleges at Yale University, and the messages are just a few of the hundreds that they left for their dean, Carlos Hortas—often slipped under his door at 4 A.M.—last year.

10 But students like the ones who wrote those notes can also be found on campuses from coast to coast—especially in New England and at many other private colleges across the country that have high academic standards and highly motivated students. Nobody could doubt that the notes are real. In their urgency and their gallows humor they are authentic voices of a generation that is panicky to succeed.

11 My own connection with the message writers is that I am master of Branford College. I live in its Gothic quadrangle and know the students well. (We have 485 of them.) I am privy to their hopes and fears—and also to their stereo music and their piercing cries in the dead of night ("Does anybody ca-a-are?"). If they went to Carlos to ask how to get through tomorrow, they come to me to ask how to get through the rest of their lives.

12 Mainly I try to remind them that the road ahead is a long one and that it will have more unexpected turns than they think. There will be plenty of time to change jobs, change careers, change whole attitudes and approaches. They don't want to hear such liberating news. They want a map—right now—that they can follow unswervingly to career security, financial security, Social Security and, presumably, a prepaid grave.

13 What I wish for all students is some release from the clammy grip of the future. I wish them a chance to savor each segment of their education as an experience in itself and not as a grim preparation for the next step. I wish them the right to experiment, to trip and fall, to learn that defeat is as instructive as victory and is not the end of the world.

14 My wish, of course, is naive. One of the few rights that America does not proclaim is the right to fail. Achievement is the

national god, venerated in our media—the million-dollar athlete, the wealthy executive—and glorified in our praise of possessions. In the presence of such a potent state religion, the young are growing up old.

15 I see four kinds of pressure working on college students today: economic pressure, parental pressure, peer pressure, and self-induced pressure. It is easy to look around for villains—to blame the colleges for charging too much money, the professors for assigning too much work, the parents for pushing their children too far, the students for driving themselves too hard. But there are no villains; only victims.

16 "In the late 1960s," one dean told me, "the typical question that I got from students was 'Why is there so much suffering in the world?' or 'How can I make a contribution?' Today it's 'Do you think it would look better for getting into law school if I did a double major in history and political science, or just majored in one of them?'" Many other deans confirmed this pattern. One said: "They're trying to find an edge—the intangible something that will look better on paper if two students are about equal."

17 Note the emphasis on looking better. The transcript has become a sacred document, the passport to security. How one appears on paper is more important than how one appears in person. *A* is for Admirable and *B* is for Borderline, even though, in Yale's official system of grading, *A* means "excellent" and *B* means "very good." Today, looking very good is no longer good enough, especially for students who hope to go on to law school or medical school. They know that entrance into the better schools will be an entrance into the better law firms and better medical practices where they will make a lot of money. They also know that the odds are harsh, Yale Law School, for instance, matriculates 170 students from an applicant pool of 3,700; Harvard enrolls 550 from a pool of 7,000.

18 It's all very well for those of us who write letters of recommendation for our students to stress the qualities of humanity that will make them good lawyers or doctors. And it's nice to think that admission officers are really reading our letters and looking for the extra dimension of commitment or concern. Still, it would be hard for a student not to visualize these officers shuffling so many transcripts studded with *A*s that they regard a *B* as positively shameful.

19   The pressure is almost as heavy on students who just want to graduate and get a job. Long gone are the days of the "gentleman's C," when students journeyed through college with a certain relaxation, sampling a wide variety of courses—music, art, philosophy, classics, anthropology, poetry, religion—that would send them out as liberally educated men and women. If I were an employer I would rather employ graduates who have this range and curiosity than those who narrowly pursued safe subjects and high grades. I know countless students whose inquiring minds exhilarate me. I like to hear the play of their ideas. I don't know if they are getting As or Cs, and I don't care. I also like them as people. The country needs them, and they will find satisfying jobs. I tell them to relax. They can't.

20   Nor can I blame them. They live in a brutal economy. Tuition, room, and board at most private colleges now comes to at least $7,000, not counting books and fees. This might seem to suggest that the colleges are getting rich. But they are equally battered by inflation. Tuition covers only 60 percent of what it costs to educate a student, and ordinarily the remainder comes from what colleges receive in endowments, grants, and gifts. Now the remainder keeps being swallowed by the cruel costs—higher every year—of just opening the doors. Heating oil is up. Insurance is up. Postage is up. Health-premium costs are up. Everything is up. Deficits are up. We are witnessing in America the creation of a brotherhood of paupers—colleges, parents, and students, joined by the common bond of debt.

21   Today it is not unusual for a student, even if he works part time at college and full time during the summer, to accrue $5,000 in loans after four years—loans that he must start to repay within one year after graduation. Exhorted at commencement to go forth into the world, he is already behind as he goes forth. How could he not feel under pressure throughout college to prepare for this day of reckoning? I have used "he," incidentally, only for brevity. Women at Yale are under no less pressure to justify their expensive education to themselves, their parents, and society. In fact, they are probably under more pressure. For although they leave college superbly equipped to bring fresh leadership to traditionally male jobs, society hasn't yet caught up with this fact.

22   Along with economic pressure goes parental pressure. Inevitably, the two are deeply intertwined.

23 I see many students taking premedical courses with joyless tenacity. They go off to their labs as if they were going to the dentist. It saddens me because I know them in other corners of their life as cheerful people.

24 "Do you want to go to medical school?" I ask them.

25 "I guess so," they say, without conviction, or "Not really."

26 "Then why are you going?"

27 "Well, my parents want me to be a doctor. They're paying all this money and . . ."

28 Poor students, poor parents. They are caught in one of the oldest webs of love and duty and guilt. The parents mean well; they are trying to steer their sons and daughters toward a secure future. But the sons and daughters want to major in history or classics or philosophy—subjects with no "practical" value. Where's the payoff on the humanities? It's not easy to persuade such loving parents that the humanities do indeed pay off. The intellectual faculties developed by studying subjects like history and classics—an ability to synthesize and relate, to weigh cause and effect, to see events in perspective—are just the faculties that make creative leaders in business or almost any general field. Still, many fathers would rather put their money on courses that point toward a specific profession—courses that are pre-law, pre-medical, pre-business, or, as I sometimes heard it put, "pre-rich."

29 But the pressure on students is severe. They are truly torn. One part of them feels obligated to fulfill their parents' expectations; after all, their parents are older and presumably wiser. Another part tells them that the expectations that are right for their parents are not right for them.

30 I know a student who wants to be an artist. She is very obviously an artist and will be a good one—she has already had several modest local exhibits. Meanwhile she is growing as a well-rounded person and taking humanistic subjects that will enrich the inner resources out of which her art will grow. But her father is strongly opposed. He thinks that an artist is a "dumb" thing to be. The student vacillates and tries to please everybody. She keeps up with her art somewhat furtively and takes some of the "dumb" courses her father wants her to take—at least they are dumb courses for her. She is a free spirit

on a campus of tense students—no small achievement in itself—and she deserves to follow her muse.

31 Peer pressure and self-induced pressure are also intertwined, and they begin almost at the beginning of freshman year.

32 "I had a freshman student I'll call Linda," one dean told me, "who came in and said she was under terrible pressure because her roommate, Barbara, was much brighter and studied all the time. I couldn't tell her that Barbara had come in two hours earlier to say the same thing about Linda."

33 The story is almost funny—except that it's not. It's symptomatic of all the pressures put together. When every student thinks every other student is working harder and doing better, the only solution is to study harder still. I see students going off to the library every night after dinner and coming back when it closes at midnight. I wish they would sometimes forget about their peers and go to a movie. I hear the clacking of typewriters in the hours before dawn. I see the tension in their eyes when exams are approaching and papers are due: *"Will I get everything done?"*

34 Probably they won't. They will get sick. They will get "blocked." They will sleep. They will oversleep. They will bug out. *Hey Carlos, help!*

35 Part of the problem is that they do more than they are expected to do. A professor will assign five-page papers. Several students will start writing ten-page papers to impress him. Then more students will write ten-page papers, and a few will raise the ante to fifteen. Pity the poor student who is still just doing the assignment.

36 Once you have twenty or thirty percent of the student population deliberately overexerting," one dean points out, "it's bad for everybody. When a teacher gets more and more effort from his class, the student who is doing normal work can be perceived as not doing well. The tactic works, psychologically."

37 Why can't the professor just cut back and not accept longer papers? He can, and he probably will. But by then the term will be half over and the damage done. Grade fever is highly contagious and not easily reversed. Besides, the professor's main concern is with his course. He knows his students only in relation to the course and doesn't know that they are also

overexerting in their other courses. Nor is it really his business. He didn't sign up for dealing with the student as a whole person and with all the emotional baggage the student brought along from home. That's what deans, masters, chaplains, and psychiatrists are for.

38 To some extent this is nothing new: a certain number of professors have always been self-contained islands of scholarship and shyness, more comfortable with books than with people. But the new pauperism has widened the gap still further, for professors who actually like to spend time with students don't have as much time to spend. They also are overexerting. If they are young, they are busy trying to publish in order not to perish, hanging by their finger nails onto a shrinking profession. If they are old and tenured, they are buried under the duties of administering departments—as departmental chairmen or members of committees—that have been thinned out by the budgetary axe.

39 Ultimately it will be the students' own business to break the circles in which they are trapped. They are too young to be prisoners of their parents' dreams and their classmates' fears. They must be jolted into believing in themselves as unique men and women who have the power to shape their own future.

40 "Violence is being done to the undergraduate experience," says Carlos Hortas. "College should be open-ended: at the end it should open many, many roads. Instead, students are choosing their goal in advance, and their choices narrow as they go along. It's almost as if they think that the country has been codified in the type of jobs that exist—that they've got to fit into certain slots. Therefore, fit into the best-paying slot.

41 "They ought to take chances. Not taking chances will lead to a life of colorless mediocrity. They'll be comfortable. But something in the spirit will be missing."

42 I have painted too drab a portrait of today's students, making them seem a solemn lot. That is only half of their story; if they were so dreary I wouldn't so thoroughly enjoy their company. The other half is that they are easy to like. They are quick to laugh and to offer friendship. They are not introverts. They are unusually kind and are more considerate of one another than any student generation I have known.

43   Nor are they so obsessed with their studies that they avoid sports and extracurricular activities. On the contrary, they juggle their crowded hours to play on a variety of teams, perform with musical and dramatic groups, and write for campus publications. But this in turn is one more cause of anxiety. There are too many choices. Academically, they have 1,300 courses to select from; outside class they have to decide how much spare time they can spare and how to spend it.

44   This means that they engage in fewer extracurricular pursuits than their predecessors did. If they want to row on the crew and play in the symphony they will eliminate one; in the '60s they would have done both. They also tend to choose activities that are self-limiting. Drama, for instance, is flourishing in all twelve of Yale's residential colleges as it never has before. Students hurl themselves into these productions—as actors, directors, carpenters, and technicians—with a dedication to create the best possible play, knowing that the day will come when the run will end and they can get back to their studies.

45   They also can't afford to be the willing slave of organizations like the *Yale Daily News*. Last spring at the one-hundredth anniversary banquet of that paper—whose past chairmen include such once and future kings as Potter Stewart, Kingman Brewster, and William F. Buckley, Jr.—much was made of the fact that the editorial staff used to be small and totally committed and that "newsies" routinely worked fifty hours a week. In effect they belonged to a club; Newsies is how they defined themselves at Yale. Today's student will write one or two articles a week, when he can, and he defines himself as a student. I've never heard the word Newsie except at the banquet.

46   If I have described the modern undergraduate primarily as a driven creature who is largely ignoring the blithe spirit inside who keeps trying to come out and play, it's because that's where the crunch is, not only at Yale but throughout American education. It's why I think we should all be worried about the values that are nurturing a generation so fearful of risk and so goal-obsessed at such an early age.

47   I tell students that there is no one "right" way to get ahead—that each of them is a different person, starting from a different point and bound for a different destination. I tell them that change is a tonic and that all the slots are not codified nor the frontiers

closed. One of my ways of telling them is to invite men and women who have achieved success outside the academic world to come and talk informally with my students during the year. They are heads of companies or ad agencies, editors of magazines, politicians, public officials, television magnates, labor leaders, business executives, Broadway producers, artists, writers, economists, photographers, scientists, historians—a mixed bag of achievers.

48   I ask them to say a few words about how they got started. The students assume that they started in their present profession and knew all along that it was what they wanted to do. Luckily for me, most of them got into their field by a circuitous route, to their surprise, after many detours. The students are startled. They can hardly conceive of a career that was not preplanned. They can hardly imagine allowing the hand of God or chance to nudge them down some unforeseen trail.